American Indian Wars

American Indian Wars

THE ESSENTIAL REFERENCE GUIDE

Justin D. Murphy, Editor

ABC-CLIO®

An Imprint of ABC-CLIO, LLC
Santa Barbara, California • Denver, Colorado

Library of Congress Cataloging-in-Publication Data

Names: Murphy, Justin D., editor.
Title: American Indian Wars : the essential reference guide / Justin D.
  Murphy, editor.
Description: Santa Barbara, California : ABC-CLIO, [2022] | Includes
  bibliographical references and index.
Identifiers: LCCN 2021023076 (print) | LCCN 2021023077 (ebook) | ISBN
  9781440875090 (hardcover) | ISBN 9781440875106 (ebook)
Subjects: LCSH: Indians of North America—Wars.
Classification: LCC E81 .A488 2022 (print) | LCC E81 (ebook) | DDC
  973.04/97—dc23
LC record available at https://lccn.loc.gov/2021023076
LC ebook record available at https://lccn.loc.gov/2021023077

ISBN: 978-1-4408-7509-0 (print)
       978-1-4408-7510-6 (ebook)

26 25 24 23 22   1 2 3 4 5

This book is also available as an eBook.

ABC-CLIO
An Imprint of ABC-CLIO, LLC

ABC-CLIO, LLC
147 Castilian Drive
Santa Barbara, California 93117
www.abc-clio.com

This book is printed on acid-free paper ∞

Manufactured in the United States of America

Contents

List of Entries

List of Documents

Preface

The American Indian Wars were a prominent part of American history in the four centuries that followed the arrival of Christopher Columbus in the New World in 1492. Indian warfare differed radically from warfare elsewhere in the world. It did not consist of the conventional set-piece battles that characterized European wars, featuring maneuvering units, artillery, and stand-up attacks and withdrawals by infantry and cavalry. Rather Indian warfare more accurately deserves the term guerrilla warfare, featuring ambush, surprise, and sudden attacks on enemy concentrations that involved noncombatants. If not surprised, Indians declined to fight unless virtually certain of winning. When their women and children were threatened, even in a direct surprise attack, Indians usually fled and scattered while men provided rearguard actions.

Traditional Indian weaponry consisted principally of bow and arrow, lance, tomahawk, knife, and a defensive hide shield. Gradually, however, Native Americans acquired European firearms, usually in trade and usually inferior to those of their opponents. The principal arms of Europeans and Americans were muskets followed in the 19th century by rifles and metallic cartridges. Pistols and later revolvers constituted sidearms. Cavalry sabers proved useless in fighting Indians. Artillery played a minor role. In the Eastern woodlands, Indians traveled and fought largely on foot—ideal for ambushing formally organized European or American troops moving in conventional formation on roads. In the western plains, mountains, and deserts, nomadic tribes moved and sometimes fought on horseback. (Spaniards brought horses to the New World, allowing pedestrian tribes to become nomads.)

In combatting Native Americans, European colonial powers and Americans waged an especially brutal form of "total war." They located Indian villages, drove out the inhabitants, burned the dwellings, and destroyed food stores and other means of subsistence. Native Americans were then hounded relentlessly until exhaustion, hunger, and insecurity compelled them to surrender.

Finally, the Indian wars of America not only pitted Indians against Europeans and Americans but also Indians against Indians. Tribes had been fighting one another for centuries, largely over hunting grounds but by long tradition as well. The advent of Europeans and their successor Americans failed not only to unite the tribes in the common defense but also to interrupt the long history of intertribal wars. Indeed, intertribal warfare often played an important role in Indian wars with Europeans and Americans.

This work is designed to provide readers a broad overview of the American Indian Wars. The entries and documents focus on key tribes, battles, campaigns, warriors, and leaders over four centuries of conflict. Deciding what to include and exclude was a difficult process, but an attempt has been made to select entries and documents that are most representative of the American Indians Wars and to focus primarily upon Native Americans, rather than Europeans and white Americans. The bibliography includes the most prominent works and most recent works. Each entry also features a Further Reading section with sources over that specific topic. The introduction provides a broad overview of the American Indian Wars and also addresses the question of whether they constituted genocide.

In preparing this work, I must acknowledge Dr. R. David Edmunds and Dr. Spencer C. Tucker. I had the great fortune to study under each at Texas Christian University. Dr. Edmunds introduced me to Native American history and directed my master's thesis. Dr. Tucker instilled in me a love for military history, while serving as my major professor for my doctoral work and directing my dissertation, and he gave me the opportunity to work with him on numerous publications.

Justin D. Murphy

Introduction

When Christopher Columbus and members of his crew waded ashore in the Bahamas on October 12, 1492, they were greeted warmly by the island's Taino inhabitants. As the natives and newcomers examined one another, some of the curious Tainos grasped the Europeans' swords, not realizing the sharpness of the blades, and accidentally slashed their hands and fingers. This bloodshed on the very first day of contact, although inadvertent, foreshadowed 400 years of warfare that would eventually devastate the native population of the Americas and, by the time the last battle was fought in 1890 at Wounded Knee in the United States, see the surviving natives subjugated by the Europeans and their descendants.

Columbus and those Europeans who came after him were not entering empty lands. Although population estimates vary widely, perhaps 8–12 million people inhabited the region north of present-day Mexico; some 4 million lived on the islands of the Caribbean; another 18 million or more inhabited Mexico and Central America; and about 10–11 million people were subjects of the Inca Empire in South America, between the Andes mountains and the Pacific Ocean. Adding the inhabitants of South America east of the Andes gives the New World an aggregate population of more than 40 million people and possibly as many as 60 million in 1492. American natives spoke hundreds of languages and dialects, and their cultures varied from small bands of nomadic hunters in Canada to semisedentary agriculturalists in most of North America to the complex, highly organized, and stratified empires of the Aztecs in Mexico and the Incas in South America.

Despite later romantic notions of native life imagined by Europeans, the inhabitants of the Americas did not live in peaceable kingdoms, free from conflict. The Tainos in the Caribbean warred sporadically with their Carib neighbors, while the Aztecs in central Mexico had built an empire through conquest, celebrating their victories and honoring their gods with thousands of human sacrifices every year. In western South America, the Incas had conquered a geographically larger if less populous empire. The inhabitants of North America also battled for resources and to avenge wrongs, albeit on a smaller scale than the wars waged by the great empires in Mexico and South America. These tribal rivalries worked to the advantage of European powers and colonists by allowing them to play tribes against each other—a practice that the United States would later employ.

Initial encounters between natives and Europeans were usually cordial. Natives greeted Europeans in accordance with their traditions of hospitality to strangers, enhanced by curiosity about the physically different newcomers and their strange and marvelous weapons, goods, and livestock, which some natives took as signs of great spiritual power. Europeans also preferred to establish good relations, since they needed information that would enable them to survive in an unfamiliar environment while also learning what resources and potential riches the new land possessed.

The Spanish Conquest

Despite the peaceful beginnings of the relationship between natives and Europeans, violence soon became commonplace. Columbus and the 1,500 Spanish colonists who accompanied him on his second voyage in 1493 quickly began to exploit the Tainos. Building on the existing Taino tribute system, the Spaniards demanded that Taino caciques (chiefs) turn over a portion of the food and other goods that their people produced. When caciques balked at the demands, they were killed and their people enslaved. Columbus, as governor of the colony, divided native lands among the colonists and put the inhabitants to work clearing land, farming, and mining for gold. Natives laboring in this encomienda system were treated harshly. Columbus insisted that some of the natives on Hispaniola turn a specified quantity of gold over to the Spaniards every three months, and those who did not meet the quota had their hands cut off. Natives revolted but were quickly suppressed, as their weapons were no match for Spanish soldiers in armor who wielded crossbows and muskets and were supported by artillery, mounted cavalry, and attack dogs.

More detrimental to natives were the new diseases brought by Europeans. Because natives lacked immunity to common European diseases, such as measles, mumps, influenza, and, most devastating of all, smallpox, epidemics decimated native populations. Hispaniola, home to an estimated 1 million Tainos in 1492, had no native survivors left in 1535 despite the Spaniards' capture and importation of tens of thousands of natives from other islands, the South American mainland, and Florida. To meet their demand for labor, the Spanish began importing African slaves.

After securing control of the Caribbean islands, the Spanish moved to establish themselves on the mainland of North America and South America. In 1519, Hernán Cortes landed on the coast of Mexico. Ordered to establish a trading post, Cortes instead marched inland, lured by reports of the wealth of the Aztec Empire. Spanish military technology enabled Cortes to defeat some of the Aztecs' subject peoples, who in turn allied with the Spaniards in the hope of overthrowing their Aztec overlords. Cortes thus established a pattern that would be followed by other Europeans: taking advantage of existing native rivalries to gain assistance from one native group against another. Aided by disease, superior weaponry, and his native allies, Cortes completed the conquest of the Aztec Empire in 1521. Francisco Pizarro subjugated the Inca Empire in 1533, although Inca elements held out in Andean strongholds and continued to resist the Spaniards for several years.

Spanish incursions north of Mexico met with less success. Although Spaniards subdued the Pueblo peoples and other tribes in the present-day American Southwest, they faced frequent revolts. In 1539, Hernando de Soto led 1,000 soldiers into what is now the southeastern United States, marching across a vast expanse of territory and using violence and intimidation to supply his men. De Soto's expedition devastated the native societies of the region before deaths from combat and disease forced the survivors to escape to Mexico.

French-Native Relations

French exploration of North America began in the 16th century, but it was not until 1604 that the French succeeded in establishing a permanent colony in Acadia (Nova Scotia). Four years later, a second colony was established at Quebec. Unlike the Spanish, the French had neither the military might nor the desire to forcibly subdue the natives. Few French colonists were willing to brave the harsh Canadian climate and settle in North America, so Native Americans always heavily outnumbered the French. Furthermore, the main goal of French colonization was to profit from the fur trade, and since traders relied on the natives to trap beaver and other fur-bearing animals, the French could not afford to alienate their native trading partners.

Samuel de Champlain, founder and first governor of Quebec, set the tone for relations between the French and Native Americans. He scrupulously purchased the land on which his colonists settled and integrated the French within the existing native trade and alliance system. French traders, the *coureurs de bois*, settled in native communities and married native women, strengthening ties between the two societies. Missionaries, notably the Jesuits, pursued a similar course, learning native languages and then settling among the various nations to carry out their work of conversion. While the Jesuits were not always welcome, they eventually won acceptance, if few converts, in the native communities where they lived and added another link to the relationship between the French and the natives.

Champlain's judicious conduct forged a strong military alliance with the natives.

Unlike other Europeans, he insisted that natives be treated on their own terms; thus, he refused to force them to submit to French law. Natives who killed French colonists paid an indemnity in goods, a traditional native practice, rather than being punished by French standards with the imposition of the death penalty, a practice not employed by most native societies. On the other hand, when a French colonist killed a native, Champlain not only compensated the native's family with trade goods but also executed the French offender. This fairness earned Champlain and his successors the respect of natives, who often turned to French governors to mediate disputes among themselves.

French willingness to accommodate natives came with a price, however, as Champlain learned in 1609. Huron and Algonquian diplomats called at Quebec and asked Champlain for warriors to join in an expedition against their Iroquois enemies to the south. Realizing that his alliance with them obligated him to participate, Champlain and one or two French soldiers accompanied the Native force, and French firearms proved crucial in the defeat of a Mohawk war party. The battle helped to not only cement the French alliance with the Hurons and various Algonquian-speaking tribes of Canada but also drew the French into their long-standing conflict with the Iroquois Confederacy, of which the Mohawks were a member. The resulting warfare would continue until the Grand Paix of 1701 ended French-Iroquois hostilities, which resumed with the outbreak of the French and Indian War five decades later.

The alliance between the French and the natives persisted, with some disruptions, until France was expelled from North America in 1763. Many native nations fought alongside France in the various colonial wars against Great Britain that raged intermittently beginning in 1689. Nevertheless, French relations with some native groups were marked by hostility and violence, notably the French campaign to eliminate the Fox (Mesquakie) tribe during 1712–1737 and the French war against the Natchez people during 1729–1733.

English-Native Relations

Sir Walter Raleigh, the driving force behind English colonization in North America, believed that the Spanish experience provided the English with a textbook example of how not to treat Native Americans. Raleigh believed that fair treatment would win the goodwill of natives, resulting in their voluntary submission to the Crown of England and peaceful coexistence. By the time the first permanent English colony was established in 1607 at Jamestown, Virginia, Raleigh had lost his influence. In any case, he had failed to take into account the deep cultural divide between Native Americans and the English. Key aspects of native society, including decentralized leadership based on persuasion and consensus, communitarian property ownership that in regard to land was based on usage rights, and nature-based religious beliefs, stood in sharp contrast to the English system of rigid hierarchical government, private property and individual land ownership, and formal religious systems. Such differences, exacerbated by the English desire to take native lands and impose their political, economic, and religious practices on the natives, made conflict virtually inevitable.

In Virginia, responsibility for diplomacy with the tribes of the Powhatan Confederacy fell to John Smith, who adopted a harsh policy. Smith frequently forced natives to supply colonists with food but was careful not to press too hard and provoke open warfare. In 1609, Smith returned to England, and the following year, English demands for supplies and land sparked the first of three Anglo-Powhatan wars. Unlike the natives, who sought to minimize casualties and take captives for adoption into their tribes, the English waged total war, targeting noncombatants as well as crops and other essential supplies. When the final war ended in 1646, the once-powerful Powhatan Confederacy survived only as a remnant on a few small parcels of its original lands, which were in effect the first native reservations.

To the north in New England, relations began peacefully. A smallpox epidemic had nearly annihilated coastal tribes shortly before the Pilgrims arrived and founded Plymouth Colony in 1620; the surviving natives helped the newcomers survive the first winter and begin farming the following spring. The Puritans who settled Massachusetts Bay in 1630 also established good relations with their native neighbors, but the New England colonies soon came into conflict with the Pequot nation in the Connecticut River Valley. Irritated by the Pequots' stubborn independence and egged on by their Mohegan allies, who were rivals of the Pequots, the colonists began hostilities against the Pequots in the summer of 1636. The Pequot War ended in 1638 with the Pequots virtually annihilated.

The victory over the Pequots intimidated the other New England tribes, and the colonies met almost no opposition as they expanded during the next four decades. However, the colonists' seemingly endless desire for land and their efforts to impose their law, religion, and customs on the natives led Metacom (King Philip) of the Wampanoags to organize a coalition of tribes to oppose the English. The resulting conflict, known as King Philip's War

(1675–1676), saw many New England settlements devastated, but natives suffered immense losses. No longer able to oppose the English, many of the survivors moved farther away from the colonists.

New York succeeded in avoiding hostilities with natives by virtue of inheriting the Dutch alliance with the Iroquois upon England's conquest of New Netherland in 1664. The Dutch had waged brutal warfare against the Algonquian-speaking tribes of the Hudson River Valley, but after an early conflict with the Mohawks, the Dutch sought peace with the Iroquois, who became New Netherland's partner in the fur trade. After assuming control of the colony, English officials continued the Dutch policy of conciliating the Iroquois, both to profit from the fur trade and to keep the confederation as a buffer between New York and New France.

In the Southern colonies, which were settled in the late 17th and early 18th centuries, warfare also erupted between the English and natives. The causes were similar: the colonists' land hunger, trade abuses, and attempts to enslave natives. The two most violent conflicts were the Tuscarora War (1711–1713) in North Carolina and the Yamasee War (1715–1717) in South Carolina, both of which ended with the defeat of the natives.

Native-colonial relations were more peaceful in a few colonies. Roger Williams in Rhode Island and William Penn in Pennsylvania, both of whom sought to create religious havens for those fleeing persecution in England or in neighboring colonies, established good relations with the natives, as did James Oglethorpe in Georgia, in another utopian experiment, in the 1730s. These colonies were exceptions, however, and by the mid-18th century both Pennsylvania and Georgia were enmeshed in the seemingly endless conflict between the British colonists and the natives.

Imperial Warfare and Native Americans

In 1689, the European War of the League of Augsburg spilled over into North America as both France and England tried to strike a blow at each other's colonies. While English colonists strove, with little success, to strike Montreal and other key French posts, the French and their native allies mounted raids on the New England and New York frontiers to keep the English on the defensive. Neither side gained a decisive advantage by the time the conflict, known to the English colonists as King William's War, ended in 1697. Peace brought no change to the situation in North America, although the Iroquois, angered by the lack of English support, opted for neutrality by signing a peace agreement with New France in 1701.

Another European conflict, the War of the Spanish Succession, broke out shortly afterward and extended to the colonies. Known to English colonists as Queen Anne's War (1702–1713), the conflict pitted them against both France and Spain. English forces from South Carolina, augmented by native allies, invaded Spanish Florida in 1702 but failed to capture St. Augustine. The English and natives then overran Spanish posts to the west before being checked by the French-allied Choctaws. To the north, the French and their native allies raided the English frontier, their most notable success being an attack on Deerfield, Massachusetts, in February 1704. An expedition from New England captured Port Royal, Acadia, in 1710, and France was forced to cede that province to Britain in the 1713 Treaty of Utrecht; the British renamed the colony Nova Scotia.

King George's War (1744–1748), known as the War of the Austrian Succession in Europe, followed a similar pattern. While the British and their colonists targeted key

French positions such as the fortress of Louisbourg on Cape Breton Island, which they captured in June 1745, the French and their native allies used raiding to maintain pressure on the borders of the British colonies. The war came to an indecisive conclusion in 1748, with the British returning Louisbourg to France, much to the chagrin of Britain's New England colonists.

The peace of 1748 brought only a brief respite to North America. Seeking to shore up the links between their possessions in Canada and those along the Mississippi River, the French began constructing forts in the Ohio River Valley. This region was also claimed by the British, and when Virginia sent militia under Lieutenant Colonel George Washington in 1754 in an unsuccessful effort to oust the French, fighting erupted that sparked the French and Indian War (1754–1763).

Hoping for a quick victory, the British government sent the 44th and 48th Irish regiments under General Edward Braddock to seize French Fort Duquesne at the Forks of the Ohio River in 1755. Braddock squandered an opportunity to gain support from native nations in the Ohio Valley area when he refused to promise that the tribes could keep their land in exchange for assisting the British. Angered, the natives sided with the French and helped to rout Braddock's force, which also included colonial militia, in July 1755. The natives followed up the victory by launching devastating raids along the frontier from New England to Virginia over the next two years.

Despite the natives' important contributions to the French war effort, the French military commander, General Louis-Joseph, Marquis de Montcalm, alienated his allies in 1757 after capturing Fort William Henry in New York. Montcalm allowed the British and colonial garrison to withdraw with their possessions, depriving the natives of plunder and captives, their traditional rewards for service with the French. The infuriated natives attacked the British and the colonists as they evacuated the fort and then returned home, where most sat out the remainder of the war. With little native aid and facing a much superior British and colonial force, Montcalm was driven back to the heart of New France in the Saint Lawrence River Valley. In 1759, the Iroquois, recognizing that the tide had turned against the French and hoping to share in the spoils of victory, joined the British. That September Quebec capitulated to the British, and under the terms of the 1763 Treaty of Paris, France ceded Canada to Britain and Louisiana to Spain, ending the French presence in North America, and Spain ceded Florida to Britain.

The British and colonial victory aroused the fears of the natives in the Ohio Valley and Great Lakes region. Having lost the protection of the French, they now stood alone against an expected onslaught of land-hungry colonists. Hoping to forestall this disaster and perhaps entice the French to return, Ottawa war leader Pontiac organized a coalition of tribes and launched a series of assaults on British posts beginning in May 1763. Pontiac's Rebellion failed to drive out the British but forced a change in British policy to the natives' benefit. Officials in London, unwilling to engage in costly wars with the natives and recognizing that their own colonists' insatiable desire for land was the root of the problem, responded with the Proclamation of 1763. The edict forbade colonial settlement west of the Appalachians and strengthened the powers of the British Indian superintendents to regulate trade and the sale of native lands east of the Appalachians. The new policy angered many colonists, who believed that their victory in the French and Indian War entitled them to seize native lands.

Native Americans and the American Revolution

Although never completely effective, the new British policy won the goodwill of the natives. Thus, when the American Revolutionary War (1775–1783) began in 1775, most tribes supported the British, because they realized that an American victory would deprive them of British protection and unleash a horde of intruders onto their territory. A few tribes, such as the Catawbas in South Carolina and the Oneidas of the Iroquois Confederacy, supported the Americans in hopes of preserving their lands and independence.

In the North, Mohawk leader Joseph Brant led most of the Iroquois in support of the British. Frequently working in company with Loyalist rangers, Brant's native forces won several important victories. Brant's success forced General George Washington to dispatch an expedition under Major General John Sullivan that devastated the Iroquois homeland in 1779. Undeterred, Brant returned to the offensive the following year. The Shawnees and other Ohio Valley nations also operated against Americans on the frontier, but British forces never cooperated effectively with any of the native operations in the North, greatly reducing their overall effectiveness.

The story was similar in the South. Ignoring the advice of British Indian agents, the Cherokees attacked the Virginia and Carolina frontiers in 1776, only to suffer a disastrous defeat after initial successes. The Cherokees' failure dampened the enthusiasm of other Southern tribes, who generally remained on the sidelines until the British occupied Savannah, Georgia, at the end of 1778. Efforts to coordinate Creek attacks with British operations in Georgia failed because of slow communications and the great distances involved. After the British captured Charleston, South Carolina, in May 1780 and occupied that state and Georgia, Southern tribes offered their services, only to be rejected by the British commander in the South, Lieutenant General Charles, Earl Cornwallis. By the time Cornwallis asked for native assistance in late 1780, the Creeks and Choctaws were committed to the defense of British West Florida against Spanish attacks. Their efforts failed to prevent the loss of that province in May 1781. Meanwhile, the Americans had driven the British to the environs of Charleston and Savannah, making cooperation with the natives impossible. In the 1783 Treaty of Paris, the British ignored their native allies and ceded the region between the Appalachians and the Mississippi River to the United States and returned Florida to Spain.

U.S.-Native Relations during the Early Republic

American independence was followed by an influx of settlers onto native lands. Sporadic fighting occurred along the entire western frontier but was most serious in the Northwest, where a coalition of tribes led by Miami war chief Little Turtle and Shawnee war chief Blue Jacket effectively opposed American expansion. Although the natives defeated U.S. military expeditions in 1790 and 1791, they were defeated in the 1794 Battle of Fallen Timbers and forced to make peace the following year.

Shawnee leader Tecumseh was determined to resist American expansion. While his younger brother, the prophet Tenskwatawa, preached a native spiritual revival, Tecumseh attempted to organize a native confederacy to prevent white encroachments on native land. While Tecumseh was away on a diplomatic mission to Southern tribes in 1811, Major General William Henry Harrison marched against Tenskwatawa's village, Prophetstown, on the Wabash River. Despite Tecumseh's admonition not to give battle, Tenskwatawa attacked Harrison and was defeated in the Battle of Tippecanoe. Harrison's victory undermined Tecumseh's efforts to form a native alliance, and Tecumseh turned to the British in Canada for assistance.

During the War of 1812, Tecumseh's Shawnees and other natives fought well in conjunction with the British until October 1813, when British and Native forces were defeated and Tecumseh was killed in the Battle of the Thames in Canada. The Creek War, fought in the South during the War of 1812, was considered part of the larger conflict by Americans, although its origins were separate. Some Southern native nations had tried to adopt American culture, which sparked a civil war among the Creeks. Nativist Red Sticks opposed the accommodationist policies of the White Stick Creek faction, and the dispute erupted into civil war in 1813. When Red Sticks attacked both their White Stick rivals and American settlers, the U.S. government responded with force. In 1814, Major General Andrew Jackson crushed the Red Sticks and forced the Creek Nation to cede much of its territory in the Southeast.

Jackson's experience fighting natives in the Creek War and the First Seminole War (1817–1818) convinced him that natives and white Americans could not peacefully coexist. After his election as president of the United States in 1828, Jackson proposed forcibly removing all native nations in the East to land west of the Mississippi River. The Indian Removal Act, passed by Congress in 1830, led many nations to accept removal to Indian Territory (present-day Oklahoma) as inevitable. Many Cherokees refused to leave their homes, however, and were forcibly removed along the so-called Trail of Tears in 1838. Many Seminoles also resisted removal, igniting the Second Seminole War (1835–1842). The survivors won a reservation in their Florida homeland, but tensions with whites led to the Third Seminole War (1855–1858); by its conclusion, most of the surviving Seminoles had been sent to Indian Territory, with only a handful left in Florida.

Indian Wars of the West

The Third Seminole War marked the end of native warfare east of the Mississippi, yet a whole new field of conflict had opened in the West. The triumph of the United States in the Mexican-American War (1846–1848) secured the cession of a vast expanse of territory in the Southwest and in California. Lured by the discovery of gold in California and inspired by the ideology of Manifest Destiny (the belief that it was Americans' right to spread their superior culture across the continent even at the expense of Native Americans, Mexicans, and others deemed inferior), thousands of settlers set out for the West. The result was a series of conflicts with the natives of the Great Plains, the Rocky Mountains, the Southwest, and the Pacific Northwest.

On the southern Plains, the Kiowas, Comanches, Southern Cheyennes, and other nations signed treaties agreeing to live in peace with the settlers, but white encroachment on native lands led to tensions that quickly resulted in sporadic warfare. By 1864, several Southern Cheyenne bands were at war with the Americans, and Colorado militia and U.S. troops slaughtered a peaceful Southern Cheyenne band at Sand Creek, Colorado, in November 1864, provoking further native attacks. The Kiowas and Comanches also began fighting the Americans to protect their lands and way of life. Hostilities culminated in the Red River War of 1874–1875. U.S. forces defeated the natives, who surrendered most of their territory and were confined to reservations.

Farther west, the Navajos attempted to remain at peace but eventually began retaliating against New Mexicans who raided their food supplies and livestock. The U.S. Army, preoccupied with the American Civil War (1861–1865), did not focus its attention on the Navajos until 1863. Army officers then ordered the Navajos to a reservation in eastern New Mexico. When the Navajos refused and were defeated in 1864, they were forcibly removed to the Bosque Redondo Reservation; several hundred Navajos died in the "Long Walk."

Meanwhile, several Apache bands went to war against the United States after Cochise, a prominent Chiricahua leader, was falsely accused in 1861 of kidnapping an American boy. Cochise waged a decade-long guerrilla war against the United States before making peace in 1872. Leadership of Apache resistance was subsequently assumed by Victorio and Geronimo, who continued to fight the Americans, in Geronimo's case until his surrender in 1886.

On the northern Plains, the various Sioux bands and their allies, the Northern Cheyennes and Arapahos, resisted the tide of white settlement for nearly 30 years. Intermittent fighting began in the 1850s, and the first major Sioux war erupted in 1862. The Santee Sioux had sold much of their land and accepted a reservation in Minnesota, only to be cheated out of their annuity payments by corrupt traders and Indian agents. Frustrated and starving, the Santees led by Little Crow went to war, inflicting heavy losses on civilians and soldiers before being defeated.

Red Cloud of the Lakota Sioux led a more successful resistance during 1866–1868. An influx of settlers and the construction of forts along the Bozeman Trail in Wyoming threatened traditional Sioux hunting grounds. Red Cloud responded by attacking civilians and soldiers along the trail, isolating the forts, and annihilating a unit of cavalry in the December 1866 Fetterman Massacre. In the 1868 Fort Laramie Treaty, the U.S. government agreed to abandon the forts and close the Bozeman Trail in exchange for peace, giving the natives a rare victory in their wars to defend their territory.

Red Cloud's triumph was short-lived, however. The discovery of gold in the Black Hills of South Dakota in 1874, territory reserved to the natives by the treaty that ended Red Cloud's War, brought a rush of miners onto Native American land. Federal officials offered to purchase the territory, and when the natives refused to sell, the government appropriated the land. Native resistance culminated in the 1876–1877 Great Sioux War. The most notable action was the near destruction of Lieutenant Colonel George Armstrong Custer's command in the June 1876 Battle of the Little Bighorn. Despite this success, the Sioux and their allies could not withstand the forces brought against them. By 1877, the Sioux and their allies had surrendered except for Sitting Bull, who had led his followers to Canada, before returning to surrender in 1881.

Another war in 1877 involved the Nez Perce of Oregon. Chief Joseph and other leaders declined to move their bands to a reservation, and in spring 1877, the army threatened to remove them by force. Before Joseph could comply, some Nez Perce warriors killed a few white settlers, and when Joseph attempted to negotiate a peaceful resolution, he was attacked by troops and civilian volunteers. The Nez Perce then waged a running battle across Idaho and Montana in an epic bid to remain free, but they failed to reach Canada and were forced to surrender.

With the notable exception of the Apaches, there was little native resistance after 1877, as most tribes had been defeated and confined to reservations. However, in 1890 military authorities feared a revival of Native American warfare as a new nativist religious movement swept across the West. Inspired by Wovoka, a Paiute prophet, who predicted the resurrection of Native American dead and renewal of the earth if his followers performed the Ghost Dance ritual, thousands of Native Americans began performing the dance. As the movement spread eastward, it became more militant, especially on the Sioux reservations, and some Native Americans left their reservations to avoid white scrutiny. One proponent of the Ghost Dance movement, Big Foot of the Miniconjou Sioux, was leading his people to the Pine Ridge Reservation in South Dakota to surrender when he was confronted by U.S. troops at Wounded Knee. On December 29, as the soldiers began to disarm the Sioux, shots were fired. More than 150 Sioux and 25 soldiers died in the ensuing battle. Although the last Sioux refugees from the reservations did not surrender until January 1891, the Battle of Wounded Knee is generally accepted as marking the end of the Indian Wars in North America.

Did the American Indian Wars Constitute Genocide?

Perhaps the most hotly debated question concerning the American Indian Wars is whether they constituted genocide. Although "genocide" usually provokes images of the Holocaust, it is important to note that Raphael Lemkin, who coined the term "genocide" from the Greek word "*genos*," which means "tribe or race," and the Latin word "cide," which means "killing," did not restrict the definition of genocide to the mass extermination of a race but instead provided a much broader definition that included the destruction of a group's political, social, and cultural identity as a people. By applying Lemkin's broader definition of genocide and considering the broader policies toward Native Americans (using Prussian General Carl von Clausewitz's famous dictum that "war is a mere continuation of policy by other means"), it becomes clear that the Indian Wars constituted cultural genocide.

The policies that the United States pursued toward Native Americans followed a pattern similar to that of the first English colonists. The most important factor that created conflict between English colonists and Native Americans was the seizure of Indian lands as the colonial population expanded westward from the Atlantic seaboard. Unlike the French and Spanish, the English made little effort to incorporate Native Americans into colonial society. Although Puritan missionary John Eliot was an exception in attempting to convert Native Americans to Christianity, native converts were segregated into "Praying Towns" and forced to adopt English cultural customs. By depriving Native Americans of their ancestral hunting lands, upon which their existence and culture depended, or forcing them to convert and adopt white culture, these policies amount to cultural genocide. In some instances, such as the Pequot War (1636–1638) and King Philip's War (1675–1676), the Puritans of New England virtually annihilated their Pequot and Narragansett opponents, meeting the standard of genocide.

The success of the United States in achieving its independence from Great Britain placed Native Americans in a precarious position, because the Treaty of Paris of 1783 granted the United States sovereignty over the land south of the Great Lakes and east of the Mississippi River (excluding Spanish Florida). After President Thomas Jefferson's administration successfully negotiated the Louisiana Purchase in 1803, the prospect of removing Eastern tribes to west of the Mississippi emerged as a new aspect of federal policy by encouraging trade that would lead to indebtedness and in turn force tribes to cede land. Jefferson also promoted assimilation as a policy with Congress appropriating funds to induce Native Americans to abandon hunting and adopt agriculture. In 1819, Congress established the Civilization Fund for Indian education, dispensing funds through missionary organizations, which established missions and schools among Native Americans. The five leading Southern tribes—Cherokees, Choctaws, Chickasaws, Creeks, and Seminoles—actively adopted aspects of white culture, including plantation agriculture, Black slavery, schools, churches, newspapers, and written laws and constitutions.

The passage of the Indian Removal Act in 1830 is one of the most controversial aspects of federal Indian policy, especially as applied to the Southern tribes that had assimilated so closely to white culture. Although Jackson has been vilified for the resulting "Trail of Tears" in which approximately 25 percent of Cherokees, Choctaws, Chickasaws, Creeks, and Seminoles died of exposure and starvation during their forced removal to Indian Territory, it should be emphasized that this resulted from the policy's flawed implementation rather than a stated objective of the policy per se. In addition, Francis Paul Prucha forcefully argues that Jackson's policy was not based on hatred of Indians but was more a practical matter of denying them dual sovereignty. Those willing to enter white society could remain behind and become citizens, while those wishing to retain their tribal identity could do so by removing to Indian territory, where they would gain the time to evolve further on the path to civilization, which in Jackson's view would prevent their extinction. Although the "Trail of Tears" was

tragic, it does not quite meet the standard of genocide, and the extent to which tribes were allowed to retain their identity, albeit by removal, does not quite meet the standard of cultural genocide.

The annexation of Texas in 1845, the acquisition of the Oregon Territory in 1846, and the Mexican Cession following the Mexican-American War (1846–1848) marked the beginning of a new phase in the Indian Wars that included numerous individual actions that in themselves were genocidal. In the infamous Sand Creek Massacre on November 29, 1864, Colorado militiamen under Colonel John M. Chivington attached Cheyenne Chief Black Kettle's peaceful village of 500 Indians located approximately 40 miles northeast of Fort Lyon and ruthlessly slaughtered almost 150 Cheyennes, mostly women and children. Four years later, on November 27, 1868, Lieutenant Colonel George Armstrong Custer led the 7th Cavalry on a dawn attack of Black Kettle's peaceful village on the Washita River, killing Black Kettle and more than 100 Cheyennes, mainly women and children. A few months later, Lieutenant General Philip H. Sheridan is reputed to have stated, "The only good Indians I ever saw were dead." Although this infamous phrase may be anecdotal, it represented the outlook of many individuals and soldiers on the frontier even if it was not official government policy.

Many aspects of federal Indian policy systematically sought to destroy Native American culture. The irony is that most who promoted this effort were well-intentioned, although misguided reformers, such as Senator Henry L. Dawes of Massachusetts, Editor Lyman Abbot of *The Christian Union*, and Reverend F. F. Ellinwood of the Presbyterian Board of Foreign Missions. Along with leading educators, they launched a "reform" movement beginning in the 1880s designed to destroy traditional Native American culture, eliminate tribal land ownership, and replace native religions and social customs with Christianity and white culture. Their efforts resulted in Senator Dawes's General Allotment Act of 1887, which divided reservations into individual homesteads with the extension of citizenship to those receiving allotments. It also opened 90 million acres of excess tribal land left over from allotments to white settlement. Education policy sought to eradicate native culture by moving children to off-reservation boarding schools, where children were often punished for speaking their native language, were given Anglo names, and were often placed into white families to further acculturation. Meanwhile, clergymen serving as Indian agents made a concerted effort to suppress native religions. The Curtis Act of 1898, ironically sponsored by U.S. Senator Charles Curtis of Kansas, a mixed-blood Native American, voided treaties with the tribes within Indian Territory by abolished their tribal governments, implementing individual allotment of tribal lands, and opening excess land for white settlement. In short, reformers sought to save Native Americans from physical extinction by trying to destroy the very characteristics that made them Native Americans. These policies clearly amount to cultural genocide.

Nevertheless, it must be noted that Native Americans resisted efforts to eradicate their culture. Ironically, Native Americans, such as Dr. Charles A. Eastman and Dr. Carlos Montezuma, who were products of the very educational system designed to destroy their culture, emerged as leaders in the early 20th century to champion Indian rights. They found an ally in John Collier, Commissioner of Indian Affairs from 1933 to 1945, who convinced Congress to pass the Indian Reorganization Act of 1934, which prohibited further allotments, allowed tribes to create their own businesses, and recognized their right to create their own constitutions and elect their own governments. Although the Eisenhower Administration attempted to reverse aspects of Collier's policies by terminating federal relations with tribes and relocating Indians from reservations to cities to accelerate their assimilation, the Civil Rights Movement of the 1960s led to the Indian Civil Rights Act of 1968, which accepted tribal laws based on tribal culture, although it required tribes to protect civil rights guaranteed by the Constitution. More important, the Indian Self-Determination and Education Assistance Act of 1975 empowered tribal governments by allowing them to administer federal assistance programs. As a result of their incredible perseverance, Native Americans have managed to survive and retain their cultural heritage, even though the extreme poverty and appalling health conditions on reservations clearly demonstrate that Native Americans continue to suffer the long-term effects of the cultural genocide inflicted upon them.

A

Abenaki Wars

Start Date: 1675
End Date: 1727

Conflict between the Abenakis and English settlers began as a result of King Philip's War (1675–1676). The Abenaki Wars were not true warfare in the classic sense, as they involved little actual combat; instead, they were marked chiefly by a massive Abenaki population displacement along the northern frontier. Constituent bands of the Algonquian-speaking Abenakis included the Androscoggin, Kennebec, Maliseet, Passamaquoddy, Pennacook, Penobscot, Saco, and Wawenock peoples who lived in the areas of Maine, New Hampshire, and New Brunswick. These bands had formed a loose confederacy by the end of the 16th century. A second group of Abenakis lived in Vermont, but this group acted largely independently of the more eastern bands.

From their first contact with Europeans, the Abenakis traded with them and had enjoyed good relations with the English in the first half of the 17th century; however, by the 1650s, the Abenakis had gravitated toward the French. Catholic French missionaries, dispatched to the Abenaki, promised them protection against their aggressive Iroquois neighbors. French interest in the fur trade strengthened ties. The English to the south, by contrast, had little interest in commercial ties with the Abenakis. The gradual expansion of the English toward Abenaki territory also heightened tensions between English colonists and the Abenakis.

The First Abenaki War (1675–1678) began as an outgrowth of King Philip's War. Algonquian-speaking refugees from New England fled to the Abenakis in an attempt to avoid the campaigns of the English. Contributing to the already tense situation, Massachusetts settlers living near the Abenakis demanded that the Abenakis relinquish their firearms to demonstrate that they were not in league with the Wampanoags. Without firearms and cut off from trade with the English on which they depended, the Abenakis faced starvation and hardship. The English failed to help matters when they overturned the canoe containing the children and wife of Abenaki chieftain Squando into the Saco River, leaving them to drown. In 1675, several Abenaki bands moved north to the French-established missions, while other bands remained neutral. In general, the Abenakis retreated northward rather than engage the English, but English raiding parties continued to push the Abenakis off of their lands.

Following the end of King Philip's War in 1676, English colonists in Massachusetts saw little need to compromise with the Abenakis, who continued to flee Massachusetts. In 1678, New York Governor Edmund Andros negotiated a peace treaty with the Abenaki, which officially ended the war but did little to address its root causes. Continuing tension over English expansion onto Abenaki lands ensured persistent conflict. Furthermore, Abenaki alignment with the French meant that the French would seek their aid against the English whenever war in Europe broke out.

The Abenaki Wars contributed to a sense of crisis in the Massachusetts Bay Colony following King Philip's War. English refugees from fighting along the Maine frontier sojourned across Massachusetts, and their stories of Native American brutality convinced many that Satan was at work. The evident union of the heathen Native Americans with the Catholic French offered further proof of satanic agency to New Englanders.

The end of the First Abenaki War failed to secure a lasting settlement, leading to three more distinct wars between the Abenakis and the English. The Second Abenaki War (1688–1699) erupted in 1688 and merged into King William's War (1689–1697) as the French attempted to capitalize on the conflict to further their fight against the English. The Third Abenaki War likewise overlapped with Queen Anne's War (1702–1713). The Abenakis seized the opportunity of renewed conflict between France and England to settle old scores. For instance, a party of Abenakis accompanied the group of French soldiers and Indians that attacked Deerfield, Massachusetts, in 1704. Conflict erupted again in the Fourth Abenaki War of 1722–1727 largely because of continued English expansion into Maine. Abenaki auxiliaries accompanied French soldiers into battle as late as the French and Indian War of 1754–1763. The French defeat in that conflict spelled disaster for the Abenakis, who dispersed and were driven from their land.

Peter C. Luebke

Further Reading

Calloway, Colin G. *The Western Abenakis of Vermont, 1600–1800: War, Migration, and the Survival of an Indian People*. Norman: University of Oklahoma Press, 1990.

Morrison, Kenneth M. *The Embattled Northeast: The Elusive Ideal of Alliance in Abenaki-Euramerican Relations*. Berkeley: University of California Press, 1984.

Algonquins

Native American people who occupied the Ottawa River Valley, the border between the present-day Canadian provinces of Ontario and Quebec. Both Algonquin and Algonkin are acceptable spellings of the tribal name, although in their own language the Algonquins call themselves Anishnabe or Anishinabe, meaning "original person" (the plural is Anishnabek or Anishnabeg). The word "Algonquian" (Algonkian) refers to a group of languages that include those of not only the Algonquins but also the Cheyennes, Arapahos, Crees, Blackfeet, and Ojibwas, among others. Algonquian is in fact the largest North American native language group. The Iroquois, however, referred to the Algonquins as the Adirondacks (literally "they eat trees").

In 1603, when they first encountered the French, the Algonquins probably numbered some 6,000 people. In 1768, the British estimated the Algonquin population at 1,500 people. The Algonquins were a seminomadic people, being too far north for settled agriculture. In contrast to the neighboring Iroquois to the west and the south, who lived primarily by agriculture in large fortified communities, the Algonquins were hunter-gatherers and trappers who lived in villages. Their shelters were of birchbark, known as waginogans or wigwams, and Algonquins traveled by water in birchbark canoes. In winter, the villages split into smaller extended family units for hunting. The harsh winter conditions would not allow additional burdens, and the Algonquins were, in consequence, often known to kill the sick or badly injured among them. Algonquins were patrilineal, with hunting rights passed down from father to son. The Algonquins were known as fierce warriors, and they dominated the Iroquois until those tribes came together in the Iroquois Confederacy.

When Jacques Cartier first arrived in the Saint Lawrence River Valley in 1534, he found only Iroquoian-speaking people living in the area between Stadacona (Quebec) and Hochelaga (Montreal), but following near-continual warfare between the Iroquois and the Algonquins from 1570 and the resultant formation of the Iroquois Confederacy, the Iroquois drove the Algonquins north from the Adirondack Mountains and the upper Hudson River Valley. The Alqonquins in turn displaced or absorbed Iroquoian-speaking native peoples along the Saint Lawrence.

In 1603, Samuel de Champlain made contact with the Algonquins when he established a French trading post along the Saint Lawrence at Tadoussac. He soon learned that the Hurons rather than the Algonquins dominated the upper Saint Lawrence. Anxious to secure both free passage and furs, in 1609 Champlain aided the Algonquins, Montagnais, and Hurons in an expedition against the Mohawks of the Iroquois Confederacy. Although by the time of the battle the French contingent numbered only Champlain and two others, their firearms proved the difference in battle, and the Mohawks fled.

This victory brought a formal alliance between the French and the Algonquins and also brought about trade in furs in exchange for the European tools and weapons sought by the Native Americans. By 1610, the Algonquins, led by their chief, Piskaret, dominated the Saint Lawrence Valley. In

the process, however, the French had made an implacable enemy of the Mohawks. In 1614, Champlain participated in an Algonquin-Huron attack on the Oneida and Onondaga nations of the Iroquois Confederacy, cementing Iroquois enmity toward the French. Soon the French were doing most of their fur trading with the Hurons rather than the Algonquins, much to the displeasure of the latter.

Intermittent fighting continued between the Mohawks and the Algonquins and Montagnais. In 1629, the Mohawks attacked the Algonquins and Montagnais near Quebec in a precursor to the so-called Beaver Wars (1641–1701). This fighting was prompted by the desire of the Iroquois to expand northward. From 1629 to 1632, the Mohawks, taking advantage of the temporary defeat of the French by the English, drove the Algonquins and Montagnais from the upper Saint Lawrence Valley. Peace terms allowed the French to return to Quebec in 1632, when they sought to restore their alliances by furnishing firearms to native groups. This effort proved unsuccessful, especially as the Dutch in turn provided the Mohawks with large quantities of the latest firearms. By the end of the 1640s, the Mohawks and Oneidas had driven the remaining Algonquins and Montagnais from the upper Saint Lawrence and lower Ottawa River areas. The Iroquois had also defeated the Hurons.

The arrival of a contingent of regular French troops in 1664 allowed the Quebec government to conclude peace with the Iroquois three years later. The French then resumed trading with the western Great Lakes region. The peace also permitted the Algonquins, now greatly reduced in number, to begin returning to the Ottawa Valley.

Although only some Algonquins converted to Catholicism, they were bound to the French cause during the French and

Indian War (1754–1763). In August 1760, after British forces had taken Quebec, the Algonquins and other Native American allies of the French made peace with the English, agreeing to remain neutral in any future fighting between the English and the French. This agreement helped to seal the fate of New France.

The Algonquins continued their new loyalty to the British, fighting on their side during the American Revolutionary War (1775–1783) and taking part in Lieutenant Colonel Barry St. Leger's campaign in the Mohawk Valley in 1777. Following the war when many British Loyalists fled to Canada, the British government settled many of them on lands in the lower Ottawa Valley. Despite this, the Algonquins also fought on the British side in the War of 1812, helping to defeat U.S. troops in the Battle of Chateauguay in October 1813. The reward to the Algonquins for their loyalty was to be continually pushed off their ancestral lands.

Ultimately, purchases by the Canadian government resulted in the establishment of reserves (reservations) for the Algonquins in their former homeland. Today, the majority of remaining Algonquins live on nine reserves in the province of Quebec and one reserve in Ontario.

Spencer C. Tucker

Further Reading

Clement, Daniel, ed. *The Algonquins*. Hull and Quebec: Canadian Museum of Civilization/Musée Canadien des Civilisations, 1996.

Couture, Yvon H. *Les Algonquins*. Quebec: Éditions Hyperborée, 1983.

White, Richard. *The Middle Ground: Indians, Empires, and Republics in the Great Lakes Region, 1650–1815*. New York: Cambridge University Press, 1991.

Anglo-Powhatan Wars

Start Date: 1610
End Date: 1646

A series of wars in Virginia between English colonists and the Powhatan Confederacy. The main catalyst for war was European encroachment on native lands. By the end of the wars, the Powhatans were forced to retreat into the interior west of the Tidewater region.

From the beginning of the English settlement at Jamestown in 1607, sporadic violence between colonists and the Powhatans had taken place, even though leaders on both sides tried to exercise restraint. The concept of land ownership was the chief cause of antagonism. The natives used land communally, while colonists believed strongly in private land ownership and erected fences and walls to demarcate such ownership. As more colonists arrived in Virginia, they cut down the forests and killed or drove away the game on which the Indians depended for both food and clothing.

The First Anglo-Powhatan War began in 1610 after Powhatan, the leader of the confederacy of tribes that bore his name, informed the Jamestown settlers that he would tolerate no further exploration of the region. He also warned the English to restrict themselves to Jamestown. Later that summer, Thomas West, Lord de la Warr, the newly arrived governor of Virginia, chose to ignore Powhatan's warnings and sent a group of explorers up the James River to search for valuable minerals. At the Indian village of Appomattox, the natives invited the explorers to eat and rest and then killed all but one. In retaliation, on August 9, 1610, acting on de la Warr's orders, George Percy, a member of the powerful Northumberland family and a deputy in the colony's government, led 70 men to the village of Paspahegh. There the English took captive a wife and children of Chief Wowinchopunch, who ruled the town but was subordinate to Powhatan. The wife was taken into the woods and killed. Once they reached the James River, the English threw the children into the water and shot them as they struggled to escape. In all, some 50 natives were slain. Percy's men burned some other Indian villages and seized their stocks of corn before returning to Jamestown. Fighting quickly escalated as native warriors, led by Opechancanough, Powhatan's younger brother, attacked Jamestown and laid siege to its fort, while colonists raided native villages and burned crops. Over a three-year span, both sides continually harassed the other, although no pitched battles occurred. The actual number of fatalities on both sides is unknown.

The First Anglo-Powhatan War was fought native style, replete with ambushes, kidnappings, and torture. In April 1613, Powhatan's favorite daughter, Pocahontas (Matoaka), had been lured aboard an English ship, captured by Captain Samuel Argall, and held hostage. Three months later, Powhatan offered food to the English in return for his daughter's release. Argall saw the value of his prisoner and made greater demands. Powhatan accordingly offered a considerable ransom for Pocahontas's return. Meanwhile, English reinforcements arrived, lifting the native siege of Jamestown.

In the end, the English arrived at a political solution in 1614 to end the First Anglo-Powhatan War. John Rolfe had settled in Jamestown in 1610. He introduced tobacco as a cash crop and was among the wealthiest Virginians. Rolfe married Pocahontas at Jamestown on April 5, 1614, sealing a peace agreement, which required Powhatan to return all English captives, runaways, tools, and firearms in his people's possession.

Despite the agreement in 1614, hostilities between the English and Powhatans simmered. Although Powhatan remained paramount chief until his death in 1618, Opechancanough and others hostile to the English dominated Powhatan diplomacy after that time. The Powhatans were frustrated by English exploration, demands for food, and attempts to impose their culture and religion on the natives. More important, the cultivation of tobacco changed the balance of power in Virginia as some 3,000 English settlers arrived between 1617 and 1622 to take advantage of the tobacco boom. English settlement spread far beyond Jamestown and put unprecedented pressure on Powhatan territory.

The Second Anglo-Powhatan War (1622–1632) began on March 22, 1622, with a massive surprise assault by the Powhatans on the English settlers near Jamestown. For years, Opechancanough lulled the colonists into a sense of security with friendly overtures and by ignoring their abuses. While Opechancanough was appeasing the English, he quietly negotiated with the various Powhatan tribes to join in a fight that would eliminate the English threat. Just before the first assault on March 22, 1622, two Powhatans betrayed Opechancanough's plans and warned the English of the coming attack. Nonetheless, the Powhatans killed 347 settlers that day, about one-fourth of the entire English population in the colony.

Once the colonists regrouped from the devastating attack, bitter fighting ensued. The English launched raids against Powhatan villages and sniped at any native in the range of their firearms. Nearly another quarter of the English population died in 1624 from small-scale native raids, starvation, dysentery, and other diseases. The climax of the war came in a large-scale battle at the town of Pamunkey in 1624 in which the English were victorious. The native threat to the English diminished greatly afterward, and warring parties finally negotiated a peace in 1632.

The Second Anglo-Powhatan War permanently changed English views toward Native Americans. Prior to 1622, many settlers envisioned living harmoniously among the natives, whom they expected to convert to Christianity and English cultural mores. After the conflict, the English no longer desired to incorporate Powhatans as English subjects. Most English now wanted to rid the land of natives altogether or at the least to keep them as servants or slaves. Another result of the war was that King James I declared Virginia a royal colony, revoking the charter of the Virginia Company of London for mismanaging the colony and endangering the lives of colonists.

Following their defeat in the Second Anglo-Powhatan War, natives watched the growing number of settlers in Virginia occupy more Powhatan land. Eager to profit from the sale of tobacco, a crop that rapidly depleted the soil, the English expanded their settlements throughout the Tidewater region along the James, York, Rappahannock, and Potomac rivers. As Virginia's settler population grew rapidly, reaching an estimated 8,000 people in 1640, Opechancanough had few options. His people, whose population had declined in size, had been pushed to the far western reaches of their land. If they chose to abandon their homes and try to reestablish themselves among their native enemies farther to the west, the Powhatans would lose their cultural identity and possibly their lives. To allow the English to occupy their remaining territory would leave the Powhatans powerless and render the destruction of their culture certain.

Although Opechancanough was elderly (nearly 70 years old) and frail, he opted for war, even though the odds were against the Powhatans and defeat would mean annihilation. On March 18, 1644, Opechancanough, borne on a litter by some of his men, launched the Third Anglo-Powhatan War (1644–1646) as the Powhatans and their allies attacked English settlements along the James, York, and Rappahannock rivers. The assaults took colonists by surprise, killing 400–500 in the initial onslaught. Many others abandoned their farms and took refuge in fortified buildings. Although the Powhatans killed many more settlers than they had in their attack of 1622, the impact of the new attack was less significant given the increase in the number of colonists. While the attack of 1622 killed 25 percent of English colonists, that of 1644 brought about the deaths of just 8.3 percent of settlers. Regrouping swiftly, the Virginians launched counterattacks against native towns, burning buildings and crops and killing any natives they found. Within six months, colonists had reoccupied all abandoned plantations. Sporadic fighting continued until the late summer of 1646, when Opechancanough was captured, brought to Jamestown, and murdered by one of his guards.

Opechancanough's death marked the end of Powhatan resistance. His successor, Necotowance, signed a treaty in October 1646 by which the Powhatans ceded most of their remaining land to the English. The natives would henceforth be confined to the territory allotted to them north of the York river by the victors, in effect the first Indian reservations in North America. The Powhatans also agreed to surrender all English prisoners and firearms, return any runaway servants who might come to them, and pay an annual tribute of furs. Unfortunately, only a few years passed before the English grew covetous of the land left to the Powhatans in the treaty. Thus, in less than 40 years, the powerful Powhatan Confederacy had been destroyed and English domination of the Tidewater region of Virginia had been secured.

Thomas John Blumer,
Jennifer Bridges Oast, and Jim Piecuch

Further Reading

Cave, Alfred A. *Lethal Encounters: Englishmen and Indians in Colonial Virginia.* Santa Barbara, CA: Praeger/ABC-CLIO, 2011.

Gleach, Frederic W. *Powhatan's World and Colonial Virginia.* Lincoln: University of Nebraska Press, 1997.

Rountree, Helen C., and E. Randolph Turner III. *Before and After Jamestown: Virginia's Powhatans and Their Predecessors.* Gainesville: University Press of Florida, 2002.

Apache Wars

Start Date: 1861
End Date: 1886

Series of conflicts in the Southwest between the Apaches and United States. No formal declaration of hostilities signaled the beginning of the bloody Apache Wars. Instead, two separate incidents, one in 1860 and another in 1861, sparked a decades-long conflict that did not end until 1886, when Chiricahua leader Geronimo surrendered to U.S. forces.

In May 1860, prospectors discovered gold in the heart of Mimbres territory in southern New Mexico, causing an influx of more than 700 miners. Mangas Coloradas, a well-respected Mimbres chief, visited a mining camp and was immediately captured, bound, and whipped. Two years later, Mangas became a prisoner of the military at Fort McLane. Two army privates taunted him by pressing hot bayonets to his feet. When he strenuously objected, they killed him. The Apaches considered both events worthy of revenge.

At about the same time Cochise, Mangas's son-in-law, was the victim of similar abuse. Cochise ranged with his Chiricahua Apache band across the deserts, grasslands, and mountains of southeastern Arizona. Known by the Americans as a friendly and cooperative Apache, Cochise had an agreement with the U.S. government to supply wood to the Butterfield Stage Station in the Sulphur Springs Valley. In February 1861, he received word that a contingent of soldiers had arrived and that they wanted to speak with him. Cochise complied only to be mistakenly accused by young army lieutenant George N. Bascom of kidnapping a rancher's son. Although wounded, Cochise escaped, but his five companions, three of whom were relatives, were held and subsequently killed. Apache custom demanded reprisal, so Cochise killed frontiersmen, drovers, stagecoach passengers, mail riders, soldiers, and anyone else who set foot in his territory.

The Apache Wars raged for 25 years. During those decades, a tide of miners, merchants, businessmen, missionaries, schoolteachers, soldiers, mercenaries, scalp hunters, and settlers all risked their lives entering Apache territory. Whites expected protection from the forts that had been established across the Southwest after the Treaty of Guadalupe Hidalgo in 1848 and the Gadsden Purchase in 1853.

The Apaches remained in small bands, each independent of the other and with each warrior completely acclimated to the harsh terrain and arid climate and able to travel 40 miles a day on foot without food or water. Relying on guerrilla warfare, traveling at night, and hiding during the day in rocky points and high places, Apaches attacked, murdered, plundered, scattered, and then regrouped at predetermined sites, carrying with them the weapons and ammunition taken from their enemies.

Despite the advantages that a guerrilla force has when protecting its homeland and the Apaches' extremely competent leadership, one fight in particular, the Battle of Apache Pass (July 15–16, 1862), showed how vulnerable Native Americans were to superior American firepower. Apache Pass, located in southeastern Arizona, is a narrow defile between the Chiricahua Mountains to the south and the Dos Cabezas range to the north. The area contained a flowing spring, the only reliable water supply for miles around. As Brigadier General James H. Carleton led a regiment of California volunteers eastward to fight the Confederates in New Mexico during the American Civil War (1861–1865), he entered Apache Pass on July 15. Apache warriors were on the cliffs high above the spring. Kicking down rocks and boulders and using traditional weapons as well as firearms, they killed two soldiers and wounded two others. When the army's howitzers responded, however, the terrified Apaches fled from their positions but not before losing an estimated 10–40 warriors. Cochise's warriors halfheartedly resumed the battle the next day, but the troops again fired their howitzers, and the Apaches scattered once more. As a consequence of the Battle of Apache Pass, Carleton recommended that a fort be established in the vicinity; it was built and was designated Fort Bowie.

Throughout the Civil War years, Carleton and other officers established new forts and camps, while volunteer units campaigned relentlessly against the Apaches and other groups. The Mescalero Apaches were particularly hard hit during this period. Despite the return of the regular army in 1867, various bands of Apaches and Yavapais continued to raid settlements and mining camps. Complicating matters for the army was a civilian population with little interest in peaceful coexistence with the Indians. Depredations perpetrated by settlers, such as the infamous Camp Grant Massacre of 1871 in which perhaps 150 Apaches, mostly women and children, were murdered, made President Ulysses S. Grant's peace policy almost impossible to implement.

In 1872, Brigadier General Oliver O. Howard arrived in Arizona in hopes of establishing peace with the Apaches. Although Howard negotiated a settlement with Cochise and established a more workable reservation system, Apache and Yavapai raiding continued, prompting department commander Lieutenant Colonel George Crook to launch his highly successful Tonto Basin Campaign during the winter of 1872–1873. Crook established a new model for operating against the Apaches, including the extensive use of Indian scouts and pack mule trains in place of cumbersome wagons. The peace overtures of Howard combined with Crook's inspired campaigning brought a temporary peace.

Following the death of Cochise in 1874, his son Naiche (Nachez) and the shaman Geronimo continued to defy U.S. plans to settle the Southwest. Apaches used the reservations in Arizona and New Mexico as protected bases from which to raid northern Mexico. The government's decision to consolidate most Apaches on the inhospitable San Carlos Reservation in 1876 contributed to a resumption of major hostilities. Several hundred Apaches, including Geronimo's Chiricahuas, raided both sides of the border, which brought a renewed effort to confine the Chiricahuas and their Warm Springs Apache allies from New Mexico on the San Carlos Reservation.

The Warm Springs faction led by Victorio broke from the reservation in 1879, resulting in a bloody rampage on both sides of the border in what became known as the Victorio War. For two years, Victorio occupied considerable numbers of U.S. and Mexican troops, including most of the 9th and 10th U.S. Cavalry regiments, before he and his band were wiped out by Mexican irregulars in the mountains of northern Mexico in October 1880.

In 1881, prompted by the deplorable conditions at the San Carlos Reservation and the killing of a popular shaman in a fight at Cibecue Creek, Apaches left the reservation in large numbers. Some attacked nearby Fort Apache, while Geronimo and some 70 Chiricahuas bolted for Mexico, where they joined the remnants of Victorio's band and raided furiously on both sides of the border. In September 1882, Crook returned to command the Department of Arizona. Crook's arrival coincided with the implementation of a reciprocal crossing agreement between the United States and Mexico that Crook soon exploited, leading a large expedition into Sonora in May 1883. Pressured by U.S. and Mexican troops, Geronimo, Nana, Natchez, and others met with Crook and agreed to return to the reservation.

Geronimo's return to San Carlos in March 1884 proved short-lived, as he led another breakout in May 1885. Bloody raiding across Arizona, New Mexico, and northern Mexico followed. Crook sent two columns into Mexico, while hundreds of other troops picketed the border and protected key areas. The campaign proved fruitless, which only encouraged more raids. In late 1885, Crook dispatched two more columns, largely comprising Indian scouts. The detachment led by the gifted Captain Emmet Crawford located the fugitive Apaches, but so too did Mexican militia, who attacked the soldiers and scouts, killing Crawford. In March 1886, Crook, Geronimo, and other Apache leaders met at the Cañon de los Embudos.

When Geronimo failed to report as promised, Crook asked to be relieved and was replaced by Brigadier General Nelson A. Miles, who launched a massive effort to catch Geronimo, including a grueling 2,000-mile march through northern Mexico led by Captain Henry Lawton. Meanwhile, Miles ordered the relocation of all Chiricahua and Warm Springs Apaches on the reservation to prisons in Florida. Having failed to catch Geronimo and his small band of followers with upward of 5,000 regular troops, Miles sent Lieutenant Charles B. Gatewood and two Indian Scouts into Mexico to bring in Geronimo. In early September 1886, Gatewood's scouts located Geronimo. Upon learning that his people had been moved to Florida, Geronimo recognized the futility of continued resistance and agreed to return with Gatewood to U.S. soil, where he surrendered to Miles in Skeleton Canyon, Arizona, on September 4, 1886. Within days, Geronimo and the remaining Chiricahuas, including the loyal scouts so instrumental during the long campaign, were loaded on trains for the trip to prisons in Florida.

H. Henrietta Stockel and David Coffey

Further Reading

Aleshire, Peter. *Reaping the Whirlwind: The Apache Wars.* New York: Facts on File, 1998.

Sweeney, Edwin R. *Cochise: Chiricahua Apache Chief.* Norman: University of Oklahoma Press, 1991.

Sweeney, Edwin R. *From Cochise to Geronimo: The Chiricahua Apaches 1874–1886.* Norman: University of Oklahoma Press, 2012.

Thrapp, Dan L. *The Conquest of Apacheria.* Norman: University of Oklahoma Press, 1967.

Apaches

Generic term used to describe numerous separate Native American groups who traditionally habituated the American Southwest (principally Arizona and New Mexico). The term "Apache" means "enemy" and was a name given to these people by the Zuni tribe of New Mexico. The Apaches referred to themselves as "the people." They spoke a variety of different but related Athabaskan dialects, including Chiricahua, Jicarilla, Mescalero, Mimbreño, White Mountain, and Aravapai.

Because the Apaches were a seminomadic people who were never united as a nation but instead identified themselves by family or clan relationships and the region in which they ranged, anthropologists and historians have often differed when identifying specific bands, leading to much confusion in the historical record. Perhaps the best approach is to group them into the six geographic regions that comprise Apacheria. First, the Lipan Apaches ranged in what is now western Texas from the Edwards Plateau to the Rio Grande. Second, the Jicarilla Apaches ranged in what is now northeastern New Mexico, east of the Rio Grande and north of Sante Fe and Las Vegas to Taos. Third, the Mescalero Apaches ranged in the Sierra Blanca and Sacramento Mountains of south-central New Mexico. Fourth, the Gila Apaches, which included the Mimbres, Warm Springs, and Mogollon bands, ranged in the upper regions of the Gila River along the New Mexico–Arizona border from the Datil Mountains south to Chihuahua. Fifth, the Western Apaches included the Coyotero or White Mountain Apaches, who ranged in the middle Gila River region of eastern Arizona, and the Aravapai, San Carlos, and Tonto bands, who ranged in eastern and central Arizona. Sixth, the Chiracahua Apaches ranged from the Dragoon Mountains of southern Arizona into northern Mexico. Because many of these regions overlapped, it is not surprising that one band often viewed another with suspicion and mistrust and that some bands occasionally warred against other Apache bands, a likely reason they never unified as a cohesive group or nation.

The Apaches drew a clear distinction between raiding and warfare. Raiding was undertaken solely for the purpose of stealing goods, principally horses and livestock. Raiding parties, which usually engaged no more than 15 individuals, launched stealth attacks to avoid detection or a larger conflict. The Apaches also hunted small and large game, gathered wild foods, and engaged in small-scale agriculture. Corn was a principal crop, as were beans and squash. Most Apaches also engaged in trade among themselves and with other Native American groups as well as non-natives. Warfare, usually undertaken to avenge a hostile act or to eliminate an imminent threat, was more methodical and was mainly designed to kill as many of the enemy as possible. War chiefs would sometimes raise several hundred warriors to engage in a military attack.

Throughout the 17th and 18th centuries, the Apaches resisted Spanish efforts to move into their lands. The Apaches also raided into northern Mexico to acquire horses and take captives, who were incorporated into the tribe. The efforts of Spain (and Mexico after its independence) to suppress the Apaches resulted in lasting enmity. Indeed, hatred of the Mexicans was so strong, in large measure because of the bounties that Mexico paid for Apache scalps, that most Apaches welcomed the arrival of American forces during the Mexican-American War (1846–1848). Once it became clear that the Americans intended to stay in the Southwest, the Apaches proved to be among the most difficult foes that the United States would face during the Indian Wars of the 19th century.

The Lipans were among the first to suffer the consequences of American expansion, which is ironic because they had befriended the first American immigrants who settled in Texas and had supported them during the Texas Revolution against Mexico (1835–1836). After Texas won independence in 1836, the Lipans not only joined Texans in military actions against the Comanches but also helped defend Austin, Houston, and other Texas cities in 1842 when Mexico's Army of the North invaded Texas. In addition, when Alexander Somervell led a daring punitive expedition into Mexico in November 1842, Lipan warriors rode alongside him, prompting Texas president Sam Houston to promise that Texas would always be "kind" to the Lipans.

Unfortunately for the Lipans, after the United States annexed Texas in 1845, the U.S. government subjected the state's Native Americans to its national policies of Indian removal. Throughout the 1850s, the U.S. Army increased troop strengths at forts on or near Lipan lands and mounted punitive raids against Lipan encampments. Although the American Civil War (1861–1865) halted attacks against the Lipans for a time, the army reentered Texas in force after the war and in 1872 and 1873 conducted a brutal campaign of annihilation against the Lipans. By 1880, most of the surviving Lipans had scattered, giving up their land and traditional way of life to hide among the Tejano populations (Hispanic Texans), especially around San Antonio, Corpus Christi, and the Rio Grande, while others moved onto the Mescalero Reservation in New Mexico. Today the Lipan Apache tribe is petitioning the State of Texas for official recognition.

The Mescaleros, from the Spanish term for "mescal makers," had traditionally warred against the Comanches and routinely raided the Pueblos. During the early 1850s, the Mescaleros also began attacking white settlers in New Mexico and stagecoaches on the San Antonio–El Paso road. In January 1855, Captain Richard S. Ewell and Captain Henry W. Stanton led a two-pronged invasion of the Capitan Mountains that resulted in the deaths of 15 Mescalero warriors, including war chief Santa Anna, and just 2 American deaths, including Stanton. In addition, Lieutenant Samuel D. Sturgis led 18 dragoons and 6 civilians in a chase of a Mescalero raiding party that had attacked the Eaton Ranch outside Santa Fe. Sturgis and his men pursued the raiders for more than 100 miles before finally cornering them, killing 3 warriors, wounding 4, and recovering all the stolen livestock. Following the 1855 campaign, the Mescaleros pursued peace and promised to refrain from future raids in exchange for annual government subsidies. They also allowed the government to build Fort Stanton near Bonita in New Mexico Territory.

Although the Mescaleros remained at peace for the next six years, the outbreak of the American Civil War and the abandonment of Fort Stanton in 1861 caused the Mescaleros to resume raiding, in part because promised government subsidies were not provided. In August 1862 alone, government authorities reported that the Mescaleros killed 46 whites and captured several others. After Brigadier General James H. Carleton assumed command of the Department of New Mexico in September 1862, he ordered Christopher "Kit" Carson and the 1st New Mexico Cavalry to reactivate Fort Stanton and dispatched four companies of California volunteers under Captain William McClean and Captain Thomas L. Roberts against the Mescaleros. Although approximately 100

Mescalero fled to the Guadalupe Mountains, the majority went to Fort Stanton to seek peace. Carleton forced Chiefs Cadete, Chato, and Estrella to agree to removal to the Bosque Redondo Reservation in eastern New Mexico. Facing harsh conditions and forced to share the reservation with the Navajos, the Mescaleros fled Bosque Redondo in December 1863 and returned to the Sierra Blanca. Although a few Mescaleros would join other Apache bands in raids afterward, the majority remained peaceful, and the tribe remains in the Sierra Blanca today.

Like the Mescaleros, the Jicarillas, the Spanish term for "little basket," had alternately traded with and raided against the Pueblos. The Jicarillas also frequently raided both Mexican and white settlers. After a series of Jicarilla attacks threatened to close the Santa Fe Trail in 1854, the U.S. Army launched a series of campaigns against them. On March 5, 1854, Lieutenant David Bell and 30 men of the 2nd Dragoon Regiment attacked a Jicarilla camp along the Canadian River approximately 50 miles from Fort Union, killing several warriors, including Chief Lobo Blanco. A few weeks later, Chief Chacon retaliated by ambushing Lieutenant John W. Davidson's company of the 1st Dragoons approximately 25 miles south of Taos, killing 22 and wounding 36. Upon receiving news of the ambush, army officials dispatched 200 dragoons and 100 riflemen under Lieutenant Colonel Philip St. George Cooke to Taos, where they were joined by 36 Pueblos and Mexicans under Captain James Quinn. Guided by Carson, Cooke's force pursued Chacon to the Rio Caliente, where on April 8 they surprised Chacon's camp, killing 5 warriors and wounding 8. Seventeen Jicarilla women and children later froze to death in the flight following the battle. Two months later, Carson led Carleton's 100 dragoons and Quinn's

Pueblo-Mexican force in a devastating expedition northeast of Taos. On June 4, they surprised a Jicarilla camp at Raton Pass, killing several warriors, destroying 22 lodges, and capturing 38 ponies. The 1854 campaign effectively ended Jicarilla resistance. Chacon settled his tribe at Chama and attempted to farm. The Jicarillas would be moved several times, including a brief tenure on the Mescalero Reservation, before finally receiving their current reservation in northern New Mexico in 1887.

Although the Gila Apache bands had remained fairly peaceful in the early years of American occupation of New Mexico and Arizona, this began to change after the Gadsden Purchase of 1853 opened a southern route to California and Gila Apache raids prompted military action. In March 1856, army officials ordered a two-pronged invasion by dragoons and infantry into the Gila region. Lieutenant Colonel David T. Chandler led a column into the Mogollon Mountains and attacked a Mogollon Apache camp in southwestern New Mexico, killing several Apaches and capturing several hundred head of livestock. Chandler's forces then converged with Lieutenant Colonel John H. Eaton's column along the upper Gila River and marched into Arizona, where they mistakenly attacked Chief Delgadito's peaceful Mimbres band.

In 1857, Brigadier General John Garland, commander of the Department of New Mexico from 1853 to 1857, launched a much larger invasion into the Gila region. Colonel William W. Loring moved from the north with three companies of Mounted Riflemen, two companies of the 3rd Infantry Regiment, and a company of Pueblo warriors, while Lieutenant Colonel Dixon S. Miles advanced from the south with three companies of the 1st Dragoons, two companies of Mounted Riflemen, two companies of the 3rd Infantry Regiment, and one company of the 8th Infantry Regiment. Although the Mogollon and other Gila Apaches evaded Garland's forces, the Western Apaches were not as fortunate. On June 27, a detachment of the American force under Captain Richard S. Ewell attacked a Coyotero Apache camp along the Gila River, killing or wounding 40 warriors and capturing 45 women and children.

In the aftermath of the attack on the Coyotero Apaches, the U.S. Army soon confronted the Chiricahua Apaches, who proved to be by far the most difficult Apache band to suppress. Although the Chiricahuas had long engaged in raids against Mexicans and other Native American groups, they had cooperated with Brigadier General Stephen W. Kearny when he moved through their territory into California during the Mexican-American War. Throughout the 1850s, the Chiricahuas remained at peace with the United States. In October 1860, however, things changed dramatically when a Coyotero raiding party attacked John Ward's ranch in the Sonoita Valley and abducted Ward's six-year-old stepson. Ward incorrectly blamed the raid on Cochise's band of Chiricahuas, who had heretofore had peaceful relations with Americans. Lieutenant Colonel Pitcairn Morrison, commander of Fort Buchanan, responded in January 1861 by dispatching Lieutenant George N. Bascom and a company of mounted infantry to Cochise's camp at Apache Pass to demand the return of the livestock and Ward's stepson. When Cochise and five others met with Bascom and denied involvement in the raid, fighting broke out after Bascom attempted to seize Cochise. Although Cochise escaped, the other five Chiricahuas, three of whom were related to Cochise, were taken hostage. Cochise then responded by seizing three whites and placing Bascom under siege. After Bascom was reinforced, Cochise executed his captives and fled to Mexico. Bascom retaliated by hanging three of his Chiricahua hostages and three Coyoteros.

The so-called Bascom Affair resulted in 25 years of bitter conflict with the Chiricahuas. In the immediate aftermath, Cochise joined forces with Mimbres chief Mangas Coloradas in attacking settlements in eastern Arizona and western New Mexico, including Pinos Altos, where a gold strike in 1860 had brought an influx of 2,000 miners by 1861. The withdrawal of federal troops from the region after the outbreak of the American Civil War further emboldened the Chiricahuas. By the summer of 1862, however, the tide began to turn against them. On July 15, Cochise and Mangas ambushed an army detachment under Captain Thomas L. Roberts in Apache Pass, but Roberts's skillful use of howitzers turned the ambush into a crushing defeat, with the Apaches losing many warriors. After Carleton took command of the Department of New Mexico in September 1862, he made suppression of the Chiricahuas a top priority. On January 18, 1863, Mangas was captured and killed after being lured into Captain E. D. Shirland's camp under a flag of truce. By the end of the following year, Mangas's band was virtually exterminated.

After the American Civil War, the U.S. Army increased its presence in the Southwest. In addition, gold and silver strikes in New Mexico and Arizona increased the number of white settlers. The resulting tensions led to events such as the Camp Grant Massacre on April 30, 1871, when 148 Tucson settlers attacked an Aravapai and Pinal Apache village at dawn, ruthlessly slaughtering as many as 150 Apaches, mainly women and children, in their sleep and taking 29 children captive. Outrage in the East compelled President Ulysses S. Grant to extend his peace policy to the Apaches. Brigadier General Oliver O. Howard traveled to Cochise's camp in autumn 1872 and succeeded in negotiating a peace whereby Cochise would go to the Chiricahua Reservation near Fort Bowie. Similar agreements were made with the Warm Springs, Mimbres, Mogollon, San Carlos, Aravaipa, Pinal, and White Mountain Apaches.

Although many Apaches genuinely wanted peace and attempted to live on the reservations, just as many found it difficult to adjust to a sedentary lifestyle and had no interest in adopting the white man's culture. Consequently, many Apaches simply used the reservations as a staging point for raids. Officials estimated that 54 raids were carried out between September 1871 and September 1872, resulting in the deaths of 44 people and the loss of 500 head of livestock. Apaches also revolted in response to the government's broken promises. Membres chief Victorio, who was Cochise's son-in-law, is perhaps the best example of this. Having been promised a reservation at Ojo Caliente, their traditional home by which the band is known, the Warm Springs Apaches were forcibly removed to San Carlos in 1877. Over the next two years, Victorio and his band would flee San Carlos twice, leading the army on a fruitless chase across New Mexico and western Texas. Eventually Victorio fled to Mexico, where he was killed by Mexican militia in 1880.

Of all the Apaches who resisted reservation life, the shaman Geronimo proved to be the most difficult to apprehend. On October 1, 1881, he fled San Carlos with 74 Chiricahuas and headed to the Sierra Madre in Mexico, where he joined other renegade Apaches under Nana. Over the next five years Geronimo launched repeated raids across the border. By 1886, however, the combination of unprecedented cooperation between U.S. and Mexican forces, Brigadier General George Crook's skillful use of Apache scouts, and relentless pressure applied by Crook's replacement, Brigadier General Nelson A. Miles, forced Geronimo to capitulate. After a period of exile in Florida, he and his followers were permanently settled at Fort Sill, Oklahoma. Geronimo died there in 1909. Although 187 of his followers were allowed to relocate to the Mescalero Reservation in 1914, 84 chose to remain at Fort Sill, where slightly more than 600 lived in 2010.

Although Americans have tended to view the Apaches as one of the more bellicose tribes in North America, such a view is clearly one-sided. For the most part, the Apaches were no more warlike than any other Native American group. Rather, white encroachment and bad dealings with the U.S. government forced them to resort to violence to preserve their lands and way of life.

Justin D. Murphy and Patrick R. Ryan

Further Reading

Aleshire, Peter. *Reaping the Whirlwind: The Apache Wars.* New York: Facts on File, 1998.

Sweeney, Edwin R. *From Cochise to Geronimo: The Chiricahua Apaches 1874–1886.* Norman: University of Oklahoma Press, 2012.

Thrapp, Dan L. *The Conquest of Apacheria.* Norman: University of Oklahoma Press, 1967.

Worcester, Donald E. *The Apaches: Eagles of the Southwest.* Norman: University of Oklahoma Press, 1979.

B

Beaver Wars

Start Date: 1641
End Date: 1701

Series of wars beginning in the 1640s fought by the five nations of the Iroquois Confederacy (the Mohawks, Oneidas, Onondagas, Cayugas, and Senecas) against the French and their Native American allies. The Iroquois had two primary goals for their offensives. First, in need of a reliable source of European goods, the Iroquois sought to gain control of the fur-trading routes to their north and west and then move the beaver pelts from the upper Great Lakes to their Dutch (later English) trading partners at Fort Orange (present-day Albany, New York). The Iroquois seem to have trapped most of the beavers in their territory by the beginning of the 1640s. Even if there were sufficient beaver pelts in Iroquoia by this time, they were not the thicker (and more valuable) pelts from the upper Great Lakes. The second goal was an extension of the traditional practice of the Mourning War by which the Iroquois sought captives who would be adopted to replace their dead.

By virtue of their location, the Wyandots (Hurons) served as middlemen in the fur trade, acquiring pelts from tribes such as the Nipissings to their north and the Ottawas to their west in exchange for maize and then trading the pelts to the French for European goods. The Iroquois attacked the Hurons in 1648 and followed up with attacks that devastated Huronia in March 1649. Several aspects of the 1649 attack on the Hurons signaled that the Iroquois were practicing a new form of warfare. The Five Nations attacked during a time of year when warfare was usually suspended because of the difficulty of travel, and they struck in great force (estimated at 1,000 men) rather than in small groups. They were also very far from their homes in Iroquoia. In addition, they unveiled a new tactic: fighting at night.

While the Hurons had the military capacity to respond in the wake of the 1649 attacks, the Iroquois assault seems to have had an unnerving effect on them. The majority of the Hurons chose to flee in an effort to escape the Iroquois. Most Hurons went to Ganadoe (now Christian) Island in Lake Huron's Georgian Bay, where many of them perished from starvation during 1649–1650. Some went to Quebec, whereas others fled and were dispersed throughout the Great Lakes region and the Ohio Country.

The Iroquois followed up with other attacks in 1650. Many of the Hurons were captured or fled to the western Great Lakes or the Ohio Country. Presumably, the confederation asked the Eries and a confederacy known as the Neutrals to join the Longhouse (the metaphor for the Iroquois League). When they refused, the Iroquois, well equipped with firearms obtained from the Dutch, devastated both nations, carrying off many of their people into captivity.

If the Iroquois goal in these campaigns was to gain control of the Huron fur-trading routes, they failed. Instead, the elimination of the Hurons shifted the epicenter of the trade westward, and Algonquian-speaking peoples, such as the Ottawas, replaced the Hurons as middlemen. The Five Nations, moreover, could not sustain this conflict without resting and rebuilding their stocks of muskets and ammunition. To facilitate this and to keep New France from attacking them, the Iroquois allowed the French to send missionaries among them.

The Iroquois, however, soon found themselves at war again, this time with the Iroquoian-speaking Susquehannocks. Backed by Maryland and Delaware and supplied with powder and firearms from Swedish traders, the Susquehannocks were a formidable foe. Unable to fight the Susquehannocks and to continue their campaign in the Great Lakes region, the Iroquois made peace with their enemies to the north and west. The Susquehannock threat was eliminated in 1676, however, when they were attacked by Virginians in the opening phases of Bacon's Rebellion. Afterward, many Susquehannock were incorporated into the Seneca tribe.

Freed of the threat to their south, the Iroquois renewed their assault on the peoples of the Ohio Country and the Great Lakes. But over time the ongoing conflict served to weaken the Five Nations. The French even invaded Iroquoia and burned a Seneca town. Moreover, neither the French nor the Iroquois could hope to control the fur trade after the founding of the English Hudson's Bay Company shifted much of the fur trade northward.

In 1701 with the Iroquois weakened and having failed to gain control over the fur trade, the Iroquois leader Decanisora came up with a cunning diplomatic solution to their difficulties. In what came to be known as the Grand Settlement of 1701, the Five Nations began a new policy best described as armed neutrality. In separate treaties, the Iroquois promised the French that they would remain neutral in future conflicts and assured New York that they would aid that colony, provided it fulfilled certain promises that the Iroquois knew would not be kept. The Iroquois would invoke these agreements to ensure a steady flow of gifts. This diplomatic maneuvering would end only toward the end of the French and Indian War (1754–1763), when the Iroquois joined the English in the conflict.

Roger M. Carpenter

Further Reading

Carpenter, Roger M. *The Renewed, the Destroyed, and the Remade: The Three Thought Worlds of the Iroquois and the Huron, 1609–1650*. East Lansing: Michigan State University Press, 2004.

Hunt, George T. *The Wars of the Iroquois: A Study in Intertribal Trade Relations*. Madison: University of Wisconsin Press, 1940.

Black Hawk War

Event Date: 1832

Conflict fought between factions of the Sauk (Sac) and Fox (Mesquakie) people and the United States. The fighting occurred throughout northern Illinois and southern Wisconsin. As with most Native American wars, the root cause of the conflict was land, particularly disputes that arose from the Treaty of 1804.

The Algonquian-speaking Sauk and Fox tribes had originally lived near the Saint Lawrence River, but with the arrival of European settlers onto their ancestral homelands, the tribes were slowly forced south and west to territory in Illinois and Wisconsin. After the American Revolutionary War, the American government repeatedly attempted to negotiate a treaty that called for the Sauks and Foxes to vacate their lands. In 1804, a delegation of Sauk and Fox leaders went to St. Louis to negotiate with William Henry Harrison, governor of the Indiana Territory, whose jurisdiction encompassed lands occupied by the Sauks and Foxes. Although the Sauk and Fox delegates agreed to vacate all lands east of the Mississippi River and move into present-day Iowa, the 1804 treaty was immediately repudiated by a number of tribal elders and young leaders, including Black Hawk, who argued that the delegation had not been authorized to cede lands. Most Sauks and Foxes remained on their lands and refused to relocate west of the Mississippi.

Following the War of 1812 in which Black Hawk's band of Sauks and Foxes backed the British, the U.S. government continued to press the Sauks and Foxes to move across the Mississippi to Iowa. In 1829, Keokuk, a rival of Black Hawk, signed a treaty whereby a significant portion of the tribe moved to Iowa. Black Hawk and his followers remained near present-day Rock Island, Illinois, however, vowing to resist any attempts to move them. In 1831, Black Hawk and his followers were forced off their land by Illinois militiamen and into Iowa, where they took up residence with Keokuk's band. In 1832, however, Black Hawk led some 400 warriors and their families back into Illinois, initiating the Black Hawk War. The Illinois militia and federal troops pursued Black Hawk and his followers across northern Illinois and southern Wisconsin.

The Black Hawk War was short but bloody. Black Hawk's forces scored a stunning victory in the Battle of Stillman's Run on May 14, 1832, routing a contingent of the Illinois militia. The war soon turned against Black Hawk, who was defeated on July 21 in the Battle of Wisconsin Heights near modern Madison, Wisconsin, by Brigadier General James D. Henry's regulars. Black Hawk then moved to the mouth of the Bad Axe River in southern Wisconsin, where his band was attacked on August 1–2, while attempting to cross the Mississippi River. As many as 150 Native Americans died in the battle. Although Black Hawk escaped, only 150 of the original 1,000 members of his band remained. Captured on August 25 near Wisconsin Dells, Black Hawk was held hostage to ensure compliance with the terms of the Treaty of Fort Armstrong (September 21, 1832), by which the Sauks and Foxes ceded approximately one-fifth of present-day Iowa. The defeat of Black Hawk signaled the collapse of Native American resistance to white expansion east of the Mississippi.

Rick Dyson

Further Reading

Jung, Patrick J. *The Black Hawk War of 1832*. Norman: University of Oklahoma Press, 2007.

Trask, Kerry A. *Black Hawk: The Battle for the Heart of America*. New York: Holt, 2006.

Black Kettle

Birth Date: ca. 1803
Death Date: November 27, 1868

Southern Cheyenne leader Black Kettle (Mo-to-vato, Mo-keta-va-ta) was born around 1803, possibly near the Black Hills of present-day South Dakota. As a youth, he distinguished himself in warfare against the Utes, Pawnees, and Comanches, emerging as a leader of the Southern Cheyennes by 1861. That year, he joined several Cheyenne and Arapaho leaders in signing the Treaty of Fort Wise by which the tribes gave up most of their land claims in exchange for a reservation south of the Arkansas River.

Black Kettle's assent to the treaty was consistent with his efforts to coexist with American settlers rather than resist them, a policy that earned him a reputation as a peace chief. He constantly sought accommodation despite suffering repeated abuses at the hands of the Americans.

In 1864, Colonel John M. Chivington of the Colorado Volunteers responded to sporadic Native American attacks on settlers by launching a campaign against area tribes. Black Kettle and 400 followers encountered some of Chivington's troops in May on the Smoky Hill River. Soldiers opened fire and killed 28 Native Americans before Black Kettle ordered the Cheyennes to cease resistance. The incident triggered reprisals by other Native American groups, and soon war engulfed the Colorado region.

Still hoping for peace, in mid-September 1864, Black Kettle accompanied Major Edward Wynkoop to Denver for talks with Chivington, who ordered Black Kettle to take his people to Fort Lyon. Black Kettle complied. Upon reaching the fort, he was ordered by Major Scott Anthony to camp at Sand Creek, 40 miles away. Early in the morning of November 29, 1864, however, Chivington and his troops attacked the camp even though Black Kettle held a pole with an American flag and waved it. Approximately 150 people died in what became known as the Sand Creek Massacre.

Although the Sand Creek Massacre led many Cheyennes to renew their campaign against the Americans, Black Kettle led his remaining supporters south of the Arkansas River to avoid the fighting. He persisted in his efforts to secure peace, signing the Little Arkansas Treaty in 1865 and the Medicine Lodge Treaty in 1867. The latter required the southern Plains nations to give up their remaining land and settle in Indian Territory (Oklahoma).

In autumn 1868, Major General Philip Sheridan ordered all peaceful Native Americans to report to Fort Cobb in Indian Territory. Black Kettle did so, but Colonel William B. Hazen told him that he had no authority to protect his people, who would have to surrender to Sheridan. Black Kettle returned to the Cheyenne camp on the Washita River, where Lieutenant Colonel George Armstrong Custer's 7th Cavalry attacked them on November 27, 1868. Black Kettle, true to his principles, did not resist and was killed while trying to flee.

Jim Piecuch

Further Reading

Hatch, Thom. *Black Kettle: The Cheyenne Chief Who Sought Peace but Found War*. Hoboken, NJ: Wiley, 2004.

Hoig, Stan. *The Peace Chiefs of the Cheyennes*. Norman: University of Oklahoma Press, 1980.

Bloody Knife

Birth Date: ca. 1840
Death Date: June 25, 1876

Native American scout of mixed Arikara and Hunkpapa Sioux ancestry. Bloody Knife (Tamena Way Way or Nes I Ri Pat in Arikara) was perhaps the most famous Native American scout to serve the U.S. Army. Lieutenant Colonel George Armstrong Custer once called Bloody Knife his favorite scout. Bloody Knife's life is surrounded by myth, however, and it is difficult to separate the legend from the actual man. Details of Bloody Knife's early life are sketchy. He was probably born around 1840, but his place of birth is not known. His mother was an Arikara, and his father was a Hunkpapa Sioux, but Bloody Knife grew up among his father's people. According to legend, during his childhood Bloody Knife and future Hunkpapa war leader Gall developed an intense hatred for each other. When his parents separated in 1856, Bloody Knife moved with his mother back to his Arikara relatives near Fort Clark in present-day North Dakota.

Sioux war parties frequently attacked Arikaras who ventured out from the village. Even though he was part Hunkpapa, Bloody Knife was not safe from such attacks. Once he was ambushed by Gall's Hunkpapas, stripped of his clothes, and beaten severely with coup sticks. In 1862, another Sioux war party killed two of his brothers in an ambush.

After working as a hunter and messenger for the American Fur Company for several years, Bloody Knife joined Brigadier General Alfred Sully's Sioux expedition as a scout in 1865. Later that year, Bloody Knife led a group of soldiers to a Hunkpapa village to arrest Gall. On this occasion, the soldiers bayoneted Gall but prevented Bloody Knife from killing him. Bloody Knife later served as a scout at Fort Stevenson, Fort Buford, Fort Rice, and Fort Lincoln. He took part in the first Yellowstone Expedition in 1872. In 1873, Bloody Knife joined Custer on the second Yellowstone Expedition, during which the troops fought several battles with the Sioux. In 1874, Bloody Knife served in the Black Hills Expedition and was awarded an additional $150 for his "invaluable assistance."

In 1876, Custer appointed Bloody Knife head scout during the expedition that led to the Battle of the Little Bighorn (June 25–26, 1876). Bloody Knife reportedly cautioned Custer against an attack but rode into battle with Major Marcus A. Reno's battalion. Bloody Knife was killed while standing next to Reno. Bloody Knife's remains were later mutilated by the Sioux.

In 1879, Bloody Knife's widow, Young Owl Woman (also known as She Owl), applied for and eventually received her husband's outstanding pay. After the Battle of the Little Bighorn, the surviving Arikara scouts composed a song in Bloody Knife's honor.

Mark van de Logt

Further Reading

Dunlay, Thomas W. *Wolves for the Blue Soldiers: Indian Scouts and Auxiliaries with the United States Army, 1860–90.* Lincoln: University of Nebraska Press, 1982.

Innis, Ben. *Bloody Knife: Custer's Favorite Scout.* Bismarck, ND: Smoky Water, 1994.

Blue Jacket

Birth Date: ca. 1743
Death Date: ca. 1810

Shawnee war chief who played a prominent role in resisting British and then American western encroachment into the Old Northwest. Weyapiersenwah, better known as Blue Jacket, was born probably in 1743 in south-central Ohio. Details of Blue Jacket's early life are so obscure that a persistent myth that he was actually a white Shawnee captive named Marmaduke Van Swearingen gained credence after the 1870s. This myth is now annually celebrated in an outdoor play performed each year in Xenia, Ohio. Blue Jacket's most recent biographer, John Sugden, has conclusively shown, however, that Van Swearingen and Blue Jacket were two different individuals.

Blue Jacket first came to prominence in Lord Dunmore's War (1774), which pitted Virginia against the Shawnee and Mingo tribes. Shawnee displeasure at the Iroquois' sale of their land to Virginians at Fort Stanwix in 1768 burst into open warfare when

American frontiersmen brutally murdered the pregnant sister of Mingo chief Logan. This murder was one of many brutal slayings along the Ohio River in 1774. Shawnee and Mingo forces attempted to stem the tide of settlers into their Kentucky hunting grounds, only to be defeated at Point Pleasant (in present-day West Virginia) on October 10, 1774.

The Shawnees were initially neutral during the early years of the American Revolutionary War (1775–1783), but the murder of Chief Cornstalk in October 1777 led many Shawnees to fight with the British, and Blue Jacket rose to great prominence during the ensuing years. By 1778, however, his town on Deer Creek (35 miles south of Columbus in present-day Ohio) near the Scioto River was abandoned, and Blue Jacket moved to present-day Bellefontaine, Ohio. British defeat in the American Revolution removed a valuable ally in the defense of Shawnee lands. Regardless, the Shawnees and many other northwestern nations continued to fight against the newly independent United States. Following the destruction of his Ohio settlement by frontiersmen under Brigadier General Benjamin Logan in 1786, Blue Jacket negotiated a peace treaty at Limestone, Kentucky, in 1787 and moved into the region of the Miami River in northwestern Ohio.

In 1788, Blue Jacket raided Kentucky and together with Miami chief Little Turtle (Michikinakoua) led confederated Indian forces in the defeat of an American military force under Brigadier General Josiah Harmar in October 1790. This was followed by a convincing defeat of another American army under Major General Arthur St. Clair, governor of the Northwest Territory, at the Wabash River on November 4, 1791. These battles were all part of Little Turtle's War (1785–1795). On August 20, 1794, however, Blue Jacket was decisively defeated by Brigadier General "Mad" Anthony Wayne at Fallen Timbers, Ohio. While many Shawnees, including Tecumseh, refused to admit defeat, Blue Jacket signed the Treaty of Greenville on August 3, 1795, which ceded most of present-day Ohio to the United States and ended Little Turtle's War.

Following his defeat, Blue Jacket lived near Fort Wayne and later Detroit. In July 1805, he signed the Treaty of Fort Industry, which ceded the rest of northwestern Ohio to the United States. In his later life, Blue Jacket witnessed the rise of Tecumseh and the new Pan-Indian movement that continued to resist American westward expansion prior to the War of 1812, and there is evidence to suggest that for a time Blue Jacket was a follower of Tecumseh's half-brother Tenskwatawa (the Prophet). Blue Jacket, one of the most prominent Shawnee leaders of his time, probably died in 1810 in northern Indiana or southern Michigan. Two of his surviving sons, George Blue Jacket and Jim Blue Jacket, continued his path of resistance, following Tecumseh into his ill-fated alliance with the British during the War of 1812.

Rory T. Cornish

Further Reading

Calloway, Colin G. *The Shawnees and the War for America.* The Penguin Library of American Indian History. New York: Penguin Books, 2008.

Sugden, John. *Blue Jacket: Warrior of the Shawnees.* Lincoln: University of Nebraska Press, 2000.

Braddock's Campaign

Start Date: March 1755
End Date: July 1755

Failed British offensive against French Fort Duquesne in 1755 during the French and

Indian War (1754–1763). When news of the French victory over the Virginia militia at Fort Necessity arrived in London in September 1754, the British cabinet debated a new course of action against the French. The Earl of Albemarle, governor of Virginia in absentia and a career soldier, recommended that "officers and good ones," be sent to North America. The Duke of Cumberland, the king's son and captain general of Britain's armed forces, proposed two Irish regiments (the 44th and 48th) and a commander in chief for the forces in America. Major General Edward Braddock was named commander in chief for North America and ordered to attack Fort Duquesne, Fort Niagara, Crown Point, and Fort Beauséjour. It was left to his discretion whether to attack them in succession or simultaneously.

On his arrival at Williamsburg, Virginia, in March 1755, Braddock found that Massachusetts governor William Shirley had raised an extra 2,000 troops. Shirley and British Indian agent William Johnson proposed that the main British attack be directed against Fort Niagara, but Braddock chose to focus on Fort Duquesne. Nevertheless, Braddock allowed Shirley and Johnson to attack Fort Niagara and Crown Point, respectively, while he took his own force of 2,200 men to Fort Duquesne. The remaining colonial forces, under Nova Scotia governor Charles Lawrence and Colonel Robert Monckton, were to attack Fort Beauséjour.

Braddock envisioned a road building project through the wilderness punctuated by a European-style siege. At first he proposed to take a large contingent with supplies for a major siege, but he soon split his force into roughly equal parts: one to transport the immense train of baggage and artillery and the other, a flying column, to scout ahead and prepare for the siege. Alert to the dangers of wilderness warfare, Braddock regularly employed more than a third of his force for screens and patrols. In June and July, the army advanced steadily and thwarted French commander Claude-Pierre Pécaudy de Contrecoeur's attempts to disrupt its progress. Despite native raids on the colonial frontier, Braddock continued forward, increasing the panic at Fort Duquesne.

On July 8, as Braddock forded the Monongahela River 10 miles from Fort Duquesne, Contrecoeur sent half of his garrison against Braddock. With 36 officers, 72 colonial regulars (troupes de la marine), 146 Canadian militiamen, and 637 American Indian allies under his command, Captain Daniel Liénard de Beaujeu was supposed to attack Braddock's column east of the Monongahela, but his force was dispatched too late. Ultimately the two forces met just west of the river shortly after noon on July 9.

As he advanced on Fort Duquesne, Braddock sent forward a vanguard of about 300 men followed by an independent company and 250 workers. The main body of 500 men followed with the artillery, and another 100 men covered the rear. Braddock missed a key terrain feature on the morning of July 9, a hill to his right and front from which scouts would have been able to detect Beaujeu's approach and prepare an adequate defense. Braddock's screening forces were unusually small and close to the main body, which was split along the road, with only two ranks to either side of the artillery train. This deployment may have reflected Braddock's confidence in his progress, but it left his force more vulnerable to surprise.

When the French and Native Americans attacked, Braddock's men fought bravely but paid for their commander's errors. The opening volleys went well for the British, killing Beaujeu. But Braddock's vanguard, flanked by Beaujeu's native allies, fell back on the main body. The units became intermingled, and Braddock's regulars, strung out on either side of the baggage train, struggled to form a line of battle. Having fallen victim to an ambush, Braddock was unable to use the light infantry tactics that had served him throughout his march.

To make matters worse, the battlefield was a Native American hunting ground that concealed hunters and exposed prey. Braddock's men, still trying to form ranks, soon became targets for Indian marksmen; officers on horseback were the most vulnerable. Although the British and some colonials fought bravely for more than three hours, they were unable to form units larger than a platoon, and most of their fire proved ineffective. Unaccustomed to the military tactics of the natives, British regulars attempted to form companies, fire in volleys, and look for the visual cues of the European battlefield. Panic in the British ranks caused several incidents of friendly fire, increasing the confusion. Braddock's force also became an increasingly dense mass as the terror of battle drove men closer together, making them an easier target.

Discipline crumbled when Braddock was shot from his horse. The workers, the rear guard, and most of the provincial troops had already fled, leaving no one to cover the retreat. Constant pressure from Canadians and Indians turned the retreat into a rout, entirely reversing the previous month of British progress. Braddock's force lost two-thirds of its numbers and most of its supplies and equipment. French and native losses totaled fewer than 40. The progress made on Braddock's road once promised a steady flow of supplies from Virginia and Maryland to Fort Duquesne; that same road now rendered the British colonies more vulnerable.

The French victory on the Monongahela released forces from their defense of Fort Duquesne and rendered abortive Shirley's proposed expedition to Fort Niagara. Although Shirley took over command of colonial forces from the deceased Braddock, he and Johnson squabbled over supplies at Albany. Johnson later allied with Lieutenant Governor James DeLancey of New York and Thomas Pownall of New Jersey to intrigue against Shirley, undermining his authority by the spring of 1756. Major General John Campbell, Earl of Loudoun, then replaced Shirley as commander in chief. Campbell made several important logistical and administrative reforms but proved militarily ineffective. Only when Major General Jeffrey Amherst took over British military operations in 1758 did British forces return to the offensive against Fort Duquesne—this time successfully—under Brigadier General John Forbes.

Matt Schumann

Further Reading

Anderson, Fred. *Crucible of War: The Seven Years' War and the Fate of the Empire in British North America, 1754–1766.* New York: Vintage Books, 2001.

Kopperman, Paul E. *Braddock at the Monongahela.* Pittsburgh: University of Pittsburgh Press, 1977.

Brant, Joseph

Birth Date: ca. 1742
Death Date: November 24, 1807

Mohawk leader. Joseph Brant was born Thayendanega around 1742 at an Iroquois settlement in present-day Ohio and was related by marriage to British northern Indian superintendent Sir William Johnson. Johnson took an interest in young Brant and groomed him as one of his protégés, arranging for him to be educated with a small group of native youths at Eleazar Wheelock's Indian Charity School.

As a young man, Brant twice visited England and made a favorable impression on London society, counting the Prince of Wales among his friends. Brant was also admired for his membership in the Masons and for having translated the Bible (and later the Book of Common Prayer) into Mohawk. His last visit to England coincided with the outbreak of the American Revolutionary War (1775–1783). In July 1776, Brant arrived in New York and made his way back to Mohawk country.

Brant offered his services to the British Crown and led Mohawk warriors in several campaigns, participating in the battles at Oswego and Fort Stanwix in 1777. He also led Mohawk warriors—in the first battle in which Iroquois fought Iroquois—at Oriskany that same year. Late the next year, he led a raid on Cherry Valley, New York.

Along with his effectiveness as a leader, Brant acquired a reputation as a humane warrior. At Cherry Valley, he was said to have protested to the British commander over the killing of noncombatants. Others argued that this reputation was unjustified, pointing out that Brant could be as harsh as any other Native American warrior with his prisoners, expecting them to keep pace with a retreating war party.

As with other Native American allies of the British, Brant was angered by the terms of the Treaty of Paris that ended the American Revolutionary War. Particularly galling was the transfer of native lands to the Americans. Brant argued that the Americans had beaten the British, not the Iroquois. However, believing that the Iroquois position was untenable in the new United States, Brant used his influence to secure reserves for the Mohawks along the Grand River in Ontario and convinced many of his people to move there.

In the early 1790s, a native confederacy under the Miami chief Little Turtle defeated American military expeditions led by Josiah Harmar and Arthur St. Clair in the Ohio Country. Brant and other Iroquois leaders recommended that Little Turtle, Blue Jacket, and other leaders negotiate a peace with the Americans that would leave their gains in place. Brant died on November 24, 1807, at Burlington, Ontario.

Roger M. Carpenter

Further Reading

Graymont, Barbara. *The Iroquois in the American Revolution*. Syracuse, NY: Syracuse University Press, 1972.

Kelsay, Isabel Thompson. *Joseph Brant, 1743–1807: Man of Two Worlds*. Syracuse, NY: Syracuse University Press, 1984.

Buffalo Soldiers

Term used to refer to African American troops who served on the western frontier from 1866 to 1917. The name "buffalo soldiers" was given to these troops by the Cheyennes, who asserted that the Black soldiers fought as fiercely and courageously as a wounded buffalo. The appellation was proudly adopted by all African American troops on the frontier. Buffalo soldiers served in the 9th and 10th Cavalry regiments and 24th and 25th Infantry regiments. These units were born out of regiments of the United States Colored Troops (USCT) that had served in the Union Army during the American Civil War (1861–1865). During their existence, the buffalo soldiers fought in every major war with Native Americans on the western frontier, often bearing the brunt of the fighting. Buffalo soldiers also fought at the 1898 Battle of San Juan Hill in the Spanish-American War, assisted in fighting Filipino insurgents in the Philippines during 1899–1902, and participated in the pursuit of Mexican revolutionary Pancho Villa during the 1916–1917 Punitive Expedition.

At the conclusion of the Civil War, a significant number of African American troops wished to remain in the U.S. Army. As reward for their wartime service, Congress responded by authorizing six Black regiments (two cavalry and four infantry) that were later consolidated into four regiments. The pay was steady at $13 a month; soldiers were also provided with room, board, clothing, a pension, and a modicum of protection from the worst abuses of discrimination suffered in Jim Crow America. The buffalo soldiers were greatly admired by the African American community. In addition to serving as occupation forces in the Reconstruction-era South, they were also sent to forts throughout the American West, where they protected white settlers against warring Native American tribes and prevented whites from encroaching upon tribal lands. The buffalo soldiers ably assisted in subduing the Cheyenne, Kiowa, Comanche, Apache, Sioux, and Arapaho tribes.

Army life on the frontier was hard, with soldiers living in isolated forts, riding and marching for days on end, and fighting Native Americans. Life for the buffalo soldiers could be even harder, as they faced hostility and ostracism from their white comrades in arms and many times from their white officers. Often the very people whom the buffalo soldiers were ordered to protect despised them, and in many towns, they were barred from saloons, hotels, and stores.

Nonetheless, buffalo soldiers served with distinction, drawing praise from their white officers and respect from their Native American adversaries. The Black regiments were known for low desertion and high reenlistment rates and for continuity of leadership. Twenty buffalo soldiers were awarded the Medal of Honor, the highest honor in the American military. Without doubt, they served capably and honorably.

Rick Dyson

Further Reading

Carlson, Paul H. *The Buffalo Soldier Tragedy of 1877.* College Station: Texas A&M University Press, 2003.

Fowler, Arlen L. *The Black Infantry in the West, 1869–1891.* Norman: University of Oklahoma Press, 1996.

Leckie, William H., and Shirley A. Leckie. *The Buffalo Soldiers: A Narrative of the Black Cavalry in the West.* Norman: University of Oklahoma Press, 2003.

C

Camp Grant Massacre

Event Date: April 30, 1871

Massacre of as many as 150 western Apaches, mostly unarmed children and women, who had surrendered to the U.S. Army at Camp Grant, just north of Tucson, Arizona. Another 30 or so children were taken captive.

Following the Gadsden Purchase in 1853, American settlers began to enter the San Pedro Valley, the fertile land to the east of present-day Tucson, where Western Apache groups such as the Aravaipa and Pinal bands resided. To protect pioneers and subdue Native Americans who refused to submit to U.S. authority, the government established military posts in the region, including Fort Aravaipa, which was erected on May 8, 1860, at the confluence of the San Pedro River and the Aravaipa Creek. In 1865, the fort was renamed Camp Grant in honor of Ulysses S. Grant.

On February 28, 1871, Lieutenant Royal E. Whitman, then in charge of Camp Grant, reported that a small group of elderly Apache women had come to the post looking for several stolen children. Whitman encouraged the Apaches to come in, and soon dozens of Aravaipa and Pinal Apaches were encamped at the fort and receiving rations of corn, flour, beans, coffee, and meat. By late March, more than 400 Apaches had arrived, settling at a traditional site called gashdla'á cho o'aa ("Big Sycamore Stands There"), five miles from Camp Grant up the Aravaipa Creek.

Although the Apaches at Camp Grant were peaceful, residents of Tucson blamed them for raids carried out by the Chiricahua Apaches. After the government refused pleas for protection, William Oury conspired with another prominent Tucson citizen, Jesus Maria Elías, to attack the Apaches near Camp Grant. They recruited dozens of local residents and scores of Tohono O'odham warriors. On the afternoon of April 28, 1871, the group was provided weapons and provisions by the adjutant general of Arizona, Samuel Hughes.

In the early morning hours of April 30, the vigilantes attacked the Big Sycamore Stands There encampment, catching the Apaches off guard. The attack was over in half an hour. Soldiers at Camp Grant did not hear the screams and gunshots because of the distance from the Apache settlement. As many as 150 Apaches, nearly all women and children, were slaughtered, as children were hacked apart and girls were raped. Some 30 children were taken captive. A half dozen of the children lived for a while with highly regarded Tucsonans, such as Leopoldo Carrillo and Francisco Romero, but were returned to Apache relatives in 1872. The rest of the children were sold into slavery in Sonora, Mexico, for $100 each.

The vigilantes returned to a jubilant Tucson, but the reaction on the East Coast and even among military personnel was horror and disbelief. When local authorities did not press charges, President Ulysses S. Grant threatened to impose martial law to prosecute those responsible. On October 23, 1871, a grand jury handed down 111 indictments, 108 for murder and 3 for misdemeanors, with Sidney R. DeLong as the lead defendant. A weeklong trial was held in December 1871. The jury deliberated for 19 minutes before announcing a verdict of not guilty on all counts.

After the massacre, the Apaches at Camp Grant dispersed throughout southern Arizona. They returned to the post in spring 1872 for peace talks and agreed to settle on the San Carlos Reservation to the north. Although this pact did not relinquish Apache territory, Anglo-American and Mexican American pioneers soon spread into the San Pedro Valley and made it their home. When the Apaches later tried to return and settle in the San Pedro Valley during the 1880s, they were run off their traditional lands.

Chip Colwell-Chanthaphonh

Further Reading

Colwell-Chanthaphonh, Chip. *Massacre at Camp Grant: Forgetting and Remembering Apache History*. Tucson: University of Arizona Press, 2007.

Colwell-Chanthaphonh, Chip. "Western Apache Oral Histories and Traditions of the Camp Grant Massacre." *American Indian Quarterly* 27, no. 3–4 (January 2003): 639–666.

Canby's Campaign

Start Date: 1860
End Date: 1861

Abortive U.S. military campaign against the Navajos in New Mexico Territory during 1860–1861. After the United States established its authority in New Mexico following the Mexican-American War (1846–1848), conflict with the Navajos escalated throughout the 1850s as whites, supported by the U.S. Army, began seizing Navajo grazing lands. Indeed, territorial governor Abraham Rencher (1857–1861) placed primary blame for the growing conflict on Colonel Benjamin L. Bonneville, who in 1858 had forced a harsh treaty on the Navajos, taking away most of their land in New Mexico proper, and on local white militia who attacked the Navajos without authorization. Given these conditions, Rencher warned officials in Washington that the Navajos would have little recourse but to turn to banditry, making a full-scale war inevitable.

Just as Rencher predicted, hard-pressed Navajo warriors began attacking supply trains in western New Mexico, leading to a vicious cycle of reprisals by the army and white settlers and counter-reprisals by the Navajos. Angered that whites had burned his home and killed some 50 of his sheep, Chief Manuelito led some 1,000 Navajo warriors in an attack on April 30, 1860, that nearly overran Fort Defiance, located near present-day Window Rock, Arizona. Rencher now had no choice but to seek army assistance, and federal officials ordered Brevet Lieutenant Colonel Edward R. S. Canby to lead elements of the 10th Infantry Regiment at Fort Garland, New Mexico, to Fort Defiance, where they would be joined by the 5th and 7th Infantry regiments and the 2nd Dragoon Regiment.

Canby departed Fort Defiance in November 1860 with 600 soldiers accompanied by Ute scouts and a small contingent of New Mexico volunteers under Captain Blas Lucero. Canby divided his force into three detachments, leading one himself and placing the other two under Major Henry Hopkins Sibley and Captain Lafayette McLaws. During the next month, Canby's men killed some 35–40 Navajos, seized more than 1,000 Navajo horses, and killed several thousand Navajo sheep. Lack of water and forage caused by the severe drought of 1860 forced Canby to return to Fort Defiance in December. The following month, he launched a second campaign from Fort Defiance, focusing primarily on the destruction of Navajo crops and livestock. By April 1861, Canby had succeeded in negotiating a series of treaties with 54 Navajo chiefs, guaranteeing food, clothing, and the army's protection in return for peace.

Unfortunately, the outbreak of the American Civil War (1861–1865) in April 1861 prevented the federal government from fulfilling its promises to the Navajos. Canby, appointed colonel of the new 19th Infantry Regiment, took command of the Department of New Mexico, but his chief concern was to defend New Mexico from Confederate attack. Consequently, the Navajos took advantage of the situation by renewing attacks on white settlements, for which they were subsequently forced to pay a heavy price during the Long Walk to Bosque Redondo in 1864.

Justin D. Murphy

Further Reading

Keleher, William A. *Turmoil in New Mexico.* Facsimile of 1952 ed. Santa Fe, NM: Sunstone, 2008.

Larson, Carole. *Forgotten Frontier: The Story of Southeastern New Mexico.* Albuquerque: University of New Mexico Press, 1993.

Utley, Robert M. *Frontiersmen in Blue: The United States and the Indian, 1848–1865.* Lincoln: University of Nebraska Press, 1967.

Carleton's Campaign

Start Date: 1863
End Date: 1864

Campaign against the Mescalero Apaches and Navajos between 1863 and 1864 that culminated in the forced removal of the Navajos, known as the Long Walk, to the Bosque Redondo Reservation in eastern New Mexico. Although Brevet Lieutenant Colonel Edward R. S. Canby had established peace with the Navajo in early 1861, the outbreak of the American Civil War (1861–1865) prevented the United States from fulfilling its promises to provide food, clothing, and protection to the tribe. More important, Canby, who had been appointed brigadier general of volunteers and given command of the Department of New Mexico, was soon preoccupied with defending New Mexico against a Confederate invasion mounted by Brigadier General Henry Hopkins Sibley in 1862. Consequently, the Navajos took advantage of the situation by raiding white settlements and disrupting mail service to California. Unfortunately for the Navajos, once the Confederate invasion was defeated, the full brunt of federal power was directed against them.

Brigadier General James H. Carleton, who succeeded Canby as commander of the Department of New Mexico on September 18, 1862, was determined to crush Native American resistance in New Mexico. Having under his command the 1st New Mexico Cavalry led by Colonel Christopher "Kit" Carson, the 1st California Cavalry, the 5th U.S. Infantry, the 1st New Mexico Infantry, and the 1st and 5th California Infantry, Carleton moved against the Mescalero Apaches in the spring of 1863 and then turned his attention to the Navajos, ordering Navajo chiefs Barboncito and Delgadito to relocate to the new reservation established for the Mescalero Apaches at Bosque Redondo near Fort Sumner along the Pecos River in eastern New Mexico.

When the Navajos refused to submit, Carleton ordered Carson to lead the 1st New Mexico Cavalry to Fort Wingate (near present-day Grants, New Mexico) and Fort Defiance (near present-day Window Rock, Arizona), which was renamed Fort Canby, in preparation for a campaign against the Navajos. In June 1863, Carson's men, joined by Ute and Zuni warriors, began attacking Navajo farms and seizing Navajo livestock. During the next six months, Carson kept steady pressure on the Navajos, killing a reported 78 warriors and destroying crops, orchards, and dwellings. By January 1864, the majority of the Navajos had been forced into their traditional stronghold of Canyon de Chelly, which Carson and his men entered on January 12, 1864.

By mid-March, the Navajos were on the verge of starvation, and approximately 6,000 assembled at Fort Wingate and Fort Canby to surrender. Approximately 2,400 Navajos were then marched to Bosque Redondo, with at least 200 dying en route. By the end of 1864, almost 8,000 Navajos had surrendered and relocated to Bosque Redondo.

Although Carleton's Campaign had brutally and effectively crushed the Navajos, his attempt to "civilize" the Navajos at Bosque Redondo proved an abject failure. There was insufficient land to support the Navajos and their livestock, and the attempt to force them to live alongside their traditional enemy, the Mescalero Apaches, resulted in continual turmoil. Indeed, the Mescalero Apaches fled the reservation in late 1865, and Carleton was relieved of his command in autumn 1866. Even hard-nosed Lieutenant General William Tecumseh Sherman, who met with Navajo leaders at Fort Sumner in 1868, recognized the futility of the Bosque Redondo experiment and agreed to a new treaty allowing Navajos to return to their traditional homeland.

Justin D. Murphy

Further Reading

Bailey, Lynn R. *The Long Walk: A History of the Navajo Wars, 1848–68*. Los Angeles: Westernlore, 1964.

Keleher, William A. *Turmoil in New Mexico*. Facsimile of 1952 ed. Santa Fe, NM: Sunstone, 2008.

Utley, Robert M. *Frontiersmen in Blue: The United States and the Indian, 1848–1865*. Lincoln: University of Nebraska Press, 1967.

Carson, Christopher Houston

Birth Date: December 24, 1809
Death Date: May 23, 1868

Fur trapper, mountaineer, military officer, and renowned Indian fighter. Christopher Houston "Kit" Carson was born in Madison County, Kentucky, on December 24, 1809. Before he was two years old, his family moved to Missouri, where he spent most of his youth. At age 14, Carson was apprenticed to a saddle maker but later ran away and joined a wagon train headed west to Santa Fe, New Mexico. Carson traveled all over the West as far as California hunting, trapping, and ranching. Often living with various Native American tribes, Carson took at least two Native American wives and learned at least four Native American languages.

Although Carson deservedly gained a reputation as one who had fought Native Americans, he also became known as someone who could work with them and served as an Indian agent for the Ute tribe from 1854 to 1861. With the outbreak of the American Civil War (1861–1865), Carson joined the Union forces as a lieutenant colonel in the New Mexico volunteers, was quickly promoted to colonel, and fought against invading Confederate forces at

Glorieta Pass (March 26–28, 1862). Native American tribes, including the Mescalero Apaches, Comanches, Kiowas, and Navajos, took advantage of the disruption brought by the Civil War and attacked settlers in New Mexico.

In mid-1862, Brigadier General James H. Carleton became commander of the Department of New Mexico. Carson was his principal field commander. Carleton believed that there could be no peace between whites and Native Americans unless Native Americans were removed to remote locations away from white settlements. Although Carson did not relish fighting Native Americans and tried to resign his post, claiming that he had joined the army to fight Confederates, he finally agreed to stay on. He then led military campaigns against several different tribes. But it would be his campaign against the Navajos that would prove most controversial.

In December 1862, Carleton informed Navajo leaders that he intended to relocate the tribe several hundred miles from their current homeland to the Bosque Redondo reservation on the Pecos River in eastern New Mexico. He gave the Navajos until July 20, 1863, to comply with the order or face war. When the Navajos refused to surrender, war became certain.

Beginning in late July 1863, Carson led five separate missions through Navajo country, conducting a total war campaign. Carson used his contacts with the Utes to bring them into the fighting against the Navajos. He reported that during one single mission he and his men confiscated or destroyed more than two million pounds of grain. This seizure or destruction of foodstuffs, homes, and even clothes, combined with continued attacks by the Utes and other traditional enemies, had a pronounced effect on the Navajos' ability and willingness to continue fighting. Carson's invasion of the Navajo stronghold in Canyon de Chelly proved overwhelming, and soon small bands of Navajos began to surrender. By the end of January 1864, between 6,000 and 8,000 Navajos (one-half to two-thirds of the tribe) had come forward to be removed to Bosque Redondo.

Charges at the time that Carson had ordered Navajos to be shot down without first offering them the chance to surrender now appear inaccurate. There were, of course, some treacherous acts such as soldiers killing innocent Navajos who had surrendered, but Carson roundly decried these, realizing that they worked against the overall goal of rounding up the Navajos. Recent scholarship also discounts as exaggerations the accounts of thousands of Navajos starving to death because of devastation wrought by Carson's forces.

In late November 1864, with the Mescalero Apache and Navajo tribes either at Bosque Redondo or on their way there, Carleton sent Carson and several hundred soldiers in search of the Kiowas, leading to the inconclusive First Battle of Adobe Walls (November 25, 1864), during which Carson was fortunate to retreat from a much larger Native American force. Nevertheless, Carson's forces did inflict considerable casualties during the fight, mainly with howitzers.

Carson was neither an avowed friend nor an enemy of Native Americans. At times he fought them, and at other times he befriended them, a behavior and attitude not uncommon to many whites of the time. Carson was awarded a brevet to brigadier general of volunteers in 1865. He then moved to Colorado to command Fort Garland before leaving the post in 1866 because of poor health. Carson died near Fort Lyons, Colorado, on May 23, 1868.

David Sloan

Further Reading

Gordon-McCutchan, R. C., ed. *Kit Carson: Indian Fighter or Indian Killer?* Niwot: University Press of Colorado, 1996.

Remley, David A. *Kit Carson: The Life of an American Border Man.* Norman: University of Oklahoma Press, 2011.

Trafzer, Clifford E. *The Kit Carson Campaign: The Last Great Navajo War.* Norman: University of Oklahoma Press, 1990.

Cavalry, Native American

The term "cavalry" traditionally refers to soldiers or warriors who fight mounted on horseback, although the term is not usually applied to irregular mounted units such as the Native Americans. When the Spanish introduced horses into North America in the late 1500s, Western tribes quickly incorporated them into their way of life. Horses transformed native societies in the West and Southwest, inducing tribes, such as the Sioux, Cheyennes, and Comanches, to abandon agriculture and adopt a nomadic or seminomadic lifestyle based on hunting the vast herds of bison on the Great Plains, which had been largely devoid of tribes prior to the arrival of the horse.

Horses revolutionized Western Indian warfare by turning warriors from foot soldiers into cavalrymen. Surprise attacks by small but highly mobile mounted war parties replaced pitched battles fought by large native armies. Instead of clubs, the mounted warrior depended almost exclusively on the bow and arrow until the introduction of firearms. Since Native Americans did not use saddles, the lessened weight gave their horses an advantage in speed and distance over the saddled horses of European and later U.S. cavalry. Native Americans also had an advantage in knowing where water sources could be found on the Plains. Consequently, American Indian war parties could generally outrun their pursuers. Ultimately, destruction of the buffalo herds, superior American firepower and numbers, and intertribal rivalries enabled the United States to defeat Native Americans in the Indian Wars.

Among the first tribes to take full advantage of the military opportunities afforded by horses was the Apaches. Horses made the Apaches the supreme military power on the southern Plains until their expansion was checked by the Pawnees, Osages, Kiowas, Comanches, and other tribes. Because of the great economic and strategic importance of horses, horse raids became the most common type of intertribal warfare. Capturing horses, which were always kept close to their owners' lodges at night, required great skill and daring.

Native Americans perfected mounted warfare. At an early age, boys learned to ride without stirrups or saddles, to shield their bodies by hanging down the side of the horse while handling the bow and arrow or firing rifles from underneath its head, and to lift up fallen comrades at high speed. By the time boys reached adulthood, they were expert horsemen. While highly trained, Native American cavalrymen were not as well organized as their U.S. Army counterparts, and combats tended to be of an individual nature.

By contrast, U.S. cavalrymen typically did not fight on horseback but instead used horses only to get close to the enemy and then dismounted for battle. The idea of employing Native Americans as cavalry troops for the U.S. Army did not take hold until the American Civil War (1861–1865). During this conflict, Cherokee-born Brigadier General Stand Watie commanded two Confederate Indian cavalry regiments and achieved several successes in battles in Indian Territory (Oklahoma).

After the Civil War, the U.S. Army began to experiment with Native American cavalry. The Army Reorganization Act of 1866 authorized the army to enlist up to 1,000 Indian scouts. Most were organized as cavalrymen and attached to regular army units as guides, but a few all-Indian units were also organized. Perhaps the best known of these was the Pawnee Battalion commanded by Frank North that was intermittently active between 1864 and 1877. Other Indian units (usually not larger than company size) included Apache scouts in the Southwest and Arikara and Crow scouts who served with Lieutenant Colonel George Armstrong Custer at the 1876 Battle of the Little Bighorn. Most Western tribes furnished scouts for the army at some point.

Native Americans signed up as scouts with the army for a variety of reasons: to escape the confines of the reservation, to earn income, to fight traditional enemies, to earn war honors, to capture horses, or to improve their bargaining position when dealing with the U.S. government. When serving against people of their own nationality, scouts sometimes hoped to persuade their opponents to surrender and avoid bloodshed. Apache scouts, for example, persuaded Geronimo to surrender in 1886.

Compared to white soldiers, Indian scouts performed remarkably well. Lieutenant John G. Bourke, who served alongside Indian scouts in several military campaigns, called them "the finest light cavalry in the world." Sixteen Indian scouts were awarded the Medal of Honor.

Although the Indian Wars ended in 1890, the U.S. Army continued to experiment with Native American troops. In 1891, the army initiated a program that created Native American companies attached to regiments stationed in the West. Among these units were Lieutenant Edward Casey's company of Cheyenne soldiers of the 8th Cavalry Regiment and Captain Hugh L. Scott's all–Native American company of the 7th Cavalry Regiment. Unfortunately, racial prejudice among the upper echelon of the army led to the disbandment of the last Indian units in 1897.

In 1916, however, following Mexican bandit Pancho Villa's attack on Columbus, New Mexico, the U.S. Army authorized the formation of a small unit of Apache scouts that took part in Brigadier General John J. Pershing's Punitive Expedition into Mexico. Although the success of Pershing's Apache scouts revived the idea in some quarters of forming new all-Indian units, the War Department rejected such proposals. By then, Native Americans had been successfully integrated into the army. During World War I (1914–1918), American Indians served alongside whites not only in the cavalry but also in all branches of the military.

Mark van de Logt

Further Reading

Dunlay, Thomas W. *Wolves for the Blue Soldiers: Indian Scouts and Auxiliaries with the United States Army, 1860–90.* Lincoln: University of Nebraska Press, 1982.

Roe, Frank G. *The Indian and the Horse.* Norman: University of Oklahoma Press, 1979.

Cavalry, U.S. Army

During the Indian Wars, cavalry units of the U.S. Army served as the primary combat force against western Native American tribes. Practicing the traditional missions of reconnaissance, security, and mounted assault, cavalry units had a mixed record of battlefield success against various tribes.

In the conflicts with the Indians of the Southeast and the Old Northwest Territory that followed the American Revolutionary War (1775–1783), most fighting took place in wooded areas and challenging terrain that were unsuited for cavalry actions. However, by the 1840s, the conflict between the U.S. government and Native Americans shifted to the West, where the United States acquired new lands via the 1848 Treaty of Guadalupe Hidalgo that ended the Mexican-American War (1846–1848). With the discovery of gold in California in 1848 encouraging thousands of white Americans to move west, the U.S. government was pressured to provide protection for its citizens and establish sovereignty over territories claimed by native tribes.

A series of western forts that delineated the frontier stretched from the Rio Grande in the South to the Red River in the North. In theory, these posts served as lines of communication, protected Western travelers, and enabled cavalry patrols to keep the Native Americans peaceful and confined to their reservations. Because mounted troops were more expensive to maintain than infantry, Congress had historically been reluctant to fund a large mounted force. Although the 1st and 2nd Dragoons were established in 1833 and 1836, respectively, and a regiment of Mounted Riflemen was established in 1846, these were used more as mounted infantry than as European-style cavalry. It was not until 1855 that the 1st and 2nd Cavalry regiments were established through the efforts of Secretary of War Jefferson Davis. The 2nd Cavalry in particular gained distinction as a training ground for officers during the American Civil War (1861–1865), including in its ranks Albert Sidney Johnston, Robert E. Lee, John Bell Hood, and George H. Thomas. With the beginning of the Civil War, all mounted forces were redesignated as cavalry.

Although Congress initially set the number of cavalry regiments at 6 in the immediate aftermath of the war, in 1866 Congress voted to increase the number of regiments to 10 in order to meet the needs of Reconstruction in the South and conflict with Native Americans on the frontier. Each cavalry regiment comprised 12 troops (officially listed as companies prior to 1883). The 9th and 10th regiments were composed of African American enlisted men (buffalo soldiers) commanded mostly by white officers. Despite subsequent reductions in the total overall strength of the U.S. Army, the basic structure of the cavalry remained the same during the American Indian Wars of the post–Civil War era. Indeed, after George Armstrong Custer's defeat at Little Bighorn in 1876, Congress authorized an increase of 2,500 men in the army's strength in order to bolster the numbers of each cavalry troop to 100 enlisted men. In reality, the actual strength of a troop was much lower, averaging just 58 men in 1881. Cavalry squadrons (officially listed as battalions prior to 1889) consisted of 2 or more troops and fluctuated in strength according to the needs of a campaign. With such a skeleton force stretched across frontier outposts, cavalrymen rarely assembled together as entire regiments. Consequently, the first loyalty among cavalrymen was to their troop.

The average cavalryman found army service to be routine and monotonous. The food was usually poor, the pay was low, and desertion rates were extremely high (less so in the Black 9th and 10th regiments). With reenlistment rates very low, cavalry ranks were often filled with inexperienced men. Cavalrymen were usually armed with a single-shot carbine and a pistol in preference to the traditional saber, which was rarely carried in the field, and cavalry doctrine dictated that soldiers fight dismounted with a combination of controlled fire against attacking warriors. The drawn-saber and bugle-sounded charges of Hollywood almost never occurred.

Campaigning required extensive supply trains that carried rations and extra ammunition and pulled small howitzers or sometimes Gatling guns. Even the food for the cavalry's grain-fed horses had to be hauled. This long logistical tail hindered the army's mobility against Native Americans and frustrated soldiers, who soon learned that warriors refused to fight according to cavalry doctrine.

As conflicts between white settlers and Native Americans escalated, the primary mission of the cavalry was to enforce the numerous treaties signed between the government and the western tribes. When the Native Americans violated these treaties by leaving the reservation or raiding white settlements, cavalry units were dispatched to punish the guilty and force the others back onto reservations. Interdicting small bands of well-mounted warriors proved to be virtually impossible, however, leading army planners to develop a new strategy of winter campaigning in the late 1860s by using the cavalry to attack Native Americans camps and destroying their food, shelter, and pony herds. Army leaders also exploited traditional animosities between various tribes by employing Native Americans as scouts.

When gold was discovered in the Black Hills in 1874, the government tried to force the Sioux to cede that territory to the United States, although the territory had been reserved to the tribe by the 1868 Treaty of Fort Laramie. The resulting Great Sioux War (1876–1877) witnessed the most famous cavalry engagement of the Indian Wars, when the 7th Cavalry attacked a Native American encampment along the Little Bighorn River on June 25, 1876. Lieutenant Colonel George Armstrong Custer and 225 men in his battalion were surrounded and killed. Unlike Little Bighorn, most of the fighting between U.S. Army cavalry units and Native American warriors consisted of brief small-unit engagements.

By the 1880s, the Indian Wars were practically over. Much of the U.S. Cavalry's attention was focused on defeating Geronimo and his small band of Apache warriors who raided on both sides of the U.S.–Mexico border. Eventually 6th Cavalry lieutenant Charles Gatewood and his Indian scouts located and compelled Geronimo to surrender in September 1886. The final engagement came on December 29, 1890, at Wounded Knee in South Dakota, where the 7th Cavalry attacked Chief Big Foot's band of Miniconjou Sioux, resulting in the deaths of at least 150 Native Americans, including women and children, and 25 cavalrymen.

During the Indian Wars, regular cavalry units participated in more than 1,000 engagements and suffered more than 2,000 total battle casualties. Although defeats such as Custer's were rare, highly mobile Native American warriors proved to be capable adversaries.

Donald L. Walker Jr. and
Justin D. Murphy

Further Reading
Herr, John K., and Edward S. Wallace. *The Story of the U.S. Cavalry, 1775–1942*. Boston: Little, Brown, 1953.

Utley, Robert M. *Frontier Regulars: The United States and the American Indian, 1866–1891*. New York: Macmillan, 1973.

Utley, Robert M. *Frontiersmen in Blue: The United States and the Indian, 1848–1865*. Lincoln: University of Nebraska Press, 1967.

Cherokee War

Start Date: October 5, 1759
End Date: November 19, 1761

A protracted and devastating frontier conflict that weakened the Cherokee Nation but did not break its traditional alliance with Great Britain. Numbering as many as 21,000 people in 1735, the Cherokees, an Iroquoian-speaking assemblage of tribes, were the largest ethnic bloc along the southern Appalachian highlands, an area encompassing parts of present-day West Virginia, Virginia, Kentucky, Tennessee, Georgia, and the Carolinas.

Early on, the Cherokees had established friendly trade relations with English colonists in Virginia and the Carolinas and fought alongside them and against their traditional Creek and Yamasee rivals in 1716. The English saw the Cherokees as a potential ally against the French-influenced Shawnees and Creeks, situated, respectively, to the north and south. In 1730, several leading Cherokee chiefs, the most prominent being Oconostota, who held the title "Great Warrior," and Attakullakulla, a peace chief, arrived in London, where a formal treaty of alliance was sealed.

The next 25 years proved both peaceful and prosperous, but the onset of the French and Indian War (1754–1763) plus a rising tide of white encroachment on Cherokee territory led to increasing friction. The British, for their part, sought to protect the Cherokees from French attacks and influence by constructing Fort Prince George near Keowee (South Carolina) in 1753 and Fort Loudoun near Chota (Tennessee) in 1756. Whatever military benefits these posts conferred were negated by growing resentment among Cherokees that their territorial rights were being violated.

Although many elements within the tribe waxed openly hostile toward the British, in 1758 the Cherokees dutifully dispatched war bands to assist Brigadier General John Forbes in his campaign against Fort Duquesne. On their return home, these same warriors were attacked and killed by Virginia militiamen who claimed that the warriors had stolen their horses. The tribesmen were understandably enraged when their slain warriors were then scalped by the militiamen, who subsequently collected bounties on the scalps. These acts triggered a spate of retaliatory raids against British settlements across the southern frontier, resulting in the deaths of at least 20 whites and both sides taking up arms against each other.

On October 5, 1759, Governor William Henry Lyttelton of South Carolina officially declared war against the Cherokees and prepared to lead an armed expedition of 1,300 men against them. Word of this spurred several Cherokee chiefs, including Oconostota, to visit Charles Town (present-day Charleston, South Carolina) in an attempt to forestall hostilities. The chiefs were taken prisoner by Lyttelton and marched under guard to Fort Prince George. There the governor met with Attakullakulla and demanded that 24 warriors known to have murdered settlers be turned over for punishment. The peace chief agreed to comply on December 26, 1759, and arranged the release of Oconostota. However, the remaining 24 chiefs and tribal leaders were to be retained as hostages.

A short truce ensued until February 16, 1760, when Oconostota lured the commander of Fort Prince George into the open for a parley and had him killed. The enraged British garrison then slaughtered all the hostages in retaliation, ending any chance for a peaceful negotiated settlement.

For many weeks into the war, Cherokee bands raided and terrorized frontier settlements with impunity, forcing Lieutenant Governor William Bull, Lyttelton's successor, to appeal to Major General Jeffrey Amherst, supreme British commander, for assistance. Amherst responded by dispatching several British regiments under Lieutenant Colonel Archibald Montgomery, who arrived at Charles Town on April 1, 1760. Augmented by supplies and militia, Montgomery marched 1,600 soldiers and militiamen to the relief of Fort Prince George and then embarked on a punitive expedition against the Cherokee Lower Towns.

The British first moved against the nearby village of Keowee, which they devastated on June 1, 1760. They then proceeded against a larger settlement at Echoe (in North Carolina), where the Cherokees sprung an effective ambush on June 27, 1760. Montgomery suffered 20 killed and 70 wounded before driving off his antagonists and withdrawing to Charles Town.

Considering the disparity in numbers and equipment, this was a considerable Cherokee victory and inspired the Overhill bands of the tribe to continue fighting. Oconostota's warriors managed to blockade Fort Loudoun and starve it into surrender. Captain Paul Demere, the commander, had been promised free passage back to British territory, but on August 8, 1760, angry Cherokees attacked his column, killing Demere and 32 others and taking the remainder hostage. This proved to be the largest humiliation for British troops during the entire war.

The loss of Fort Loudoun prompted Amherst to detail 2,500 British troops under Lieutenant Colonel James Grant to Charles Town as reinforcements in the spring of 1761. Grant took the offensive on March 20 by marching to Fort Prince George, where he conferred with Attakullakulla. The colonel brushed off the chief's peace offer and marched in force toward the Middle Towns. On June 10, 1761, only two miles from where Montgomery's force had been ambushed, the Cherokees launched another devastating attack. Grant managed to repel the warriors, driving them from the field, but at a cost of 10 killed and 50 wounded. The victorious British then spent an entire month systematically devastating native villages, crops, and fields, forcing upward of 5,000 Cherokees to flee into the wilderness. The natives proved unable to sustain this swath of destruction, and many chiefs, unable to secure assistance from neighboring tribes, sued for peace.

Attakullakulla, Oconostota, and other tribal leaders subsequently conferred with Grant at Fort Prince George and formalized a peace treaty on September 23, 1761. The treaty stipulated that the Cherokees would cease all contacts with the French and recognize the sovereignty of British courts over fugitives hiding on native land. In addition, the terms of the treaty pushed the South Carolina border 26 miles past the village of Keowee. The British demanded that the Cherokees hand over several chiefs for execution, but Attakullakulla, having ventured to Charles Town to confer with the lieutenant governor, had this demand rescinded. A separate arrangement signed with Virginia on November 19, 1761, brought the Cherokee War to an end.

Afterward, the Cherokees and the British normalized relations to the extent that lingering anger and resentment on both sides allowed. The natives in particular had sustained considerable loss of life, displacement of entire communities, and the surrender of valuable hunting grounds. In their weakened condition, the Cherokees were unable to stem the rising tide of colonial encroachment along the frontier. But whatever reservations they may have entertained against the British, the tribe trusted the emerging American nation even less. In 1776, the Cherokees went to war as an ally of Great Britain and suffered commensurately for it.

John C. Fredriksen

Further Reading

Hatley, Tom. *The Dividing Paths: Cherokees and South Carolinians through the Revolutionary Era*. New York: Oxford University Press, 1995.

Oliphant, John. *Peace and War on the Anglo-Cherokee Frontier 1753–63*. Baton Rouge: Louisiana State University Press, 2001.

Cherokees

One of the so-called Five Civilized Tribes and the largest single Native American group in the American Southeast upon first European contact. The name "Cherokee" is probably from the Creek tciloki, meaning "people who speak differently." Cherokee is an Iroquoian language and had three dialects, which were mutually intelligible with difficulty. Their self-designation was Ani-yun-wiya, meaning "Real People." Along with the Creeks, Choctaws, Chickasaws, and Seminoles, the Cherokees were designated the Five Civilized Tribes by Americans because by the early 19th century many members of these tribes dressed, farmed, and governed themselves much like white Americans.

The tribe's chief deity was the sun, which may have had a feminine identity. The people conceived of the cosmos as being divided into three parts: an upper world, this world, and a lower world. Each contained numerous spiritual beings that resided in specific places. The four cardinal directions were replete with social and spiritual significance. Tribal mythology, symbols, and beliefs were complex, and there were also various associated taboos, customs, and social and personal rules.

The various Cherokee villages formed a loose confederacy. There were two chiefs per village: a red (or war) chief and a white chief (Most Beloved Man or Woman) who was associated with civil, economic, religious, and juridical functions. Chiefs could be male or female, and there was little or no hereditary component. There was also a village council in which women sat, although usually only as observers. The Cherokee were not a cohesive political entity until the late 18th century.

Towns were located along rivers and streams. They contained a central ceremonial place and in the early historic period were often surrounded by palisades. People built rectangular summer houses of pole frames and wattle with walls of cane matting and clay plaster and gabled bark or thatch roofs. The houses, about 60 or 70 feet by 15 feet, were often divided into three parts: a kitchen, a dining area, and bedrooms. Some were two stories high, with the upper walls open for ventilation. There was probably one door.

The Cherokee were primarily farmers. Women grew corn, beans, squash, sunflowers, and tobacco, the latter used ceremonially. Wild foods included roots, crab apples, persimmons, plums, cherries, grapes, hickory nuts, walnuts, chestnuts, and berries. Men hunted various animals, including deer, bears, raccoons, rabbits, squirrels, turkeys, and rattlesnakes. The men also fished occasionally; they also collected maple sap in earthen pots and boiled it into syrup.

Cherokee pipes were widely admired and easily exported. The people also traded maple sugar and syrup. They imported shell wampum that was used as currency. Their plaited cane baskets, pottery, and masks carved of wood and gourds were of especially fine quality.

In addition to the red (war) chief in each village, there was also a War Woman, who accompanied war parties. She fed the men, gave advice, and determined the fate of prisoners. Women also distinguished themselves in combat and often tortured prisoners of war. The people often painted themselves as well as their canoes and paddles for war. The party carried an ark or medicine chest to war and left a war club engraved with its exploits in enemy territory.

The Cherokees probably originated in the upper Ohio Valley, the Great Lakes region, or someplace else in the present-day northeastern United States. They may also have been related to the Mound Builders. The town of Echota, located on the Little Tennessee River, may have been the ancient capital of the Cherokee Nation.

The Cherokees encountered Hernando de Soto around 1540, probably not long after they arrived in their historic homeland. Spanish attacks commenced shortly thereafter, although new diseases probably weakened the Cherokees even before Spanish soldiers began killing them. There were also contacts with the French and especially the English in the early 17th century. Traders brought guns around 1700, along with debilitating alcohol.

The Cherokees fought a series of wars with the Tuscaroras, Shawnees, Catawbas, Creeks, and Chickasaws early in the 18th century. In 1759–1761, the Cherokees, led by Chief Oconostota, fought the British as a protest against unfair trade practices and violence against them. The Cherokees raided settlements and captured a British fort but were defeated by the British scorched-earth policy. The peace treaty cost the Cherokees much of their eastern land, and in fact, they never fully recovered their prominence after that time.

Significant depopulation resulted from several epidemics in the mid-18th century. Cherokee support for Britain during the American Revolutionary War (1775–1783) brought retaliatory attacks by southern state militias. Finally, some Cherokees who lived near Chattanooga relocated in 1794 to Arkansas and Texas and in 1831 to Indian Territory (Oklahoma). These people eventually became known as the Western Cherokees.

After the American Revolutionary War, the Cherokees adopted American-style farming, cattle ranching, business relations, and government, becoming relatively cohesive and prosperous. They also owned slaves and sided with the United States in the Creek War (1813–1814). The tribe enjoyed a cultural renaissance between 1800 and 1830, although they were under constant pressure for land cession and were plagued by internal political factionalism.

The Cherokee Nation was founded in 1827 with Western democratic institutions and a written constitution (which specifically disenfranchised African Americans and women). By then the Cherokees were intermarrying regularly with nonnatives and receiving increased missionary activity, especially in education. Sequoyah (also known as George Gist) is credited with devising a Cherokee syllabary and thus providing his people with a written language. During the late 1820s, the Cherokee people began publishing a newspaper, the *Cherokee Phoenix*.

The discovery of gold in Cherokee territory led in part to the 1830 Indian Removal Act, requiring the Cherokees (among other tribes) to relocate west of the Mississippi

River. Gold also brought squatters and prospectors onto Cherokee land. The tribe sought federal assistance from the U.S. Supreme Court. In *Cherokee Nation v. Georgia* (1831), Chief Justice John Marshall ruled that the court had no jurisdiction in the case but that the Cherokees had an "unquestionable right" to their lands. In *Worcester v. Georgia* (1832), the Marshall court ruled that the Cherokee Nation was a "distinct political community" in which Georgia law did not apply. President Andrew Jackson refused to enforce the court's rulings or support the Cherokees in their fight against illegal encroachment.

When a small minority of Cherokees signed the Treaty of New Echota, ceding the tribe's last remaining eastern lands, local whites immediately began appropriating their land and plundering their homes and possessions. Cherokees were forced into internment camps where many died, although more than 1,000 escaped to the mountains of North Carolina, where they became the progenitors of what came to be called the Eastern Cherokees.

The removal, known as the Trail of Tears, began in 1838. The Cherokees were forced to walk some 1,000 miles through severe weather without adequate food and clothing. About 4,000 Cherokees, almost a quarter of the total, died during the removal, and more died once they reached Indian Territory (Oklahoma), where they joined—and largely absorbed—the group already there. Following their arrival in Indian Territory, the Cherokees quickly adopted another constitution and reestablished their institutions and facilities, including newspapers and schools. Under Chief John Ross, most Cherokees supported slavery and joined the Confederate cause in the Civil War.

The huge "permanent" Indian Territory was often reduced in size, however. When the northern region was removed to create the states of Kansas and Nebraska, Native Americans living there were again forcibly resettled. One result of the Dawes Severalty Act (1887) was the "sale" (the virtual appropriation) of roughly two million acres of Native American land in Oklahoma. Although the Cherokees and other tribes resisted allotment, Congress forced them to acquiesce in 1898. Their land was individually allotted in 1902, and their tribal governments were officially terminated.

Ten years after the Cherokee removal, the U.S. Congress ceased efforts to round up the Eastern Cherokees. The Cherokees received North Carolina state citizenship in 1866 and incorporated as the eastern band of Cherokees in 1889. In the early 20th century, many Eastern Cherokees were engaged in subsistence farming and in the local timber industry. Having resisted allotment, the tribe took steps to ensure that it would always own its land.

In the 1930s, the United Keetoowah Band (UKB), a group of full-bloods opposed to assimilation, formally separated from the Oklahoma Cherokees. (The name "Keetoowah" derives from an ancient town in western North Carolina.) The group originated in the anti-allotment battles at the end of the 19th century. In the early 20th century, the UKB reconstructed several traditional political structures, such as the seven clans and white towns, as well as some ancient cultural practices that did not survive the move west. They received federal recognition in 1946.

Barry M. Pritzker

Further Reading

Conley, John R. *The Cherokee Nation: A History.* Albuquerque: University of New Mexico Press, 2005.

Ehle, John. *Trail of Tears: The Rise and Fall of the Cherokee Nation*. New York: Doubleday, 1988.

Woodward, Grace Steele. *The Cherokees*. Norman: University of Oklahoma Press, 1982.

Cheyenne Campaign

Start Date: May 1857
End Date: September 1857

U.S. military campaign against Cheyennes during spring and summer 1857. Although the Cheyennes had agreed in the 1851 Fort Laramie Treaty to refrain from attacking white settlers traveling across Kansas and Nebraska to Oregon and California and to remain at peace with other tribes, chiefs found it virtually impossible to enforce treaty restrictions on younger warriors. Indeed, Cheyenne raids against their traditional enemies, the Pawnees, not only violated the treaty but also made incidents with settlers crossing the Plains inevitable.

Numerous incidents escalated tensions during 1856. In June, Captain Henry W. Wharton attempted to arrest three Cheyenne warriors at Fort Kearny because a white settler had been killed not far from the fort. In August, Wharton dispatched elements of the 1st Cavalry under Captain George H. Stewart against the Cheyennes after they attacked a stagecoach. In an attack on a Cheyenne camp along the Platte River, Stewart's troops killed 10 Cheyennes, wounded 10 more, and seized camp provisions. When the Cheyennes retaliated by attacking white settlers crossing the Plains, Secretary of War Jefferson Davis authorized a campaign against them in the spring of 1857.

In May 1857, the campaign commenced from Fort Leavenworth with three columns under the overall command of Colonel Edwin Vose Sumner, a veteran of the Mexican-American War (1846–1848) who had assumed command of the new 1st Cavalry Regiment in 1855. Sumner's column of two companies from the 1st Cavalry and two companies from the 2nd Dragoons was to advance up the Platte along the Overland Trail to Fort Laramie and then swing south. Major John Sedgwick's column of four companies from the 1st Cavalry was to advance up the Arkansas along the Sante Fe Trail to the foothills of the Rockies (near present-day Pueblo, Colorado) and then swing north to converge with Sumner. Lieutenant Colonel Joseph E. Johnston headed a third column of four companies from the 1st Cavalry and two companies from the 6th Infantry Regiment charged with surveying the southern boundary of Kansas and providing support to Sumner if possible.

Each column was supported by two howitzers. During their advance, neither Sumner nor Sedgwick encountered hostiles, and the two companies of the 2nd Dragoon Regiment were detached from Sumner's column and transferred to Utah to suppress the Mormons. Upon arriving at Fort Laramie, three companies of the 6th Infantry were attached to Sumner's column, which then moved south to meet Sedgwick. Johnston meanwhile completed the survey of Kansas's southern border without incident but was too far away to play a role in the Cheyenne Campaign.

After converging with Sedgwick's column near present-day Greeley, Colorado, in mid-July, Sumner led the combined force eastward in search of the Cheyennes. On July 29, scouts located a large force of Cheyennes along the Solomon River. Approximately 300 Cheyenne warriors, who had been told by their medicine man that they could not be harmed by the

American guns because they had bathed in a "holy lake," formed a line from the banks of the Solomon to nearby bluffs and prepared to meet the American forces in a pitched battle. To their surprise, Sumner ordered his cavalry, approximately 300 strong, to draw their sabers and charge instead of opening fire and waiting to bring up his infantry or howitzers. The ferocity of the charge and the realization that the medicine man's magic protected them against guns, not sabers, caused the Cheyennes to flee in panic. Sumner's cavalry followed in hot pursuit for seven miles. Casualties were relatively light on both sides, with nine Cheyenne warriors killed and two cavalrymen killed and another eight wounded, including Lieutenant J. E. B. Stuart.

After spending two days building an earthen embankment on the Solomon, where Sumner left his infantry behind to take care of the wounded, he pursued the trail left by the Cheyennes, eventually finding their hastily abandoned village and burning their lodges. Sumner then proceeded to Bent's Fort on the Arkansas River, where he confiscated the allotment of firearms and ammunition that the Indian agent was supposed to distribute to the Cheyennes and Arapahos. Although Sumner planned to continue the campaign, in early September he received orders to send most of his men to Utah. Consequently, the Cheyenne Campaign of 1857 ended rather abruptly. In the weeks that followed, the Cheyennes launched a series of raids along the Platte, leading general in chief of the army Brevet Lieutenant General Winfield Scott to criticize Sumner's effectiveness. In reality, the Cheyenne Campaign had produced an important psychological victory over the Cheyennes. For the next seven years, the Cheyennes remained relatively peaceful despite an onrush of miners and settlers into Colorado.

Justin D. Murphy

Further Reading

Bonvillain, Nancy. *The Cheyennes: People of the Plains.* Brookfield, CT: Millbrook, 1996.

Chalfant, William Y. *Cheyennes and Horse Soldiers: The 1857 Expedition and the Battle of Solomon's Fork.* Norman: University of Oklahoma Press, 1989.

Utley, Robert M. *Frontiersmen in Blue: The United States and the Indian, 1848–1865.* Lincoln: University of Nebraska Press, 1967.

Cheyennes

Great Plains tribe located during the 1800s between the Yellowstone River to the north and the Arkansas River to the south, encompassing a large region from the Black Hills in South Dakota to southeastern Colorado. The Cheyennes, an Algonquian-speaking nation, were first encountered by Europeans as woodland Indians in Minnesota west of the headwaters of the Mississippi River. The name "Cheyenne" was from the Sioux term meaning "foreign speakers." The Cheyennes were sedentary during this period, harvesting wild rice and planting maize, beans, and squash. They also hunted for deer and ventured onto the prairies for bison. There is evidence that they produced some pottery during this period, a skill they later abandoned.

During the first half of the 18th century, the Cheyennes and Sioux were pushed by the Ojibwas out of the extensive woodland lakes region of Minnesota to the prairies of southern and western Minnesota and the eastern Dakotas. Continuing their westward migration in the late 18th century, the

Cheyennes again adopted a semisedentary lifestyle while still hunting bison on a seasonal basis. They had now settled in a number of walled villages along the present boundary between North and South Dakota. While the younger men left on the available horses to hunt bison, the older men, most women, and the children would remain behind. Several villages were destroyed in the late 1700s by Ojibwa war parties. Because of the Ojibwa threat and the lure of the bison- and horse-rich Great Plains, the Cheyennes abandoned agriculture once more and advanced farther onto the Plains. By 1800, they were west of the Missouri River and possessed enough horses to become fully nomadic.

The Cheyennes split into two groups—Northern and Southern—comprising several smaller bands. The Northern division remained close to the Lakotas in Wyoming, Nebraska, Montana, and South Dakota. The Southern division moved farther south into Colorado and Kansas, where they began to push the Kiowas out. The Cheyennes were often willing to wage a more intense form of warfare than their neighbors. By the mid-1830s, skirmishes between the Kiowas and the Cheyennes had become quite intense.

In 1838, the Cheyennes (now partnered with the Arapahos) declared war on the Kiowas. At the 1838 Battle of Wolf Creek, the two met in a set-piece battle. The Cheyennes approached a large Kiowa village and attacked. Although the Battle of Wolf Creek was a draw, both sides realized that the level of casualties involved in further fighting would be devastating. In 1840, a peace was concluded between the Cheyennes and Kiowas whereby the Cheyennes agreed to remain north of the Arkansas River and the Kiowas agreed to remain south of it.

Movement along the Oregon Trail led to tension with whites but little direct conflict until the 1850s, when the discovery of gold in the Colorado Rockies led to a large migration of whites across Cheyenne hunting grounds. In 1857, the army conducted a brief campaign against Cheyennes on the southern Plains, which forestalled wider conflict for a number of years.

A third band of Cheyennes, the Dog Soldiers, now developed. The Dog Soldiers were originally a warrior society, many of whose members had intermarried with Lakota women and were more aggressive than other Cheyennes. By 1864, small-scale raids on whites by Dog Soldiers resulted in open war. Some Cheyenne elders, in particular, Chief Black Kettle, sought accommodation with the whites. Assured that if he encamped near Fort Lyon along Sand Creek he and his band would be safe, Black Kettle went so far as to raise a white flag and an American flag over his encampment. On November 29, 1864, however, the 3rd Colorado Cavalry Regiment and other militia units under Colonel John Chivington, a Methodist minister and politician, attacked Black Kettle's camp at sunrise. The attack, known as the Sand Creek Massacre, ended with approximately 150 Cheyennes killed. Among the dead were a number of Arapahos as well. Two-thirds of the casualties were women and children. Although the attack was condemned by the U.S. Army, the Cheyennes and their allies—the Lakotas, Arapahos, Kiowas, and Comanches—were incensed by the massacre.

In retribution, Cheyennes attacked farmers, ranchers, and stagecoaches throughout Wyoming, Colorado, western Kansas, and Nebraska. Continuing throughout 1865 and into 1866, the conflict merged with Red Cloud's War (1866–1868) in the Powder River Country of Wyoming and Montana. During the war, the Cheyennes fought around Fort Phil Kearny, which precipitated the December 21, 1866, Fetterman Massacre. Many Cheyennes were also at the Beecher's Island fight between September 17 and 24, 1868. Here Major George Forsyth and 51 volunteer scouts were surrounded and unhorsed on a small island in the Arickaree Fork of the Republican River. Although the losses were light on both sides, Cheyenne war leader Roman Nose was killed on the afternoon of the first day as he led a charge on the scouts.

Black Kettle, meanwhile, had fled to Indian Territory (Oklahoma), preventing his young men from taking revenge. On the morning of November 27, 1868, the 7th U.S. Cavalry under Lieutenant Colonel George Custer, on the trail of a band of hostiles made up of Kiowas, Comanches and Cheyennes, attacked Black Kettle's camp along the Washita River. Black Kettle and dozens of Cheyenne men, women, and children were killed.

The Southern Cheyennes aligned with the Kiowas and Comanches as they attempted to slow settlement on the southern Plains and the massive slaughter of the bison herd. They participated with the Kiowas and Comanches in the Second Battle of Adobe Walls (June 27, 1874) and during the subsequent Red River War (1874–1875), after which they remained largely peaceful and settled on their reservation in Indian Territory.

The Northern Cheyennes generally rode with their Lakota allies and participated in actions throughout the late 1860s and mid-1870s. Chief Dull Knife's band fought at the Battle of the Little Bighorn (June 25–26, 1876) against Custer's 7th Cavalry. The last major action of the Cheyennes was the defeat of Dull Knife's band in winter camp by Colonel Ranald S. Mackenzie's 4th Cavalry on November 26, 1876. Led by Pawnee scouts, Mackenzie destroyed Dull

Knife's village, forcing the chief's surrender.

The Northern Cheyennes were then moved south to Indian Territory. In 1878, homesick for their northern Plains, 300 Cheyenne warriors, women, and children under chiefs Little Wolf and Dull Knife broke away from the Fort Reno area in Oklahoma and evaded patrols. Dull Knife's band was eventually caught and imprisoned at Fort Robinson until it moved onto the reservation in Montana at Fort Keogh, where they were joined by Northern Cheyennes who had been at Pine Ridge with the Lakotas and some Southern Cheyennes from Oklahoma.

John Thomas Broom

Further Reading

Bonvillain, Nancy. *The Cheyennes: People of the Plains*. Brookfield, CT: Millbrook, 1996.

Grinnell, George Bird. *The Cheyenne Indians*, 2 Vols. Lincoln: University of Nebraska Press, 1972.

Moore, John H. *The Cheyenne*. Malden, MA: Blackwell, 1996.

Church, Benjamin

Birth Date: 1639
Death Date: January 17, 1717

New England soldier and frontiersman and the first of the so-called border captains who figure so prominently in the history and mythology of the colonial wars against Native Americans. Benjamin Church was born in 1639 at Duxbury in Plymouth Colony, the son of a carpenter and veteran of the Pequot War (1636–1638). Church advocated adopting Native American ways of fighting (the so-called skulking way of war), instructing colonists under his command to move silently through the forests and swamps, to "scatter" as the Native Americans did if attacked, and to "never fire at an Indian if you can reach him with a hatchet." Church also urged the use of Native American allies to defeat Metacom (King Philip) and his warriors in King Philip's War (1675–1676).

Ranging through Massachusetts and Rhode Island, Church's mixed band of Native Americans and colonial militia burned enemy villages and crops and took native prisoners. Finally, on August 12, 1676, Church and his rangers tracked Metacom to his camp near Mount Hope, Rhode Island, and killed him when he tried to escape. The dead chief's head was cut off and taken to Plymouth, where it remained atop a pole for some 25 years as a trophy of English victory. For his exploits, the Plymouth authorities awarded Church the sum of 30 shillings.

Church frequently fell out with colonial leaders over treatment of native foes. On more than one occasion, Native Americans he had convinced to surrender or who had been captured were sold into slavery, to his great fury. This was the fate of Metacom's wife and son, taken by Church and his rangers 10 days before they killed the Native American leader.

When King William's War (1689–1697) began, Church was commissioned a major and led militia in the fight against the French and their Native American allies in Maine. His troops participated in the Battle of Brackett's Woods, which helped lift the siege of Fort Loyal. Church led three more expeditions into Maine and what is today New Brunswick in 1690, 1692, and 1696.

In March 1704, Church, although by now a rotund 65-year-old, was granted a commission as colonel of Massachusetts troops and was ordered to raid into Acadia to retaliate for the French and Indian destruction of Deerfield, Massachusetts, the month before. Fortified by a promise of £100 for each Native American scalp and moving from place to place by whaleboat and taking to snowshoes when necessary, Church's 550 New England volunteers attacked native villages, seized and burned the towns of Les Mines (Grand Pré) and Chignecto, and threatened the French base at Port Royal.

The Acadia raid was Church's last campaign. He retired to his farm at Little Compton, Rhode Island, where he and his son Thomas composed the two volumes of his memoirs of King Philip's War and the struggles against the French and Native Americans. The volumes are noteworthy for the author's insistence on the importance of human agency—his own, primarily—in the victories of the colonists over their enemies. Other contemporary historians of the wars, such as William Hubbard and Cotton Mather, had seen the triumphs as evidence of God's will. Publication of his memoirs made Church a model for other border captains, such as Robert Rogers, to follow. Church died on January 17, 1717, near his home at Little Compton, Rhode Island.

Bruce Vandervort

Further Reading

Leach, Douglas Edward. *Flintlock and Tomahawk: New England in King Philip's War.* East Orleans, MA: Parnassus Imprints, 1992.

Lepore, Jill. *The Name of War: King Philip's War and the Origins of American Identity.* New York: Vintage Books, 1999.

Schultz, Eric B., and Michael J. Tougias. *King Philip's War: The History and Legacy of America's Forgotten Conflict.* Rev. ed. Woodstock, VT: Countryman Press, 2017.

Cochise

Birth Date: ca. 1810
Death Date: June 8, 1874

Chiricahua Apache leader. Born circa 1810 probably in present-day southeastern Arizona, Cochise spent much of his youth fighting Mexicans who routinely trespassed on Chiricahua lands. He also launched devastating raids into the Mexican provinces of Chihuahua and Sonora, often in concert with his father-in-law, Mangas Coloradas, leader of the Mimbres Apaches. Cochise's keen intelligence and finely honed military skills led to his emergence as leader of the Chiricahuas by 1856.

Although he continued to battle the Mexicans after the United States acquired his Arizona homeland from Mexico in 1848, a result of the Mexican-American War (1846–1848) and the 1848 Treaty of Guadalupe Hidalgo, Cochise remained at peace with the Americans. The Chiricahuas took no hostile action against the stagecoach stations built in their territory along the road from the Rio Grande to Tucson, nor did they harass travelers.

The situation changed in February 1861, however, when U.S. Army lieutenant George Bascom summoned Cochise to a conference at Apache Pass, located in far southeastern Arizona in present-day Cochise County. Bascom falsely accused Cochise of stealing cattle and kidnapping a boy. Cochise explained that the raid that Bascom described had been carried out by Coyotero Apaches and offered to negotiate for the boy's release, but Bascom attempted to arrest him. Cochise escaped by cutting through the wall of the tent where the meeting took place. However, Bascom seized five of Cochise's companions (three of whom were relatives) who had accompanied him to the meeting.

In an effort to free the hostages and secure bargaining power, Cochise captured three whites. Bascom refused to exchange Cochise's relatives, insisting that Cochise must return the boy and the cattle. The Chiricahua leader responded by surrounding the troops at Apache Pass and launching a series of raids against travelers and other soldiers in the area. Seeing that Bascom would not yield, Cochise executed his prisoners. Bascom retaliated by hanging the Chiricahua hostages. Cochise responded with further raids.

Soon afterward the U.S. government withdrew most of its troops from the Southwest for service in the American Civil War (1861–1865). Cochise and Mangas Coloradas took prompt advantage by intensifying their attacks on settlers and travelers and besieging the mining camp at Pinos Altos, forcing most of the prospectors to flee. They met no resistance from the small Confederate detachment that had occupied Tucson.

In summer of 1862, a unit of California Volunteers under Brigadier General James H. Carleton marched into Arizona and drove out the Confederates. Cochise and Mangas Coloradas ambushed Carleton's force at Apache Pass on July 15. After their initial assault was repulsed, the troops fought their way through to Apache Springs. Apache sharpshooters tried to deny the soldiers access to the water but were driven off by artillery fire.

From his nearly inaccessible stronghold in the Dragoon Mountains of Arizona, Cochise continued to wage a guerrilla war against soldiers and civilians, although his 300 Chiricahua fighting men were vastly outnumbered. His determination to continue resistance increased after U.S. troops captured Mangas Coloradas under a flag of truce and then murdered him in January 1863.

By late 1869, Cochise had grown tired of fighting and sent word through intermediaries that he was willing to make peace. The U.S. government was similarly inclined, and its emissaries proposed that the Chiricahuas and Mimbres share a reservation in New Mexico. Cochise approved, but his people preferred to remain in the Arizona mountains. He also distrusted both the government and the settlers, and therefore in the early spring of 1871, he declined an invitation to visit Washington, D.C. In April 1871, Cochise's worries were confirmed when about 150 Avaraipa and Pinal Apaches, who had accepted a reservation at Camp Grant, were massacred by white Arizona settlers.

President Ulysses S. Grant denounced the massacre and ordered the army and the Bureau of Indian Affairs to make peace with the Apaches. Cochise had been raiding in Mexico and upon his return found that Brigadier General George Crook had troops searching southern Arizona for the Chiricahuas. Cochise then led his people to New Mexico, where he contacted Brigadier General Gordon Granger. The two met at Cañada Alamosa in March 1872 and discussed peace terms, but the Chiricahuas returned to the Dragoon Mountains upon learning that the government had ordered that all Apaches were to be sent to Fort Tularosa.

On October 1, 1872, Brigadier General Oliver O. Howard, who had taken charge of the effort to negotiate with Cochise, reached the Chiricahua camp with the assistance of Cochise's friend Thomas Jeffords. After 10 days of discussions, Cochise agreed to end the fighting and accept a reservation in the mountains of southeastern Arizona.

Cochise had suffered from a stomach ailment since at least 1872 and was in declining health. He died on June 8, 1874, at his camp in the Dragoon Mountains.

Jim Piecuch

Further Reading

Cole, D. C. *The Chiricahua Apache, 1846–1876: From War to Reservation*. Albuquerque: University of New Mexico Press, 1988.

Sweeney, Edwin R. *Cochise: Chiricahua Apache Chief*. Norman: University of Oklahoma Press, 1991.

Comanche Campaign

Start Date: 1867
End Date: 1875

Series of skirmishes and small battles between the U.S. Army and white settlers against the Comanches and their Kiowa, Arapaho, and Southern Cheyenne allies. The hostilities took place mainly in Kansas, Colorado, New Mexico, and parts of Texas. After decades of incessant raids on white settlements by the Comanches throughout the southern Plains and northern Mexico, the U.S. government called for a meeting of the Comanches and other southern Plains tribes at Medicine Lodge Creek, 60 miles south of Fort Larned (Kansas), in October 1867. The Comanches believed that the resulting treaty would not be enforceable and was unlikely to resolve the differences between the tribes and white settlers but signed it anyway. Some Comanches accepted a reservation in southwestern Indian Territory (Oklahoma), which they would share with several Kiowa bands. Others refused to go to the reservation. The annuities promised by the U.S. government failed to materialize, so the Comanches and their allies continued raids against whites.

Throughout the late 1860s the raids intensified, as the Comanche were now hard pressed to provide for themselves because the buffalo herds upon which they relied were reducing at an alarming rate; the bison would be hunted nearly to extinction by the late 1870s. By 1871, U.S. Army commanding general William T. Sherman and Lieutenant General Philip Sheridan, commander of the Military Division of the Missouri, had instituted a scorched-earth policy toward the Comanches. This meant that their winter camps, supplies, and animals were to be destroyed and that noncombatants were to be killed. Although this strategy was difficult to carry out over the vast Comanche territory, the Comanches would feel the full impact of the policy, which did not end until their final surrender in 1875.

The first major U.S. military strike began in autumn 1871 with Colonel Ranald S. Mackenzie's 4th Cavalry marching through western Texas's Blanco Canyon onto the Staked Plains, where Tonkawa scouts found the Comanche war chief Quanah Parker leading a large Kwahadi Comanche band. The troops pushed the Kwahadis deep into the region until cold weather halted their drive.

In spring 1872, Mackenzie changed his strategy, instituting a border patrol system anchored by newly established forts. With 300 soldiers and Tonkawa scouts, he tracked Comanche Rancherias, charted war and hunting trails, and mapped the sites of Comancheros (New Mexican Hispanic traders). Avoiding direct confrontation, he wore down the Comanches by disrupting their seasonal cycle of activities, including trade.

In September 1872, the 4th Cavalry attacked a Kwahadi-Kotsoteka camp of 262 lodges on the North Fork of the Red River. In a brutal engagement, the soldiers killed 24 warriors, captured more than 100 women and children, seized horses and mules, and burned lodges, robes, and food. Pursuing Comanche parties managed to recapture most of the animals in night raids, but the fight left the Comanches destitute.

In 1874, the Comanches followed a mystic Kwahadi medicine man, Isatai, who promised a restoration of Comanche power. He claimed that he could raise the dead, stop bullets in midflight, and regurgitate all the cartridges that the Comanches would need. By mid-June 1874, some 700 warriors and their families had gathered on Elk Creek to follow Isatai. At dawn on June 27, 1874, Isatai and Quanah Parker attacked buffalo hunters at Adobe Walls, a small trading post in the Texas Panhandle. The assault, known as the Second Battle of Adobe Walls, failed, thanks largely to the high-powered rifles of the post's defenders and demoralization among the attackers. Isatai's horse was killed by a stray shot, and his support quickly evaporated.

The U.S. government now ordered all Comanches and Kiowas to return to their agency by August 3, 1874, at Fort Sill, but they remained in place. In what became known as the Red River War, Sherman and Sheridan sent five columns, 1,400 soldiers in all, from every direction to converge upon Comanche and Kiowa sanctuaries in the canyons along the Caprock and plains of the Texas Panhandle. The advancing troops meaningfully engaged the Comanches only once, but their looming presence prevented fleeing Comanche bands from searching for the few remaining bison and making preparations for the winter.

On September 28, 1874, Mackenzie's 4th Cavalry attacked a serpentine village of several hundred Comanches, Kiowas, and Southern Cheyennes in Palo Duro Canyon. Scattered across the canyon floor, the tribes failed to organize a united defense and fled onto the open plains, leaving their possessions behind. Mackenzie ordered the camp destroyed. Soldiers captured some 1,500 Indian ponies, most of which Mackenzie ordered killed. Following this defeat, the half-starved and worn-out Native Americans returned to their reservations for good by summer 1875, with Quanah Parker and his band being the last to submit.

John Thomas Broom

Further Reading

Ferhenbach, T. R. *Comanches: The History of a People*. New York, Anchor Books, 2003.

Hoig, Stan. *Tribal Wars of the Southern Plains*. Norman: University of Oklahoma Press, 1993.

Wallace, Ernest, and E. Adamson Hoebel. *The Comanches: Lords of the South Plains*. 1952; reprint, Norman: University of Oklahoma Press, 1986.

Comanches

A Native American group of the southern Great Plains. The Comanches were an offshoot of the Shoshones of the Upper Platte River area of Wyoming. Between 1650 and 1700, the Comanches became an autonomous group. Although never really a unified tribe, the Comanches were subdivided into as many as 12 independent groups. Their language was of the Uto-Aztekan family, and they were linguistically and in many ways culturally identical to the Shoshones, whose wider range had been in the Great Basin and Rocky Mountain area. The first European contact with the Comanches occurred in New Mexico in 1705, when the Spaniards first encountered them. The Spaniards named them "Comanche," from the Ute name "Komantcia," which translates loosely as "enemy." The Comanches' name for themselves was "Nermernuh," which means "the people."

After the split with the Shoshones, the Comanches migrated east and south toward eastern Wyoming and Colorado, western Nebraska, and Kansas before settling on the southern Plains. From the 1700s, their principal range became northwestern Texas, western Oklahoma, eastern Colorado, eastern New Mexico, and southern Kansas—an area that became known as the Comancheria. They conducted raids much farther from eastern Kansas and Nebraska deep into Mexico and from the Gulf Coast of Texas to Santa Fe, New Mexico. It is believed that at their peak the Comanches numbered about 20,000 people.

The Comanches' migration from the Rocky Mountains to the southern Plains was influenced by several factors. The abundance of bison lured them onto the Plains, while the growing power of tribes to their north, such as the Kiowas and later the Cheyennes and Lakotas, pushed them farther south, where the allure of Spanish horse herds became a major factor. The Comanches obtained horses early. By the time of their first encounter with the Spanish, the Comanches already had substantial herds. Indeed, their culture was dominated by the horse, the bison, and raiding.

The various Comanche bands did not have a single leader, or chief. Instead, each group chose a small group of leaders and advisers who carried out the governing functions of the whole band, including warfare. Thus, most Comanche clans had a war chief, a peace chief, and a small group of elders who handled other concerns, including the settling of disputes and the assignment of particular tasks.

The Comanches were divided into a shifting number of bands, the principal ones being the Honey-eaters (Penatekas), located at the southern and eastern side of their range in Texas; the Yap-eaters (Yapparikas), located along the northern side of the range; and the Antelopes (Quahadi, Kwahadi), located in the western area of the range, principally on the Staked Plains. The Wanderers (Nokonis), who ranged along the headwaters of the Brazos River in Texas, and the Buffalo-eaters (Kotsotekas), of the Canadian River Valley, were other prominent bands. Band membership was partially by family association and partially by choice. Members were free to shift from band to band.

The Comanches were aggressive, driving various Apache tribes off the southern Plains and then raiding into the regions of the Lipan Apaches in Texas and the various Apache groups of eastern New Mexico. The Comanches warred on an almost constant basis with the Utes and engaged in raids deep into Mexico until the 1870s. In addition, the Comanches warred against tribes to their east in Texas and Oklahoma and against Prairie tribes such as the Osages and Pawnees. Throughout the early 1800s, the Comanche presence on the southern Plains stopped Spanish and later Mexican expansion from New Mexico and Texas and halted French penetration of the area. Texan and American expansion, while not halted, was slowed. During the American Civil War (1861–1865), the Comanches forcefully drove back the Texas frontier by as much as 100 miles in some areas.

Despite their warlike ways, the Comanches could also make peace with long-standing enemies. In the 1790s, the Comanches made peace with the Kiowas and the associated Kiowa Apaches. Later in 1840, the Comanches and Kiowas made peace with the Cheyennes and Arapahos. These peace arrangements served to protect the Comanches from attacks from the northern end of their range. Young warriors from these tribes often joined the Comanches on long-distance raids.

In 1786, the Comanches made peace with the New Mexicans under Don Juan Bautista de Anza, and their raids on Spanish and (later) Mexican settlements in New Mexico stopped. This treaty, signed in Taos, arranged for traders from New Mexico known as Comancheros to provide trade goods, specifically guns and ammunition, previously denied to the Comanches. Despite the agreement with de Anza in New Mexico, the Comanches continued raiding into northern Mexico and Texas.

The initial purpose of warfare for the Comanches was to maintain their hold on Comancheria, their bison hunting grounds. Additionally, they raided for horses, captives, and material goods. The Comanches raided other tribes, the Mexicans, Texans, American settlers, and even the U.S. Army for horses. Indeed, the Comanches accumulated some of the largest horse herds of any Plains people. When making peace with the Cheyennes and Arapahos, the Comanches greatly impressed their northern neighbors with the number of horses given as gifts.

The Comanches angered and frightened settlers with their habit of taking captives. Young captives were often brought up within Comanche families as adopted children to increase tribal numbers. Some were kept as slaves to perform menial tasks around the band's camps, while others managed and guarded the horse herds. Women were sometimes taken as secondary wives but more often simply to be raped. In addition, the Comanches learned quickly that captured white children and women could be ransomed by white New Mexicans and other settlers with whom they traded.

Cloth, trinkets, cooking utensils, and arms and ammunition were also primary objectives of Comanche raiding. In 1840, a Comanche raiding party under Buffalo Hump raided as far east as Linnville, Texas, at Lavaca Bay on the Gulf Coast. On reaching Linnville, the Comanches captured so much booty that it slowed down their escape, and they were caught by a hastily raised group of Texas Rangers and civilian volunteers. The resulting action fought at Plum Creek on August 12, 1840, resulted in at least 80 dead Comanche warriors.

Comanches had adopted firearms but preferred bows and arrows, lances, and clubs in their warfare. In addition to the tangible results of raiding, raids also provided the path to manhood for young Comanche men. While some tribes allowed as many as four warriors to count coup, the Comanches recognized only the first two warriors to strike an enemy as coup counters, meaning that only they received primary credit for the raid or attack. Comanches rarely engaged in large-scale warfare, preferring instead a raid-and-ambush strategy. On the few occasions in which the Comanches did engage in large attacks, they suffered heavy casualties, the most notable being the Second Battle of Adobe Walls (June 27, 1874) in the Texas Panhandle.

As the 19th century progressed, increasing white settlement, the extermination of the southern bison herd, and the expansion of the railroads spelled the end of the Comancheria. The Medicine Lodge Treaty, which most Comanche bands signed, sought to concentrate the Comanches and Kiowas on a reservation in western Indian Territory (Oklahoma) around Fort Sill. Most Comanches had no faith in the treaty nor did most intend to recognize its stipulations. In fact, the treaty led to a brief but intense Comanche attempt to beat back white civilization. The reign of the Comanches on the southern Plains came to an end in June 1875 when the last of the major Comanche bands, under Quanah Parker, surrendered to Colonel Ranald S. Mackenzie and moved to the reservation at Fort Sill.

John Thomas Broom

Further Reading

Ferhenbach, T. R. *Comanches: The History of a People*. New York: Anchor Books, 2003.

Hoig, Stan. *Tribal Wars of the Southern Plains*. Norman: University of Oklahoma Press, 1993.

Wallace, Ernest, and E. Adamson Hoebel. *The Comanches: Lords of the South Plains*. 1952; reprint, Norman: University of Oklahoma Press, 1986.

Connor's Powder River Expedition

Start Date: August 11, 1865
End Date: September 24, 1865

Inconclusive campaign led by Brigadier General Patrick E. Connor against northern Native American tribes along the Powder River in 1865. With the outbreak of the American Civil War (1861–1865), Native American tribes in the western United States reasserted control over their ancestral lands. This was especially true on the northern Plains, which saw widespread attacks on isolated frontier forts and white settlements. In many cases, citizen militias took matters into their own hands, helping to spark the Sand Creek Massacre in 1864 during which Colonel John Chivington led Colorado militia in a vicious assault against Cheyenne chief Black Kettle's peaceful village. That action resulted in some 150 Native American deaths, more than half of whom were women and children. In retaliation, the Sioux, Cheyennes, and Arapahos launched raids along the Platte River and against Fort Laramie.

As the Civil War ended, the U.S. Army began shifting resources and manpower to the West and felt compelled to act swiftly because many soldiers' terms of service were soon to expire. Major General Grenville

Dodge, commander of the Department of Missouri and the Department of Kansas at Fort Leavenworth, ordered Brigadier General Patrick E. Connor, who two years earlier had led a successful attack against the Shoshones in the Battle of Bear River (sometimes described as a massacre), to lead a three-pronged punitive expedition to the Powder River.

Connor's force numbered approximately 2,400 men and comprised primarily volunteers from California, Kansas, and Nebraska. Colonel Nelson Cole's column proceeded up the Loup Fork of the Platte River to the forks of the Little Powder and Big Powder rivers and then to the Tongue River, where they were to be met by Lieutenant Colonel Samuel Walker's column, which marched north from Fort Laramie and then swung west of the Black Hills. Meanwhile, Connor led the third column from the north bend of the North Platte River to the Powder River, arriving on August 11 and building a stockade, named Fort Connor, before advancing to the Tongue River.

Arriving at the Tongue River on the morning of August 29, Connor attacked Chief Black Bear's camp of approximately 500 Arapahos. Catching the natives by surprise, Connor's forces used howitzers to devastating effect, killing approximately 60 Arapahos, including Black Bear's son. Following the victory, Connor waited in vain for the arrival of Cole and Walker. By the time Connor's scouts located their columns on September 19, Cole's and Walker's men were on the verge of starvation, primarily because Connor had brought the bulk of supplies with his column.

While Connor debated on a course of action, a courier arrived on September 24 with orders relieving him of his command. The expedition then straggled back to Fort Laramie. The limited success of the expedition, its high cost, and outrage with Connor's order that all Native American males over age 15 should be summarily shot contributed to the decision to pursue a peace policy with the Plains tribes.

Justin D. Murphy

Further Reading

Brady, Cyrus Townsend. *The Sioux Indian Wars: From the Powder River to the Little Big Horn*. New York: Barnes and Noble, 1992.

McDermott, John D. *Circle of Fire: The Indian War of 1865*. Mechanicsburg, PA: Stackpole, 2003.

Crazy Horse

Birth Date: ca. 1840
Death Date: September 5, 1877

Lakota Sioux war chief and one of the most widely known leaders of the centuries-long Native American resistance to white expansion across North America. Most sources accept that Crazy Horse was born sometime in 1840, although cases have been made for alternative dates ranging from 1841 to 1845. His father, who survived him and became one of the major sources of information about him, had also been called Crazy Horse, but when his son reached maturity and wished to take that name, his father took the name Worm. The tribal affiliation of Crazy Horse's mother is also somewhat ambiguous: most sources identify her as a Brulé Sioux, but some contend that she was a Miniconjou Sioux.

As a young warrior, Crazy Horse earned a reputation for being skilled and fearless in battles against the Arikaras, Blackfeet, Crows, Pawnees, and Shoshones, but relatively few of his exploits against these enemies survived in Lakota oral tradition. After the Lakotas allied with the Cheyennes, Crazy Horse distinguished himself in his first battles against the U.S. military at Red Buttes and Platte River Bridge Station.

Crazy Horse first came fully to the attention of the U.S. military and of the American public during Red Cloud's War (1866–1868). In violation of existing treaties, the U.S. Army had constructed forts along the Bozeman Trail, which provided an eastern route to gold-rich Virginia City, Montana. On December 21, 1866, Crazy Horse led a small contingent of warriors who lured cavalry and infantry units away from Fort Phil Kearny and into a trap. Outnumbered more than 10 to 1, Fetterman and 80 soldiers were quickly wiped out in what became known as the Fetterman Massacre. The commander of the doomed infantry unit, Captain William Fetterman, had boasted that he could subdue the whole Sioux Nation with the exact number of soldiers who perished with him in what was, to that point, the worst defeat suffered by the army during the wars with the Plains Indians.

On August 2, 1867, Crazy Horse attempted to repeat the success that he had achieved against Fetterman. The Lakotas surprised a woodcutting party sent out from Fort Phil Kearny. In what became known as the Wagon Box Fight, the soldiers surprised and eventually drove off the Lakotas with the much-enhanced firepower provided by their recently issued breech-loading rifles.

Ten years later during the Great Sioux War (1876–1877), Crazy Horse led about 1,500 Lakota and Cheyenne warriors against Brigadier General George Crook's roughly equal force of cavalry, infantry, and Native American allies in the Battle of the Rosebud (June 17, 1876). Although neither side committed fully enough to the battle to sustain sizable losses, Crook's advance into Sioux territory was temporarily checked, delaying his rendezvous with the 7th Cavalry under Lieutenant Colonel George Armstrong Custer.

All Native American sources agree that Crazy Horse had a decisive role in the annihilation of Custer's battalion at the Battle of the Little Bighorn (June 25–26, 1876), but nothing is known about Crazy Horse's specific actions during the engagement. Nonetheless, his notoriety following the massacre of Custer and his troops made Crazy Horse a prime target of the forces sent to subdue the Sioux and Cheyennes.

After Crazy Horse's surrender in May 1877, any rumors of further insurrection among the Lakotas increased the suspicion surrounding him. He was eventually killed at Camp Robinson on September 5, 1877, when such rumors led to an order for his arrest. Although there were numerous eyewitnesses, the details of how he was fatally stabbed have remained ambiguous. Even those who accept that he was bayoneted by an impetuous soldier cannot agree on the identity of that soldier or whether he was acting out of heightened anxiety or deep-seated animus.

Although Crazy Horse is honored with a mountaintop sculpture rivaling the nearby Mount Rushmore, there is only one surviving photograph of the Lakota war chief. And, fittingly, much doubt has been cast on whether the figure in the photograph is actually Crazy Horse.

Martin Kich

Further Reading

Matthiesen, Peter. *In the Spirit of Crazy Horse*. New York: Viking, 1991.

McMurtry, Larry. *Crazy Horse*. New York: Lipper/Viking, 1999.

Sandoz, Mari. *Crazy Horse: The Strange Man of the Oglalas.* 3rd ed. Lincoln: University of Nebraska Press, 2008.

Creek War

Start Date: 1813
End Date: 1814

Civil war between the White Stick Creeks (mainly Lower Creeks) and the Red Stick Creeks (mainly Upper Creeks) in which the United States intervened on the side of the White Sticks. The Creek Nation's relationship to the United States and other issues caused a major division within the tribe. The United States became involved in the war with the Battle of Burnt Corn Creek on July 17, 1813, and the massacre at Fort Mims on August 30. The Creek War is usually seen as part of the War of 1812.

Creek reactions to American encroachment onto their lands, along with the U.S. government's efforts to "civilize" the Creeks, broke the nation into two factions. Located in present-day northern and central Alabama and southern Georgia, Creek territory was prime land for growing cotton, a highly prized crop. The faction that opposed the U.S. efforts, not to mention its land policies, was the Red Sticks, so-named because they painted their war clubs red. The Red Sticks favored joining Shawnee leader Tecumseh's Pan-Indian alliance to resist white expansion and urged the rejection of white goods and culture in favor of a return to traditional native ways. By 1813, the Red Sticks were receiving support from the British, who were at war with the United States; some of the aid was funneled through Spanish Florida. The White Sticks, in contrast to the Red Sticks, believed that the Creeks should work with the United States, even if it meant ceding additional land and adopting American cultural practices.

Open fighting between the two sides broke out in 1813 when White Sticks ambushed a Red Stick war party, captured the Red Stick leader, and then executed him. The United States entered the war on July 27, 1813, with the Battle of Burnt Corn Creek. An Alabama Militia unit intercepted a group of Red Sticks returning from Pensacola, Florida, where they had received weapons and ammunition from the British and Spanish. The militia unit, commanded by Colonel James Caller, found the Red Sticks encamped near Burnt Corn Creek about 90 miles north of Pensacola and surprised them on July 27. Winning an initial easy victory, the militia did not pursue the Red Sticks, who then rallied and counterattacked, routing the militia and recapturing their supplies. The militia suffered 2 dead and 15 wounded. Creek losses in the encounter are unknown.

On August 30, 1813, the Red Sticks launched a retaliatory strike on Fort Mims, where the Alabama Militia was stationed. Numerous civilians and White Stick refugees had fled to the fort, which was about 25 miles southwest of the Burnt Corn Creek battlefield. The odds should have been in favor of the fort's defenders, but the commander of the post, Major Daniel Beasley, failed to heed warnings that a Red Stick war party was nearby. The Red Sticks gathered information about the fort and identified its weaknesses. On the day of the attack, the Red Sticks launched a surprise attack, quickly overran the fort through a gate that had been left open, and killed almost all of the inhabitants, including women and children. As many as 500 people died, while only 36 escaped.

The U.S. response to the Fort Mims massacre was swift, as Major General Andrew

Jackson and 2,500 Tennessee militia supported by 600 Cherokee and White Stick allies marched against the Red Sticks. On November 3, 1813, a detachment from Jackson's force ambushed a group of Red Sticks at Tallushatchee, Alabama. The Red Sticks suffered 186 killed, including women and children, while U.S. losses included 5 killed and 41 wounded. Later in the month, the White Sticks asked Jackson to attack the Red Sticks who were laying siege to the White Stick village at Talladega. Moving quickly, Jackson launched his attack on November 9, 1813. Jackson estimated Red Stick strength at some 1,080 warriors. Despite the large number of Red Sticks, Jackson won a victory, killing 290 Red Sticks while suffering 15 U.S. dead and 85 wounded.

Jackson spent the remainder of the year hunting down the Red Sticks, training his men, and seeking to hold his force together. The enlistment period for many of the volunteers was coming to an end, and a large number wished to return home. Jackson was also beginning to experience supply problems. At the beginning of 1814, however, he received replacement volunteers and 600 U.S. regulars of the 39th Infantry Regiment.

In March 1814, Jackson moved his force against the Red Stick encampment at Horseshoe Bend along the Tallapoosa River in Alabama, where the Red Sticks had built a fortified encampment. Jackson advanced toward the camp with 2,000 infantry, 700 cavalry and mounted riflemen, and 600 Native American allies (500 Cherokees and 100 White Stick Creeks). There were about 1,000 warriors and 300 women and children at the Red Stick camp.

The Battle of Horseshoe Bend occurred on March 27, 1814. Jackson's men arrived in front of the encampment to find it protected by a barricade of logs and earth at least eight feet in height with firing ports. Jackson sent his Native American allies and most of his cavalry around the camp on the other side of the river to prevent the Red Sticks from escaping or being reinforced. This force eventually helped support the main attack by crossing the river and moving against the encampment from the rear.

The attack on the barricade proved to be difficult, but Jackson's troops eventually breached it. This action and the attack from the rear led the Red Stick defenders to attempt to flee. They had little success. Red Stick losses in the battle included 557 killed and 400 warriors captured. Most of the women and children were captured and turned over to Jackson's Native American allies. Jackson lost 32 killed and 99 wounded among his own troops, Cherokee losses were 18 killed and 36 wounded, and the allied White Sticks lost 5 dead and 11 wounded. Although it would be several months before the Creek War officially ended, the Battle of Horseshoe Bend broke the back of Red Stick resistance.

Jackson's forces were not the only Americans to fight against the Red Sticks. In late November 1813, Georgia Militia forces under Brigadier General John Floyd attacked the Red Stick village of Auttose, killing as many as 200 Red Sticks, while suffering just 11 dead and 54 wounded. On January 29, 1814, however, the Red Sticks attacked Floyd's position at Calibee Creek (in eastern Alabama) and inflicted heavy casualties (22 dead and 140 wounded) with a loss of 37 Red Stick warriors. While Floyd's men successfully held off the Red Sticks, the general saw the attack as a defeat and withdrew. The Georgians would not launch any subsequent attacks during the remainder of the war. The Mississippi Militia under Brigadier General Thomas

Flournoy never actively engaged the Red Sticks but did destroy several Red Stick villages and outposts.

In August 1814, Jackson called all Creek leaders to a meeting at Fort Jackson (near Watumpka, Alabama) to negotiate a treaty ending the war. The only Creek leaders who attended, however, were the White Stick leaders, who were shocked when Jackson demanded 23 million acres of Creek land (about half of all their territory) and 4 million acres from the Cherokees. This land was to come not just from the defeated Red Sticks but also from the Native Americans allied with the United States during the war.

White Stick complaints had no effect on Jackson, who blamed the White Sticks as much as the Red Sticks for the war. Indeed, Jackson told the White Sticks that they should have prevented the conflict and that because they had not, they were equally responsible for it. Knowing that their only alternative to signing the treaty was to go to war against the United States, White Stick and Cherokee chiefs signed the Treaty of Fort Jackson (Horseshoe Bend) on August 9, 1814.

Dallace W. Unger Jr. and
Paul G. Pierpaoli Jr.

Further Reading

Ethridge, Robbie. *Creek Country: The Creek Indians and Their World*. Chapel Hill: University of North Carolina Press, 2003.

Remini, Robert Vincenti. *Andrew Jackson and His Indian Wars*. New York: Penguin, 2001.

Creek-Cherokee Wars

Start Date: 1716
End Date: 1754

Series of wars fought between the Creeks and Cherokees in the American Southeast.

These conflicts sprang from disputes over hunting grounds, frustrations over white settlers' designs on their lands, and alliances forged with other native tribes. The fighting occurred in two phases: one from 1716 to 1727 and the other from 1740 to 1754. The Creeks and Cherokees were two of the most populous Native American nations in the Southeast, and any conflict involving them was bound to impact whites in the Carolinas and Georgia.

Hostilities between the Creeks and Cherokees began in 1716 during the Yamasee War (1715–1717) when the Cherokees assassinated Creek diplomats sent to the Lower Cherokee towns to secure support for an assault on South Carolina. During the war, Cherokee warriors, assisted by Carolina settlers, repeatedly raided Upper Creek towns. The settlers, made aware of the precariousness of their southern frontier during the Yamasee War, aided the Cherokees in the expectation that intertribal warfare would weaken both nations and prevent them from attacking British settlements. The situation was further complicated by warfare between the Creeks and the pro-French Choctaws.

Attempts of officials in Charles Town (present-day Charleston, South Carolina) to influence the Creek-Cherokee War to British advantage were not successful. As the fighting on the frontier escalated, South Carolinians increasingly feared for their safety. In 1725, the British sent Tobias Fitch, agent to the Creeks, to secure an end to the war. Despite this and other British efforts, the Creeks and Cherokees continued the fight.

In March 1726, several hundred Cherokee and Chickasaw warriors moved against the Creeks. Operating under the British flag in the false belief that they enjoyed the support of the Crown, the warriors destroyed most of the Creek village of Cussita. The attack alarmed British settlers, who feared that it would bring closer ties between the Spanish and Creeks. After a small force of about 40 Creek warriors attacked and defeated some 500 Cherokee and Chickasaw warriors, officials in Charles Town renewed their push for peace and by January 1727 negotiated an end to war.

Fighting between the Creeks and Cherokees resumed in 1740 shortly after the onset of the War of Jenkins' Ear (1739–1744) between Britain and Spain. The Creeks initially remained largely neutral, whereas many Cherokees allied themselves with the British. Hostilities began when Creeks attacked a Cherokee war party that had entered Creek country. The Cherokee warriors, who were on their way to attack the Choctaws and their French allies, believed that an ongoing war between the Creeks and Choctaws would allow them to march safely through Creek territory. In this the Cherokees miscalculated.

Fighting between the Creeks and the Cherokees continued for several years until the onset of King George's War (1744–1748) between Britain and France. British officials then sought to secure Indian allies and end the Creek-Cherokee dispute. In 1745, despite a recently negotiated truce with the Creeks, the Cherokees allowed the Senecas to use their territory as a staging ground for attacks on the Creeks. When Cherokee warriors joined the fighting, Creek-Cherokee hostilities resumed. In late 1748, Governor James Glen of South Carolina tried to arrange another truce. The French, correctly assuming that peace between the two Native American nations would benefit the British, sought to disrupt the peace talks by arranging for Creek headman Acorn Whistler to lead an attack on the Cherokees. Despite this action, the Creeks and Cherokees came to an agreement. They settled on boundaries for their hunting grounds, and the Cherokees agreed to stop allowing northern natives passage through their lands to attack the Creeks. Glen guaranteed the agreement, promising to punish transgressors.

The treaty did not hold. In 1750, several Lower Creek towns waged war on their Cherokee neighbors. This fighting was prompted primarily by Lower Creek frustration over Cherokee control of valuable hunting grounds and continued Cherokee assistance to northern tribes attacking the Creeks. Seeking to seize control of hunting grounds from the Cherokees, in April 1750 Malatchi, Creek headman of the important Coweta village, and 500 Lower Creek warriors attacked and razed the Lower Cherokee towns of Echoi and Estatoe. When South Carolina restricted trade with the Cherokees for a series of frontier depredations in 1751, the Creeks escalated their campaign to acquire Cherokee lands. This effort was largely successful. All but three of the Lower Cherokee towns were destroyed, and many Cherokees became refugees as the Creeks secured much of the disputed hunting ground between the Little River and the Broad River north of present-day Savannah, Georgia.

In 1752, Acorn Whistler and other Creeks assassinated Cherokee diplomats while they were in Charles Town. Governor Glen demanded justice, and under great pressure from British officials, the Creeks finally executed Whistler. In May 1753, Creek officials traveled to Charles Town to negotiate another peace treaty with the Cherokees. Small skirmishes plagued the region during the following year, but in April 1754 at Coweta, the Creeks and Cherokees negotiated a formal end to the war and secured a peace settlement.

Andrew K. Frank

Further Reading

Corkran, David. *The Cherokee Frontier: Conflict and Survival, 1740–1762.* Norman: University of Oklahoma Press, 1962.

Hahn, Stephen C. *The Invention of the Creek Nation, 1670–1763.* Lincoln: University of Nebraska Press, 2004.

Saunt, Claudio. *A New Order of Things: Property, Power, and the Transformation of the Creek Indians, 1733–1816.* New York: Cambridge University Press, 1999.

Creeks

Multiethnic Native American group, also known as the Muskogees, who in the colonial and early national period lived in what is now Florida, Georgia, and Alabama. The location of the Creeks in British Georgia and South Carolina, French Louisiana, and Spanish Florida allowed them to play the colonial powers against one another and protect their own interests throughout the colonial period. The Creeks tended to pursue a policy of neutrality when it came to the wars that consumed their European neighbors and vigorously protected their interests against their Choctaw and Cherokee neighbors.

Organized in the 17th century after the disease-induced collapse of the southeastern Mississippian Culture chiefdoms that once dominated the region, the Creeks obtained their name from the English, who noted that their villages were always built near inland waters. The Spanish similarly called them Tallapoosa Indians, after one of the rivers along which they primarily lived. At its height, the Creek Confederacy included approximately 60 villages.

Comprising a diversity of ethnic and linguistic groups, the Creeks remained decentralized throughout the colonial period. Nevertheless, Muskogee became the dominant language of the confederacy. A series of rituals, such as the Green Corn Ceremony, and a system of matrilineal clans unified them as a people. The Creeks were an agricultural society, with women farming corn, beans, and squash. Men hunted in order to augment their diet and provide skins for trade.

An amorphous polity known as the Creek Confederacy slowly emerged, but at best the Creeks were an alliance of loosely affiliated villages. Rather than a centralized nation, Creeks primarily associated themselves with their village. During the colonial period, they typically referred to themselves as Cowetas, Abihkas, Hichitis, and Alabamas rather than as Creeks. Unbeknownst to colonial officials, many of the most prominent leaders represented only a minority interest or a single village. For example, Tomochichi, one of Georgia governor James Oglethorpe's closest allies, represented the Yamacraws, one of several conquered groups among the Creeks. The Creek spokesperson Brims, frequently called "Emperor Brims," was simply the mico ("head chief") of Coweta, one of the most powerful Creek villages, in the early 17th century.

Power in Creek society was primarily organized around villages and matrilineal clans, and authority was extended to individuals who could convince rather than coerce others into agreement. Consequently, Creek power was extremely localized and fluid, and Creek villages were largely autonomous. The confederacy served as an organizing principle for trade and war but did not act as a centralized nation. Marriages, trade, and clan ties connected the villages, but individual villages were free to make alliances or war. As a result, during the colonial wars Creek villages were often divided, either fighting against one another or remaining neutral while others went to war.

The emergence of the deerskin trade and the presence of Spanish and British neighbors shaped the diplomatic history of the Creeks. Connections and resistance to slave raiders also helped define the position of the Creeks in the region. During the Yamasee War (1715–1717), the Creeks primarily allied themselves with the French in order to counter trade abuses by the British. The Cherokees took this opportunity to secure an alliance with the British. As a result, the devastating Creek-Cherokee Wars (1716–1754) ensued.

After the Yamasee War, most Creek towns created trading alliances with the British and allowed traders to reside in their village and often marry the daughters of influential leaders. Upper Creek villages in the west, however, encouraged the French to build Fort Toulouse (Alabama) to bring supplies and trade goods into the region. Similarly, several Creek villages negotiated alliances with the Spanish in Florida. Despite the hopes of many European diplomats, trade connections and pledges of peace did not necessarily lead to allies during wartime. Although some Creek warriors accompanied Governor Oglethorpe in his invasion of Florida in 1743, most Creeks refrained from participating. During King George's War (1744–1748), most Creek villages remained neutral even as some villages felt pulled by British or French relationships.

Creek neutrality in terms of their European neighbors did not result in peace with neighboring tribes. The Creek-Cherokee Wars began during the Yamasee War and were renewed in the 1740s and early 1750s from conflicts over hunting grounds and as attempts to conquer each other's territory.

The Creeks also fought a series of bloody wars with the Choctaws, known as the Creek-Choctaw Wars (1702–1776). The conflicts began as reciprocal slave raids and as extensions of the French-English rivalry in the region. These slave raids were often encouraged by European neighbors. In 1711, for example, the British armed more than 1,000 Creek warriors as they marched on their French-Choctaw enemy.

Hostilities between the Creeks and Choctaws were the most severe after the French and Indian War (1754–1763). When the British called for a congress at Augusta, Georgia, the Creeks sought to exclude their longtime Choctaw enemies. The British provided guns and ammunition to both sides in the ensuing war, and the Creeks and Choctaws remained at arms until the American Revolutionary War (1775–1783), during which some—but not all—Creeks sided with the British. Thereafter, the Creeks had to contend with the new state of Georgia and the U.S. government, neither of which had much regard for former treaties or Creek land rights.

In the early 19th century, continued white encroachment onto Creek lands threatened open warfare. By 1810, most Creeks were divided on how to deal with white encroachment. The Red Sticks, the more militant faction, favored war, while the White Sticks sought peace. The War of 1812 provided the perfect context for the Red Sticks, influenced by Shawnee chief Tecumseh's concept of unified Native American resistance, to go on the offensive. In January 1813, a contingent of Red Sticks took part in a battle with U.S. forces at the Raisin River in which the Americans were badly mauled. That August, Red Eagle (William Weatherford) commanded some 1,000 Red Stick warriors in an attack on Fort Mims, resulting in the deaths of some 500 white settlers.

By now the Creek War (1813–1814) was in full swing, and Major General Andrew Jackson was charged with defeating the Red Stick Creeks and their allies. Sporadic warfare ensued until the Red Sticks were convincingly defeated in the Battle of Horseshoe Bend (March 27, 1814).

On August 9, 1814, Jackson imposed the punitive Treaty of Fort Jackson upon the Creeks—both the Red Sticks and White Sticks. The agreement compelled the Creeks to surrender some 23 million acres of their land to the U.S. government, which would then be opened to white settlers. In 1836, as part of the 1830 Indian Removal Act, the Creeks were relocated by force to Indian Territory (Oklahoma). The resulting Trail of Tears was catastrophic to the Creeks, who lost 3,500 people (out of a total of 15,000) during the forced march and relocation. Today most surviving Creeks continue to reside in Oklahoma, but a small number remain in Georgia, Alabama, and Florida.

Andrew K. Frank

Further Reading

Ethridge, Robbie. *Creek Country: The Creek Indians and Their World*. Chapel Hill: University of North Carolina Press, 2003.

Hahn, Stephen C. *The Invention of the Creek Nation, 1670–1763*. Lincoln: University of Nebraska Press, 2004.

Saunt, Claudio. *A New Order of Things: Property, Power, and the Transformation of the Creek Indians, 1733–1816*. New York: Cambridge University Press, 1999.

Crook, George

Birth Date: September 8, 1828
Death Date: March 21, 1890

U.S. Army officer. Born near Dayton, Ohio, on September 8, 1828, George Crook graduated from the U.S. Military Academy in 1852 and was commissioned a second lieutenant in the 4th Infantry. His first assignment was in the Pacific Northwest.

Crook rose to prominence during the American Civil War (1861–1865). Promoted to captain at the war's outset, in September 1861 Crook entered the volunteer establishment as colonel of the 36th Ohio Infantry and participated in actions in western Virginia. Promoted to brigadier general of volunteers on September 7, 1862, Crook commanded a brigade in the Kanawha Division in the Battle of South Mountain (September 14, 1862) and in the ensuing Battle of Antietam (September 17, 1862). In early 1863, he played a prominent role in operations in eastern Tennessee before assuming command of the 2nd Cavalry Division in the Army of the Cumberland in July 1863. Given command of the Kanawha District in February 1864, Crook led a series of operations to disrupt Confederate communications between eastern Tennessee and Lynchburg, Virginia. During Major General Philip Sheridan's Shenandoah Valley Campaign (August 7, 1864–March 2, 1865), Crook commanded the Department of Western Virginia and the Army of Western Virginia (VIII Corps) and played a conspicuous role in the succession of Union victories during that campaign. In October 1864, Crook was promoted to major general and continued to command the Department of Western Virginia from his headquarters in Cumberland, Maryland. On February 21, 1865, Crook and Brigadier General Benjamin Kelley were captured by Confederate partisans in a daring raid. Exchanged on March 20, Crook subsequently led a cavalry division in the Army of the Potomac as it drove toward Appomattox. Crook was brevetted major general in the regular army on March 27, 1865.

After the Civil War, Crook reverted to lieutenant colonel in the regular army and assumed command of the 23rd Infantry Regiment. He spent the next few years fighting the Paiutes in the Idaho Territory. In 1871, Crook was assigned to command the Department of Arizona while still a lieutenant colonel. There he met Captain John G. Bourke, an outstanding officer who would later immortalize Crook in such books as *On the Border with Crook* and *With General Crook in the Indian Wars.*

In Arizona, Crook developed three key methods that helped him to become the nation's premier Indian fighter. First, he employed Native Americans not only as scouts but also to provide insight into the possible courses of action of his foes. Second, he used only mule trains instead of wagons, giving him greater flexibility and speed. Third, he followed his adversaries wherever they went, even into northern Mexico, until he could bring them to battle. After the notable success of his 1872–1873 campaign, he was promoted directly to brigadier general. Crook's approach paid off, and by early 1875, the hostile Apaches had been temporarily subdued. Crook then worked to improve the lot of the Apache people and show them that the benefits of peace outweighed those of war.

In March 1875, Crook was named commander of the Department of the Platte, headquartered in Omaha, Nebraska. He participated in the Great Sioux War (1876–1877) and commanded one of three converging columns during the army's spring offensive. In the Battle of the Rosebud (June 17, 1876), Crook's men engaged Native Americans under Chief Crazy Horse in a spirited stand-up fight unusual for Native Americans. Forced to fall back and regroup, Crook was unable to support the other columns or to communicate news of his setback. Following the devastating defeat of Lieutenant Colonel George Armstrong Custer's 7th Cavalry at the Little Bighorn, Crook largely directed the army's response, including Colonel Ranald S. Mackenzie's destruction of Cheyenne chief Dull Knife's village.

In 1882, Crook returned to Arizona, where he again employed his innovative approaches, including a heavy reliance on Indian scouts and small expeditions, but his efforts to deal with the Apaches encountered strong opposition from civilian agents and his old roommate, now commanding general of the army, Lieutenant General Philip Sheridan. Crook's opponents were strengthened when Geronimo led a group of Chiricahuas off the San Carlos Agency on May 17, 1885. Crook's forces wore Geronimo down, and the Apache leader finally agreed to surrender. Sheridan rejected Crook's terms, however, and demanded Geronimo's unconditional surrender. Geronimo and some of his men again fled U.S. control. Sheridan blamed Crook, and on April 1, 1886, Crook requested to be relieved of his command. Sheridan replaced him with Brigadier General Nelson A. Miles.

Crook spent the last years of his life attempting to win the return of Apaches from imprisonment in Florida to Arizona and battling with Miles and Sheridan in print. President Grover Cleveland promoted Crook to major general in April 1888 and assigned him to command the Division of the Missouri. Crook died in Chicago on March 21, 1890, while still on active duty.

Alan K. Lamm

Further Reading

Aleshire, Peter. *The Fox and the Whirlwind: General George Crook and Geronimo, A Paired Biography.* New York: Wiley, 2000.

Robinson, Charles M., III. *General Crook and the Western Frontier*. Norman: University of Oklahoma Press, 2001.

Crows

A northern Plains tribe whose traditional territory was located in the Yellowstone River Valley. The Crows are part of the Siouan language group. The name they apply to themselves is Absaroka, which is derived from a bird of the Great Plains. The Crows are most closely related to the Hidatsa tribe of the upper Missouri River Valley. The Hidatsas were sedentary farmers relying primarily on maize for their diet, supplemented with some gathering efforts and hunting of the ubiquitous bison of the Plains. Anthropologists disagree as to the date when the Crows and Hidatsas split, but it was definitely prior to contact with whites and most likely pre-Columbian.

The Crows evolved into a seminomadic tribe and would travel every summer to visit and trade with their Hidatsa cousins along the Missouri River. The Crows would bring meat, furs, buffalo hides, and sometimes horses to exchange for grain, trade goods, and guns. It was on one of these summer trading migrations that the Crows encountered the Lewis and Clark expedition in 1805. By that time, the Crows had become typical northern Plains Indians. They had substantial horse herds, primarily hunted bison, lived in tepees, and engaged in the Sun Dance ritual. Crow society was both matrilineal and matriarchal, and it was not uncommon to find women in their governing hierarchy.

The Crows were divided into three principal bands: the River Crows, who lived primarily along the Yellowstone River; the Mountain Crows, who lived higher up along the tributaries of the Yellowstone River; and the Kicked-in-the-Bellies, who spent part of their time with the Mountain Crows, especially during the summer months, but moved away from them in the autumn and winter.

Warfare was central to the Crow lifestyle. Success in hunting and war was the sign of manhood and the means to respectability and wealth among the Crows. The principal mode of warfare was the raid on another tribe's village for horses, to count coup (thus displaying courage), and to take captives. Skirmishes between tribes as they hunted buffalo were also common. Large-scale set-piece battles with large bodies of warriors were quite uncommon, and casualties were assiduously avoided. Despite this, the numbers of the slain could, over time, become quite large.

The Crows were first noted by Europeans in about 1715 or 1716 by fur traders of the Hudson's Bay Company. Some 18th-century accounts refer to the Crows as "Rocky Mountain Indians." At the time, the Crows hunted from the Black Hills west along the present-day Wyoming-Montana state line to the Yellowstone Basin. This territory included some of the richest of the northern Plains hunting grounds, especially the Powder River Country. The Crows shared this area with various other tribes, including the Comanches and the Kiowas before they migrated south to the Arkansas River basin and the Red River basin of Texas. To the north and west lay the hunting grounds of the Blackfeet, the Shoshones, and the Utes, with whom the Crows often engaged in warfare. To the east and south, the Crows engaged in intermittent warfare with the Pawnees along the Platte River in present-day Nebraska.

The Crows' most notable enemies, however, were the Lakotas and the other members of the Lakota alliance, principally the Cheyennes. Probably around 1780, the Lakotas drove the Crows from the Black Hills and continued to push them farther west. By the 1850s, the Lakota were contesting the Powder River Country with the Crows.

Although the Crows initially resented white intrusion onto their hunting grounds, they were far more concerned with the aggression of the Lakotas. When the Lakotas invited the Crows to join them during the Powder River War of 1866–1867, the Crows declined, still seeing the Lakotas as the larger threat. The Crows never engaged in serious conflict with whites and often allied with them against the Lakotas. The Crows often provided scouts to U.S. Army columns, including Lieutenant Colonel George Armstrong Custer's Little Bighorn expedition in 1876. Crow and Arikara scouts tried to warn Custer of the danger involved because of the unprecedented size of the horse herds they observed. Custer chose to attack anyway. The Crows, in spite of their awareness of the size of the Lakota alliance, rode with the column. The Little Bighorn battlefield is located on the present-day Crow Reservation in Montana.

The Crows continued to provide scouts to the U.S. Army even after the Custer disaster and continued to engage the Lakotas unilaterally. With the end of large-scale campaigning, the Crows settled down on a large reservation covering much of southern Montana within their old home range. They were eventually relocated on a much smaller reservation in south-central Montana but still within the heart of their home territory. The Crows gradually adopted ranching, retained mineral rights to their lands, and were reasonably successful in adapting to the new conditions, maintaining a strong identity and strong tribal sense on their own terms.

John Thomas Broom

Further Reading

Hoxie, Frederick E. *Parading through History: The Making of the Crow Nation in America, 1805–1935*. New York: Cambridge University Press, 1997.

Lowie, Robert H. *The Crow Indians*. Lincoln: University of Nebraska Press, 1983.

Custer, George Armstrong

Birth Date: December 5, 1839
Death Date: June 25, 1876

U.S. Army officer. One of the youngest generals in the American Civil War (1861–1865) who went on to an infamous career on the frontier in the Indian Wars, George Armstrong Custer was born on December 5, 1839, in New Rumley, Ohio, although he spent part of his childhood with his half-sister in Monroe, Michigan. Custer often accompanied his father to local militia drills and by the age of four could go through the manual of arms perfectly. At age 16, he was admitted to the U.S. Military Academy, graduating last in his class in 1861.

Despite his mediocre record as a student, Custer excelled during the Civil War. Shortly after graduating from West Point, he was assigned to a regiment on its way to the First Battle of Bull Run (July 21, 1861). His daring reconnaissance patrols and valor brought him to the attention of Union Army commander Major General George B. McClellan. As a captain and a staff officer for McClellan and Major General Alfred Pleasonton, Custer demonstrated his potential to such an extent that he was promoted to brigadier general on June 29, 1863, and given command of the 2nd Brigade of the 3rd Cavalry Division at the age of 23. From the Battle of Gettysburg (July 1–3, 1863) through the end of the war, he was renowned for his fearless and often decisive cavalry charges. In October 1864, he took charge of the entire 3rd Cavalry Division and became a close confidant of Major General Philip Sheridan during the Shenandoah Valley Campaign (August 7, 1864–March 2, 1865), leading his force in the Third Battle of Winchester (September 19, 1864), the Battle of Fisher's Hill (September 22, 1864), and the Battle of Five Forks (April 1, 1865). By the end of the war, he had been promoted to major general and was considered one of the most brilliant cavalry officers in the Union Army.

Following the war, Custer returned to the regular army with the permanent rank of lieutenant colonel and was assigned to the 7th Cavalry Regiment. Because his commanding officer was frequently absent, the 7th Cavalry was, for all intents and purposes, Custer's regiment. He quickly made a name for himself on the Plains. Dressed in fringed buckskin instead of a traditional uniform, he was the embodiment of the dashing Indian fighter. His best-selling book *My Life on the Plains* (1874) and several popular magazine articles helped to reinforce his reputation as a military genius. Yet the Custer myth did not always square with reality.

Custer's first experience fighting Native Americans in 1867 ended in humiliating failure during a campaign against the Cheyennes. He not only failed to win a victory, but was court-martialed and sentenced to a year's suspension from rank and pay for being absent without leave. He rebounded from this personal setback in 1868 when he surprised Chief Black Kettle's Cheyenne village in a brutal and

strategically questionable attack at the Battle of the Washita (November 27, 1868). This victory helped to burnish Custer's public reputation.

In 1874, Custer and the 7th Cavalry escorted a large exploratory expedition that located gold in the Black Hills of the Dakota Territory, and the U.S. government subsequently attempted to buy the Black Hills from the Sioux. When this effort failed, the government essentially appropriated the land and attempted to confine the Sioux and Northern Cheyennes to significantly reduced reservations. In 1876, thousands of Sioux and Cheyennes left the reservation for hunting grounds in the Powder River and Yellowstone River valleys, resulting in the Great Sioux War of 1876–1877. The 7th Cavalry spearheaded Brigadier General Alfred Terry's column, part of a large three-pronged campaign to subdue the wayward Indians.

On June 25, 1876, Custer's scouts located a massive village on the Little Bighorn River in southwestern Montana. Custer divided his 7th Cavalry into three battalions and without waiting for the commands of Terry and Colonel John Gibbon to arrive rashly attacked the village of Sioux leaders Sitting Bull and Crazy Horse. Sending a battalion under Major Marcus Reno to strike the village directly, Custer and his battalion of some 225 men attempted to outflank the Sioux. Reno's force was quickly repulsed with heavy loses but managed to retreat to a ridge where they were joined by Captain Frederick Benteen's battalion and held out until the Indians withdrew. Custer, meanwhile, found himself outnumbered 10 to 1 and surrounded. In one of the most famous and controversial battles in American history, the Sioux slaughtered "Long Hair"—the name the Sioux had given Custer—and all of his men, including Custer's younger brother Tom. Custer's Last Stand at Little Bighorn stunned Americans and attached to Custer an immortality that fit with his reputation and public persona. The shocking development galvanized the army, which mobilized resources from across the West for a punitive campaign that brought an end to Sioux and Cheyenne dominance.

Andy Johns

Further Reading

Connell, Evan S. *Son of the Morning Star: Custer and the Little Bighorn.* New York: North Point Press, 1984.

Monaghan, Jay. *Custer: The Life of General George Armstrong Custer.* Lincoln: University of Nebraska Press, 1971.

Wert, Jeffrey D. *Custer: The Controversial Life of George Armstrong Custer.* New York: Simon and Schuster, 1996.

D

Deerfield, Massachusetts, Attack on

Event Date: February 29, 1704

Raid on and near destruction of the English settlement of Deerfield, Massachusetts, on February 29, 1704, by a combined force of Native Americans and French, resulting in the deaths of 41 English colonists and the capture of 112 more. As the northwesternmost town in Massachusetts, Deerfield had been a frequent target of Native American assaults during King Philip's War (1675–1676) and King William's War (1689–1697). To the English, Deerfield was merely a small, exposed settlement in the middle Connecticut River Valley, but to Native Americans, the town symbolized English intrusion onto their lands as well as a source for potential captives for ransom or adoption.

With the outbreak of Queen Anne's War (1702–1713), Deerfield was again at direct risk for assault. In May 1703, New York's governor received word of a French and Native American raiding party gathering at Fort Chambly and intent on attacking Deerfield. Similar warnings would come four more times during 1703 and early 1704. In October 1703, two Deerfield men were captured while working in the nearby fields. In response to this raid and repeated alarms, Deerfield's inhabitants temporarily crowded into the stockade that surrounded several houses in the center of the town. Massachusetts also sent 20 militiamen from neighboring towns to defend Deerfield, but when nothing else happened, the people of Deerfield began to let down their guard.

In the winter of 1703–1704, French Lieutenant Jean Baptise Hertel de Rouville led a force composed of 48 French and Canadians and 200–250 Pennacooks, Abenakis, Hurons, Kahnawake Mohawks, and Iroquois of the Mountain toward Deerfield. Just before daybreak on February 29, 1704, de Rouville's forces struck. Some of the raiders climbed a snowdrift that had accumulated at the base of the stockade and opened the north gate. The remainder then streamed in. Native American warriors spread throughout the town, bent on acquiring captives for ransom and adoption. Many families in the northern part of town were quickly captured, but the uncoordinated nature of the attack allowed some to mount a defense or hide. Settlers in Benoni Stebbins's house managed to hold out for more than two hours. Alerted by sounds of the fight and a few Deerfielders who managed to flee, militiamen from nearby Northampton, Hadley, and Hatfield came to Deerfield's relief and managed to drive de Rouville's raiders from the village. As the English militiamen chased the French and Native Americans through the town's North Field, however, they fell into an ambush and were forced back after losing nine men.

Although de Rouville's expedition suffered 10 dead (3 French and 7 Native Americans) and 22 French and an unknown number of Native American wounded, his force had devastated Deerfield, completely destroying 17 houses and barns, killing 41, wounding uncounted others, and carrying off 112 captives, including the town's minister, John Williams. Two young men escaped soon after, but 21 captives did not survive the march to French and Native American communities to the north. Although 62 Deerfield captives eventually returned to New England, many of them resettling in Deerfield, others chose to remain among their captors. Eight young girls, including Eunice Williams, daughter of the town's minister, married natives and remained among the Kahnawake Mohawks or the Iroquois of the Mountain (although 1 of the girls subsequently returned to New England). Ten women and 6 men married French colonists, while 2 captives married each other.

The Deerfield raid was a great success for the French. By spreading fear among the English and putting them on the defensive, de Rouville had helped protect France's underpopulated colonies.

David M. Corlett

Further Reading

Demos, John. *The Unredeemed Captive: A Family Story from Early America*. New York: Knopf, 1994.

Haefeli, Evan, and Kevin Sweeney. *Captors and Captives: The 1704 French and Indian Raid on Deerfield*. Amherst: University of Massachusetts Press, 2003.

Dog Soldiers

One of the six Cheyenne warrior bands, perhaps the most warlike of all the Plains tribes, also known as Dog Men (the Cheyenne phrase is Hotamétaneo'o). Dog Soldiers were critical to Cheyenne governance and led the Cheyenne resistance to American westward expansion from the 1830s until they were defeated in the Battle of Summit Springs in northeastern Colorado on July 11, 1869. Even after that, however, they were involved in other Cheyenne struggles against U.S. troops.

Dog Soldiers were held in reverence by other Cheyennes because of their bravery and prowess in battle and were known for their sashes, called dog ropes, made of tanned skins and decorated with porcupine quills and human hair that the four designated bravest Dog Soldiers wore into battle. The dog rope hung over the right shoulder and would be staked to the ground with a sacred arrow or metal pin during battle. This symbol of resolve meant that the Dog Soldier was left to defend his piece of ground to the death, if necessary, in order to cover the possible retreat of the rest of the band.

Dog Soldiers policed Cheyenne encampments during war and peace and were in charge of tribal buffalo hunts and the distribution of meat. Dog Soldier policing was especially important during wartime, as it kept individual warriors from seeking personal glory, thus allowing large bands to approach their enemies unawares. For example, Dog Soldier policing enabled some 3,000 Cheyennes to remain undetected until they began their assault on Camp Dodge in 1865.

The Dog Soldiers came together in the late 1830s under the leadership of Porcupine Bear, who was deemed an outlaw after he murdered his cousin. Porcupine Bear and his followers were alienated from the tribe, which led to their independence because they were then only governed by what became the war leaders of the Dog Soldier Clan. Soon the Dog Soldiers became more than half the military arm of the Cheyennes.

Dog Soldiers staunchly opposed white expansion and refused to sign treaties with the U.S. government or be limited to reservations. Instead, they fought to retain their freedom, even when the Council of Forty-Four (a civil council of chiefs) had voted for peace. This aggressive posture made the Cheyennes the target of American military aggression that culminated in the massacre of Black Kettle's tribe at Sand Creek, Colorado, in November 1864.

In 1865, the Dog Soldiers led a coalition of Cheyenne, Arapaho, and Lakota warriors to avenge the Sand Creek Massacre. Under the leadership of Roman Nose, Dog Soldiers devastated nearly 400 miles of white settlements from Kansas through Colorado and laid siege to Denver. The U.S. government threatened the Cheyennes with extermination unless the raiding stopped. Until 1877, the Dog Soldiers led the Cheyennes in continual conflict against American expansion and played key roles in many critical engagements with U.S. forces, including the Battle of the Little Bighorn (June 25–26, 1876) in which Dog Soldiers along with Arapaho and Lakota Sioux warriors almost destroyed the 7th Cavalry. In response to Little Bighorn, the U.S. Army, working with Pawnee and Shoshone mercenaries, pursued the Dog Soldiers and eventually subdued them.

B. Keith Murphy

Further Reading

Afton, Jean, David Fritjof Halaas, and Andrew E. Masich. *Cheyenne Dog Soldiers: A Ledgerbook History of Coups and Combat*. Niwot: University Press of Colorado, 1997.

Broome, Jeff. *Dog Soldier Justice: The Ordeal of Susanna Alderdice in the Kansas Indian War*. Lincoln, KS: Lincoln County Historical Society, 2003.

Dull Knife Outbreak

Start Date: September 1878
End Date: March 1879

Cheyenne trek led by Dull Knife that began in August 1878 from Indian Territory (present-day Oklahoma) to the Bighorn Mountains in Wyoming near the headwaters of the Powder River. The harrowing march of Dull Knife and his Cheyenne compatriots from U.S. Army captivity toward their homeland in present-day Wyoming added a sad chapter to the tragic closing stages of the Great Sioux War.

Northern Cheyenne leaders Dull Knife (Morning Star was his Cheyenne name, but called Dull Knife by the Lakota Sioux) and Little Wolf had allied with the Lakota Sioux and defeated Lieutenant Colonel George Armstrong Custer and his battalion of the 7th Cavalry Regiment in the Battle of the Little Bighorn (June 25–26, 1876). Dull Knife, Little Wolf, and their followers were pursued by the army and surrendered in May 1877. They were then relocated to Indian Territory (Oklahoma).

Promises of adequate resources on the reservation proved untrue. Game was nearly nonexistent, government rations failed to arrive on time and in sufficient quantity, and many Cheyennes either starved to death or died from disease. In August 1878 with half of the Cheyennnes who had been sent to Indian Territory now dead, Dull Knife and Little Wolf pleaded with Indian agent John Miles to let the survivors return to their ancestral homes in the Powder River basin of Wyoming and Montana. Miles refused.

On September 9, Dull Knife and Little Wolf led some 350 Cheyennes from the reservation and began a march on foot to their homelands. There were perhaps only 70 warriors among them. Pursuing cavalry and Arapaho scouts caught up with them on the Little Medicine Lodge River, but the Cheyennes refused to surrender. Three soldiers and an Arapaho scout were killed, and the

Northern Cheyennes continued their trek, repelling attacks, capturing arms, and taking food from settlements that they encountered. After crossing the Arkansas and South Platte rivers, the Indians split into two groups at White Clay Creek, Nebraska. Little Wolf led 115 Cheyennes to the Sand Hills, while Dull Knife led the remainder to the Red Cloud Agency, where they would surrender.

Finding the Red Cloud Agency in Nebraska abandoned, Dull Knife and his followers trekked to Fort Robinson, where they surrendered on October 23. Two months later, they were informed that they would have to return to Indian Territory, but they refused. Denied food, water, and heat until they relented, on the night of January 9, 1879, the Cheyennes killed two guards in an escape attempt. Some 50 Cheyennes were shot down by soldiers as they ran from the fort. Others were discovered nearby in the course of the next days and ordered to surrender. Many chose to fight to death. Fewer than 100 were herded back to Fort Robinson. Traveling at night on foot, Dull Knife, his wife, and son made it to the Pine Ridge Agency 18 days later. They and their few remaining followers were eventually allowed to stay there until receiving a reservation of their own, which occurred a year after Dull Knife's death in 1883.

Meanwhile, Little Wolf and his band had proceeded to the Nebraska Sand Hills, where they managed to survive that winter. Along the Little Missouri River in Montana, Little Wolf surrendered his band to Lieutenant William P. Clark of the 2nd Cavalry Regiment on March 27, 1879. They were escorted to Fort Keogh, where Little Wolf and many of his followers signed on to help U.S. troops fight the Sioux.

Bruce E. Johansen

Further Reading

Sandoz, Mari. *Cheyenne Autumn*. 1953; reprint, Lincoln: University of Nebraska Press, 1992.

Wiltsey, Norman B. *Brave Warriors*. Caldwell, ID: Caxton, 1963.

Dummer's War

Start Date: July 25, 1722
End Date: 1727

War between New England colonists and various Native American groups, primarily the Abenakis. The 1713 Treaty of Utrecht, ending the War of the Spanish Succession—known in America as Queen Anne's War (1702–1713), which ended with the Treaty of Portsmouth (1713)—had brought a temporary halt to violence in northern New England. As New England settlers and traders once again expanded into the northern and eastern frontiers of the region, intruding on Abenaki lands and disrupting their lives, however, tension mounted. In September 1721, the Abenakis responded to British encroachments with open insolence and property destruction, causing many British families to flee exposed areas. Hoping to coerce the natives into a settlement, the Massachusetts legislature halted all trade with the Abenakis in September 1721. Religion also furthered the divide between natives and the English as Jesuit priests such as Sébastien Râle at Norridgewock continued to proselytize among the Abenakis. When Massachusetts attempted to arrest Râle in January 1722 and plunder his church, open warfare erupted.

During summer 1722, the Abenakis raided the lower settlements of the Kennebec River near Brunswick, where they burned homes and took more than 60 captives (most of whom they later released) but avoided indiscriminate bloodshed. On July 25, 1722, Governor Samuel Shute of Massachusetts denounced the eastern natives as rebels, essentially declaring war. Shute soon left for England, leaving the conduct of the war to Lieutenant Governor William Dummer, who served as acting governor and for whom the conflict was named.

Native American raiding parties struck across Maine, New Hampshire, and western Massachusetts. New England went on the offensive in 1723, burning the Penobscot village of Panawanske (Old Town) in February. Convinced that Râle was inciting the natives to violence, New England leaders were determined to stamp out his influence for good. After unsuccessful winter expeditions in 1723 and 1724, captains Johnson Harmon and Jeremiah Moulton led forces up the Kennebec River in August 1724. Undetected, the New England forces attacked Norridgewock, killing Râle and several Abenaki leaders and burning the village. The Abenakis were less aggressive following this defeat.

In addition to organized expeditions, British colonial governments encouraged private actions against hostile natives by offering an extraordinarily high bounty of £100 for each scalp of male Abenakis over 12 years of age. Private citizens organized and equipped armed companies, essentially business ventures, to range against the natives in hopes of gathering scalps and sharing the profits. Captain John Lovewell led one such company toward Pigwacket, where on May 8, 1725, native warriors attacked his party, killing Lovewell and nearly a third of his men.

Peace negotiations eventually followed, but Dummer wanted peace on his terms and had difficulty obtaining agreement among the various Abenaki bands. Androscoggins, Kennebecs, and Canadian mission Native Americans continued sporadic raids on eastern frontier settlements into 1726. A formal peace was declared with Dummer's Treaty in 1727.

Fighting continued, however, in western New England in 1727, where the war was known as Grey Lock's War. Grey Lock, a Western Abenaki leader and possible refugee from King Philip's War (1675–1676), led numerous raids against British settlements in the Connecticut River Valley. He ignored repeated efforts by New York, the Iroquois, and the Penobscots to end the war. However, once the Eastern Abenakis had come to terms with the British, Grey Lock ended his war but without signing a peace agreement.

Peace was followed by another spurt of British expansion as the Massachusetts government approved the creation of a series of new townships across northern New England to establish a buffer against northern and eastern natives, satisfy the land demands of veterans of King Philip's War and King William's War, and strengthen its claims to the region.

Following Dummer's War, the Massachusetts government took greater control of the Indian trade, establishing three truck houses in frontier regions as the only sanctioned locations for trade with the natives. As a result of aggressive British actions against Abenaki villages, the Abenakis dispersed north and eastward in small groups, many moving to Canada.

David M. Corlett

Further Reading

Leach, Douglas Edward. *Arms for Empire: A Military History of the British Colonies in North America, 1607–1763*. New York: Macmillan, 1973.

Morrison, Kenneth M. *The Embattled Northeast: The Elusive Ideal of Alliance in Abenaki-Euramerican Relations*. Berkeley: University of California Press, 1984.

Dutch-Indian Wars

Start Date: 1640
End Date: 1664

A series of conflicts between colonists in New Netherland and neighboring Algonquian-speaking tribes. Tensions flared into four periods of open warfare: Kieft's War (1640–1645), the Peach War (1655), the First Esopus War (1659–1660), and the Second Esopus War (1663–1664).

Residents of New Netherland carried on a profitable fur trade with the Mohawks of the upper Hudson River Valley but increasingly viewed the Algonquian people—the Hackensacks, Raritans, and Wecquaesgeeks, among others—of the lower Hudson as an obstacle to the colony's expansion. Director General Willem Kieft had purchased several large tracts of land around New Amsterdam from the Algonquian tribes. Dutch settlers quickly moved onto the tracts and established farms. The European practice of fencing fields and letting livestock roam clashed, however, with the natives' open-field agriculture. When European hogs and cattle damaged native crops, the Native Americans retaliated by killing and eating the livestock.

Kieft aggravated the growing native hostility by ordering the tribes to pay a tribute to the colonial government. Indeed, Kieft sent a boat to collect the tribute from riverside native villages. At one village in early 1640, the crew began loading furs without permission and sparked an armed skirmish. Shortly thereafter, Kieft received word of Raritans killing hogs belonging to a Dutch planter on Staten Island, although in fact Dutch seamen were the culprits. On July 16, 1640, Kieft sent a punitive expedition of some 70 soldiers and sailors against a band of Raritans near Staten Island with orders to demand satisfaction and, if that was not forthcoming, to destroy the Raritans' corn crop and take prisoners. During the expedition, Dutch commander Cornelis Van Tienhoven walked away rather than restrain his men, and the troops immediately began to kill Raritans.

Kieft mistakenly believed that his attack would subdue the Raritans, but it only enraged them. Although conflicting reports obscure whether a particular incident triggered Kieft's War, a picture emerges of a cycle of murder and revenge, some of it fueled by alcohol, the colonists' main stock in trade. On September 1, 1641, the Raritans retaliated for the July 1640 expedition, killing four Dutch men and burning several houses on Staten Island. Kieft then called for the other tribes to turn on the Raritans. Enough of them did so that the Raritans sued for peace by the end of the year.

Meanwhile, in August 1641 a Wecquaesgeek man robbed and murdered a Dutch craftsman, claiming that he was avenging the long-ago murder of his uncle by Dutch traders. Kieft demanded that the killer be turned over to him for punishment. The end of hostilities with the Raritans freed Kieft to seek redress from the Wecquaesgeeks. He mounted an expedition against them in March 1642, but soldiers failed to find the native encampment. Frightened by how near they had come to being attacked, the Wecquaesgeeks sued for peace. They promised to turn over the fugitive but never did. In summer 1642, the son of a Hackensack sachem, while drunk, shot and killed a Dutch farmer on Staten Island and then fled the area. Again Kieft demanded custody of the fugitive but to no avail.

In February 1643, Kieft decided to mount an attack so brutal that it would end all native resistance. He chose two targets: an encampment at Pavonia, where several hundred Tappan and Wecquaesgeek people had taken refuge after an attack by the Mohawks, and an encampment of Hackensacks on Manhattan Island. On the night of February 25, 1643, Kieft ordered his militia to massacre the refugees. Eighty Dutch soldiers torched the Pavonia encampment as their victims slept and killed some 80 defenseless men, women, and children. Some 50 volunteers attacked the refugees on Manhattan Island, killing another 40.

Kieft's massacre ignited a general Indian uprising against colonial settlements throughout New Netherland. Eleven tribes mounted attacks on farms and settlements, and the colonists fled to the New Amsterdam fortifications. Many Dutch families desperately sought passage back to the Netherlands. In late April 1643, the tribes accepted the terms of a peace treaty, but Kieft insulted the sachems by giving them only the bare minimum of the expected gifts. The young men of the tribes agitated for a return to war, and violent incidents proliferated. In August 1643, the Wappingers began attacking trading ships on the Hudson. The violence quickly escalated, and within a month, 1,500 warriors from seven tribes had attacked and occupied much of Manhattan.

Kieft then hired John Underhill, the New England officer who had taken part in the 1637 massacre of the Pequots, to lead a militia force of some 40 English volunteers. Underhill's troops, supported by Dutch militia, swept through the countryside, killing more than 100 Native Americans and mutilating several prisoners. A third of the war's native casualties occurred one night in February 1644. In an action similar to the Pequot massacre, Underhill led a 130-man force in the slaughter of more than 500 Wecquaesgeeks and Wappingers in present-day Westchester County, New York, setting fire to their village and killing them as they fled.

In April 1645, some of the Algonquian tribes sued for peace, and by August, all parties had signed a treaty. Kieft's War ended with more than 1,500 Algonquians killed and the countryside virtually emptied of Dutch settlers. Colonists complained bitterly about Kieft's incompetence, some calling him too bellicose and others saying that he failed to prosecute the war with sufficient vigor. Their complaints spurred the West India Company to replace him with Petrus Stuyvesant, who arrived in May 1647. European immigration surged, and once again natives and colonists struggled for control of the land. Isolated killings occurred, but unlike his predecessor, Stuyvesant showed restraint.

The so-called Peach War began in 1655 when nearly 2,000 Mahicans, Esopuses, and Hackensacks came down the river to attack an enemy people, the Canarsies of Long Island. Camped on Manhattan, they foraged for food, and a hot-tempered Dutch landowner killed a native woman as she picked peaches from his orchard. To avenge her death, on September 15 hundreds of warriors invaded Manhattan Island, Staten Island, and Long Island. During a three-day rampage, they burned farms and orchards and captured nearly 100 women and children. The attack took place while Stuyvesant was in Delaware subjugating the Swedes. On Stuyvesant's hurried return, colonial forces retaliated against native villages and farms, although peace negotiations began in October. While the combatants did not bring the war to a formal conclusion, hostilities ceased, and Native Americans began ransoming their prisoners. The episode caused the deaths of some 50 colonists and 60 Native Americans, the loss of some 500 cattle, and the destruction of 28 farms.

Although Stuyvesant instructed colonists to live together in defensible villages rather than on their scattered farms, settlers preferred to live independently and thus remained isolated and vulnerable to attack. They also gave the natives brandy in exchange for furs. Young men of the Esopus tribe, fueled by the brandy, harassed colonists around the village of Esopus, a Dutch settlement between New Amsterdam and Fort Orange (Albany). Stuyvesant visited Esopus in 1657 and sternly admonished both settlers and natives to refrain from liquor trafficking. He insisted on the fortification of Esopus and stayed long enough to see it accomplished. The situation returned to a semblance of tranquility, but resentment simmered on both sides.

On September 20, 1659, a colonist gave 8 Native Americans brandy in payment for harvesting his corn. They proceeded to have a loud party just outside of Esopus. Several settlers attacked them after they had fallen asleep and killed 1 of them. The next day some 500 Esopuses and Wappingers retaliated, attacking farms and villages along the Hudson River and besieging Esopus for 23 days. Stuyvesant raised an army of some 300 men and came to its aid on October 10, but the natives had already abandoned the siege.

After a quiet winter, Stuyvesant and his force again sailed north in March 1660 to finish the war. After a series of skirmishes and the killing of the eldest Esopus chief, the combatants signed a treaty in July 1660.

Still resentful that Stuyvesant had deported 11 captives to slavery in the West Indies during the previous war, the Esopuses began a new series of attacks on June 7, 1663. They massacred the inhabitants of Wiltwyck (formerly Esopus), including women and children, leaving more than 20 dead and taking nearly 50 prisoners. Calling for volunteers among the panic-stricken populace, Stuyvesant mustered only 150 men, 80 of whom were mercenaries. Their capable leader, Martin Cregier, received a description of the terrain from a woman who had escaped from her captors. On September 3, Cregier led a successful expedition from Wiltwyck, killed some 30 of the Native Americans, and recovered numerous prisoners.

Esopuses continued to harass settlers until a second expedition in October destroyed what was left of their crops. The surviving Esopuses took refuge with the Wappingers. Although the two tribes planned a joint attack, they lacked the resources to carry it out. Instead, they sued for peace near the end of 1663. Distracted by the growing English threat, Stuyvesant accepted their offer. A treaty concluded on May 16, 1664, divested the Esopus people of all their land near Wiltwyck.

Roberta Wiener

Further Reading

Merwick, Donna. *The Shame and the Sorrow: Dutch-Amerindian Encounters in New Netherland.* Philadelphia: University of Pennsylvania Press, 2006.

Richter, Daniel K. *The Ordeal of the Longhouse: The People of the Iroquois League in the Era of European Colonization.* Chapel Hill: University of North Carolina Press, 1992.

Van der Zee, Henri, and Barbara Van der Zee. *A Sweet and Alien Land: The Story of Dutch New York.* New York: Viking, 1978.

E

Endicott Expedition

Event Date: August 1636

Military expedition mounted by Massachusetts Bay Colony against Native Americans on Block Island (now part of Rhode Island) that precipitated the Pequot War (1636–1638). In July 1636, a ship captained by John Gallop came on John Oldham's pinnace near Block Island. Seeing a number of Block Island natives on board, Gallop investigated. A fight ensued in which Gallop and his men killed 10 or 11 of the natives before discovering Oldham's body below deck.

Since the Block Islanders paid tribute to the Narragansetts, Governor Henry Vane of Massachusetts sent a delegation to the Narragansetts to investigate Oldham's murder. The investigators reported that the leading Narragansett sachems (chiefs) were loyal and willing to punish those responsible. Nonetheless, Vane ordered John Endicott (also spelled Endecott) to lead a force of volunteers to seize Block Island, kill all native adult males there, and capture women and children (who would then be sold as slaves). Endicott was then to sail to Pequot territory and demand the surrender of natives responsible for the 1634 murder of a Virginian, John Stone. The Pequots were to pay damages in wampum and turn over several Pequot children as hostages to ensure the tribe's future good behavior.

Endicott's force of some 90 men set sail on August 24. Endicott had the assistance of captains John Underwood, Nathaniel Turner, and William Jenningston and ensign Richard Davenport as well as two native guides. High waves and wind at Block Island prevented their ships from landing, and the men had to disembark offshore and wade in, whereupon they promptly came under native attack. Musket fire soon compelled the natives to retreat.

For two days, Endicott and his men attempted to do battle with the natives, who had sought refuge in the swamps on the island. The colonists burned two abandoned villages and set fire to much of the island, including its cornfields. After having killed perhaps as many as a dozen natives and being unable to locate the remainder, Endicott ordered his men to return to their ships to fulfill the second part of his orders.

Endicott first sailed to Fort Saybrook at the mouth of the Connecticut River on Long Island Sound. The commander of the fort, Lieutenant Lion Gardiner, was a strong critic of the expedition. Fearing native retribution on Saybrook, he questioned why Massachusetts leaders would be mounting a military expedition to avenge the murder of a Virginian and warned Endicott of the likely repercussions.

When Endicott's ships finally sailed up the Pequot River (now known as the Thames River), the Pequots inquired as to the reason for the English presence. Endicott remained on his ship and did not answer. The next day, the Pequots sent an emissary to meet with Endicott, who then revealed the purpose of his expeditionary force, saying that he had come to avenge the killing of Stone. The envoy replied that the sachem Sassacus and others had killed Stone in retaliation for the murder of the sachem Tatobem. The Dutch had captured and killed the grand sachem, and the Pequots had taken revenge on Stone, not recognizing that he was English. The envoy asked the English to wait for a response and departed.

Fearing a trick, the English went ashore, ready to do battle. The Pequots asked for time, claiming that their principal sachems were away. Endicott took this as a ruse by which the Pequots would gain time to prepare for battle, and he ordered an attack. As on Block Island, the Pequots refused to fight; they simply fled. Endicott repeated the tactics of Block Island, destroying the Pequot settlements and crops. Endicott's force then returned to Massachusetts Bay, having failed to accomplish any of the mission's objectives.

As Gardiner predicted, Endicott's actions led to war. Despite defense of the action by new governor John Winthrop (1637–1640) as being necessary to avenge the deaths of two Englishmen, colonial settlements and trading posts on the Connecticut River soon came under attack by angry Pequots. This fighting soon expanded into the destructive Pequot War.

Sarah E. Miller and Spencer C. Tucker

Further Reading

Cave, Alfred A. *The Pequot War.* Amherst: University of Massachusetts Press, 1996.

Hauptman, Laurence M., and James D. Wherry, eds. *The Pequots in Southern New England: The Rise and Fall of an American Indian Nation.* Norman: University of Oklahoma Press, 1990.

F

Fallen Timbers, Battle of

Event Date: August 20, 1794

Significant engagement fought near present-day Toledo, Ohio, between U.S. troops and Native Americans that secured control of much of Ohio from Native Americans. In the 1783 Treaty of Paris ending the American Revolutionary War (1775–1783), the British government acknowledged U.S. claims west of the Appalachians and made no effort to protect Native American lands in the Ohio Valley. Although between 1784 and 1789 the U.S. government persuaded some chiefs to relinquish lands in southern and eastern Ohio, most Native American leaders and tribes refused to acknowledge the validity of these treaties or recognize U.S. authority north of the Ohio River. Consequently, incursions by American settlers led to conflict.

Encouraged by the British, leaders of the Miami and Shawnee tribes insisted that the Americans fall back to the Ohio River. When the settlers refused, the Miamis attacked them, prompting Northwest Territory governor Arthur St. Clair to send U.S. troops and militia against Native Americans along the Maumee River. Brigadier General Josiah Harmar led an expedition in October 1790, the first for the post-Revolution U.S. Army. Setting out with 1,300 men, including 320 regulars and Pennsylvania and Kentucky militiamen, Harmar divided his poorly trained force into three separate columns. Near present-day Fort Wayne, Indiana, the Miamis and Shawnees, led by Miami chief Little Turtle, defeated Harmar in detail, the troops sustaining 300 casualties.

In autumn 1791, St. Clair, commissioned as a major general, led a second expedition of the entire 600-man regular army and 1,500 militia. On November 3, the men camped along the upper Wabash River at present-day Fort Recovery, Ohio. The next morning, Little Turtle and his warriors caught them by surprise and administered the worst defeat ever by Native Americans on the British or Americans, inflicting some 800 casualties. Native American losses were reported as 21 killed and 40 wounded.

President George Washington did not attempt to conceal these twin disasters from the American people, and in December 1792, Congress voted to establish a 5,000-man Legion of the United States, commanded by a major general and consisting of four sub-legions led by brigadier generals. Washington appointed retired general Anthony "Mad Anthony" Wayne to command the legion.

Wayne set up a training camp 25 miles from Pittsburgh, Pennsylvania, at a site he named Legionville and put the men through rigorous training. In May 1793, he moved the legion to Fort Washington (Cincinnati) and then a few miles north to a new camp, Hobson's Choice. In early October, Wayne moved north with 2,000 regulars to Fort Jefferson, the end of his defensive line. When Kentucky mounted militia arrived, Wayne moved a few miles farther north and set up a new camp, naming it Fort Greeneville (now Greenville, Ohio) in honor of his American Revolutionary War commander, Major General Nathanael Greene.

In December 1793, Wayne sent a detachment to the site of St. Clair's defeat on the

Wabash. On Christmas Day, the Americans occupied the battlefield and constructed Fort Recovery on high ground overlooking the Wabash. Aided by friendly Native Americans, the soldiers recovered most of St. Clair's cannon, which Native Americans had buried nearby. These were incorporated into Fort Recovery, which was manned by an infantry company and a detachment of artillerists.

Wayne's campaign timetable was delayed because of unreliable civilian contractors, Native American attacks on his supply trains, the removal of some of his men elsewhere, and a cease-fire that led him to believe that peace might be in the offing. But Little Turtle, Shawnee war chief Blue Jacket, and other chiefs rejected peace negotiations, in part because British governor-general in Canada Sir Guy Carleton had pledged British support for the Native Americans. In February 1794, Carleton ordered construction of Fort Miami on the Maumee River to mount cannon larger than those that Wayne might be able to bring against it, further delaying Wayne's advance.

On June 29, 1794, Little Turtle struck first at Fort Recovery, Wayne's staging point for the invasion. A supply train had just arrived and was bivouacked outside the walls when 2,000 warriors attacked. Although several soldiers were killed, Native Americans suffered heavy casualties and withdrew two days later. The repulse prompted some of the smaller tribes to quit the coalition and led to the eclipse of Little Turtle, who was replaced as principal war leader by the less effective Blue Jacket.

Wayne now had 2,000 men. In mid-July, some 1,600 Kentucky militia under Brigadier General Charles Scott began to arrive. Wayne also could count on 100 Native Americans, mostly Choctaws and Chickasaws, from Tennessee. On July 28, Wayne departed Fort Greeneville for Fort Recovery. Washington warned that a third straight defeat "would be inexpressibly ruinous to the reputation of the government."

The Native Americans were concentrated at Miami Town, the objective of previous offensives, and the rapids of the Maumee River around Fort Miami. A 100-mile-long road through the Maumee River Valley connected the two. Wayne intended to build a fortification at midpoint on the road, allowing him to strike in either direction and forcing Native Americans to defend both possible objectives. By August 3, he had established this position, Fort Adams, and had built Fort Defiance at the confluence of the Auglaize and Maumee rivers. Wayne then sent the chiefs a final peace offer. Little Turtle urged its acceptance, pointing out the strength of Wayne's force and expressing doubts about British support. Blue Jacket and British agents urged war, which a majority of the chiefs approved.

Having learned of a Native American concentration near Fort Miami, Wayne decided to move there first. After a difficult crossing of the Maumee River, on August 15 Wayne's men were still 10 miles from the British fort. Sensing an impending fight, Wayne detached unnecessary elements from his column to construct a possible fallback position, Fort Deposit, manned by Captain Zebulon Pike and 200 men.

On August 20, Wayne again put his column in motion, anticipating battle that day with either Native Americans or the British. Indeed, more than 1,000 warriors and some 60 Canadian militiamen were lying in wait, hoping to ambush the Americans from the natural defenses of a forest of trees that had been uprooted by a tornado and transformed into a chaos of twisted branches and broken tree trunks.

Blue Jacket had expected Wayne to arrive on August 19, not anticipating the daylong delay. In preparation for battle, the Native Americans began a strict fast on August 18 and then continued it the next day. When the Americans did not arrive, many warriors, hungry and exhausted, departed to Fort Miami.

Wayne marched his men to be ready to meet an attack from any quarter. His infantry were in two wings: Brigadier General James Wilkinson on the right and Colonel John Hamtramck on the left. A mounted brigade of Kentuckians protected the left flank, while legion horsemen covered the right. Additional Kentucky horsemen protected the rear and served as a reserve. Well to the front, Major William Price led a battalion to trigger the Native American attack and allow Wayne time to deploy the main body.

When Native Americans opened fire, Price's men fell back into Wilkinson's line. Wayne rallied his men and sent them to defeat the ambush with an infantry frontal attack driven home with the bayonet, while his horsemen closed on the flanks. Native Americans were routed, fleeing the battle toward Fort Miami. The killing went on to the very gates of the fort while the British looked on. Wayne's losses in the battle were 33 men killed and 100 wounded (11 of them mortally), while Native American losses were in the hundreds.

Although Wayne disregarded Fort Miami, he destroyed Native American communities and British storehouses in its vicinity. The soldiers then marched to Miami Town, occupied it without opposition on September 17, and razed it. They then built a fort on the site of Harmar's 1790 defeat, naming it Fort Wayne.

The Battle of Fallen Timbers broke forever the power of the Native Americans in the eastern region of the Northwest Territory, led the British to evacuate their garrisons below the Great Lakes, and did much to restore U.S. military prestige. Wayne is justifiably known as the father of the U.S. Army.

On August 3, 1795, chiefs representing 12 tribes signed the Treaty of Greenville, Wayne having revealed to them that the British had agreed in Jay's Treaty to withdraw their forts and recognize the boundary set in the 1783 Treaty of Paris. The Treaty of Greenville set a definite boundary in the Northwest Territory, forcing Native Americans to cede most of the present state of Ohio and part of Indiana. Increased settler movement into the Ohio Country and ensuing Native American resentment and support from the British helped set the stage for the War of 1812 in the Old Northwest.

Spencer C. Tucker

Further Reading

Nelson, Paul David. *Anthony Wayne: Soldier of the Early Republic*. Bloomington: Indiana University Press, 1985.

Sword, Wiley. *President Washington's Indian War: The Struggle for the Old Northwest, 1790–1795*. Norman: University of Oklahoma Press, 1985.

Tebbel, John W. *The Battle of Fallen Timbers, August 20, 1794*. New York: Franklin Watts, 1972.

Fetterman Massacre

Event Date: December 21, 1866

Massacre of 81 U.S. soldiers by Sioux, Cheyenne, and Arapaho warriors on December 21, 1866, near Fort Phil Kearny in Wyoming. The Fetterman Massacre took place within the context of Red Cloud's War (1866–1868). The U.S. Army had constructed a series of forts along the Bozeman

Trail, with Fort Phil Kearny as the major installation. The post was designed and commanded by Colonel Henry Carrington of the 18th Infantry Regiment. Fort Phil Kearny was strategically located but was several miles away from the nearest stand of timber, required as a fuel source in the winter. Each day a small detachment of soldiers was sent about an hour distant to obtain wood, and on most days, the men were attacked by Native Americans.

In November 1866, 33-year-old Captain William Fetterman arrived at Fort Phil Kearny. Fetterman's wartime experiences during the American Civil War (1861–1865) led him to look with contempt upon Native Americans who fought using hit-and-run tactics. He also believed that Colonel Carrington was too timid and that more aggressive action was needed against hostile tribes. Indeed, Fetterman often bragged that with just 80 soldiers, he could defeat the entire Sioux Nation.

By early December 1866, Oglala Sioux chief Red Cloud and Northern Cheyenne chief Roman Nose had gathered several thousand warriors (mainly Sioux, Cheyennes, and Arapahos) a mere 50 miles from the fort. When another army wood train ventured out on December 6, a large party of warriors attacked it and then nearly defeated a relief party that Carrington sent out. Carrington now forbade any more retaliatory operations. On December 19, another wood train was attacked and was rescued by a detachment under Captain James Powell that drove the attackers off. As ordered, Powell refused to pursue the warriors and fall into their trap. The next day, a heavily armed detachment accomplished its mission without incident. Carrington planned one last wood train for the season before taking a break for winter.

That last wood train headed out on December 21 and came under attack. This time, according to the most widely accepted account, Fetterman insisted that he be permitted to lead the rescue party. Carrington relented but ordered Fetterman not to pursue the warriors beyond Lodge Trail Ridge. Ironically, Fetterman led exactly 80 men, the precise number that he claimed he would need to defeat the Sioux Nation.

When Fetterman arrived on the scene with his mixed command of infantry and cavalry, the warriors broke off their attack and began to retreat. An Oglala warrior named Crazy Horse stopped to check his horse to entice the pursuing soldiers to move faster. Others followed Crazy Horse's lead and taunted the soldiers with insults and obscene gestures. Ignoring his orders, Fetterman pursued the Native American party beyond Lodge Trail Ridge until he and his men suddenly found themselves confronted by some 2,000 warriors. Within 20 minutes, Fetterman's force had been annihilated.

When a relief force arrived, what they found stunned them: 81 dead soldiers had been stripped, and their bodies had been mutilated. The sight of the grotesquely mutilated dead sent the remaining men at Fort Phil Kearny into an understandable panic. The fort's women and children were placed in the powder magazine with orders to blow it up should the fort fall.

The Native Americans did not attack the fort but instead moved on. Initially, Fetterman was proclaimed a hero. Only later did people begin to view his rash actions differently. He had clearly disregarded Carrington's order not to pursue the warriors too aggressively.

Months later, an agreement was reached with Red Cloud to close the trail if Native Americans would permit a railroad line to be built across their lands to the south. As agreed, on July 31, 1868, the last U.S. troops abandoned Fort Phil Kearny, and the Sioux promptly burned the fort to the ground. The Fetterman Massacre was the heaviest U.S. military loss in any battle with Native Americans in the West to that date.

Alan K. Lamm

Further Reading

Brown, Dee. *The Fetterman Massacre*. Lincoln: University of Nebraska Press, 1984.

Johnston, Terry C. *Sioux Dawn: The Fetterman Massacre, 1866*. New York: St. Martin's, 1991.

Monnett, John H. *Where a Hundred Soldiers Were Killed: The Struggle for the Powder River Country in 1866*. Albuquerque: University of New Mexico Press, 2008.

Fort Laramie, Treaty of (1868)

The second of two important mid-19th-century treaties signed by Native American nations of the Great Plains and the U.S. government. The Treaty of Fort Laramie, signed on April 29, 1868, effectively ended Red Cloud's War (1866–1868).

The terms of the treaty guaranteed ownership of the Black Hills to the Lakota Sioux and the removal of military forts along the Bozeman Trail in the Powder River Country, and the establishment—on Lakota land—of the Great Sioux Reservation, a reserve of land covering 26 million acres that ran from the northern boundary of the state of Nebraska to the 46th Parallel, was bordered on the east by the Missouri River and ran westward to the 104th degree of longitude. Moreover, the treaty closed the Powder River Country and the Bozeman Trail to military and settler incursions. The treaty, however, also prophetically designated this same country as "unceded Indian Territory" and therefore left the Lakotas in

only temporary ownership of the land outside the official reservation. Additionally, the treaty articles specified the intention of the U.S. government to pursue its stated long-term goals of forced assimilation with agriculture, education, and the division of land held in common.

The treaty document itself is lengthy and relies heavily on dense legal language that often contradicts its own provisions. Red Cloud himself would later claim that the only provisions of the treaty that he was able to understand were the continued tenure of the Lakotas on their own land and the expulsion of the U.S. military from the Powder River Country.

The Fort Laramie Treaty of 1868 was signed by 25 chiefs and headmen of the Brulés, the Oglalas, the Miniconjous, the Hunkpapas, the Blackfeet, the Pabaskas (Cut Heads), the Itazipacolas (Sans Arcs), the Oohenupas (Two Kettles), and Santee bands of the Lakota Nation; by the Yanktonais of the Nakota Nation; by the Mdewakantons and Wahpekutes of the Dakota (Santee) Nation; by members of the Inunaina (Arapaho) Nation; and by members of a U.S. treaty commission. The treaty document and a yearlong process of negotiating for signatures were the result of a successful war waged against the United States by the Lakotas, led by Red Cloud. Red Cloud's War was fought in the Wyoming and Montana territories for control over the important hunting grounds of the Powder River Country in north-central Wyoming. The Fort Laramie Treaty was ratified by the U.S. Congress on February 16, 1869.

The Fort Laramie Treaty failed to preserve peace for a variety of reasons: discovery of gold in the sacred Black Hills by Lieutenant Colonel George Armstrong Custer's governmentally sanctioned expedition resulted in the Black Hills Gold Rush, increased pressure on Lakota land by white settlement, decimation of the great buffalo herds, demands of the Northern Pacific Railroad, and unstable and changing governmental and military policy. In September 1875, President Ulysses S. Grant sent a special commission to Lakota territory to negotiate for the sale of "unceded Indian Territory" of the 1868 Fort Laramie Treaty and the Black Hills themselves. The Lakotas refused to sell. In November 1875, the Bureau of Indian Affairs ordered all Lakotas who were in the "unceded" hunting lands to come onto the reservation and submit to agency control by January 31, 1876. The government then launched a military campaign against Lakotas who were unwilling or unable to comply with the order. The campaign, which began in the spring of 1876 and lasted into the spring of 1877, is known as the Great Sioux War and included the Battle of the Little Bighorn (June 25–26, 1876). The Sioux and their allies fought to maintain the ownership of the land that they believed the Fort Laramie Treaty of 1868 had guaranteed them.

The Fort Laramie Treaty of 1868 remained an important document in the struggle over native rights and land claims in the 20th century. Two important events in the history of the Indian Movement during the 1960s and 1970s were predicated on the language and history surrounding the 1868 Fort Laramie Treaty: the occupation of Alcatraz in 1964 and again in 1969 and the occupation of Wounded Knee in 1973.

In the 21st century, the Fort Laramie Treaty of 1868 continues to be an important aspect of the long-standing Black Hills Land Claim wherein the Lakota Nation continues to press the U.S. government for the return of the Black Hills that were guaranteed to them by the 1868 treaty. The U.S. Supreme Court itself ruled in 1980 that the sacred land was indeed unlawfully seized by the government and ruled that the monies that were never paid to the Lakotas, along with interest accrued over time (more than $100 million), be given to them. The Lakotas refused the payment and continue to argue for the return of their land.

Kathleen Kane

Further Reading

Deloria, Vine, Jr. *Behind the Trail of Broken Treaties: An Indian Declaration of Independence.* 3rd ed. Austin: University of Texas Press, 1990.

Prucha, Francis Paul. *American Indian Treaties: The History of a Political Anomaly.* Berkeley: University of California Press, 1994.

Fox Wars

Start Date: 1712
End Date: 1737

A series of armed conflicts between the Foxes (also known as the Mesquakies or Outagamis) and New France and its Native American allies between 1712 and 1737. The Fox Wars became a genocidal conflict as the French sought essentially to exterminate the Fox Nation. By 1737, the Foxes numbered fewer than 1,000 people, whereas at the start of the conflict, their population was more than 5,000.

The causes of the Fox Wars, although largely attributed to the bellicose nature of the Foxes, had their beginnings in the Beaver Wars (1641–1701) and the reemergence of the fur trade in the Great Lakes. In the 17th century, the Foxes were driven from Michigan lands by the Iroquois, Hurons, and Ojibwas. By the 18th century, the Foxes had resettled in Wisconsin and engaged in conflict with the Sioux. In the late 1600s,

French traders had entered the Wisconsin region, where they initially traded with the Foxes and eventually added the Sioux as customers of European goods, particularly weaponry. The Foxes responded to French trade with their Sioux enemies by harassing and killing French traders, especially those carrying muskets. These actions led the Foxes to seek allies outside the French sphere of influence, and by 1701, they had allied with the Iroquois Confederacy. By 1710, Foxes from several villages had relocated to the Detroit region. This move not only brought the Foxes closer to the Iroquois and the British but also placed the Foxes among natives who were pro-French and former enemies.

The immediate catalyst of the Fox Wars was an attack by the Ojibwas and Pottawatomis on a group of Mascoutens, who were allied with the Foxes. In the raid, 200 Mascoutens died, and the survivors fled to a nearby Fox village. In retaliation, Fox and Mascouten warriors attacked the French and their allies, eventually laying siege to Fort Pontchartrain de Detroit. Following several days of siege, the Foxes attempted to flee during a thunderstorm. The fort's commander, François de La Forest, fearful of reprisals from France's native allies for failing to aid them, pursued the Foxes and Mascoutens, killing more than 1,000. Those captured were either executed or sold into slavery. Fewer than 100 managed to escape. After news of the defeat at Detroit reached the Foxes and the Mascoutens in Wisconsin, they made the area unsafe for French traders and their allies between 1712 and 1716. This conflict in the Great Lakes forced the French to construct Fort Michilimackinac in 1715 across the Mackinac straits from Fort Buade.

In 1716, 400 French soldiers, including a battery of artillery, and 1,000 native allies advanced into Wisconsin to attack the Foxes. After a brief siege of one of their villages, the Foxes agreed to keep the peace, reopening French trade in the Wisconsin region. Despite this, the refusal by Illinois to return captives combined with Illinois and other French allies raiding Fox villages and attacking Fox hunting parties soon resulted in continued warfare. Pressure from Louisiana governor Étienne de Périer (1726–1733), Jesuits, and Canadian merchants compelled Quebec governor Charles de la Boische, Marquis de Beauharnois to dispatch 1,500 men against the Foxes in 1728, an expedition that failed to locate any Fox villages.

In the 1720s, the Foxes reaffirmed their alliance with the Iroquois and built new alliances with the Chickasaws and the Abenakis. Kiala, a Fox war chief, recognized the need for a united stance against the French. Indeed, his efforts not only challenged the French alliance system but also threatened to cut Louisiana off from New France. Importantly, the French also sought to stop anti-French Abenakis, led by Nescambiouit, from joining the Foxes in the interior. Such a move by the Abenakis would have strengthened the Foxes while removing a buffer between New England and New France. Hence, Beauharnois saw the destruction of the Foxes as imperative.

In 1730, the Foxes experienced a second disastrous defeat, when they left their villages in the Illinois-Wisconsin region and attempted to join the Senecas in New York. Trapped during their flight across the Illinois prairie, the Foxes fortified a grove of trees (Fox Fort) and after a siege attempted to sneak away during an intense summer storm. Detected by their attackers and slowed by their families, as many as 1,000 men, women, and children were killed, and dozens were taken captive.

The Foxes sued for peace in 1733, and a delegation of four leaders, including Kiala, arrived in Montreal in 1734 to finalize their surrender. The French arrested the peace delegates, sending one to France to serve in the galleys, selling Kiala into slavery, and scattering the remainder among the missions and towns of Quebec. As the French intensified their campaign to exterminate the Foxes, other Great Lakes tribes began to fear the outcome if they allowed the Foxes to be destroyed. During 1734–1735, French native allies released Fox prisoners and refused assistance to the French in what had become a genocidal conflict. When a group of Great Lakes nations and Foxes arrived in Quebec to seek peace in 1737, Governor Beauharnois agreed for several reasons: conflicts in the Mississippi region such as the Natchez War (1729–1733) and the Chickasaw Wars (1731–1745) drew away French troops and supplies; British attempts to increase their presence in the interior and lure away French native allies; and increasing tensions in Europe.

The Fox Wars are noteworthy not only as an example of attempted genocide but also because the conflict reshaped French policies in the pays d'en haut ("upcountry"). First, the Fox Wars made it clear that the French presence in the interior depended on the cooperation and sufferance of Native Americans. Second, the tribes of the Great Lakes learned that the French could be dangerous and that the existence of a benign middle ground was tenuous at best. Third, the wars revealed that canoe routes from Lake Michigan to the Mississippi were not secure and that control of the Ohio River system was vital to France's American empire. The resulting expansion of the French presence in the Ohio River Valley greatly contributed to the series of conflicts with the British that ended with the conquest of New France in 1760. Finally, the wars demonstrated the French alliance

system in the Great Lakes was neither stable nor absolute.

Karl S. Hele

Further Reading

Edmunds, R. David, and Joseph L. Peyser. *The Fox Wars: The Mesquakie Challenge to New France.* Norman: University of Oklahoma Press, 1993.

Skinner, Claiborne, Jr. "'They Would Not Suffer the French to Live among Them': The Fox Wars, the Emergency of 1747, and the Origins of the Seven Years' War, 1671–1752." In *Entering the 90s: The North American Experience*, edited by Thomas E. Schirer, 27–39. Sault Ste. Marie, MI: Lake Superior State University Press, 1991.

French and Indian War

Start Date: 1754
End Date: 1763

The last and largest North American conflict between Britain and France and their respective Native American allies. The French and Indian War (1754–1763) began on May 28, 1754. It involved battles on at least three distinct fronts and served as the catalyst for a wider conflict that came to be known in Europe as the Seven Years' War that began there on August 28, 1756, and ended on February 15, 1763. The war saw fighting on land and sea in North America, Europe, India, West Africa, and the Caribbean. The fighting in North America not only confirmed British hegemony on the eastern half of that continent but also affected the war in Europe and set forces in motion that would later influence the American drive for independence. Native Americans played an important role in the conflict.

During the long struggle, alliances sometimes shifted, and Native Americans warred against each other as well as against

European powers. The French often claimed the Delawares (Lenni Lenapes), Ottawas, Algonquins, Wyandots, Abenakis, Senecas, Mohawks, and Onondagas as allies. The British, at various points, claimed independent Iroquois bands as allies (although the Iroquois Confederacy declared neutrality) as well as select bands of the Mohawks and Cherokees. The alliance with the Cherokees, however, was short-lived. By 1759, the Cherokees were engaged in their own war with the British.

On August 28, 1753, Robert d'Arcy, Earl of Holdernesse, British secretary of state for the Southern Department (which included North America), sent a circular order to the British North American colonial governors. In it he authorized them to demand a French withdrawal from several disputed territories and, failing that, to force the French out using colonial militia.

Acting on this order, Virginia lieutenant governor Robert Dinwiddie dispatched 21-year-old Major George Washington to Fort Le Boeuf, the nearest known French outpost, in what is now northwestern Pennsylvania. On December 16, 1753, Washington arrived with 11 men and was graciously received by commandant Jacques Legardeur de St. Pierre. St. Pierre patiently received Dinwiddie's demand to withdraw but went only so far as to forward the summons to his superiors in Quebec. This set in motion the second clause of Holdernesse's circular order.

On April 15, 1754, the French presence in western Pennsylvania turned from construction to conquest. A force of 500 men under French captain Claude Pierre Pécaudy, Seigneur de Contrecoeur, forced the surrender of 40 English workmen under Ensign Edward Ward and transformed their Ohio Company trading post into the nucleus of Fort Duquesne at the Forks of the Ohio River. Meanwhile, Washington returned to the frontier with 150 Virginia militiamen and some native allies. On May 28, a detachment of 47 men from this force surprised a party of 35 French and native allies from Fort Duquesne, firing the first shots of the war. Among the 10 French dead was their commander, Ensign Joseph Coulon de Villiers de Jumonville, who received a hatchet blow to the head delivered by Tanaghrisson, the leader of Washington's native allies.

While ministers in Britain and France sought to negotiate their differences in North America, the colonists further heightened tensions. Before the news of Fort Duquesne and Jumonville's death could reach Europe, French captain Louis Coulon de Villiers, Jumonville's brother, led a force of 600 Canadians and 100 native allies against his brother's supposed murderer. Washington's 500-man militia fought from hastily erected Fort Necessity, where they were compelled to surrender after a 10-hour fight.

For 1755, both governments planned a proxy war in North America, reinforcing colonial militia with regular European troops. The ministers in London planned one campaign for 1755, but colonial officials requested four smaller ones. The first, during June 2–16, witnessed Nova Scotia lieutenant governor Charles Lawrence and Colonel Robert Monckton leading 250 British regulars and 2,000 colonials to Fort Beauséjour and Fort Gaspéreau on the isthmus connecting Nova Scotia to the Canadian mainland. There the British force defeated 150 French regulars and a few hundred unsteady Acadians. On September 8, 1755, Major General William Johnson's operation against Crown Point achieved a defensive victory at Lake George, capturing the French commander, Maréchal de Camp

Jean Armand, Baron de Dieskau. Major General William Shirley's campaign to Fort Niagara, however, ended at Fort Oswego when supplies ran short and 2,000 colonial militia fell ill. Meanwhile, on July 9, British major general Edward Braddock's expedition to Fort Duquesne ended in the loss of more than 900 out of his 2,200 troops in the Battle of the Monongahela.

By year's end, ministers in London and Versailles planned new campaigns, expanding operations from North America into the Atlantic and from the Atlantic to the shores of Europe, where nothing short of a diplomatic revolution had occurred. Maria Theresa, the Habsburg empress of Austria, sought to recapture Silesia, which Frederick II of Prussia had seized in the War of the Austrian Succession (1740–1748), known as King George's War in America. She arranged an alliance with Louis XV of France, while Britain allied with Prussia. Tsarina Elizabeth of Russia also agreed to enter the war against Prussia. Frederick II, aware of the forces massing against him, did not wait to be attacked. Frederick mobilized his own army and on August 28, 1756, began what would become known as the Seven Years' War (1756–1763) with an invasion of Saxony en route to the Habsburg kingdom of Bohemia.

There was little in the way of large-scale campaigning in North America during 1756. The British commander in chief in North America, John Campbell, Fourth Earl of Loudoun, reorganized British forces, which increased by the end of 1757 to 17 regular regiments and more than 10,000 colonial militiamen. Meanwhile, Maréchal de Camp Louis-Joseph, Marquis de Montcalm, commanded some 7,200 French regulars and as many as 17,000 Canadian militiamen. Whereas Loudoun remained quiescent, aborting two projected British operations against Louisbourg on Cape Breton Island, Montcalm won several important victories and attracted large numbers of native allies to the French cause.

Accompanied by 250 native allies, 1,300 French regulars and 1,500 Canadian militiamen raided Fort Oswego late in 1756, leaving the British without their trading and logistical base on Lake Ontario. Abandoned by their Oneida allies, the British garrison of 1,135 men was surprised in their poorly constructed works on the afternoon of August 11 and were compelled to conclude an ignominious surrender.

By 1757, the British attempted to gather their own intelligence and employed Captain Robert Rogers and his 100-man company of green-clad American troops, known as Rogers' Rangers. Discovered and routed in their attempt to reconnoiter Fort Carillon (Ticonderoga) in January 1757, the rangers left Fort William Henry as vulnerable to surprise as Fort Oswego had been in 1756, and the prestige of French victories attracted increasing numbers of native allies. In mid-March, a raid on Fort William Henry by Captain François Pierre Rigaud and 1,500 natives, French, and Canadians exposed British weaknesses and destroyed supplies, but Major William Eyre's capable defense saved the fort from immediate capture.

Fort William Henry was in no better shape on August 3 when Montcalm arrived there with some 6,000 French regulars and Canadian militia and 2,000 native allies. British lieutenant colonel George Monro had brought reinforcements to Fort William Henry in the spring and received additional reinforcements later, giving him a total garrison strength of 2,300 British regulars and American colonials. This force held out bravely for a week before surrendering.

On August 9, 1757, Monro negotiated a European-style surrender. Granted the full honors of war, the British garrison was assured safe conduct down the 14-mile road to Fort Edward. Unfortunately for the British, Montcalm had not consulted with his native allies. The natives, seeking plunder and scalps, engaged in what the British and colonial press called a massacre, inflaming public opinion throughout the Anglophone world. Moreover, by trying to restrain his native allies, Montcalm damaged French credibility and gave British Indian commissioner William Johnson an unprecedented opportunity to swing native opinion to Britain's side.

British North American forces under the overall command of Major General James Abercromby in 1758, and Amherst from 1759, had great advantages in numbers and organization and in the quality and creativity of their officers. With the American Indian threat largely removed by the Treaty of Easton of August 5, 1757, British colonial forces, backed by regular troops, began a large and virtually continuous three-year offensive. Although Montcalm blunted the English advance at Fort Ticonderoga on July 8, 1758, British ships and troops under Major General Jeffrey Amherst and Colonel (later Brigadier General) James Wolfe conducted a successful amphibious operation that took Louisbourg on July 26, 1758. Lieutenant Colonel John Bradstreet captured Fort Frontenac during August 25–27, 1758, threatening the French Canadian war economy. Brigadier General John Forbes seized Fort Duquesne on September 14, 1758, driving the French from western Pennsylvania. Indian commissioner Major General William Johnson convinced the Iroquois to join the struggle as a British ally in 1759 and then successfully besieged Fort Niagara during July 6–26, 1759, clearing French influence from New York and the western Great Lakes region and securing British authority over the Ohio Country. Finally, Wolfe continued with Vice Admiral Charles Saunders up the Saint Lawrence River and on September 13, 1759, captured Quebec, the capital of New France. Although French forces under Chevalier Gaston de Lévis almost retook Quebec following the Battle of Sainte Foy on April 28, 1760, the British seizure of Montréal on September 8, 1760, effectively completed its conquest of New France.

With the fall of Louisbourg, Fort Frontenac, Fort Niagara, and Quebec, French trade with Canada collapsed. With the cancellation of payment on Canadian bills of exchange, merchants trading with Canada were compelled to declare bankruptcy. The Ministry of Marine declared bankruptcy as well in November 1759, and financial problems spread throughout the French government soon thereafter. As French territories in Canada and the Caribbean fell, French subsidies to its European allies, notably Austria, dwindled, and French military efforts around the globe weakened substantially after 1760. Meanwhile, the British made regular subsidy payments to Frederick II that kept Prussia in the war, although just barely.

The British were also successful at sea and in operations in the Caribbean and in India. The last French operation by sea was a successful assault on Newfoundland in 1762. British colonists in Massachusetts organized a relief expedition of more than 1,500 men under Colonel William Amherst and soon recovered the island. The French campaign in Newfoundland did not truly envision the conquest of that island as an end in its own right; rather, like the British invasion of Belle Isle with 8,000 men on June 7, 1761, it was an attempt to affect their bargaining positions at a future peace negotiation.

The first attempt to start peace talks was the Hague Declaration, presented by British and Prussian envoys in the Dutch Republic to their Austrian, French, and Russian counterparts in October 1759. These negotiations failed but led to efforts at a peace congress in Augsburg (Breda) in 1760 and 1761. Britain and France also attempted to negotiate a separate peace in 1761 with envoys Hans Stanley and Sieur de Bussy. Negotiations broke down, however, mostly under Austrian and Spanish pressure and because of concerns over fishing rights off Newfoundland and the return of conquests in Germany. Talks were restarted through Sardinian envoys in 1762 and ended in success near the end of the year.

The negotiations in 1762 were more complex than those of 1761 for several reasons. Changes in the leadership in Spain, in Britain, and finally in Russia altered the international playing field. Spain had slowly edged toward the French camp after the accession of King Carlos III in 1759, and the two states concluded the Third Family Compact on August 15, 1761. With the accession of King George III on October 25, 1760, Britain moved quickly from the hawkish stance of William Pitt the Elder to the more dovish agenda of John Stuart, Third Earl of Bute, and John Russell, Fourth Duke of Bedford. Finally, on January 5, 1762, Tsarina Elizabeth of Russia died and was succeeded by Tsar Peter III, an ardent admirer of the Prussian king. At his command, the Russian Army switched sides and helped the Prussians achieve victory over the Austrians in July at Burkersdorf. Although Peter III was soon overthrown in a palace coup that made his wife, Catherine of Anhalt-Zerbst, Tsarina Catherine II, the die had been cast: Russia declared neutrality, and Frederick II and Prussia survived.

When Russia left the conflict, Sweden also declared neutrality. Europe experienced a second diplomatic revolution so that Prussia had an advantage over Austria. Although exhausted financially and militarily, Prussia gained several victories over Austria in 1762. British and allied forces meanwhile invaded Havana in Cuba and Manila in the Philippines while repelling a Spanish invasion of Portugal.

At the prodding of their respective allies, Austria and Prussia made peace at Hubertusburg on February 15, 1763, reaffirming the prewar status quo of 1756 and providing for the definitive secession of Silesia by Austria to Prussia. On February 10, Britain, France, and Spain concluded the Treaty of Paris, formalizing a substantial exchange of territories, greatly in Britain's favor. In North America, the agreement involved the cession of all of New France to British control except for Louisiana, which France ceded to Spain, and the small fishing islands of Saint-Pierre and Miquelon, which France retained. Britain also acquired Florida from Spain.

Although the British acquired large amounts of territory, Britain had to contend with the difficulties and contradictions inherent in administering its new lands, including the toleration of Catholicism in New France, which was anathema to the Puritan colonists of New England. More important, the war left Britain with a huge debt, leading the British to seek tighter political and economic control over its American colonies, which provoked a series of increasingly hostile reactions among the colonists. By 1775, American discontent erupted into full-scale revolt against the mother country, presenting the

French with the opportunity for revenge during the American Revolutionary War (1775– 1783).

Matt Schumann

Further Reading

Anderson, Fred. *Crucible of War: The Seven Years' War and the Fate of the Empire in British North America, 1754–1766.* New York: Vintage Books, 2001.

Fowler, William, Jr. *Empires at War: The French and Indian War and the Struggle for North America, 1754–1763.* New York: Walker, 2004.

Jennings, Francis. *Empire of Fortune: Crowns, Colonies, and Tribes in the Seven Years War in America.* New York: Norton, 1988.

G

Gatewood, Charles Bare

Birth Date: April 6, 1853
Death Date: May 20, 1896

U.S. Army officer who secured Chiricahua Apache leader Geronimo's surrender in 1886. Born at Woodstock, Virginia, on April 6, 1853, Charles Bare Gatewood graduated from the U.S. Military Academy, West Point, in 1877. Commissioned a second lieutenant in the 6th Cavalry Regiment, he was posted to the Southwest, mostly working out of Camp (later Fort) Apache, and participated in the Victorio War of 1879–1880. Gatewood devoted himself to understanding Native American culture and language, becoming something of an expert of Native American ways in the process. Promoted to first lieutenant, Gatewood had already established himself as a capable leader of Apache scouts when Brigadier General George Crook assumed command of the Department of Arizona in 1882. Crook placed officers with the best grasp of the Apaches in charge of the various reservations and gave Gatewood charge of the difficult White Mountain Agency at Fort Apache.

As the Apaches grew increasingly restive on the reservation, raiding across the Southwest and into Mexico, Crook mounted a series of partially successful campaigns in which Gatewood and his Apache scouts figured prominently. Gatewood's integrity, sense of justice, and growing sympathy for the Apaches brought him into conflict with Crook. The escape of Geronimo following his much-celebrated surrender to Crook in March 1886 prompted Crook's removal and caused many to question his methods, including the broad use of Indian scouts.

When a large and grueling campaign into Mexico directed by Crook's replacement, Brigadier General Nelson A. Miles, failed to capture Geronimo, Miles turned reluctantly to Gatewood and his Indian scouts. Gatewood was the only officer available whom Geronimo knew and trusted. Gatewood located Geronimo and convinced him to surrender to Miles in September 1886. Miles, apparently concerned that Gatewood might garner too much credit for bringing in the dreaded warrior, isolated the lieutenant, resulting in another troubled relationship with a superior.

Repeatedly overlooked for much-deserved promotion to captain, Gatewood was subsequently sent to the Dakota Territory but was not engaged in the final campaign against the Sioux that culminated in the tragedy at Wounded Knee in December 1890. The following year, the 6th Cavalry was rushed to Wyoming in response to the so-called Johnson County Range War. In May 1892, Gatewood was badly wounded in the bombing of a building at Fort McKinney by one faction in that conflict. He never fully recovered from his injuries, and his health soon rendered him unfit for field duty. Gatewood died of abdominal cancer at Fort Monroe, Virginia, on May 20, 1896, still a first lieutenant after almost 20 years of service.

David Coffey

Further Reading

Gatewood, Charles B. *Lt. Charles Gatewood and His Apache War Memoir*. Edited by Louis Kraft. Lincoln: University of Nebraska Press, 2005.

Kraft, Louis. *Gatewood and Geronimo*. Albuquerque: University of New Mexico Press, 2000.

Geronimo

Birth Date: June 16, 1829
Death Date: February 26, 1909

Chiricahua Apache war leader and shaman. Geronimo, named Goyahkla at birth, was born on June 16, 1829, on the upper Gila River near the present-day Arizona–New Mexico border. He was given the name "Geromino" by the Mexicans; Geronimo is Spanish for Jerome, and Saint Jerome is the Catholic saint of lost causes. Legend has it that Mexican soldiers invoked Saint Jerome's name when fighting against Geronimo's raiding parties. Geronimo was born into the Bedonkohe band, which was closely associated with the Chiricahuas. As a youth, Geronimo honed his skills as a hunter and marksman and learned survival skills that would serve him well throughout his storied career.

Although never a chief himself, Geronimo engaged in raids on both sides of the U.S.-Mexican border with many notable Apache chieftains, such as Mangas Coloradas, Cochise, Juh, and Victorio. While Geronimo was absent on an 1850 raid with Mangas Coloradas into Chihuahua, a group of Mexicans attacked his family's encampment, killing his mother, wife, and three young children and leaving Geronimo with a lasting hatred of Mexicans. Geronimo is thought to have joined Cochise in the Battle of Apache Pass (July 15–16, 1862). In May 1871, when Nednhi Apache war chief Juh led an ambush against a U.S. cavalry detachment commanded by renowned Indian-fighter Lieutenant Howard B. Cushing, Geronimo may have been responsible for Cushing's death. In 1877, Geronimo joined Victorio and his followers in New Mexico at the Ojo Caliente Reservation, where the Indian agent had him arrested and placed in irons. This began a long series of intrepid breakouts and arrests. By 1878, he was back in Mexico, where he raided with Juh and his followers. When Juh's band subsequently took up residence at the San Carlos Reservation in southern Arizona, Juh and Geronimo were forbidden to leave by U.S. authorities. Nevertheless, in 1881, they escaped and led their followers into Mexico's Sierra Madre, where they settled for about a year. In 1882, Geronimo and Juh led a daring raid on the San Carlos Reservation, to win the release of Chief Loco. Although several hundred Apaches decided to follow Geronimo and Juh into Mexico, unprecedented cooperation between the United States and Mexico enabled Brigadier General George Crook to pursue them. After locating the renegades in Mexico with the aid of Apache scouts, Crook compelled Geronimo and others to agree to return to San Carlos.

Although Geronimo returned to San Carlos in March 1884 and voluntarily surrendered to American authorities, he found reservation life hard to accept. In April 1885, he fled San Carlos again and remained at large until March 1886, when he agreed to surrender to Brigadier General George Crook at Cañon de los Embudos, just south of the U.S.-Mexican border. Geronimo and his followers halted temporarily in southeastern Arizona, where an unscrupulous Tombstone trader clandestinely entered the encampment and proceeded to provide enough liquor to inebriate Geronimo and his followers. The trader then convinced Geronimo that he and his followers would likely be killed by U.S. forces, leading Geronimo and his followers to flee once again. Pursued tenaciously by U.S. forces over the next six months, Geronimo finally surrendered on September 4, 1886, to Brigadier General Nelson A. Miles in Skeleton Canyon, Arizona. Four days later, he and his followers were placed on a train bound for Florida.

Eventually Geronimo and other Apache leaders were detained at Fort Marion in St. Augustine. Their families, however, were sent to Fort Pickens near Pensacola, some 300 miles away. This violated the terms of the surrender, which had guaranteed that families would not be split up. By May 1888, the Apaches were reunited in Mount Vernon, Alabama. Geronimo embraced his new life, cooperating with U.S. officials and missionaries, converting to Christianity, and even becoming a local justice of the peace. In 1892, the Apaches were relocated again, this time to Indian Territory (Oklahoma). Geronimo died at age 79 at Fort Sill, Oklahoma, on February 26, 1909.

Paul G. Pierpaoli Jr.

Further Reading

Debo, Angie. *Geronimo: The Man, His Time, His Place.* Norman: University of Oklahoma Press, 1976.

Skinner, Woodward B. *The Apache Rock Crumbles: The Captivity of Geronimo's People.* Pensacola, FL: Skinner Publications, 1987.

Stockel, H. Henrietta. *Survival of the Spirit: Chiricahua Apaches in Captivity.* Reno: University of Nevada Press, 1993.

Geronimo Campaign

Start Date: 1881
End Date: 1886

Prolonged U.S. Army campaign to capture Apache warrior Geronimo and his band of followers. Although not a chief, Geronimo had emerged as the leader of disenchanted Chiricahua and Warm Springs Apache warriors at the San Carlos Reservation in southeastern Arizona, where the U.S. government had concentrated numerous Apache bands. Dissension among the bands combined with increased white settlement in Arizona, where the American population doubled from 40,000 to 80,000 between 1880 and 1882, dramatically increased tensions.

Amid this atmosphere, Nakaidoklini, a White Mountain Apache shaman, began preaching that a special dance would bring dead Apaches back to life and cause whites to disappear. When the U.S. Army suppressed the movement on the White Mountain Apache Reservation, many White Mountain Apaches fled to San Carlos. Fearing retribution, Geronimo, along with Apache leaders Juh, Nachez, and Chato, fled San Carlos on October 1, 1881, with 74 Chiricahuas and headed to the Sierra Madre in Mexico, where they joined Nana's small band of Apache survivors from Victorio's War (1879–1880).

After resting in the Sierra Madre, in April 1882 Geronimo, Juh, Nachez, and Chato returned to the United States to recruit more warriors. Slipping around forces that District of New Mexico commander Colonel Ranald S. Mackenzie had stationed along the border, on April 19 Geronimo's warriors attacked the Camp Goodwin subagency, freeing Warm Springs leader Loco and several hundred Apaches. They then advanced up the Gila River before heading to the Peloncillo Mountains along the Arizona–New Mexico border, killing 30–50 whites as they went.

The Apaches would be pursued by both U.S. and Mexican forces. On April 23, Lieutenant Colonel George A. Forsyth, leading five troops from the 4th Cavalry Regiment and one scout troop, attacked the Apaches in Horseshoe Canyon, losing five dead and seven wounded and failing to prevent Geronimo's forces from escaping into northern Mexico. Captain Tullius C. Tupper with two troops of the 6th Cavalry pursued the Apaches into Mexico, catching up with them on April 28 but failing to dislodge them from well-defended positions. Although the Apaches forced Tupper to withdraw, on April 29 Colonel Lorenzo Garcia and 250 Mexican soldiers ambushed the Apaches, killing some 78 Apaches (mostly women and children) at a cost of 22 dead and 16 wounded. Meanwhile, Forsyth had joined forces with Tupper. On April 30, however, Garcia confronted the combined Americans and ordered them out of Mexico.

Growing unrest among the Apaches convinced General William Tecumseh Sherman, commanding general of the army, who was touring Arizona at the time of Geronimo's raid on Camp Goodwin, to replace Colonel Orlando B. Willcox with Brigadier General George Crook as commander of the Department of Arizona. Upon assuming command at Whipple Barracks on September 4, 1882, Crook sought to secure the reservations by improving conditions and placing trusted officers on each reservation to avoid unnecessary confrontations. He then turned his attention to Geronimo's forces in the Sierra Madre. This task was made easier by improved cooperation with Mexico, which in July 1882 had agreed to a treaty that allowed both Mexican and American troops to cross the border when in pursuit of Apaches. Crook augmented his forces with trusted Apache scouts and replaced supply wagons with pack mules in order to keep his forces provisioned when operating in rugged terrain. These measures would prove to be highly effective in the ensuing campaign.

After Apaches under Chato launched a raid into Arizona and New Mexico in late March 1883 that left at least 11 whites dead, Crook began stockpiling supplies and concentrating forces at Willcox, Arizona, and met with MacKenzie in Albuquerque and Mexican officials in Chihuahua and Sonora to coordinate the campaign. By May 1, 1883, Crook had posted portions of the 3rd and the 6th Cavalry at key border crossings and crossed into Mexico with a column of 193 scouts, including 1 of Chato's raiders who had been apprehended, under Captain Emmet Crawford and Lieutenant Charles B. Gatewood, 45 troopers of the 6th Cavalry under Captain Adna Chaffee, and a pack train of 350 mules. On May 15, Crawford's scouts attacked a camp led by Chato and Benito, killing 9 warriors and destroying 30 lodges before the Apaches escaped. When a captured Apache girl revealed to Crook that most of the Native Americans would be willing to surrender, he sent her as an emissary to the Apache leaders. Over the next two days, Chiricahua and Warm Spring Apaches, including Geronimo, Chato, Benito, Nachez, Nana, and Loco, came to Crook's camp to discuss terms of surrender.

After a week of negotiations, the Apaches agreed to surrender, although Geronimo asked for time to gather his scattered followers. Running low on provisions, Crook was forced to assent to Geronimo's terms and departed Mexico on June 10 with 52 Apache warriors and 273 women and children. Although Crook was somewhat concerned about whether the Apache leaders would honor their promise to surrender, by mid-March 1884, Nachez, Chato, Mangas, and Geronimo had led their bands to San Carlos. Only a few renegade Apaches remained in the Sierra Madre, but they were not enough to present a major threat. Crook's strategy had proven highly effective. His use of pack mules not only ensured that his troops could remain in the field for a longer amount of time but also enabled them to enter the rugged Sierra Madre, where even few Mexicans had dared to venture. More important, his use of Apache scouts had enabled him to find the Apache camps and demoralized the Apaches by having their own people assisting the enemy.

Securing the peace proved to be difficult. Power struggles between the U.S. Army and the Indian agents on the reservations undermined Crook's efforts to maintain positive relations. On May 17, 1885, 42 Apache warriors and 92 women and children under Geronimo, Nachez, Chihuahua, Nana, and Mangas fled San Carlos. Geronimo and his followers escaped directly to Mexico, while Chihuahua and his followers raided southeastern Arizona and southwestern New Mexico for three weeks, eluding 20 cavalry troopers and 100 scouts before crossing into Mexico.

Although Crook responded similarly to the 1883 campaign, concentrating approximately 3,000 soldiers along the border and sending scouting expeditions into Mexico, this time he enjoyed less success. Crook's scouting expeditions attacked Apache camps on June 23, July 28, August 7, and September 22, but the Apaches quickly dispersed with minimal losses. In late September, 20 Apache warriors successfully crossed the border into southeastern Arizona and stole several horses. This was followed in November by a raid in which Chihuahua's brother, Josanie, led a dozen warriors into Arizona and New Mexico in a raid that covered some 1,200 miles. The warriors successfully evaded all army units sent after them, while killing 38 people and capturing 250 head of livestock.

On November 29, Lieutenant General Philip Sheridan, commanding general of the army, arrived at Fort Bowie to confer with Crook and demand more vigorous action. Crook dispatched two columns into Mexico. Crawford commanded two companies composed almost exclusively of White Mountain and Chiricahua scouts led by lieutenants Marion P. Maus and William E. Shipp. Captain Wirt Davis commanded a company of Apache scouts and one cavalry troop. Davis and Crawford moved deep into Mexico, where on January 9, 1886, Crawford succeeded in locating the main Apache camp on the Aros River, approximately 200 miles south of the border. Although the Apaches had fled, Crawford sent an Apache woman as an emissary to the Apache leaders, including Geronimo, who agreed to meet with Crawford at the captured Apache camp on January 11. Before the meeting could take place, however, a force of 150 Mexican militia attacked the camp, thinking that they were attacking Geronimo and his band. Crawford was killed in the unfortunate engagement, and Maus ordered the column to withdraw. Nevertheless, on January 13, Geronimo, Nachez, Chihuahua, and Nana met with Maus and promised to surrender to Crook within two months. Nine Apaches, including Nana and Geronimo's wife, were offered as hostages to demonstrate good faith.

Geronimo and the other Apache leaders met with Crook on March 25 and 27 at Cañon de los Embudos, where they agreed to surrender on the condition that they would not be removed from the Southwest for more than two years. On March 28, however, Geronimo and Nachez, who had obtained mescal from a traveling trader and drank to excess, escaped along with 20 men and 13 women from the escort column that was leading them to Fort Bowie. Meanwhile, Sheridan informed Crook that the agreed-upon terms of surrender were unacceptable.

Once informed of Geronimo's flight, Sheridan demanded a more conventional military strategy of relying on regular troops rather than Apache scouts. On April 1, Crook requested to be relieved of his command. Sheridan happily complied and promptly appointed Brigadier General Nelson A. Miles commander of the Department of Arizona.

After assuming command at Fort Bowie on April 12, 1886, Miles stationed mobile forces along the border and placed heliograph stations on 27 mountains and high points to keep troops informed about enemy movements. When Apache raiding parties crossed the border on April 27, they were vigorously pursued but not captured. On May 5, Miles dispatched Captain Henry W. Lawton into Mexico with an expeditionary force consisting of 35 troopers from the 4th Cavalry, 20 infantrymen from the 8th Regiment, 20 Apache scouts, and 100 pack mules and 30 drivers.

Over the next four months, Lawton pursued the Apaches across northern Mexico, marching some 2,000 miles, but failed to force an engagement. Meanwhile, Miles rounded up the Warm Springs and Chiricahua Apaches from the reservations and removed them by train to Florida. In addition, he sent Gatewood and two Apache scouts to join Lawton in Mexico and attempt to negotiate with Geronimo. When Gatewood met with Geronimo on August 24 and informed him that the Chiricahuas were being shipped to Florida, Geronimo agreed to surrender to Miles personally. On September 4, 1886, Miles accepted Geronimo's

surrender at Skeleton Canyon on the promise that the lives of the Apaches would be spared and that they would be allowed to rejoin their families in Florida. Although President Grover Cleveland had wanted and even ordered that they be turned over to civil officials for trial in Arizona, he eventually, albeit reluctantly, accepted the terms that Miles had negotiated.

Geronimo's surrender brought an end to the Indian Wars in the Southwest but did not bring an end to controversy. Despite Miles's promises, Geronimo and his warriors were initially held at Fort Marion instead of being reunited with their families at Fort Pickens. The Indian Rights Association, which included Crook, successfully pressured the government into reuniting the warriors with their families in 1887. In 1894, the Chiricahuas were transferred to Fort Sill in Indian Territory (Oklahoma). Four years after Geronimo's death at Fort Sill in 1909, 187 Chiricahuas were allowed to join the Mescalero Reservation in New Mexico, but the remainder stayed at Fort Sill.

Justin D. Murphy

Further Reading

Aleshire, Peter. *The Fox and the Whirlwind: General George Crook and Geronimo, A Paired Biography.* New York: Wiley, 2000.

Sweeney, Edwin R. *From Cochise to Geronimo: The Chiricahua Apaches, 1874–1886.* Norman: University of Oklahoma Press, 2010.

Thrapp, Dan L. *The Conquest of Apacheria.* Norman: University of Oklahoma Press, 1967.

Grant's Peace Policy

President Ulysses S. Grant's initiative to establish peace and help Native American tribes assimilate into American society.

Upon Grant's inauguration to the presidency on March 4, 1869, the principal source of trouble between whites and Native Americans was white encroachment on Native American lands. For years, settlers had established homesteads, extracted minerals, grazed cattle, and hunted or habitually passed through tribal lands in violation of numerous treaties signed by the U.S. government and Native American tribes. These encroachments led to a never-ending series of conflicts between Native Americans and white settlers and the U.S. Army.

Native American policy was at a crossroads at the beginning of Grant's first term in office. It was clear that most Americans and U.S. politicians did not care what happened to Native Americans and only wished to use their land as they pleased. Others wished to assimilate Native Americans into American society. Some extremists even favored the extermination of Native Americans.

Grant sought both to safeguard the future of Native Americans and to prevent bloodshed between them and white Americans. He instituted his peace policy in 1869 soon after taking office. Its primary purpose was to assimilate Native Americans into American society by educating them, converting them to Christianity, and training them to become self-sufficient farmers. Grant hoped to prevent conflict by guaranteeing Native Americans land upon which whites would be forbidden. This was certainly not a new concept, but the activities sponsored on the reservations and those who administered them were new.

Tribes that refused to move to a reservation were to be forced to do so by the army. The reservation system set aside federal lands for Native Americans that would be governed by federal officials. The reservations would be run by the Bureau of Indian Affairs (BIA) with assistance by Indian agents from various religious orders, philanthropic organizations, and the army. It was hoped that they would be less susceptible to the graft and corruption that had been endemic to political appointees for many decades. Indeed, one of Grant's first actions was to fire all Indian agents and replace them with individuals from churches and religious organizations and orders. Twelve Christian denominations took part in Grant's plan and administered 73 agencies.

In addition, Grant transferred the BIA from the Department of War to the Department of the Interior, a powerful gesture by which he hoped to de-emphasize armed conflict with Native Americans. One of Grant's most daring moves was to appoint genuine reformers to important positions to implement and enforce the new policy. Jacob D. Cox, a noted advocate of civil service reform, became secretary of the interior, while Grant appointed Ely S. Parker commissioner of Indian affairs. Parker, a member of the Seneca Iroquois tribe, was the epitome of what Grant and the reformers hoped to accomplish with their policy of assimilation. Parker was educated in white church-run schools and went on to become a self-educated engineer as well as a lawyer. Indeed, Parker had been a valued member of Grant's staff during and after the Civil War and became a close friend of the president.

Unfortunately, Grant's peace policy failed for several reasons. The federal government provided inadequate financial support to Indian agencies, forcing many agents to abandon their posts or to turn to graft to supplement their meager salaries and making it almost impossible to provide promised provisions. Land provided for reservations was poor for grazing livestock or cultivating crops and failed to support a tribe's needs. This contradicted the government's goal of turning Native Americans into successful farmers. Additionally, many Native Americans did not wish to assimilate into white society. Although there were some success stories, the well-meaning peace policy can only be viewed as a noble failure. In fact, it proved to be a catalyst for destructive conflicts, including the Great Sioux War on the northern Plains and the Nez Perce War in the northwest. Grant's peace policy virtually disappeared after he left office in 1877.

Rick Dyson

Further Reading

Bender, Norman J. *New Hope for the Indians: The Grant Peace Policy and the Navajos in the 1870s.* Albuquerque: University of New Mexico Press, 1989.

Bolt, Christine. *American Indian Policy and American Reform.* London: Unwin Hyman, 1987.

Prucha, Francis Ford. *American Indian Policy in Crisis: Christian Reformers and the Indian, 1865–1900.* Norman: University of Oklahoma Press, 1976.

Great Sioux War

Start Date: 1876
End Date: 1877

Conflict in Montana, Wyoming, and the Dakotas during 1876–1877 pitting the U.S. Army against Lakota Sioux and their allies. It is also known as the Black Hills War, the Centennial Campaign, or Sitting Bull's War. The most famous engagement of the war was the Battle of the Little Bighorn (June 25–26, 1876), also known as Custer's Last Stand.

Several factors contributed to the Great Sioux War: ongoing white encroachment into the Black Hills region; Lakota and Cheyenne raids against the Crows, who were U.S. allies; and Lakota resistance to railroad and settler expansion in the Dakota Territory and Montana. The most important cause, however, was Lakota resistance to a U.S. government order to move onto their assigned reservations in the Dakota Territory. Led by Oglala chief Crazy Horse and Hunkpapa shaman Sitting Bull, various Lakota bands steadfastly resisted relocation and remained in the Powder River and Yellowstone River country of Wyoming and Montana, where they were joined by hundreds of other Native Americans from reservations.

The army campaign was to begin in early 1876 with three columns moving from the south, the northwest, and the northeast into the Powder River and Yellowstone River country in winter strikes on the Lakota and Cheyenne encampments. This plan miscarried, however, because of the severity of the winter weather. Brigadier General George Crook's Bighorn expedition finally got under way in February, but after the army's success in a fight along the Powder River on March 17, the Lakotas counterattacked Crook's subordinate, and Crook lost the ponies he had captured. He then withdrew to refit his command. Colonel John Gibbon's column did not depart from Fort Ellis in Montana Territory until March 30 and only scouted along the northern bank of the Yellowstone River. Brigadier General Alfred H. Terry did not depart Fort Abraham Lincoln until May 17, so the notion of winter offensives had by then completely fallen through.

By mid-June 1876, the summertime movement of tribes on reservations to their hunting territories was already under way. Bands led by Sitting Bull and Crazy Horse were now augmented by hundreds of young aggressive warriors. Crook resumed his northward movement into Montana Territory from what is today Sheridan, Wyoming. On June 17, 1876, his troops were attacked by a force of more than 1,000 warriors. In a daylong fight along Rosebud Creek, the attackers were repulsed, as Native Americans sustained heavy casualties. Crook was taken aback by the willingness of the Native Americans to fight a stand-up battle and pulled back to reorganize his force. He was unable to directly communicate news of his setback to the other converging columns, which proceeded unawares.

Meanwhile, Gibbon continued to scout the Yellowstone but made no significant contact with hostile tribes. In mid-June, he linked up along the Yellowstone River with Terry's force, which included the 7th U.S. Cavalry Regiment under Lieutenant Colonel George Armstrong Custer. Terry, Gibbon, and Custer together planned a combined assault on a Native American encampment in the Little Bighorn Valley. Custer would move south along the Rosebud with the fast-moving 7th Cavalry and turn west toward the Little Bighorn to prevent the hostile warriors from escaping south. Gibbon would take his slower-moving infantry down the Little Bighorn, trapping Native Americans between them.

On June 25, Custer began his westward swing, becoming aware of a large Native American encampment in the Little Bighorn Valley. In the afternoon, without waiting for Gibbon and Terry, Custer split the 7th Cavalry into three battalions and commenced an attack on the camp, which was the combined encampment of Sitting Bull's and Crazy Horse's warriors reinforced with hundreds of others. Major Marcus Reno's battalion was repulsed and retreated to a hill while under constant attack. Custer's battalion moved north along the river to encircle the village, but this proved impossible because the village was too large. His battalion was surrounded and annihilated in an engagement that lasted a mere 30 minutes. Custer had, however, already summoned Captain Frederick Benteen's battalion forward. Benteen encountered and joined Reno's troops instead of continuing to the north. Their commands were immobilized because of the loss of horses until June 27, when Gibbon's column arrived. By then the Native Americans had scattered, and Reno's, Benteen's, and Gibbon's men had the grim task of burying the 268 soldiers and civilian scouts who had died at the Battle of the Little Bighorn.

Marches and countermarches engaged U.S. soldiers throughout the summer and early autumn. The only bright spot for the army was an engagement on Warbonnet Creek on July 17 in which Colonel Wesley Merritt and his 5th U.S. Cavalry Regiment intercepted several hundred Cheyennes attempting to escape the Red Cloud Agency on the Platte River to join their cousins in the hunting territory.

Troops were rushed to the area from across the West, and by late summer, some 40 percent of the U.S. Army was involved in the campaign, including all the army's top Indian fighting officers. By September, many Native Americans were hungry and tired, having had no time to hunt and being perpetually on the move. On September 9, at Slim Buttes in northwestern South Dakota, Crook managed to destroy a large camp of Miniconjou Lakota under the leadership of American Horse.

Campaigning lasted throughout the autumn and winter of 1876–1877. The army established several semipermanent camps in the heart of unceded Native American hunting grounds, which served as bases from which to harass the still-resistant tribes. Colonel Nelson A. Miles and the 5th U.S. Infantry Regiment attacked several Native American villages, most successfully at Cedar Creek, Montana, on October 21, 1876.

Under Crook's overall command, Colonel Ranald S. Mackenzie and his 4th Cavalry also hit Native American camps, destroying Cheyenne chief Dull Knife's camp during November 25–26. Sitting Bull and his band fled to Canada in January 1877 because of the relentless pressure from Miles, and Crazy Horse surrendered on May 6, 1877, at Camp Robinson, Nebraska, ending the Great Sioux War.

John Thomas Broom

Further Reading

Goodrich, Thomas. *Scalp Dance: Indian Warfare on the High Plains, 1865–1879.* Mechanicsburg, PA: Stackpole, 1997.

Gray, John S. *Centennial Campaign: The Sioux War of 1876.* Norman: Oklahoma University Press, 1988.

Hedren, Paul L., ed. *The Great Sioux War, 1876–77.* Helena: Montana Historical Society Press, 1991.

Greenville, Treaty of (1795)

Major treaty between the United States and tribes of the Old Northwest. The treaty was signed on August 3, 1795, near Waterville, Ohio, after negotiations between Major General Anthony ("Mad Anthony") Wayne, commander of the Legion of the United States, and several regional tribes—the Delawares, Shawnees, Ottawas, Ojibwas, Miamis, Kickapoos, and Pottawatomis. Formally ending Little Turtle's War (1790–1794), the treaty also sought to prevent tensions between Native Americans and whites by setting the boundaries between their lands.

Although many tribes in the Old Northwest had joined a confederacy to resist American settlement, some tribes made separate treaties with the United States, ceding large portions of native land without authority to do so. The resulting change in power and loss of land caused resentment among many tribes, who began attacking white settlers. After Native Americans defeated American military expeditions in 1790 and 1791, Wayne's Legion of the United States soundly defeated the confederated tribes under Shawnee chief Blue Jacket in the Battle of Fallen Timbers (August 20, 1794), just south of present-day Toledo, Ohio. Native Americans then fled to British-held Fort Miami, where they had been promised protection. In November 1794, however, the United States and Great Britain signed Jay's Treaty, which formalized the border between the United States and British-controlled Canada and forced the British to evacuate their posts inside U.S. boundaries.

Abandoned by the British, several tribal leaders met with Wayne to negotiate a new treaty. After eight months of talks, they signed the Treaty of Greenville. In it the tribes ceded most of the Ohio River Valley; part of Indiana; 16 sites on Michigan waterways; Mackinac Island; and land around Forts Niagara, Detroit, and Michilimackinac. They also gave up all land south and east of the boundary beginning at the mouth of the Cuyahoga River and then extending southward to Fort Laurens, westward to Fort Laramie and Fort Recovery, and southward to the Ohio River. The Ojibwas, the Ottawas, and the Pottawatomis also ceded Bois Blanc Island, hoping to demonstrate their goodwill toward the Americans. For their part, the Native Americans received cash payments and a promise of annual payments.

The Treaty of Greenville ultimately failed to prevent future conflict because Americans continued to settle on Indian land. It is significant, however, because it marked the end of British power in the Old Northwest Territory, revealed the strength of the new federal government, and dashed hopes for a Native American confederation to oppose white settlement.

Billie Ford

Further Reading

Hinderaker, Eric. *Elusive Empires: Constructing Colonialism in the Ohio Valley, 1673–1800*. New York: Cambridge University Press, 1997.

Prucha, Francis Paul. *American Indian Treaties: The History of a Political Anomaly*. Berkeley: University of California Press, 1994.

H

Harrison, William Henry

Birth Date: February 9, 1773
Death Date: April 4, 1841

U.S. Army officer, politician, and ninth president of the United States (March–April 1841). William Henry Harrison was born on February 9, 1773, on his family's plantation in Charles City County, Virginia. He studied classics at Hampden-Sydney College and medicine at the University of Pennsylvania.

Harrison joined the 1st U.S. Infantry Regiment as an ensign in August 1791. During the winter of 1791–1792, he led patrols into Native American territory and learned the rudiments of military life. In 1793, he served as an aide to Major General "Mad" Anthony Wayne, commander of the Legion of the United States. Harrison fought with distinction in the Battle of Fallen Timbers (August 20, 1794). The following year, he was a signatory to the Treaty of Greenville.

Harrison remained in the army until June 1798, when he resigned to become secretary of the Northwest Territory. Although appointed by Federalist president John Adams, Harrison's politics aligned more with Democratic-Republican Thomas Jefferson. In 1799, Harrison was elected the Northwest Territory's delegate to Congress.

In 1800, Congress divided the Northwest Territory with one part becoming the state of Ohio in 1803 and the remainder becoming Indiana Territory. As governor of Indiana Territory until December 1812, Harrison negotiated 10 treaties by which Native American tribes ceded millions of acres of land. Shawnee leader Tecumseh refused to recognize their validity and worked to create a confederation of tribes to prevent further white incursions. Harrison and white settlers in the Northwest believed that the British were inciting Native Americans and providing them weapons.

These tensions and the murder of white settlers prompted Harrison, who was also a brigadier general in the militia, in late September 1811 to lead 970 men into Indian country. On November 6, Harrison's force arrived near Prophetstown, where Tenskwatawa (known as the Prophet), the half-brother of Tecumseh, held sway while Tecumseh was in the South recruiting tribes for his confederation. Although he agreed to meet with Harrison the next day, Tenskwatawa, acting against Tecumseh's orders, goaded warriors into attacking Harrison's camp.

Harrison had posted a strong guard and warned his men to be prepared for a night attack, but he neglected to throw up entrenchments or consider that his men might be silhouetted against their own campfires. Nonetheless, when warriors struck early on November 7, Harrison's men rallied and won what became known as the Battle of Tippecanoe. Having lost almost a quarter of his force, Harrison burned Prophetstown and then withdrew. The battle made Harrison a national figure and caused many Native Americans to side with the British in the War of 1812.

At the beginning of the War of 1812, Harrison was appointed a major general of the Kentucky Militia. After helping lift the siege of Fort Wayne in September 1812, Harrison was commissioned a major general in the regular army and replaced Brigadier General James Winchester as commander of the Army of the Northwest. During May 1–9, 1813, he fought a siege and battle at Fort Meigs, near Perrysburg, Ohio. Following Commodore Oliver Hazard Perry's victory in the Battle of Lake Erie (September 10, 1813), Perry ferried Harrison's forces to Detroit, which he recaptured in late September. Harrison then pursued British and Native American forces led by Brigadier General Henry A. Procter and Tecumseh down the Thames River to near Chatham, Ontario, defeating them on October 5 in the Battle of the Thames. Tecumseh was among those killed.

Harrison resigned his commission in May 1814 following disputes with Secretary of War John Armstrong and returned to his Ohio home in North Bend, near Cincinnati. Harrison's strong showing in the War of 1812 established his reputation as a bona fide military hero, which enhanced his subsequent political career. From 1816 to 1819, he served in the U.S. House of Representatives. After serving in the Ohio Senate, Harrison lost elections for the U.S. Senate in 1821 and U.S. House of Representatives in 1822 before winning election to the U.S. Senate in 1825. Harrison served in the Senate until 1828, when President John Quincy Adams appointed him minister to Colombia, a post he held until 1829.

Returning to North Bend in 1829, Harrison became clerk of the Hamilton County Court of Common Pleas in 1834. One of three candidates nominated by the Whig Party for president in 1836, Harrison received the second most votes, losing to Democratic nominee Martin Van Buren. Harrison was again nominated by the Whigs in 1840 with John Tyler as his vice-presidential running mate. Their campaign is often referred to as the first modern campaign and included the slogan "Tippecanoe and Tyler Too." Harrison handily defeated Van Buren. After giving the longest inaugural address in U.S. history (100 minutes), despite a freezing rainstorm, Harrison fell ill and died of pneumonia on April 4, 1841, after serving just one month. Harrison was the first American president to die in office.

William Toth

Further Reading

Horsman, Reginald. "William Henry Harrison: Virginia Gentleman in the Old Northwest." *Indiana Magazine of History* 96 (June 2000): 125–149.

Millett, Allan R. "Caesar and the Conquest of the Northwest Territory: The Harrison Campaign, 1811." *Timeline* 14 (August 1997): 2–19.

Owens, Robert M. *Mr. Jefferson's Hammer: William Henry Harrison and the Origins of American Indian Policy.* Norman: University of Oklahoma Press, 2007.

Horses

Before horses diffused into Native American territory from Spanish settlements, the only beast of burden used by North Americans was the dog, which could pull small loads on a travois (a frame slung between trailing poles). Not surprisingly, horses were first greeted as a larger, stronger kind of dog. Native peoples who acquired horses usually affixed travois to them before learning to ride them. Ultimately horses, having both economic and military applications, radically transformed Native American culture.

Horses may have been introduced to some Native American peoples by Francisco de Vázquez de Coronado's expedition of the early 1540s, but the Native American horse culture probably sprang from the herds that the Spanish kept at Santa Fe following the expedition of Juan de Oñate a half century later. Some horses escaped Spanish herds and bred wild in New Mexico and Texas. Although these fast and agile wild horses averaged less than 1,000 pounds in weight and were smaller than modern-day riding horses, they were later interbred with larger horses acquired by trade with or theft from the Spanish and later Anglo-Americans. The Pawnees especially became among the best and most prolific horse traders on the Plains.

By 1659, Spanish reports indicate that the Apaches were stealing horses (the Apaches and Pueblos also traded for horses). By 1700, the Utes and Comanches had acquired mounts. After that, horses spread among tribes throughout the continent. By 1750, the horse frontier had reached a line stretching roughly from present-day eastern Texas northward through eastern Kansas and Nebraska and then northwest through Wyoming, Montana, Idaho, and Washington. The horse was widely recognized as a unit of barter and wealth. Horses became such an essential part of many Native American cultures that the Apaches, for example, incorporated them into their oral history as gifts of the gods.

After acquiring horses, many native peoples migrated to the Plains because mounts made economic life there, especially the buffalo hunt, easier. Some of these natives were also forced westward by the expansion of European-American settlements. The various Lakota-Nakota-Dakota bands moved westward before widespread white contact. The horse extended the range of native peoples as well as control over their environment. A native group on foot was limited to a few miles' travel a day, while horses allowed camps to move 30 miles or more a day. A small party of warriors on horseback could cover 100 miles of rough country in a day or two.

Native Americans explored different ways of training horses. Unlike Europeans, the Cheyennes, for example, did not usually break their horses. Instead they gentled them. Boys who tended horses stroked them, talked to them, and played with them. An owner of a horse might sing to it or smoke a pipe and blow smoke in its face. At age 18 months, the horse would begin more intense training but was still gentled. Gradually the horse was habituated to carrying a human being and gear. Horses meant for war or hunting were trained specifically in those skills.

The horse shaped Native American life in many ways. One was the productivity of raiding. By the early 19th century, raiding on horseback was the Apaches' major economic activity. The greatest fame that a Crow could earn came by snatching a tethered horse from under the nose of an enemy. The horse turned a subsistence lifestyle on the harsh High Plains of North America into a festival of abundance because tribes could follow the buffalo herds. Horses changed some peoples' housing styles from fixed lodges to mobile tepees. The size of the average tepee increased because a horse could haul a tepee as large as 20 feet in diameter, much larger than a dog or a human being could carry. Some tepees weighed as much as 500 pounds and required three horses to carry. The horse reduced economies of scale in hunting, especially of buffalo, making hunting parties smaller. The increased mobility brought by horses energized trade as well as intertribal conflict because ease of transport brought more contact between diverse peoples, friendly and not. When fighting whites, Native Americans found in the horse a reliable, sturdy mode of transportation that was every bit the equal of white transportation. This along with the introduction of firearms helped even the odds.

Bruce E. Johansen

Further Reading

Denhardt, Robert M. *The Horse of the Americas.* Norman: University of Oklahoma Press, 1975.

Wissler, Clark. "The Influence of the Horse in the Development of Plains Culture." *American Anthropologist* 16 (1914): 1–25.

Horseshoe Bend, Battle of

Event Date: March 27, 1814

Decisive American victory by Major General Andrew Jackson of the Tennessee Militia during the Creek War (July 1813–August 1814). In 1813, a civil war erupted within the Creek Nation in Alabama between the White Sticks (Lower Creeks), who favored accommodation and assimilation with whites, and the Red Sticks (Upper Creeks), who advocated resistance to whites. The United States would be drawn into the conflict because of Red Stick attacks on white settlers. Since the British provided aid to the Red Sticks, the Creek War is also considered part of the War of 1812.

On August 30, 1813, a Red Stick war party led by Peter McQueen and William Weatherford sacked Fort Mims, commanded by Major Daniel Beasley. In autumn 1813, Americans responded with a series of expeditions against the Red Sticks, including a force of 2,500 Tennessee militia led by Jackson and supported by 600 Cherokee and White Stick allies. Jackson's force destroyed Red Stick settlements at Tallushatchee (November 3) and Talladega (November 9) before withdrawing to resupply. In January

1814, Jackson resumed the offensive with 1,000 militiamen and defeated the Red Sticks at Emuckfaw Creek on January 22 and Enitachopco Creek on January 24, sustaining about 100 casualties while inflicting twice that number.

By February 1814, Jackson's force had grown to almost 5,000 men, mostly militia but also including the 600-man 39th U.S. Infantry Regiment as well as several hundred Cherokee and White Stick allies. The Red Sticks, some 1,200 strong, fortified their encampment on a peninsula of about 100 acres formed by the Tallapoosa River and called Horseshoe Bend. They constructed a log breastwork across the neck of the peninsula and collected canoes to escape across the river if necessary.

Jackson arrived at Horseshoe Bend on the morning of March 27, 1814, with some 3,000 men. Sensing the weakness of the Red Stick defensive position, he sent Brigadier General John Coffee of the Tennessee Militia with mounted infantry and allied Native Americans to take position behind the bend to prevent the Red Sticks from escaping. Some of the Cherokees swam across the river and seized the canoes. At about 10:00 a.m., Jackson ordered his two small cannons to shell the fortifications. Coffee then used the captured canoes to get some of his men across the Tallapoosa and assault the Creeks from the rear. Flaming arrows fired by Jackson's Native American allies set much of the Creek settlement on fire. At about 12:30 p.m., Jackson ordered the 39th Infantry to execute a frontal assault with bayonets against the breastworks. Although the Red Sticks fought desperately, they were quickly overwhelmed and driven back. Fighting in small bands, the survivors were soon pinned against the river.

The battle turned into a massacre as many Red Sticks refused to surrender and others were shot while swimming across the river to escape. Jackson, a hardened soldier, described the carnage as "dreadful." Perhaps 800 Red Sticks were killed, and another 350, mostly women and children, were captured. Casualties among the militia and U.S. regulars were 26 killed and 106 wounded, while the Cherokees and White Sticks suffered 23 killed and 47 wounded.

The Battle of Horseshoe Bend brought major combat in the Creek War to an end. Weatherford fled with a few survivors into Spanish territory but soon surrendered. On August 9, 1814, Jackson compelled the Creeks, both friend and foe, to sign the Treaty of Fort Jackson, ceding half of Alabama and part of Georgia to the United States.

Paul David Nelson

Further Reading

Heidler, David S., and Jeanne T. Heidler. *Old Hickory's War: Andrew Jackson and the Quest for Empire.* Mechanicsburg, PA: Stackpole, 1996.

Owsley, Frank L., Jr. *Struggle for the Gulf Borderlands. The Creek War and the Battle of New Orleans, 1812–1815.* Gainesville: University Presses of Florida, 1981.

Howard, Oliver Otis

Birth Date: November 8, 1830
Death Date: October 26, 1909

U.S. Army officer. Oliver Otis Howard was born in Leeds, Maine, on November 8, 1830. Graduating from Bowdoin College in 1850 and the U.S. Military Academy, West Point, in 1854, Howard was a first lieutenant teaching mathematics at West Point when the American Civil War (1861–1865) began. He resigned his regular commission to become colonel of the 3rd Maine Regiment. Leading a brigade during the First Battle of Bull Run (Manassas) on July 21, 1861, Howard helped cover the Union retreat and won promotion to brigadier general of volunteers for his performance. On May 31, 1862, Howard was wounded twice at Seven Pines during the Peninsula Campaign. His right arm was amputated close to the shoulder. For his actions at Seven Pines, he received the Medal of Honor in 1893.

During Howard's convalescence, he became convinced that God had spared his life for the purpose of liberating the slaves. After rejoining his troops, Howard fought with distinction in the Second Battle of Bull Run (Manassas) (August 28–30, 1862) and the Battle of Antietam (September 17, 1862). Promoted to major general of volunteers, Howard led his division in the desperate frontal assault at Fredericksburg on December 13, 1862. At Chancellorsville on May 2, 1863, Howard commanded XI Corps, which virtually disintegrated when Confederate lieutenant general Thomas "Stonewall" Jackson struck his flank. During Confederate general Robert E. Lee's second invasion of the North, on the morning of July 1, 1863, Howard selected Cemetery Ridge as the key defensive position at Gettysburg. After Gettysburg, Howard was shifted to the western theater, where he commanded a corps at Chattanooga and took command of the Army of the Tennessee following the death of Major General James McPherson during the 1864 Atlanta Campaign. Howard then commanded the right wing of Major General William Tecumseh Sherman's army in its march to Savannah and through the Carolinas. At the close of the war, he was appointed brigadier general in the regular army.

Throughout the war, Howard won the admiration of his men for his great personal bravery and attracted attention for his churchgoing and for his puritanical ways.

Howard's straight-laced demeanor led President Andrew Johnson to appoint him head of the Bureau of Refugees, Freedmen, and Abandoned Lands in May 1865. While in this post, Howard championed African Americans in various ways. In 1867, he became the key figure in the establishment of one of the earliest Black institutions of higher education, which was named in his honor (now Howard University); he served as its first president until 1874.

Howard also played an active role in the Indian wars. In 1872, he had taken time off from his post to travel with an aide and three civilian guides (two of whom were Apaches) to the remote camp of the Chiricahua Apaches who had taken up arms against the whites. He entered the camp unarmed and, following 11 days of talks, negotiated a lasting peace settlement with Chiricahua leader Cochise. In 1874, Howard assumed command of the Department of the Columbia, going west to Fort Vancouver. Here he was forced to deal with white settler demands that the Nez Perces under Chief Joseph be removed from the Wallowa Valley. Howard ordered his adjutant, Major Henry Clay Wood, a trained lawyer, to study the 1855 and 1863 treaties. Wood concluded that the Nez Perces had a legal claim to the land in question. Howard himself wrote in a report of 1876 that "I think it is a great mistake to take from Joseph and his band of Nez Perces Indians that valley . . . and possibly Congress can be induced to let these really peaceable Indians have this poor valley for their own." It was not to be.

The Nez Perce War broke out in 1877 after Howard reportedly lost his temper in a meeting with the Nez Perce and, in the words of Yellow Wolf, "showed the rifle."

(In Chief Joseph's famous speech in Washington, D.C., in 1879, he said that if Howard had given him sufficient time to gather his stock there would have been no war.) Although Howard's force outnumbered the Nez Perces some six to one in the Battle of the Clearwater River, the Nez Perces escaped through Lolo Pass and began an epic 1,500-mile flight in an attempt to find refuge in Canada. Howard's forces pursued Joseph's small band but never directly engaged them in battle again, making Howard a target of public criticism. Four months later, Joseph surrendered to Colonel Nelson A. Miles at Bear Paw, Montana.

Howard's last engagement in the Indian Wars took place in 1878 when his forces quickly and easily defeated the Bannock Indians, some of whom had served as scouts for the army in the Nez Perce War. Howard was superintendent of the U.S. Military Academy during 1881–1882 and was promoted to major general in 1886. After various other peacetime assignments, he retired from active duty in 1894. Howard died in Burlington, Vermont, on October 26, 1909.

Malcolm Muir Jr.

Further Reading

Greene, Jerome A. *Nez Perce Summer, 1877: The U. S. Army and the Nee-Me-Poo Crisis.* Helena: Montana Historical Society Press, 2000.

Howard, Oliver O. *My Life and Experiences among Our Hostile Indians: A Record of Personal Observations, Adventures, and Campaigns among the Indians of the Great West.* 1907; reprint, New York: Da Capo, 1972.

McCoy, Robert. *Chief Joseph, Yellow Wolf, and the Creation of Nez Perce History in the Northwest.* New York: Routledge, 2004.

Indian Removal Act (1830)

Congressional legislation signed into law by President Andrew Jackson on May 26, 1830, that provided for the removal of Native American tribes from the East to the West of the Mississippi River, principally Indian Territory (present-day Oklahoma and parts of Kansas). The Indian Removal Act of 1830 was the culmination of a decades-long struggle between whites and Native Americans for control over vast tracts of Native American lands. The Indian Removal Act rendered most prior agreements and treaties between the U.S. government and Native American nations null and void and provided for negotiating new treaties for their removal to Indian Territory. Jackson believed that prior Indian treaties were an "absurdity" and that Native Americans were "subjects" of the United States who could not claim any rights to sovereignty, as a foreign nation could.

The Indian Removal Act was aimed immediately at the so-called Five Civilized Tribes (the Choctaws, Cherokees, Chickasaws, Creeks, and Seminoles), who inhabited lands in the Southeast, including parts of Alabama, Mississippi, Tennessee, the Carolinas, Georgia, and Florida. Many southerners, principally wealthy planters, coveted the lands that these tribes inhabited because they were prime agricultural lands for lucrative, labor-intensive staple crops such as cotton.

During the election campaign of 1828, Jackson and the Democratic Party had made Indian removal a major issue, and Jackson saw the Indian Removal Act as a campaign pledge fulfilled. While Jackson was intent on placing relations with Native Americans within the complete purview of the federal government, some states sought to control Native American tribes themselves. In 1830, for example, Georgia enacted a law that made it illegal for whites to live on Native American lands without explicit authorization and that placed tribal lands under state jurisdiction. This was aimed at white missionaries, who in some cases were helping Native Americans resist removal to the West. When this came before the U.S. Supreme Court in 1832 in *Worcester v. Georgia*, Chief Justice John Marshall ruled that Native American tribes were indeed sovereign nations, meaning that state laws could not apply to them. Jackson derisively scorned the decision and refused to enforce it, as did his successors.

Within a decade of the 1830 Indian Removal Act, treaties providing for the removal of the five tribes had been signed. While nothing in the act suggested forcible removal per se, that in fact occurred in many cases. While some tribes or factions of tribes resisted fiercely, most saw little choice but to acquiesce. Many left their ancestral homelands under the watch of well-armed U.S. Army soldiers.

The first removal treaty was with the Choctaws (chiefly in Mississippi) and saw the movement of some 14,000 Choctaws to the Red River Valley. About 7,000, however, refused to leave and stayed behind. In the ensuing years, they came under increasingly greater white encroachment. In 1838 and 1839, the U.S. Army used force to remove thousands of Cherokees to Indian Territory, precipitating the so-called Trail of Tears during which thousands died of exposure, starvation, and disease. Only a few hundred remained behind, having fled into mountainous areas. There were in fact numerous trails of tears, as most of the affected tribes suffered similar fates. The refusal of the Seminoles to accept forcible removal triggered the Second Seminole War (1835–1842). The Seminoles fought intrepidly and were not ultimately subdued until the end of the Third Seminole War (1855–1858). The Indian Removal Act also affected tribes farther north and west, including the Shawnees, Pottawatomis, Sauks, and Foxes, who were eventually removed to Indian Territory. The Black Hawk War of 1832 was largely a result of attempts to relocate the Sauks and Foxes as well as the Kickapoos.

The Indian Removal Act was certainly not without controversy, and many Americans opposed it for varying reasons. Numerous Christian missionaries living among Native Americans denounced the act because it would result in a forcible process by which lives would likely be lost. Some northerners opposed the legislation because it would expand slavery into newly acquired lands, thereby empowering southern planters.

The Indian Removal Act was bitterly debated in Congress before its passage. In most cases, individual removal treaties involved the cession of Native American land in the East in exchange for land in Indian Territory. The exchange was almost never equal, however, as tribes gave up far more land than they gained. Most treaties also continued earlier annuity payments by the federal government and provided for additional annuities after relocation was complete.

Although a few thousand Native Americans (mainly Cherokees, Choctaws, and Seminoles) remained on part of their ancestral homelands in the East, it is estimated that as many as 100,000 Native Americans, as well as a few thousand African slaves, were relocated to Indian Territory. This mass relocation caused untold suffering. As many as one-third of those forcibly removed died from disease, starvation, dehydration, or exposure along the Trail of Tears or shortly after arriving in Indian Territory. Those who survived established their own communities and began farming with considerable success. However, by the end of the 19th century, many were once more under pressure to cede land to whites in Indian Territory, where oil attracted white speculators in droves.

Paul G. Pierpaoli Jr.

Further Reading

Cave, Alfred A. "Abuse of Power: Andrew Jackson and the Indian Removal Act of 1830." *Historian* 65 (Winter 2003): 1130–1153.

Prucha, F. P. "Andrew Jackson's Indian Policy: A Reassessment." *The Journal of American History* 56, no. 3 (December 1969): 527–539.

Satz, Ronald N. *American Indian Policy in the Jacksonian Era.* Lincoln: University of Nebraska Press, 1975.

Iroquois

At the time of European contact, the Iroquois Confederacy consisted of five tribes—the Mohawks, Oneidas, Onondagas, Cayugas, and Senecas—located in what is now upstate and western New York. A sixth nation, the Tuscaroras, joined the confederacy in the 1720s. By virtue of their numbers, geographic location, and military prowess, the Iroquois served as a potent counterweight to English and French imperial ambitions for most of the colonial period.

Organized into clans headed by a matriarch, the Iroquois lived in large villages, usually on easily defensible hilltops. According to the founding myth of the Iroquois Confederacy, the five tribes warred against one another until a supernatural being, Deganawida, and his human helper, Hiawatha, traveled among them, preaching a message of peace and unity. The founding of the confederacy created something of a paradox, however. While the Iroquois now lived in peace with one another, they increasingly engaged other native peoples in warfare to strengthen their power and to secure captives to replace their dead.

Samuel de Champlain encountered the Iroquois on July 30, 1609, when he joined his native allies in an expedition against the Mohawks, during which Champlain personally killed three warriors. Some historians have pointed to this small battle as the genesis of the century and a half of enmity between the Iroquois and the French.

For the rest of the 17th century, the Iroquois remained in conflicts with the French and their native allies that were occasionally punctuated by brief truces. To maintain access to metal, cloth, firearms, and other goods from European trading partners, the Iroquois fought other native people. The Mohawks forced the Mahicans to leave the vicinity of New Netherland's Fort Orange (now Albany, New York) after a bloody four-year conflict in the 1620s.

Unlike the Hurons, the Iroquois did not have direct access to the western Great Lakes and the regions south of Hudson Bay, where the best furs were to be found. Beginning in the 1630s and escalating in the 1640s, the Iroquois launched attacks on Huron fur-trading parties, taking furs and captives. The rerouting of furs to Dutch traders at Fort Orange and away from the French in Montreal threatened New France's economic survival.

The French and the Iroquois remained in conflict with one another for much of the 17th century. The Beaver Wars (1641–1701) benefited each economically. The Iroquois served as a barrier that separated northern Native Americans from the Dutch at Fort Orange and their high-quality and reasonably priced trade goods. Northern natives, who had access to higher-quality pelts, were forced to trade with the French in order to obtain European goods. Thus, the Dutch could not obtain better-quality furs except for those that the Iroquois pillaged from other native peoples.

In the late 1640s, the Iroquois, needing captives to replace their dead and wanting to supplant the Hurons' middleman position in the fur trade, launched a series of attacks that destroyed two major Huron towns and prompted the Hurons to abandon their country, with the majority of them becoming refugees throughout the Ohio Country and the western Great Lakes region. The assaults against the Hurons, however, were only partially successful. While the Iroquois gained an impressive number of captives—French Jesuits claimed that there were more non-Iroquois adoptees than natives among the Iroquois—they did not gain control of the fur trade. Instead, the focus of the trade shifted farther west, and peoples such as the Ottawas replaced the Hurons as middlemen. With the founding of the English Hudson's Bay Company in the 1660s, both the Iroquois and the French lost access to many of the high-quality furs of the north.

From the 1640s to the end of the 17th century, the Iroquois routinely attacked other native peoples in the Ohio Country and the Great Lakes region. In the early 17th century, the Iroquois could easily obtain firearms from the Dutch, the English, or the Swedes. After the 1660s, other native peoples were at least equally well armed, and the Iroquois suffered horrible losses as a result.

Beginning in the 1660s, a series of events forced the Iroquois to reevaluate their position. In 1664, the English seized New Netherland without firing a shot. The English promised that they, like the Dutch, would be faithful trade partners and allies. But when a French expedition devastated Seneca villages in the late 1680s, the English provided no help. Iroquois warriors continued to die in large numbers as the Beaver Wars continued. Consequently, the Iroquois established the so-called Grand Settlement of 1701, negotiating a treaty with the French by which the Iroquois promised to remain neutral in any future conflict between France and England. In a separate treaty with New York, the Iroquois promised to lend the English military assistance if the English secured the Iroquois hunting grounds in Ontario. The Iroquois, of course, realized that it was impossible for the English to fulfill this condition, which in effect allowed the Iroquois to remain neutral throughout the first half of the 18th century as they played the English and the French against one another, threatening to join one side or the other and receiving gifts intended to keep them neutral or encourage them to join in a war (which they never did).

The 1701 treaties did not diminish Iroquois influence, particularly among the English. Having dealt almost exclusively with New York, the Iroquois soon formed an alliance with Pennsylvania, evicting the Delawares (Lenni Lenapes) on the colony's behalf after the fraudulent Walking

Purchase of 1737. But the Iroquois did not always enjoy good relations with the English. Indeed, in the 1720s the Iroquois tried to persuade the Delawares and the Shawnees to join them in a war against the English, but both tribes refused.

The Iroquois became more useful to the English as time went on. The Iroquois Confederacy claimed that it owned the lands comprising the Ohio Country, and the British government, arguing that the Iroquois were their subjects, used this claim to assert its legal title to the region. The French, however, also claimed the area. Iroquois diplomats oversaw some of the Delaware and Shawnee towns in the area, and their presence caused resentment among these tribes. Offered a chance to join the French and the possibility of regaining their lands, many of the tribes went to war against the British.

For the most part, the Iroquois sat on the sidelines and watched as British forces performed poorly in the early phases of the French and Indian War (1754–1763). Despite being given wagonloads of gifts at the 1754 Albany Congress, most Iroquois, with notable exceptions such as the Mohawk sachem Hendrick, chose to remain neutral. In the later phases of the war as the British began to win some significant victories, the Iroquois recognized that a British victory could result in the eviction of the French from the continent and entered the conflict on the side of the British to be on the winning side.

After the French and Indian War, Iroquois relations with the British remained unsettled. The Senecas sent a war belt to the western tribes in an attempt to raise a rebellion against the British, but none accepted. In the 1768 Treaty of Fort Stanwix, the Iroquois ceded most of present-day Kentucky and Tennessee to the British, which led to conflicts when colonists entered the region and came into conflict with Cherokees, Shawnees, and other peoples who lived there.

With the beginning of the American Revolutionary War (1775–1783), most of the Iroquois initially opted to remain neutral. British partisans such as Joseph Brant (Thayendanega) of the Mohawks and Guy Johnson, Sir William Johnson's successor as British agent to the northern tribes, were able to make a compelling case that an American victory would be against the best interests of the Iroquois Confederacy. The Oneidas and some Onondagas, however, chose to side with the Americans, rupturing the Iroquois Confederacy. After the war ended in 1783, Brant and a sizable group of Iroquois left New York to settle in Canada, where the Crown granted them a large tract of land along the Grand River. Other bands stayed in the United States, but the cohesion of the original Iroquois Confederacy had been diluted by conflicting wartime allegiances.

The Iroquois had a highly sophisticated form of government, which among other things provided for a system of checks and balances to ensure that no individual or small group would come to dominate the political structure. Scholars have pointed out that the Iroquois' plan for political union informed the design of the U.S. Articles of Confederation. Today perhaps 40,000–45,000 people of Iroquois ancestry reside in Canada. Tribal registrations in the United States in the mid-1990s claimed about 32,000 Iroquois. Many others have claimed Iroquois ancestry, and in the 2000 census, 80,822 people claimed Iroquois ancestry.

Roger M. Carpenter

Further Reading

Jennings, Francis. *The Ambiguous Iroquois Empire: The Covenant Chain Confederation of Indian Tribes with English Colonies from Its Beginnings to the Lancaster Treaty of 1744*. New York: Norton, 1984.

Richter, Daniel K. *The Ordeal of the Longhouse: The People of the Iroquois League in the Era of European Colonization*. Chapel Hill: University of North Carolina Press, 1992.

Richter, Daniel K., and James H. Merrell, eds. *Beyond the Covenant Chain: The Iroquois and Their Neighbors in Indian North America, 1600–1800*. Syracuse, NY: Syracuse University Press, 1987.

J

Jackson, Andrew

Birth Date: March 15, 1767
Death Date: June 8, 1845

U.S. general and president (1829–1837). Born the posthumous son of a poor Scotch Irish immigrant father in the Waxhaws Settlement on the South Carolina frontier on March 15, 1767, Andrew Jackson received little formal education. During the American Revolutionary War (1775–1783), he fought in guerrilla operations against the British in the Carolinas in 1780–1781 and was captured in 1781. A British officer slashed Jackson's face with a saber, allegedly because Jackson refused to polish the officer's boots. Jackson contracted smallpox while a prisoner, and his mother and both older brothers died during the war. These events no doubt influenced Jackson's subsequent hatred for the British.

Following the war, Jackson first read and then practiced law in North Carolina before moving to Tennessee, where he became territorial prosecuting attorney in 1788. Although his poor investments almost led to bankruptcy, Jackson was a delegate in the state constitutional convention of 1796 and was Tennessee's first representative in the U.S. House of Representatives in 1796–1797. Appointed U.S. senator in 1797, Jackson resigned the next year because of financial problems. He then served as a superior court judge from 1798 to 1804 but again resigned because of financial difficulties.

Jackson found his calling when he was elected major general of the Tennessee Militia in 1802. He and his men entered federal service at the beginning of the war with Britain in June 1812. Jackson led his men to Natchez, Mississippi, in preparation for an invasion of Florida, which was canceled by Congress. He then marched his men back to Tennessee, earning the nickname "Old Hickory" for his toughness.

When a civil war between nativist and accommodationist factions split the Creek Confederacy in Alabama and Georgia during the War of 1812, Americans assumed that the nativist Red Sticks had allied with the British. Although not technically true, British traders in Spanish Florida had provided the Red Sticks with arms and ammunition. When the Red Sticks began attacking white settlers, Jackson was ordered to suppress the Red Sticks. A strict disciplinarian, he drilled his Tennessee militiamen thoroughly, believing that militia, if well trained and adequately supplied, could prove an effective fighting force. After carefully stockpiling supplies, Jackson began a campaign against the Red Sticks that November when their own food supplies were low. Part of his force, under Brigadier General John Coffee, defeated the Creeks at Tallasahatchee, Alabama, on November 3, while Jackson won a lesser victory at Talladega on November 9. After reorganizing his forces, Jackson invaded the Creek heartland in March 1814, defeating the main Red Stick force in the Battle of Horseshoe Bend on March 27.

Appointed major general in the regular army in May 1814, Jackson assumed command of the 7th Military District. After defending Mobile, Alabama, against a

British naval attack on September 15, 1814, Jackson marched into Florida without official authorization, taking Pensacola on November 7 and destroying its fortifications. He then hastened to New Orleans in December to defend the city against an expected British attack. Jackson hastily assembled a force of regulars, militia, and volunteers that repulsed British lieutenant general Sir Edward Pakenham's assault on January 8, 1815, making Jackson a national hero.

Following the War of 1812, Jackson assumed command of the Southern Division at New Orleans. Ordered to put an end to Native attacks during the First Seminole War (1817–1818), he invaded Florida. Taking advantage of the vagueness of his orders, Jackson not only seized Pensacola on May 24, 1818, but also created an international incident that April by hanging two British subjects for allegedly supplying the Seminoles with arms. The James Monroe administration used Jackson's actions to induce Spain to sell Florida to the United States in 1819.

While Jackson began his military career as a rank amateur, he proved to be a military genius. A strict disciplinarian and a careful planner, he understood the need for thorough training before committing his men to battle, yet he could act quickly in an emergency, as he had done at New Orleans.

Resigning his commission in June 1821, Jackson served briefly as military governor of Florida during March–October 1821 before returning to his plantation home, the Hermitage, near Nashville. Elected to the U.S. Senate from Tennessee in 1823, he resigned after one session to run for president in the election of 1824. Although Jackson won a plurality of the popular vote and electoral votes, he lost the election in the House of Representatives to John Quincy Adams. Jackson denounced Adams's deal with Henry Clay that secured the former's election and Clay's appointment as secretary of state as a "corrupt bargain." Jackson's supporters responded by working to expand voting rights by eliminating property requirements. Their efforts led to his election to the presidency by wide margins in 1828 and 1832.

As president, Jackson maintained U.S. neutrality but encouraged his friend Sam Houston in the Texas Revolution (1835–1836), also known as the Texas War of Independence. In 1830, he secured congressional approval for the Indian Removal Act that forced most Native Americans to move west of the Mississippi River to Indian Territory. Jackson insisted that removal was a humanitarian gesture to prevent Native Americans from being engulfed and exterminated by the growing white population, but thousands died during the moves. Removal also led to both the Black Hawk War (1832) in Illinois and the Second Seminole War (1835–1842) in Florida. Among other events during his presidency were the Nullification Crisis in South Carolina and the elimination of the Second Bank of the United States.

After his second term ended in 1837, Jackson returned to Nashville. He died at the Hermitage on June 8, 1845.

Spencer C. Tucker

Further Reading

Remini, Robert Vincenti. *Andrew Jackson and the Course of American Democracy: 1833–1845.* New York: HarperCollins, 1984.

Remini, Robert Vincenti. *Andrew Jackson and the Course of American Empire, 1767–1821.* New York: Harper and Row, 1977.

Remini, Robert Vincenti. *Andrew Jackson and the Course of American Freedom,*

1822–1832. New York: Harper and Row, 1981.

Remini, Robert Vincenti. *Andrew Jackson and His Indian Wars*. New York: Penguin, 2001.

Joseph, Chief

Birth Date: 1840
Death Date: September 12, 1904

Nez Perce chief, Wallowa headman, and leader during the Nez Perce War (1877). Chief Joseph, also known as Young Joseph or Hin-mah-too-yah-lat-kekt, was born in Oregon's Wallowa Valley in 1840, the son of Christianized Nez Perce chief Old Joseph. As a child, he was baptized and renamed Young Joseph. He spent a short time at the Spalding Mission School. Young Joseph developed diplomatic and leadership skills by accompanying his father to councils and other negotiations. Old Joseph, however, refused to sign an 1863 treaty with the United States, renounced Christianity, and influenced his son to reject any white attempts to purchase Nez Perce land. When Old Joseph died in 1871, Young Joseph became chief of the Wallowa Band.

Growing friction between settlers and the Nez Perces prompted U.S. Army brigadier general Oliver Otis Howard to meet with headmen in July 1876. Chief Joseph and his brother Ollokot represented the nontreaty Nez Perces and presented testimony regarding settlers' crimes against their people. Chief Joseph was not satisfied with Howard's response, which virtually ignored the charges brought by Joseph. In January 1877, Howard gave Joseph an ultimatum: the Wallowas were to leave for a reservation in Idaho by April 1 or face forcible removal. Joseph's refusal prompted Howard to send two companies of the 1st Cavalry from Fort Walla Walla (Washington) to the mouth of the Wallowa Valley.

Seeking to avert war, in early May Joseph met Howard at Fort Lapwai and finally agreed to move his people to the reservation. On June 14, 1877, however, three Nez Perce warriors killed four settlers. Fearing retribution, Joseph then led his tribe on a three-month trek through Oregon, Idaho, Wyoming, and Montana that ultimately covered more than 1,500 miles in an effort to reach Canada.

On June 17, troops of the 1st Cavalry caught up with Joseph's small band in White Bird Canyon, but were defeated by Joseph, Ollokot, and about 60 warriors. Leading about 800 people, Joseph evaded or engaged U.S. Army detachments throughout June and July. He earned a reputation as a civilized fighter, allowing noncombatants to escape and refusing to scalp or mutilate dead soldiers. On August 7 at Big Hole, Montana, Colonel John Gibbon, with the 7th Infantry and the 2nd Cavalry, attacked the Nez Perces. The tactical draw at Big Hole was followed by fierce fighting with Howard at Canyon Creek. Colonel Nelson A. Miles's command joined the pursuit, chasing Joseph to the Bear Paw Mountains in Montana, where he was forced to surrender with about 400 of his followers on October 5 less than 40 miles south of Canada. Some 300 Nez Perces managed to escape into Canada. Chief Joseph told Miles on his surrender that "from where the sun now stands I will fight no more forever."

The government dispersed the Nez Perces, and Joseph was eventually sent to the Colville Reservation in Washington. He remained a staunch advocate for his people for the rest of his life, always seeking to return to Wallowa, where his father was buried. Chief Joseph died on September 12, 1904, in Colville, Washington.

Dawn Ottevaere Nickeson

Further Reading

Greene, Jerome A. *Nez Perce Summer, 1877: The U. S. Army and the Nee-Me-Poo Crisis*. Helena: Montana Historical Society Press, 2000.

McCoy, Robert. *Chief Joseph, Yellow Wolf, and the Creation of Nez Perce History in the Northwest*. New York: Routledge, 2004.

Moulton, Candy. *Chief Joseph: Guardian of the People*. New York: Tom Doherty, 2005.

K

King George's War

Start Date: January 25, 1744
End Date: October 1748

One in a series of imperial wars of the 18th century involving Great Britain and France that spilled over from Europe to North America. In December 1740, taking advantage of the accession of Austrian archduchess Maria Theresa to the Austrian throne, King Frederick II of Prussia invaded and seized the rich Austrian province of Silesia. Major European powers entered the conflict, which became known as the War of the Austrian Succession (1740–1748). France sided with Prussia, whereas Britain supported Austria. This situation was complicated by the Anglo-Spanish War (1739–1744), popularly known as the War of Jenkins' Ear, which spread to North America and led to clashes involving Spanish and British forces along the North Carolina, Georgia, and Florida coasts. As a consequence of the Second Family Compact between France and Spain (October 23, 1743), France declared war on Britain on March 4, 1744, and King George II issued a counter declaration of war on March 29.

News of the declarations of war reached North America by the end of April. Perhaps wishing to steal a march on the British, the French began hostilities in North America, although neither side prosecuted the fighting there with great vigor. In May, the French launched an attack from their great Cape Breton Island fortress of Louisbourg against Canso (Canseau), a small English fishing settlement in extreme northeastern Nova Scotia. Although the French took Canso without difficulty on May 13, the attack fully alarmed New England.

A few weeks after the French took Canso, a French-allied Native American force appeared before Annapolis Royal (formerly Port Royal), Nova Scotia. The natives showed little inclination to attack a fortified position, even one defended by only about 100 men, and they soon withdrew on the arrival of 70 Massachusetts reinforcements. In August, native warriors returned, this time with some French troops, but Massachusetts reinforcements again caused the attackers to depart.

Meanwhile, Massachusetts Governor William Shirley prepared an expedition against Louisbourg for several reasons. Eliminating this important French base would, it was hoped, end French support for Native American attacks along the northern frontier. Louisbourg was also the chief base for French fishing vessels, which were in direct competition with those of New England for the rich fishing grounds of the Grand Banks. In addition, Louisbourg served as the principal wartime base for French privateers preying on New England merchant vessels as well as attacks on the British colonists' fishing boats. Exchanged British prisoners convinced Shirley that Louisbourg was undermanned and vulnerable to attack.

Other New England colonies sent men for the expeditionary force, although it was largely composed of citizens of Massachusetts. William Pepperell Jr. commanded the land force, which was supported by a

British Royal Navy squadron. The force of some 100 ships of all sorts carrying 3,500 men arrived near Louisbourg at the end of April and captured the fortress on June 17. Although the Royal Navy had made possible the capture of Louisbourg through its effective blockade, Pepperell and the colonials justly received the credit for the victory, heralded as a remarkable achievement for a militia force and indeed certainly the greatest accomplishment of colonial arms before the American Revolutionary War (1775–1783). Many colonials falsely took this to mean that militia forces were superior to regular forces. A colonial force remained in garrison at Louisbourg, but dysentery, smallpox, and yellow fever claimed a high toll.

Governor Shirley meanwhile urged an immediate assault on Quebec in order to seize all of Canada. London approved the plan and ordered other colonial governors to cooperate. The British government promised to pay for the troops raised and pledged to contribute a fleet and regular forces to meet the colonial force in Louisbourg. All the New England colonies plus New York, Maryland, and Virginia supplied troops. Mohawk warriors agreed to join as well. The colonial militia was in place by July 1746. Unfortunately for the colonists, the promised British troops and ships were never sent because European considerations led to their diversion there. The assault on Canada was called off, and the colonial troops dispersed.

The French were not able to take advantage of London's quiescence. Recognizing the importance of Louisbourg to New France, in 1746 the French mounted a considerable effort under Admiral Jean-Baptiste-Louis-Frédéric de la Rouchfoucauld de Roye, Duc d'Anville. The assembled force included 76 ships lifting 3,000 men with the goal of retaking Louisbourg and Annapolis Royal. The ships had a difficult three-month passage to America during which they were buffeted by hurricanes, and the men in the crowded ships fell prey to an outbreak of smallpox. On the fleet's arrival in American waters in September, d'Anville died of apoplexy. His successor attempted suicide and was in turn succeeded by the Marquis de la Jonquière, governor designate of New France. Before the fleet limped back to France, the infected troops inadvertently spread smallpox ashore among Native Americans. The disease would exact a higher human toll on France's allies than the latter sustained in fighting during the entire war.

New Englanders had hoped that the capture of Louisbourg would bring an end to native attacks along the northern frontier, but attacks in Maine, New Hampshire, and Massachusetts actually increased. Early in 1744, the Massachusetts General Court ordered construction of four new posts along the Connecticut River. These became Fort Shirley, Fort Pelham, Fort Massachusetts, and Fort at Number Four. Massachusetts also sent 440 militiamen to guard the northwestern frontier. These efforts came none too soon, for in July 1745 natives attacked the Great Meadow Fort in present-day Putney, Vermont, and St. George's Fort in present-day Thomaston, Maine.

In this activity, the Six Nations of the Iroquois Confederacy occupied an important position because of their geographical location and influence. Ever since King William's War (1689–1697), the Iroquois had generally pursued a policy of neutrality. During King George's War, however, the Iroquois position tilted somewhat toward the French because they did not trust the British and feared that they would be left in the lurch.

The French launched numerous raids against British settlements in upper New York and New England from the French-built Fort St. Frédéric at Crown Point near the south end of Lake Champlain. In November 1745, Lieutenant Paul Marin led a sizable party from Fort St. Frédéric consisting of some 520 Frenchmen, Iroquois, Nipissings, Wyandots (Hurons), and Abenakis and even a priest against the English agricultural community of Saratoga, New York. Located on the west bank of the Hudson River some 30 miles above Albany, Saratoga boasted a fort, but it was poorly maintained and lacked a regular garrison. Marin's raiders struck at night and achieved total surprise, setting fire to the fort, homes, farms, and mills. The raiders then withdrew, taking with them 109 prisoners and significant stocks of supplies. They arrived back at Crown Point on November 22. The Saratoga raid had a devastating effect on the morale in the British settlements of the upper Hudson River Valley. Most settlers simply abandoned their homes and fled south. There were even fears that Albany might be attacked next.

During spring 1746, natives attacked British settlements between the Kennebec and Penobscot rivers in Maine. During April–June 1746, natives struck at Fort at Number Four on the Connecticut River, located in present-day Charlestown, New Hampshire, four different times but were driven back. Attacks also occurred all along the New York frontier. In August, a strong 700-man French and native raid struck Fort Massachusetts on the upper Hoosick River only 25 miles east of Albany. There were only 29 people at the post, of whom 21 were men, but they held out until their ammunition supply ran low. The attackers took them all prisoner and then burned the fort. Colonial governments found it impossible to protect the thinly spread frontier population against such attacks. Settlers who chose to remain risked being killed in their fields, taken prisoner, or having their possessions seized or destroyed.

The situation for the British in Nova Scotia seemed particularly precarious. French forces were located nearby at Beaubassin on Chignecto Bay. The Acadian population of Nova Scotia sought to maintain a neutral stance. At Grand Pré, English colonel Arthur Noble commanded a 500-man garrison. In early January 1747, Antoine Coulon de Villiers led a force of 200 Canadians from Beaubassin through heavy snow with snowshoes and sledges. Gathering native and Acadian recruits as they proceeded, the French and native force arrived at Grand Pré at the end of the month in the midst of a snowstorm, catching the British unawares. Noble and several other officers were killed in the initial assault. After a fight lasting several hours and leaving 80 British dead and 80 wounded, the French allowed the remaining British soldiers to withdraw to Annapolis Royal. The French did not control northern Nova Scotia for long, as they soon departed, and a strong Massachusetts force reoccupied Grand Pré.

In April 1747, Ensign Boucher de Niverville led a French force of perhaps 700 men against British forts along the Connecticut River. They attacked Fort at Number Four, but after a three-day siege withdrew. At London's request, in spring 1747 British colonial leaders gathered a large force of more than 3,000 militiamen and Iroquois at Albany. With pay late in arriving from England and unrest growing among various colonial factions, the troops were dismissed in July 1747.

In late June 1747, the French attacked Saratoga with a mixed force of 500–600 men. The British suffered 15 casualties and

49 men captured before English reinforcements arrived from Albany. Deciding that the fort at Saratoga was too costly to maintain and too vulnerable to attack, New Yorkers burned the fort and abandoned the site.

Fighting along the frontier continued into 1748 with attacks by the British near Crown Point and Fort at Number Four. The French struck twice near Fort Dummer and another time near Schenectady, New York. British efforts to mollify their Native American allies continued as colonial leaders held a third Iroquois Congress at Albany in July 1748. Although the Iroquois declared themselves ready to fight, they expressed disappointment with the failure to attack Quebec in 1747. Meanwhile, relations between other Native American tribes and British colonists grew even more strained.

Both sides engaged in considerable privateering activity during the war. This consisted mostly of seizures of merchant vessels and occasional hit-and-run attacks on coastal settlements. A Rhode Island privateer attacked and sacked a Spanish town in northern Cuba, and the Spanish raided coastal settlements in South Carolina and Georgia. In 1747, the Spanish even raided Beaufort, near Cape Lookout in North Carolina. The next year, the Spanish attacked and held for a time the town of Brunswick, on the lower Cape Fear River. In 1747, French and Spanish privateers were active farther north, even penetrating some 60 miles up the Delaware River.

By 1747, the Royal Navy had reduced the French and Spanish fleets in European waters. This boded ill for the French and Spanish in America, because reinforcements of men and supplies could not get through to offset the British colonies' far larger population advantage. Indeed, shortages of goods forced the French into illicit trade with British colonists. This also impacted relations with Native Americans who increasingly turned to the better-supplied British colonists to procure needed goods. Scarcity of trade goods contributed to the revolt of the Miami tribe against the French in the Ohio Country in 1747 and strengthen the pro-British faction among the Choctaws.

The war ended with the October 1748 Treaty of Aix-la-Chapelle. The key provision for America was the restoration of colonial conquests. Revealing the disadvantage of being part of a worldwide empire, New England colonists were incensed that Britain had returned Louisbourg to France for the return of Madras in India, which the French had captured from the British. Colonists held as insufficient Parliament's reimbursement to New England of £235,000, most of which went to Massachusetts, and a knighthood for Pepperell. Some 500 British colonists died in the actual fighting, while more than 1,100 others died from disease and exposure. About 350 Frenchmen died in the fighting and at least 2,500 died from disease. Native American casualties are unknown. Although the war left both the French and British empires in North America intact, peace proved illusory as the final showdown for control of North America would erupt in 1754.

Marcia Schmidt Blaine and
Spencer C. Tucker

Further Reading

Leach, Douglas Edward. *Roots of Conflict: British Armed Forces and Colonial Americans, 1677–1763.* Chapel Hill: University of North Carolina Press, 1986.

Peckham, Howard Henry. *The Colonial Wars, 1689–1762.* Chicago: University of Chicago Press, 1964.

King Philip's War

Start Date: June 20, 1675
End Date: October 1676

Last and deadliest general war between Native Americans and English colonists in southern New England. King Philip's War was named for the Wampanoag sachem Metacom, known to the colonists as King Philip. Tensions had been building for years over issues such as land rights and the subjugation of natives to colonial law. While colonists grew in numbers and seized more and more land, natives, devastated by European diseases, diminished in number with each passing year. By 1660, colonists in Massachusetts Bay, Connecticut, Plymouth, and Rhode Island greatly outnumbered the native tribes remaining in the area.

In 1662, Metacom, the son of influential chief Massasoit, took control of the Wampanoag people on his brother Alexander's death. Metacom was not nearly as patient with the colonists as his father had been. Taken into court several times for breaking colonial law, Metacom resented colonial authorities.

For several years, it had been rumored that Metacom was plotting with nearby tribes to attack colonists. In January 1675, Metacom's former translator, John Sassamon, who had become an informant for colonial authorities in Plymouth, was found murdered shortly after warning Plymouth officials of Metacom's plans. In early June, Plymouth authorities accused, tried, and executed three Wampanoag warriors for the crime. In revenge, on June 20, 1675, Wampanoags attacked the town of Swansea in southwestern Plymouth Colony. The conflict spread rapidly thereafter, becoming known to history as King Philip's War.

A number of tribes—specifically the Pocassets, Sakonnets, and Nipmucks—joined Metacom and the Wampanoags. Other tribes, such as the powerful Narragansetts, remained neutral, while still other tribes, especially many Christian groups, sided with the colonists. Traditional enmities between tribes trumped the natives' common complaints against the English.

In June 1675, militia forces of the United Colonies tried to blockade Metacom and his followers on Rhode Island's Mount Hope peninsula. After Metacom and his followers escaped via boats into nearby swamps, colonial forces pursued them throughout July but were compelled to pull back when their ill-equipped and undertrained militiamen lost a number of skirmishes in the swamps. Where natives were accustomed to traversing the swampy landscape of southern Rhode Island, the thick brush and marshy ground slowed the English and frustrated their efforts to bring the enemy into open battle. Indeed, colonists found themselves the victims of frequent ambushes and traps. In late July, Metacom and his main force headed north to Nipmuck country, where on July 14 the Nipmucks had attacked Mendon.

Fighting then shifted to the Connecticut River Valley, where Metacom's forces attacked colonial towns across the length and width of the valley. The United Colonies sent troops west to protect the towns, deciding on a strategy that called for defending all the towns. Major John Pynchon, the founder and majority landholder of Springfield, had charge of the western theater of operations.

Natives besieged Brookfield in August and quickly devastated Northfield and Deerfield. Colonial militiamen did little better in the woods of western Massachusetts than they had in the swamps of Rhode Island. Natives ambushed Captain Richard Beers's 40-man company in September 1675. In one of the most infamous incidents of the war, Captain Thomas Lathrop and his company of 70 men from Essex County were ambushed on September 19 while securing a wagon train of food from abandoned Deerfield. Lathrop's men, many of whom had placed their muskets in carts in order to eat wild grapes along their route, were surprised by hundreds of warriors and ambushed alongside the banks of the Muddy Brook, since known as Bloody Brook. At least 60 colonists, including Lathrop, were slain.

The worst blow to the colonial cause came in October, when native forces attacked and destroyed much of Springfield, the main settlement and military command center for the entire valley. Pynchon subsequently resigned his post as western commander to help in rebuilding Springfield, and Captain (later Major) Samuel Appleton took over. Appleton and his men soon shifted their attention away from the western theater.

In November 1675, the commissioners of the United Colonies, believing that the neutral Narragansett tribe was in fact aiding Metacom, decided on a preemptive strike against them. Massachusetts Bay, Plymouth, and Connecticut put an army of more than 1,000 men in the field against the Narragansetts, with Governor Josiah Winslow of Plymouth in overall command. Charged with making the Narragansetts adhere to their treaty obligations, Winslow decided to advance against the Great Swamp Fortress, the main Narragansett stronghold. The wintry conditions, although harsh, allowed the English to march over the now-frozen swamps, and the now-thin brush allowed them to see farther in the thick forests. In place by mid-December 1675, the army based itself at Wickford, Rhode Island, and fought a number of small skirmishes before attacking the Great Swamp Fortress.

With the help of a native traitor, the colonial army found and attacked the Narragansett fort on December 19, 1675. The fighting was at first indeterminate. However, Winslow's order to burn the village with hundreds of people still inside shelters turned the tide of the battle. Initial casualties were about 20 dead and 200 wounded on the colonial side. Estimates of native dead, largely from the fires, range from 600 to more than 1,000. Having destroyed the fort, the colonial force then limped back to Wickford during a horrible winter storm in which many of the wounded died. The remainder of the colonial force, along with some fresh troops, tried to pursue the escaping Narragansetts in the infamous Hungry March during January and February 1676. Although many considered the Great Swamp Fight a decisive English victory, a large number of committed Narragansett warriors bent on revenge joined Metacom.

Metacom had hoped to spend the winter in the west, readying his men for the spring campaign. In order to do this, he needed the cooperation of the mighty Mohawk tribe. Instead of welcoming their fellow natives, the Mohawks took the opportunity to lash out at a weakened rival. In February, 300 Mohawk warriors attacked a winter camp of 500 of Metacom's men east of Albany and routed them. Other such attacks followed. Metacom was now fighting a two-front war, which had more to do with his ultimate demise than did any other development.

In the spring, Metacom once again attacked colonial towns in the western Connecticut River Valley. Some, such as Sudbury in April 1676, were amazingly close to Boston (within 20 miles). Colonists abandoned more than 12 towns as the frontier moved eastward. Yet the two-front fighting in which Metacom was now engaged, as well as English superiority in numbers, changes in tactics and militia preparedness, and the increased use of native allies as scouts and guides, began to take their toll. The Fall's Fight of May 1676, when a large group of warriors was ambushed and many perished plunging to their deaths over a high waterfall, demonstrated this fact. In her famous captivity narrative, Mary Rowlandson of Lancaster noted that her captors were tiring of the fight, and their food and supplies were dwindling by late spring 1676.

By summer 1676, many Native Americans, with almost no food (most of the native fields and food caches had been destroyed by colonial troops), surrendered. In July, forces under Captain Benjamin Church captured Metacom's wife and son who, along with hundreds (if not thousands) of captured natives, were sold into slavery in the West Indies. Metacom slipped back to the vicinity of his Mount Hope, Rhode Island, home with his most faithful followers.

On August 12, 1676, a native warrior under the command of Captain Church shot and killed Metacom. His head was taken to Plymouth town, where it was placed on a pike and displayed for several years, a grim warning to other natives who might think of resisting English authority. By October 1676, the other native leaders and their men had been captured, and the war came to an end except in Maine (then part of Massachusetts), where intermittent violence continued for several years.

King Philip's War was the deadliest war in American history in terms of numbers of casualties per capita. Colonial losses were between 800 and 1,000, with at least 12 towns totally destroyed, hundreds of houses and barns burned, and thousands of cattle killed. Native American losses were even more severe. Perhaps 3,000 warriors were killed in battle, with hundreds more men, women, and children killed or sold into slavery after the war. Native converts to Christianity did not escape unscathed. Fearing that they might aid Metacom, colonial officials rounded up the inhabitants of the so-called Indian praying towns and confined them on an island in Boston Harbor, where many died of disease and exposure. The tribes of southern New England never recovered from King Philip's War. Indeed, their ability to resist the colonial onslaught had ended.

Kyle F. Zelner

Further Reading

Leach, Douglas Edward. *Flintlock and Tomahawk: New England in King Philip's War.* East Orleans, MA: Parnassus Imprints, 1992.

Lepore, Jill. *The Name of War: King Philip's War and the Origins of American Identity.* New York: Knopf, 1998.

Mandell, Daniel R. *King Philip's War: Colonial Expansion, Native Resistance, and the End of Indian Sovereignty.* Baltimore: Johns Hopkins University Press, 2010.

Schultz, Eric B., and Michael J. Tougias. *King Philip's War: The History and Legacy of America's Forgotten Conflict.* Woodstock, VT: Countryman, 1999.

King William's War

Start Date: 1689
End Date: 1697

The North American extension of what began in Europe as the War of the League of Augsburg. The European conflict grew out of Catholic-Protestant tensions, French king Louis XIV's expansionary policies in the Low Countries and the Rhineland, and the accession of the Protestant William of Orange (King William III) and his wife

Mary II to the English throne. This occurred after the overthrow of Catholic King James II in the 1688–1689 Glorious Revolution. Nevertheless, James II still enjoyed powerful support among Catholics in England and Ireland as well as from Louis XIV, whose expansionist ambitions on the continent and desire to restore a Catholic to the English throne fueled Anglo-French rivalry.

Full-scale war in Europe commenced in September 1688 when France invaded Flanders and the Palatinate. Following the Glorious Revolution, William III brought England and the Netherlands into the League of Augsburg—an alliance of German principalities, Sweden, Austria, and Spain against France. This anti-French combination became known as the Grand Alliance.

Political and religious tensions in the New World mirrored those in the Old World. Catholic New France and the Protestant English colonies in New England and New York had been moving steadily toward confrontation. Rivalries over fishing rights and the fur trade, as well as Native American violence on the northern frontier, inflamed feelings on both sides. The resulting war produced a string of failures by the colonial forces of English America. This combined with a series of horrific native raids on the northern frontier triggered a panic in Massachusetts that influenced the Salem Witch Trials of 1692 and caused a general crisis of confidence between English colonists and the government in London.

The ensuing war stimulated domestic industry (particularly shipbuilding) in the colonies and led them to find their own methods of financing military operations. Particularly significant was the Massachusetts Bay Colony's decision to print paper money to defray the cost of the 1691 naval expedition against Quebec.

English military failures weakened relations with their closest Native American allies of the Iroquois Confederacy greatly. King William's War revealed the dangers involved in relying on separate colonies to cooperate with each other. Nevertheless, the frustrating stalemate led many colonists to question London's commitment to their interests. In neither Europe nor North America did this nine-year conflict resolve any of the issues between England and France. Indeed, the 1697 Treaty of Ryswick proved only a temporary truce before the onset of Queen Anne's War (1702–1713).

In North America, news of the Glorious Revolution gave impetus to long-nourished desires in the colonies, particularly in New England and New York, to strike against French Canada. New England Puritans had chafed under James II's prohibition of attacks on the French and raged against French encroachments on the fur trade and offshore fisheries and French incitement of Native American violence.

For their part, the French regarded the English colonies as threats to New France. They harbored their own ambitions in the Mississippi River and Ohio River valleys and in northern Maine to the Kennebec River. French agents cultivated local tribes along the northern New England and New York frontiers, especially the Abenakis. In fact, the French had established a fort along the Penobscot River in Maine (then part of Massachusetts) to funnel arms to potential native allies. The governor of New France, Count Louis de Buade de Frontenac, an abrasive but skilled career soldier, actively strengthened ties with pro-French tribes and encouraged them to attack the Iroquois and frontier settlements in northern Maine. Indeed, war between the French and the Iroquois had already broken out in August 1689, when a large Iroquois war party attacked the French village of Lachine near Montreal, slaying or capturing most of the population. News from Europe ignited this tinderbox into full-scale war.

In the ensuing conflict, English colonists set goals that were vastly different from those of their home country. In Europe, King William III's objectives were limited to protecting his throne and preventing French expansion into the Low Countries and to the banks of the Rhine. Protestant New England and New York, however, sought nothing less than the destruction of New France and the expulsion of the French from North America.

In neither the ground nor the naval dimensions of King William's War did events develop as English colonists had hoped. The English colonies began the war with three major advantages. First, they possessed a lopsided advantage in manpower. The population of English North America's colonies in 1689 was nearly 250,000 people, more than 20 times that of New France, providing governing authorities a formidable base for recruiting troops. Second, the colonists believed that they could count on military and naval support from the mother country. Third, the English colonies were allied with the largest and most powerful Native American tribal group in the Northeast, the Iroquois Confederacy.

None of these strengths proved decisive, however. Although much smaller numerically, the French could draw on a large number of males, many of whom had military experience. England, though fielding a large army, had to post most of its troops to Flanders and Ireland to parry French threats and internal unrest among the ousted James II's Catholic supporters. The ground and naval forces sent by the English government to the Western Hemisphere were deployed mostly to the West Indies to protect English possessions there. Also, English America was divided among a number of colonies, each with sovereignty over finances and military manpower, while New France was unified under the authority of one governor. Finally, the Iroquois tribes, although eager for plunder in Canada, were beset with internal divisions and relentless guerrilla attacks from their pro-French rivals.

While colonial authorities in New York and New England struggled to organize their forces, Frontenac sent mixed French and native war parties into northern New York and New England to raid remote and vulnerable English towns. On February 8, 1690, one such force raided the village of Schenectady, New York, killing 60 people and carrying off 27 and burning the settlement. The French and their American Indian compatriots struck again about a month later, hitting Salmon Falls, New Hampshire, not far from Portsmouth. The attackers killed 34 and took 54 hostages. In yet another attack in May 1690, 500 French and natives laid siege to Fort Loyal (Portland), Maine, forcing the small garrison into submission. When the English colonists surrendered, the French commanders stood by while their allies killed some 100 men, women, and children before burning the fort.

News of these attacks triggered a wave of terror among English colonists and moved authorities in New York, Massachusetts, and Connecticut to raise militias. The northern English colonies then tried to launch a two-pronged invasion of French Canada via Lake Champlain and through the Saint Lawrence Valley against Montreal and Quebec. Their efforts foundered on internal divisions growing from the upheavals of the Glorious Revolution.

In April 1690, the first intercolonial conference assembled in New York City, with representatives from Massachusetts Bay, Plymouth, Connecticut, and New York attending (Maryland and Rhode Island promised financial support). There they agreed to furnish troops for an overland expedition against Canada. In addition, the Iroquois promised to send 800 warriors.

Efforts to raise and organize militias and launch the expedition suffered amid political bickering, supply shortages, and an outbreak of smallpox that devastated both the Iroquois and the colonists. The joint expedition against Canada ended in an embarrassing failure. While the main body under Major Fitz John Winthrop, a former British Army officer, halted, Captain John Schuyler proceeded north on Lake Champlain with 29 soldiers and 120 native warriors on a raiding expedition. On August 23, having paddled the length of the lake and entered the Richelieu River, they attacked the French settlement of La Prairie, across the Saint Lawrence from Montreal. The attackers killed 6 men, took 19 prisoners, shot a number of cattle, and burned several houses, barns, and haystacks. Fearing a reaction from the large Montreal garrison and with no sign of the rest of the expedition, Schuyler withdrew. The main body under Winthrop had already returned to Albany. The collapse of this Lake Champlain expedition fanned discontent, damaged intercolonial cooperation, and undermined the confidence of the Iroquois in their English American allies.

In summer 1691 New York's new royal governor, Henry Sloughter, sent another expedition against Montreal. After shoring up support among the Iroquois at a May conference in Albany, he ordered a mixed band of colonists and natives organized by Albany mayor Peter Schuyler on another raid against Montreal. Departing Albany on June 22, Schuyler's force reached Montreal a month later in canoes, again via Lake Champlain. On August 1, the force struck La Prairie a second time, overrunning it. Schuyler and his men repulsed one counterattack but were obliged to withdraw on the appearance of reinforcements from Montreal. Fighting through a French ambush, Schuyler's detachment returned to Albany.

Although more successful than the 1690 attempt, Schuyler's raid did not significantly alter the political and strategic balance between French and English America. The French did not mount any major raids in 1691 or 1692. Hampered by the unexpected death of Sloughter in July 1691 and with only limited funds for raising troops, New York authorities were content to maintain a small garrison of 150 men at Albany and encourage the Iroquois to raid into Canada and blockade the fur trade on the Saint Lawrence.

The arrival of a new governor, Benjamin Fletcher, in August 1692 did not alter New York's quiescence. Unable to raise money from the already overtaxed colonists, Fletcher had to be content with encouraging the Iroquois and asking other colonies for help. The precariousness of New York's position became clear in July 1696 when a large French and native force, commanded by Frontenac himself, invaded central New York. The attackers terrorized the Onondaga tribe and burned several English settlements. By the time Fletcher was able to borrow money from the other colonies, the attackers had departed. The raid made clear to the Iroquois that New York authorities could not protect them.

Over the ensuing six years, the pattern established in New York persisted. The ground fighting followed a cycle of fierce raids interspersed with periods of inactivity. The French, driven by Frontenac's ambitions, continued to encourage native raids, particularly by the Abenakis, against both the Iroquois and the Anglo-Americans.

New England colonists, in turn, sought to raise sufficient manpower to protect their outlying settlements and deter French attacks. Like their counterparts in New York in the Lake Champlain Valley, leaders in Plymouth and Massachusetts Bay made independent efforts to take the offensive in northern New England. For this, they commissioned Major Benjamin Church, a veteran of King Philip's War (1675–1676), to organize troops and take the offensive in Maine. With a force of 300 men, Church sailed to Casco Bay in September 1691 and raided Abenaki villages near present-day Brunswick and Lewiston.

Although Church did not achieve decisive success, his expedition hurt the Abenakis sufficiently that they agreed to a peace treaty at Kennebec in November. This agreement lasted only until the following winter and early spring when, under French prodding, the Abenakis struck the Maine villages of York and Wells. In retaliation, the new governor of Massachusetts, Sir William Phips, accompanied Church on another expedition against the Abenakis. The attackers established a new post, Fort William Henry, on the Maine coast near Saco Bay and raided into Abenaki territory. An attempt by the French to take the fort by sea failed when the commander of the naval expedition, Pierre Le Moyne d'Iberville, decided that his forces were insufficient and withdrew without firing a shot.

The New England frontier remained stable for approximately three years. Massachusetts, by now in the throes of the Salem witch hysteria, could provide only limited forces. French authorities, smarting from their failure at Fort William Henry, were struggling to keep their native allies from negotiating with the English. A militia force of 300 under Captain James Converse kept the peace and deterred any serious native raids. In August 1693, Converse negotiated a peace with 13 Abenaki chiefs. This broke down later when 250 Abenakis, aroused by the new French commandant at Penobscot, Sieur de Villieu, overran Oyster Bay, New Hampshire, in July 1694. This force ravaged the New England frontier as far west as New York. Subsequent attempts to reestablish peace fizzled, and sporadic raiding continued throughout 1694 and 1695.

The last major clash on the New England frontier occurred in July 1696 when a mixed detachment of two French regular companies and 250 Native Americans supported by two French warships appeared off Fort William Henry and induced the commander, Captain Pasco Chubb, to surrender without resistance. The French restrained their allies from killing Chubb or any of his men but spent three days plundering the fort before withdrawing back to Penobscot.

In response, Massachusetts raised 500 men and once again called on Church to command an expedition into Canada. Supported by three English ships, Church landed at Penobscot but found that most of the French and natives had departed. He then moved his men up the coast to the Bay of Fundy, killing a few natives and burning the settlements in his path. There was no organized resistance.

Maine remained relatively secure until the war ended. News of the Treaty of Ryswick, which concluded the War of the League of Augsburg in 1697, effectively ended the fighting between the English colonists and New France but did not end warfare between the Iroquois and the pro-French tribes.

Walter F. Bell

Further Reading

Laramie, Michael. *King William's War: The First Contest for North America, 1689–1697.* Yardley, PA: Westholme Publishing, 2017.

Leach, Douglas Edward. *The Northern Colonial Frontier, 1607–1763.* New York: Holt, Rinehart and Winston, 1966.

Leckie, Robert. *"A Few Acres of Snow": The Saga of the French and Indian Wars.* New York: Wiley, 1999.

Nester, William R. *The Great Frontier War: Britain, France, and the Imperial Struggle for North America, 1607–1755.* Westport, CT: Praeger, 2000.

Peckham, Howard Henry. *The Colonial Wars, 1689–1762.* Chicago: University of Chicago Press, 1964.

Kiowas

A southern Plains tribe and member of the Kiowa-Tanoan language family, one of the smaller Native American language groupings. The traditions of the Kiowas place their earliest territory in the Rocky Mountains, probably in Wyoming and southern Montana. The other members of the Kiowa-Tanoan family were located along the Rio Grande Valley in New Mexico, yet Kiowa traditions make no mention of them. The Kiowas have many memories of northern tribes; the Crows, for example, introduced the Kiowas to the horse and the nomadic life of Great Plains bison hunting. The Kiowas exhibited the full range of Plains Indian traits, including dependence on the horse for mobility, the tepee for shelter, the travois for transportation, and the bison for survival as well as warrior societies and the Sun Dance ritual.

The Kiowas were familiar with Missouri River groups such as the Mandans and Hidatsas and also had contact with the Cheyenne and Pawnee peoples. The Lakota Sioux were remembered as the people who drove the Kiowas from the region of the Black Hills, eastern Wyoming, and western Nebraska. Eventually their territory was confined to western Texas, Oklahoma, and eastern New Mexico.

A subgroup within the Kiowa Nation, the Kiowa Apaches speak a dialect of the Athabascan language family, but were fully acculturated within the Kiowa Nation. The only significant difference between the two elements beyond the obvious linguistic difference was the higher proportion of mixed-blood families among the Kiowa Apache peoples. Full members of the tribal circle, they appear to have joined the Kiowas very early, as there is no traditional memory among either peoples of a time in which they lived apart.

The first Kiowa contact with Europeans appears to have been in the late 17th or early 18th centuries by French explorers when the Kiowas were still on the northern Great Plains. The Kiowas were then gradually pushed farther south, caught between the Lakota alliance pushing them south and the Comanche tribe, which occupied the southern Plains from the Arkansas River deep into Texas and from the Cross Timbers in central Texas and Oklahoma to the foothills of the Rocky Mountains in Colorado and New Mexico. This was the heart of the southern bison range. After 20–30 years of intermittent conflict between the Kiowas and the Comanches, a peace agreement was worked out around 1840.

From then until 1875, the Kiowas and Comanches were partners in war and in hunting. Sharing the northern part of the Comancheria, the Kiowas were the buffer to the north along the Arkansas River. The Kiowas began to accumulate massive horse herds through their long-distance raiding into Mexico and Texas alongside the Comanches. Some of these raids were as long as 1,000 miles. The objectives of the raids were horses, captives, luxury goods, and glory for young warriors. At times, women and children accompanied these raiding parties, as the duration could be many months. The Kiowas and Comanches would drive stolen livestock to the Staked Plains, where they would meet up with the Comancheros, traders from New Mexico. The Comanches had come to peace with the province of New Mexico in the 1780s and were thus free to come and go, bringing horses and cattle as well as captives for ransom. The Kiowas joined in this lucrative trade. Together the Kiowas and Comanches would delay the expansion of the Texas frontier until the mid-1870s.

In the north along the Arkansas River, the Kiowas were pressed by a very aggressive move south by the Cheyennes, supported by both their Arapaho and Lakota allies. This culminated in the Battle of Wolf Creek in 1838, when virtually the entire Cheyenne Nation and its Arapaho allies attacked a large camp of Kiowas along with some of their Comanche allies. Unlike most intertribal conflict, the Cheyennes pushed this toward a decisive engagement. Willing to accept high casualties in return for victory, the Cheyennes shocked the Kiowas who, while fearless themselves, had never encountered this intensity in war from other Native Americans and were instead used to the small-scale raid as the means of war. The result was the settlement of their differences in 1840, which resulted in a new alliance between the Cheyennes and the Kiowas, a deal that the Kiowas sealed with the gift of hundreds of horses. From that time forward, there was a solid wall of Native American warriors across the Plains who were opposed to further white encroachment.

In the 1840s, raiding in Texas intensified as more and more settlers moved first into the Republic of Texas and later the state of Texas. Although the U.S. Army established a series of forts west of the Texas settlements to try to protect the settlers, the forts were too far apart, and the Kiowas simply went around them. Prior to the American Civil War (1861–1865), army troops and Texas Rangers began to take the war to the Kiowas on their home grounds, causing the rise of a Kiowa peace party. Kiowa warriors, however, continued to raid deep into Texas and Mexico. The Civil War aggravated the situation when Union troops withdrew and the Confederacy failed to replace the garrisons. In places the Texas frontier receded by up to 100 miles.

With the end of the Civil War in 1865, U.S. troops were initially focused more on Reconstruction tasks but soon resumed attacks against the Kiowas. Many Kiowas moved to the reservation in Indian Territory (Oklahoma) during at least part of the year. Raiding continued, however, and on May 18, 1871, a group of young Kiowa warriors led by several chiefs—among them Owl Prophet and Satanta—allowed a small party including the commanding general of the U.S. Army General William Tecumseh Sherman to pass through an ambush site and later ambushed a wagon train carrying supplies. Most of the men in the wagon train were killed. An army patrol then followed the trail back to the reservation. Three chiefs—Satanta, Satank, and Big Tree—were subsequently arrested and tried in civilian court for the massacre in Texas.

Sherman then ordered Colonel Ranald S. MacKenzie, commanding the 4th Cavalry, and Colonel Benjamin Grierson, commanding the 10th Cavalry, to root out the hostile Kiowas. In a series of campaigns during the next three years, the troops penetrated into the Staked Plains, previously a Kiowa and Comanche sanctuary. The final outbreak of Kiowa resistance in 1874, punctuated by the Second Battle of Adobe Walls (June 27, 1874), was crushed during the Red River War (1874–1875), and the Kiowas were subdued and placed on a large reservation in Indian Territory.

John Thomas Broom

Further Reading

Mayhall, Mildred P. *The Kiowas*. Civilization of the American Indian Series. 1971; reprint, Norman: University of Oklahoma Press, 1984.

Meadows, William C. *Kiowa, Apache, and Comanche Military Societies: Enduring Veterans, 1800 to the Present*. Austin: University of Texas Press, 1999.

L

Little Bighorn, Battle of the

Start Date: June 25, 1876
End Date: June 26, 1876

Battle between units of the U.S. Army's 7th Cavalry Regiment, commanded by Lieutenant Colonel George Armstrong Custer, and Lakota Sioux, Arapaho, and Cheyenne warriors, led by Sitting Bull, Crazy Horse, Rain-in-the-Face, and Gall. Also known as Custer's Last Stand and to Native Americans as the Battle of Greasy Grass Creek, the battle took place along the Little Bighorn River in eastern Montana during the Great Sioux War of 1876–1877. The Battle of the Little Bighorn is arguably the most famous battle of the American Indian Wars and the most important victory by the Plains Indians over the U.S. Army.

In 1874, a U.S. Army expedition, led by Custer, confirmed the presence of gold in the Black Hills of South Dakota, sacred ground to the Lakota Sioux and off-limits to white settlement according to the 1868 Fort Laramie Treaty. As news of the discovery spread, white prospectors began pouring into the area. When the U.S. government tried to purchase the area with the gold in the Black Hills, the tribes refused to sell.

In late 1875, many Native Americans, outraged over the continued intrusions of whites onto their sacred lands, left their reservations and began raiding mining camps. The government then abrogated the Fort Laramie Treaty, and the commissioner of Indian affairs decreed that all Native Americans must return to their reservations by January 31, 1876. If they did not, they would be considered hostile. Defying the decree, several thousand Native Americans gathered in eastern Montana to fight for their lands.

The U.S. government and the army appeared to welcome the showdown. The result was the Powder River–Bighorn–Yellowstone Campaign of 1876. To force Native Americans back to the reservations, the army dispatched three large columns to the Black Hills region. Commander of the Department of Dakota Brigadier General Alfred Terry had overall command. Driving on the Sioux from the east, he had at his disposal some 1,000 men, including Custer's 7th Cavalry. Brigadier General George Crook moved north from Fort Fetterman in Wyoming with some 1,000 troops and 250 allied Native Americans. A third column of some 450 men under Colonel John Gibbon would march from Fort Ellis in western Montana. The plan was for the three columns to converge on Native Americans in eastern Montana and force them back to their reservations. With some 3,000 men involved, army leaders were confident of victory.

The coordinated attack never occurred. Crook's column fought a large group of warriors in the Battle of the Rosebud on June 17 and was forced to retire in order to regroup. Unaware of Crook's situation, Gibbon and Terry proceeded forward and joined forces in late June near the mouth of Rosebud Creek. They decided that Terry's largest unit, the 7th Cavalry under Custer, would proceed up the Rosebud while Terry and Gibbon moved toward the Bighorn and Little Bighorn rivers, hoping to trap the Native Americans between them.

Custer had won some renown as a major general of cavalry in the Union Army during the American Civil War (1861–1865) and was resentful that he had still not recovered his wartime rank 10 years later. A veteran of the Plains wars, he was a glory seeker and was contemptuous of the ability of Indians to fight. Yet the camp toward which Custer was moving was probably the greatest concentration of Indian power ever: some 10,000–15,000 people, at least 4,000 of them warriors.

Terry's strategy was to place the Indians between Custer and Gibbon's mixed force of infantry and cavalry. The plan called for Gibbon's Montana column to move west along the Yellowstone River to its confluence with the Bighorn River. At that point, Gibbon, with Terry accompanying, was to turn south to cooperate with Custer's cavalry, which it was hoped would be driving the Indians from the east. Terry made it clear to Custer that he was to strike the Indians wherever they could be found but allowed him ample latitude in which to exercise tactical judgment.

Custer's force, which departed at noon on June 22, numbered 633 men: 32 officers; 566 enlisted men; and 35 Arikara, Crow, and Dakota scouts. Discovering a large Indian trail, Custer followed it to the west, reaching the valley of the Little Bighorn River in southeastern Montana early on June 25. From the Crow's Nest, a high point on the divide separating the valleys of the Rosebud and the Little Bighorn, Custer's scouts detected the Sioux pony herd some 15 miles distant. Initially planning to rest his regiment and then attack the Indian village at dawn on June 26, Custer chose to attack immediately when it appeared that the Native Americans had discovered his presence.

Custer divided the regiment into three battalions. Breakup and dispersal of an Indian village before an attack could be launched was always of paramount concern to the officer in command of an attack, and Custer ordered a battalion of three companies under Captain Frederick Benteen to scout to the left to ensure that the Indians did not escape in that direction. Custer directed a second battalion of three companies together with the Indian scouts, under Major Marcus Reno, to cross the Little Bighorn River, charge down the valley, and attack the village. Meanwhile, the third and largest of the three battalions, five companies commanded by Custer himself, would approach the Indian village on a course roughly parallel to that of Reno's but above and to the right, hidden from Reno's view by the intervening bluffs above the river. Custer's exact strategy that sultry Sunday afternoon is unclear, but most historians believe that Reno's attack was intended as a diversionary movement, which would have allowed Custer, with the largest battalion of the regiment, to strike the village from an unexpected quarter.

Encountering much stiffer resistance than he anticipated, Reno halted his charge down the valley. He then retreated into the timber along the river and finally abandoned that location. Panicking, he withdrew in disorderly flight across the Little Bighorn River to the safety of the bluffs above it, losing perhaps a fourth of his men in the process. Here the survivors dug in.

Whether and to what extent Custer was aware of Reno's situation has been debated ever since. Also unclear is whether Custer attempted to cross the river and attack the village or was in fact himself attacked and driven back before he had an opportunity. Regardless, Custer's battalion was eventually forced to seek the higher ground north-northeast of the river. At some point, Custer's five companies were forced to assume a defensive posture and were eventually overwhelmed. The final act of the drama saw Custer and a few others gathered atop what became known as Custer Hill in the famous last stand for which the battle is best known. In the fighting, Custer himself sustained two wounds. It is not clear whether he was hit early in the fight or during the last stand. Compounding the situation for Custer was the fact that his troopers were armed with single-shot Trapdoor Springfield carbines, while many of the Indians had faster-firing Winchester repeating rifles.

Meanwhile, some five miles to the southeast at what is known as the Reno-Benteen defense site, Major Reno's three companies were joined by the pack train and Captain Benteen's battalion, returning from its earlier scout to the left. Here Reno and Benteen, although suffering substantial casualties, managed to hold out until relieved by Gibbon's column on June 27.

In the battle, the 7th Cavalry lost 268 men killed, including about 210 on what has become known as Custer Field. This was nearly 40 percent of the regiment's prebattle strength. Four other members of Custer's family were also lost: two brothers, Captain Tom Custer and Boston Custer; a nephew, Armstrong Reed; and a brother-in-law, Lieutenant James Calhoun. There is no consensus on Indian losses, although these may have been as few as 50. The battle was at once the apex and the nadir for the Sioux and their allies.

When Terry and Gibbon reached the field on June 27, there were no Indians. They had moved to the south immediately after the battle, and soon the separate clans went their own ways. Although the Indians lacked the ability to maintain a large force in the field for long, had they stayed together for a few more days, they might have defeated both Terry and Gibbon.

The Battle of the Little Bighorn shocked the entire nation. The government immediately

sent reinforcements to the northern Plains, and by spring 1877, virtually all of the hostile Sioux, including Crazy Horse, had been hunted down and removed to reservations or had followed Sitting Bull to Canada.

Robert B. Kane, Jerry Keenan, and
Spencer C. Tucker

Further Reading
Connell, Evan S. *Son of the Morning Star: Custer and the Little Bighorn*. New York: North Point Press, 1984.

Miller, David H. *Custer's Fall: The Native American Side of the Story*. Norman: University of Nebraska Press, 1985.

Philbrick, Nathaniel. *The Last Stand: Custer, Sitting Bull, and the Battle of the Little Bighorn*. New York: Viking, 2010.

Sklenar, Larry. *To Hell with Honor: Custer and the Little Bighorn*. Norman: University of Oklahoma Press, 2000.

Little Turtle's War

Start Date: 1785
End Date: 1795

A series of battles and skirmishes fought in the Old Northwest Territory between a loose confederation of Native American tribes and the U.S. Army from 1785 to 1795. Little Turtle's War, called the Miami Campaign by the U.S. Army, arose from competition over lands that are now part of Ohio and Indiana.

After the Northwest Ordinance of 1785 encouraged development of the lands newly acquired from Britain following the American Revolutionary War (1775–1783), American settlers began migrating farther west across the Ohio River. The British provided Native Americans in the region with arms and other supplies. As a result, Chief Little Turtle's Miamis and Blue Jacket's Shawnees, aided by other tribes, were strong enough to inflict more than 1,000 casualties on white settlers and prevent them from moving out of the Ohio River Valley.

The security of the Northwest Territory was a major concern for the new U.S. government, and in autumn 1790, it sent a force of 300 regulars and more than 1,000 militia under Brigadier General Josiah Harmar to secure the region. The initial engagements in the war went badly for the Americans. Harmar divided his force, and two detachments were badly mauled in ambushes, forcing Harmar to fall back to Fort Washington (present-day Cincinnati, Ohio). In all, Harmar lost some 130 men during the campaign.

In spring and summer 1791, the War Department orchestrated an enlargement of the army, and Congress commissioned Northwest Territory governor Major General Arthur St. Clair to lead two 300-man regiments of regulars and 1,400 ill-trained levies and militiamen against the main Miami town, Kekionga, (located in present-day Fort Wayne, Indiana). Little Turtle, Blue Jacket, and Tecumseh, leading a contingent of 2,000 warriors, surprised the force's poorly defended camp at present-day Fort Recovery, Ohio, near the headwaters of the Wabash River on November 4, 1791. More than half of the Americans were killed or wounded, and the survivors were forced into a haphazard retreat toward Fort Washington. In 1792, U.S. emissary Colonel John Hardin, on a peace mission to the Shawnees authorized by President George Washington, was killed by Shawnee warriors, which further intensified the ongoing war.

Convinced of the strategic necessity of securing the trans-Ohio region, Congress doubled the authorized size of the army, and President Washington appointed Major General Anthony "Mad Anthony" Wayne commander of the new Legion of the United States in late autumn 1793. Paying more attention to discipline, training, and provisioning than his predecessors, Wayne moved methodically into Native American lands in 1794, building defensive structures along the way. Seeking to avenge St. Clair's earlier defeat, Wayne ordered the construction of Fort Recovery, which Little Turtle and his warriors unsuccessfully attacked in June 1794.

On August 20, Native Americans, led by Blue Jacket, attacked Wayne's force of about 3,000 men near present-day Toledo. In the ensuing Battle of Fallen Timbers (so-named for the large number of trees felled there in an earlier tornado), Wayne's soldiers withstood the initial Native American onslaught and used a bayonet charge to push the warriors from their position onto open ground, where mounted soldiers quickly shattered the force. This stinging defeat for the Native Americans all but ended Little Turtle's War.

The defeat, coupled with the knowledge that Britain had agreed to abandon its frontier forts in accordance with Jay's Treaty (1794), effectively broke the Native Americans' resistance, and they ceded most of the disputed lands to the United States in the Treaty of Greenville, signed on August 3, 1795.

Matthew J. Krogman

Further Reading

Carter, Harvey Lewis. *The Life and Times of Little Turtle: First Sagamore of the Wabash.* Urbana: University of Illinois Press, 1987.

Dowd, Gregory Evans. *A Spirited Resistance: The North American Indian Struggle for Unity, 1745–1815.* Baltimore: Johns Hopkins University Press, 1992.

Lord Dunmore's War

Event Date: April 1774

Conflict that erupted in April 1774 when bands of frontiersmen attacked Native American settlements in the Ohio River Valley.

Subsequent retaliatory raids by the natives prompted John Murray, Fourth Earl of Dunmore and Virginia's governor since 1771, to send 2,000 men into the district that he named West Augusta. By month's end, Dunmore announced that Fort Pitt (Pennsylvania) was in imminent danger. Pennsylvanians and Virginians, particularly land speculators associated with the Loyal Company, proceeded to manipulate the evolving frontier dispute as a means of subverting the hated boundary delineated by the Proclamation of 1763. The proclamation had been the British Crown's attempt to maintain peaceful relations with potentially rebellious western natives by prohibiting settlement west of the Appalachians.

Tensions between the Shawnees and British colonists first surfaced when Sir William Johnson, British superintendent of Indian affairs for the northern colonies, and Iroquois emissaries fixed the northern boundary line, originally expressed in the Proclamation of 1763, with the Treaty of Fort Stanwix in 1768. Native American tribes in the upper Ohio Valley—particularly the Miamis, Shawnees, Wyandots, Delawares, and Mingos—rejected the right of the Iroquois to cede all of their hunting grounds south of the Ohio as far as the mouth of the Tennessee River. The tributary nations argued that their dependency was based on a compact of mutual responsibilities that did not involve the unilateral surrender of their land rights. When Daniel Boone and other American colonists claimed the ceded territory in Kentucky, angry Shawnees and Wyandots sought to turn back the encroachers. By 1771, Delaware, Mingo, Miami, Ottawa, and Illinois leaders helped fashion a confederacy to repulse the British invaders. Yet as throngs of pioneers crossed the Appalachians, one Shawnee leader, Cornstalk, advocated peaceful restraint.

Lord Dunmore's War began with a series of atrocities committed against unsuspecting Native Americans. When frontier clashes first erupted in spring 1774, John Logan, a Mingo chief, admitted that the Ohio tribes had just grounds for complaint. Unlike other native leaders who favored a more militant course of action, Logan reminded Mingo warriors of their own transgressions during council deliberations. After the tribal council ended, however, messengers arrived in early May 1774 with news that Captain Michael Cresap and frontiersmen had ambushed a party of Mingos on April 30, killing 11, including 2 of the Logan's relatives. Mingo and Shawnee warriors responded by increasing their raids against British settlements along the west bank of the Monongahela River.

Eager to subdue the hostile Native Americans, Dunmore promptly dispatched two militia columns totaling 2,000 men into the Ohio Valley. He also ordered the men to build a stronghold at Wheeling (Fort Wincastle) and to destroy neighboring Shawnee villages. Angus McDonald's subsequent expedition destroyed five Shawnee villages. Although successful, the Wapatomica campaign failed to halt Shawnee and Mingo raids against isolated frontier communities.

On July 12, 1774, Dunmore instructed Colonel Andrew Lewis, commander of the southwestern militia, to proceed from Camp Union (present-day Lewisburg, West Virginia) directly to the mouth of the Kanawha River, where Dunmore's army would join him from Fort Pitt. Lewis and his 1,100 militiamen arrived on October 6, 1774, and camped at Point Pleasant, a triangle of land at the confluence of the Kanawha and Ohio rivers. Messengers later informed Lewis that Dunmore had altered his plans. Instead of joining Lewis at Point Pleasant, Dunmore now wanted Lewis to join him in attacks against Shawnee villages along the Scioto River. Shawnee scouts, however, spotted the invaders before they had time to depart, and the Native Americans rushed to prepare an assault. Although the warriors wanted to strike the first blow, Shawnee leader Cornstalk counseled peace. After rejecting Cornstalk's pleas for negotiation, the tribal council voted to strike Lewis's force at dawn.

Cornstalk demonstrated his acceptance of the council's decision by leading some 1,000 Shawnee, Mingo, Delaware, Wyandot, and Ottawa warriors against the unsuspecting Point Pleasant encampment. The Battle of Point Pleasant began on October 10, 1774. The natives fought hard but were eventually scattered after a day of bloody combat.

Following their defeat at Point Pleasant, the Native Americans fled through the forest to their towns on Pickaway Plains. After warriors had reassembled in council, Cornstalk upbraided the other chiefs for their refusal to let him negotiate a settlement. No one moved to answer Cornstalk's questions about how to stop the advancing enemy. Thus, a furious Cornstalk rose and struck his tomahawk in a post in the council house and offered to make peace. The humbled warriors concurred, and Cornstalk assembled a Shawnee delegation to accompany him.

Cornstalk set out for Camp Charlotte, Dunmore's headquarters. Dunmore received Cornstalk's peace overture and agreed to hold a conference. During the ensuing treaty negotiations, Cornstalk described the innumerable wrongs that his people had suffered. According to the provisions of the Treaty of Camp Charlotte on October 19, 1774, members of the Shawnee delegation pledged to surrender all prisoners and valuables, to deliver hostages as a guarantee of friendship, to never again attack the frontier, and to surrender all claims to lands south and east of the Ohio River. The Mingos initially rejected the treaty, but later capitulated after Major William Crawford's frontiersmen destroyed several of their towns. In autumn 1775 at Fort Pitt, Mingo, Shawnee, Delaware, Wyandot, Iroquois, and Ottawa chiefs ratified and confirmed Dunmore's original peace terms.

Lord Dunmore's War represented the failure of the British Crown to live up to the goals enunciated in the Proclamation of 1763. Despite repeated orders to treat American Indians with justice, colonial governors and royal officials failed to enforce existing laws.

Jon L. Brudvig

Further Reading

Brand, Irene. "Dunmore's War." *West Virginia History* 40 (Fall 1978): 28–46.

Holton, Woody. "The Ohio Indians and the Coming of the American Revolution in Virginia." *Journal of Southern History* 60 (August 1994): 453–478.

McConnell, Michael N. *A Country Between: The Upper Ohio and Its Peoples, 1724–1774*. Lincoln: University of Nebraska Press, 1992.

Sosin, Jack M. "The British Indian Department and Dunmore's War." *Virginia Magazine of History and Biography* 74 (1966): 34–50.

M

Mackenzie, Ranald Slidell

Birth Date: July 27, 1840
Death Date: January 19, 1889

U.S. Army officer. Born on July 27, 1840, in New York City, the son of U.S. Navy commander Alexander Slidell Mackenzie, Ranald Slidell Mackenzie lacked the flamboyance and celebrity of George Armstrong Custer and Nelson A. Miles but was one of the army's most successful Indian fighters, eventually regarded by General William Tecumseh Sherman as the indispensable man in a crisis.

After graduating first in his class from the U.S. Military Academy at West Point in 1862, Mackenzie would win rapid promotion during the American Civil War (1861–1865) by demonstrating exceptional abilities and exemplary bravery (he was wounded six times during the war). He was badly wounded in the Second Battle of Bull Run (Manassas) on August 29, 1862. Mackenzie performed engineering duties in the Battle of Fredericksburg (December 13, 1862) and was promoted to first lieutenant and brevetted to captain after fighting in the Battle of Chancellorsville (May 1–4, 1863). Advanced to captain in the regular army after Gettysburg (July 1–3, 1863), Mackenzie fought in the 1864 battles of the Wilderness (May 5–7) and Spotsylvania Court House (May 7–19). Promoted to colonel, Mackenzie commanded a regiment in the Shenandoah Valley Campaign and in the Siege of Petersburg, where he lost two fingers on his right hand, leading Indians to call him "Bad Hand." By war's end, Mackenzie was a brigadier general of volunteers, commanding the Cavalry Division in the Army of the James. He led the division at Five Forks and during the Appomattox Campaign (April 3–9, 1865). He ended the war with brevet promotions through the rank of brigadier general in the regular army and major general of volunteers.

In 1866 on the reorganization of the army, Mackenzie remained in the army at his permanent rank of captain. In 1867, he accepted command of an African American unit, the 41st Infantry Regiment, no doubt in part to secure a rare postwar colonelcy. He molded the regiment into an efficient outfit. In 1869, he took command of the 24th Infantry Regiment, a consolidation of the 41st and 38th regiments. The following year, he took command of the 4th Cavalry, which he transformed into one of the finest regiments on the frontier.

From 1871 to 1874, Mackenzie pursued various Native American tribes in western Texas and led a controversial raid across the Rio Grande some 60 miles into Mexico to attack Lipan Apache and Kickapoo villages. In 1873, he received his seventh wound. During the Red River War (1874–1875), Mackenzie won the climactic engagement at Palo Duro Canyon on September 28, 1874, capturing some 1,500 Indian horses, most of which he ordered to be shot to prevent their recapture. Famed Comanche leader Quanah Parker personally surrendered to Mackenzie on June 2, 1875, at Fort Sill, ending the war on the southern Plains.

Following Custer's defeat at Little Bighorn (June 25–26, 1876), Mackenzie and the 4th Cavalry played a key role in the 1876 punitive campaign that ended the Great Sioux War (1876–1877). After forcing Dull Knife's Cheyennes back to the reservation with a devastating surprise attack in November 1876, Mackenzie spent the rest of the decade suppressing banditry in Texas and New Mexico. In 1881, with a bold show of force in Colorado, he singlehandedly prevented a renewed war with the Utes, a feat that he regarded as his greatest accomplishment. He then served briefly in Arizona during the early stages of the Geronimo Campaign (1881–1886). Mackenzie's operations on the frontier were distinguished by sound logistics, careful reconnaissance, surprise attacks, concentration of force, and low casualties among his own troops and his enemies.

Mackenzie's last campaign was for a brigadier general's star. His many wounds, long frontier service, and high-strung nature were eroding his health, and he sought a less strenuous posting. Sensing that time was running out, supporters convinced President Chester A. Arthur to approve Mackenzie's promotion in October 1882. Mackenzie, serving as commander of the Department of Texas, was already in a noticeable state of decline. Briefly institutionalized after a nervous breakdown in 1883, he spent the rest of his life in various stages of insanity. Recognized as one of the outstanding soldiers in American military history, Mackenzie died at his sister's home in New Brighton, Staten Island, New York, on January 19, 1889.

Raymond W. Leonard

Further Reading

Pierce, Michael D. *The Most Promising Young Officer: A Life of Ranald Slidell Mackenzie.* Norman: University of Oklahoma Press, 1993.

Robinson, Charles M., III. *Bad Hand: A Biography of General Ranald S. Mackenzie.* Austin, TX: State House Press, 1993.

Wallace, Ernest. *Ranald S. Mackenzie on the Texas Frontier.* College Station: Texas A&M University Press, 1993.

Mangas Coloradas

Birth Date: ca. 1790
Death Date: January 18, 1863

Chiricahua Apache leader during the mid-1800s. Born around 1790 near present-day Silver City, New Mexico, Mangas Coloradas, from the 1830s until his death in 1863, was the most prominent leader of the Chiricahuas in their struggles first with Mexicans and then, beginning in the late 1840s, with Americans in the southwest. The Chiricahuas were not a single tribe in political terms, but consisted of four related major bands—the Chihennes, the Chokonens, the Bedonkohes, and the Nednhis—that shared strong linguistic and cultural bonds.

Most likely born a Bedonkohe, Mangas Coloradas married into the Chihenne band. For the first decades of his life he was known as Fuerte and only later received the name Kandazis-tlishishen, or Mangas Coloradas ("Red Sleeves" or "Pink Sleeves"). He came from a prominent family and matured during a period of relative peace with the Spanish when rations and gifts were regularly distributed to the Apaches. Economic and political unrest prompted by the collapse of Spanish power, however, caused this system to crumble.

Struggling Mexican regimes could no longer afford to pay off the Chiricahuas, leading to escalating warfare during the 1830s that would continue until the 1880s. Because of their policies of extermination and treacherous acts of genocide, the Mexicans of Sonora especially gained Mangas Coloradas's deep hatred.

Mangas Coloradas excelled as a fierce fighter, a courageous leader, a generous statesman, a wise diplomat, and a loving family man, all traits valued in Chiricahua society. From the 1830s onward, he not only controlled his own local group, which was a mix of Bedonkohes and Chihennes, but also attracted a wide following of fighting men and many times led Chiricahuas from all bands. He gained even more influence by marrying his children wisely. For example, one daughter wed the Chokonen Apache leader Cochise, while others married prominent Navajo, White Mountain Apache, and Mescalero Apache men.

Overall, Mangas was exceptionally well connected with the many Apache divisions of the Southwest. Mexicans recognized him as the "general" of the Chiricahuas, the most prominent man of that militarily powerful people and whose cooperation and approval were vital for any significant peace initiative to succeed. He was also synonymous with Apache power and cruelty among many Mexicans, and the American invaders knew his reputation when they arrived in the late 1840s.

At first, Mangas Coloradas advocated peaceful relations with the Americans, who shared a common enemy with him: the Mexicans. The Americans were rich in trade commodities and thus were useful as partners. However, racial hatred, economic greed, and a lack of mutual respect brought war, and despite peace agreements, several violent incidents caused a deterioration in American–Chiricahua Apache relations throughout the 1850s and early 1860s. During the last years of the prominent chief's life, American miners, ranchers, and farmers began to inundate much of his country.

Mangas Coloradas became engaged in a destructive war with the Americans during the early 1860s and was killed by U.S. volunteers on January 18, 1863, at Fort McLane (southwestern New Mexico) after he had arrived for peace negotiations. Upon his arrival, he was captured and handed over to the American military. Soldiers taunted him and burned his feet, and when Mangas Coloradas responded, he was shot and killed. His body was thrown into a ditch after being decapitated for "scientific purposes." Military reports later contained a fabricated story of an escape attempt.

During his lifetime, Mangas Coloradas saw Chiricahua power dwindle under the double pressure of Mexican and American colonization. When he was born, the Chiricahuas were the dominant group in the region, but his death signaled the beginning of the end for Apache power. Within two and half decades, all surviving Chiricahuas would be exiled to Florida as prisoners of war.

Janne Lahti

Further Reading

Sweeney, Edwin R. *Mangas Coloradas: Chief of the Chiricahua Apaches*. Norman: University of Oklahoma Press, 1998.

Worcester, Donald E. *The Apaches: Eagles of the Southwest*. Norman: University of Oklahoma Press, 1979.

Manuelito

Birth Date: ca. 1818
Death Date: 1894

Navajo leader. Manuelito, a Spanish name given him by Mexicans, was noted for his resistance to Mexican and American invasions of Navajo territory. Born around 1818 into the Bit'ahni Clan ("Folded Arms People") near Bear Ears in present-day Utah, Manuelito trained as a medicine man who followed hózhó, the path of harmony and balance to Old Age. Manuelito's marriage to the daughter of the headman Narbona provided him with the wise leader's insight.

The arrival of Spaniards and then Mexicans into the Southwest beginning in the mid-to-late 16th century contributed to cultural changes for the Navajo, making them herders and warriors. With the horse, the Navajos ably impeded the foreigners' advances. Manuelito witnessed the shifting relationships of peace and conflict between Navajo and Mexicans. In the 1830s, Mexicans rode into Navajo territory determined to break Navajo resistance and to capture women and children for the slave trade. Slavery had been previously known in the Southwest, but the slave trade intensified with Spanish and Mexican invasions. Raiding for Navajo slaves reached a peak during the 1830s. In 1835, Narbona and Manuelito defeated the Mexicans in a battle at Copper Pass in the Chuska Mountains.

When the United States gained the Southwest after the Mexican-American War (1846–1848), Manuelito was a respected war chief. The cycle of peace and conflict among Navajos, other tribal peoples, and U.S. immigrants began anew. In 1851, the establishment of Fort Defiance on Navajo land preceded a war that would end in the Navajos' defeat. The conflict began over the pasturelands that lay outside the newly established fort. In 1858, Captain (Brevet Major) W. T. H. Brooks asserted control over the pastures for U.S. Army use. In defiance, Manuelito continued to pasture his livestock on the disputed lands, whereupon Brooks ordered the livestock slaughtered. Soon afterward, a Navajo killed Brooks's Black slave, and Brooks demanded that the Navajos produce the murderer for American justice. Eventually the Navajos produced a body, most likely that of a Mexican captive. Enraged at what he considered Navajo arrogance, Brooks went on the offensive. In 1860, Manuelito and 1,000 warriors attacked Fort Defiance several times but were unable to take the fort.

The American Civil War (1861–1865) initially turned the U.S. Army's attention away from the Navajos, however, and Fort Defiance was abandoned. With Manuelito leading the resistance to white expansion, in 1863 Brigadier General James H. Carleton ordered the removal of the Navajos to a reservation near Fort Sumner, New Mexico. Carleton enlisted Colonel Christopher "Kit" Carson for the campaign against the Navajos. Carson and his men burned Navajo settlements, destroying cornfields, peach trees, and livestock. By 1863, destitute Navajos began surrendering to the Americans. As prisoners, they endured a 300-mile journey to the internment camp. The old and sick were abandoned, and pregnant women were shot and killed if they could not keep up. Many Navajos drowned when they tried to cross the Rio Grande. At the Bosque Redondo reservation, the Navajos barely survived.

Manuelito vowed to remain free. U.S. officials, fearing that he would serve as inspiration to others who sought to elude their enemy, hoped to either capture or kill him. In 1865, Navajo leaders, including Herrera, met Manuelito and gave him the army's message to surrender. Manuelito refused. Nevertheless, in 1866 Manuelito, wounded and ill, surrendered and was interned at Bosque Rodondo.

In 1868, Carleton reluctantly admitted that Bosque Rodondo was a failure. On June 1, 1868, Manuelito and other leaders signed a treaty so that they could return to their homeland. The treaty stipulated a peaceful relationship between the Navajos and the United States, defined a boundary for a reservation, and required education for Navajo children. Seventeen days later, some 8,000 Navajos began the journey home.

Manuelito remained an influential leader who articulated his concerns for the return of his people's land. He was appointed head of the first Navajo police charged with keeping order on the reservation. In 1874, he traveled with his wife and other Navajo leaders to Washington, D.C., to meet President Ulysses S. Grant. Manuelito died in 1894 in New Mexico from disease and alcoholism.

Jennifer Nez Denetdale

Further Reading

Iverson, Peter. *Diné: A History of the Navajos.* Albuquerque: University of New Mexico Press, 2002.

Roessel, Ruth. *Navajo Stories of the Long Walk Period.* Tsaile, AZ: Navajo Community College Press, 1973.

Sundberg, Lawrence D. *Dinétah: An Early History of the Navajo People.* Santa Fe, NM: Sunstone, 1995.

Metacom

Birth Date: Unknown
Death Date: August 12, 1676

Metacom, known as Philip, Metacomet, or Pometacom, was the son of Massasoit and sachem (chief) of the Wampanoags (1662–1676). When Massasoit died in 1660, his eldest son, Wamsutta, informed the leaders of Plymouth Colony that he was now sachem. He also asked them to give him and his brother, Metacom, English names. The Plymouth officials drew on classical history and bestowed the name of Alexander Pokanokett on Wamsutta. They dubbed Metacom "Philip."

Wamsutta's cordial relations with the English ended abruptly in 1662 when rumors that he was plotting an attack on Plymouth Colony began to circulate. Wamsutta temporarily mollified the English, but tensions increased when he died of illness shortly after returning from being questioned at Plymouth in early 1662.

After assuming the role of sachem following his brother's death, Metacom entered a pact with Plymouth on August 6, 1662. Under its terms, Metacom accepted that the Wampanoags were the subjects of the English Crown, promised to adhere to treaties signed by his predecessors, vowed not to provoke a war with neighboring native tribes, and agreed not sell land to "strangers" deemed unacceptable to Plymouth. In return, Plymouth promised to treat the Wampanoags as friends and aid them, presumably militarily. Metacom thought that the document was binding for seven years, but in fact, it established the terms in perpetuity.

As the population and strength of Plymouth, Rhode Island, and Massachusetts Bay expanded over the next decade, Metacom maneuvered to maintain his power and ensure his people's welfare. He sold land to various colonists, but subsequent conflicts over colonial borders were rarely settled to Metacom's satisfaction. Indeed, colonial courts were unwilling to rule in favor of the Native Americans. The Wampanoags were angered by colonial interference in native politics. Tensions also arose as English livestock wandered into Wampanoag fields, destroying crops.

In 1667, the conflict between the Wampanoags and English settlers became more acute when Plymouth established the town of Swansea, violating the agreement with Metacom and authorizing the purchase of Wampanoag land that was also claimed by Rhode Island. Believing that his earlier agreement with Plymouth had expired, Metacom had begun selling the same land to Rhode Island colonists.

War parties appeared on the outskirts of Swansea in attempts to intimidate the colonists. At a meeting with Metacom in 1671, Plymouth compelled him to surrender his firearms and sign a treaty binding him to

Plymouth's authority and challenging prior land sales to other colonies. Plymouth also insisted on a literal interpretation of the treaty, whereby all Wampanoag guns were to be confiscated. Metacom had assumed that only the guns that he and his men carried to the signing were to be surrendered. When he refused the colony's interpretation, Plymouth announced that it would confiscate all Wampanoags' guns and ordered the Wampanoags' allies to disarm as well. Metacom sought assistance from Massachusetts Bay but found himself confronted by a joint commission from Massachusetts Bay, Plymouth, and Connecticut insisting on strict enforcement of the treaty.

There is evidence that at this time Metacom sought the backing of other native leaders and peoples, such as the Nipmucks, who also felt pressure from colonists. Metacom also appears to have sought an alliance with the Narragansetts, who were old enemies but also the most powerful tribe in the region. When rumors of his efforts reached colonial authorities, conflict ignited with the death of John Sassamon, one of Plymouth's native informers, on January 29, 1675. Sassamon had warned Plymouth officials of Metacom's plans. Although the circumstances of Sassamon's death remain unclear, Plymouth officials became convinced that the Wampanoags had murdered him. Three Wampanoags accused in Sassamon's death were tried in an English court, found guilty, and hanged. But the jury could not determine if Metacom had known about or ordered the murder.

In June 1675, a band of Pokanokets appeared at Swansea, rifling through several abandoned homes and slaying livestock. After the death of one of the Pokanokets, Native Americans attacked and destroyed Swansea. A full-scale native uprising ensued, seemingly sparked more by the rage of the Wampanoags than by any plan. Metacom was besieged at his home at Mount Hope (Bristol, Rhode Island) but escaped and joined Nipmuck and Podunk allies in attacking and burning English settlements west and south of Boston.

The New England Confederation declared war on the Wampanoags on September 9, 1675, officially beginning King Philip's War. Various Native American groups from the Connecticut River Valley and the Narragansetts joined the uprising after being attacked by English forces, but Metacom was not in formal command. He had left New England in December to seek support from the Mahicans in the upper Hudson River Valley. As attacks by colonial forces and their native allies became more effective, disease and hunger also took their toll on Metacom's allies. In spring 1676, the informal Native American alliance began to disintegrate as many tribes moved north and west to escape the fighting or made peace with the colonies. In June, Mohawks attacked Metacom and his forces, killing all but 40 of them and forcing Metacom to return to Massachusetts.

On August 12, 1676, colonial forces surrounded Metacom and his remaining warriors. He was shot and killed just outside Mount Hope by a native serving with colonial forces. Metacom's head was cut off, his body was drawn and quartered, and the pieces were sent to the colonial capitals. For the next 25 years, his head was displayed at Plymouth as a warning to other natives. Metacom's wife and son, along with hundreds (if not thousands) of captured natives, were sold into slavery in the West Indies. King Philip's War devastated the native population of southern New England, and Metacom's death marked the end of native independence in the region. The Narragansetts, the Wampanoags, the Podunks, the Nipmucks, and several smaller tribes were virtually eliminated.

Anna Kiefer

Further Reading

Drake, James D. *King Philip's War: Civil War in New England, 1675–1676*. Amherst: University of Massachusetts Press, 1999.

Leach, Douglas Edward. *Flintlock and Tomahawk: New England in King Philip's War*. East Orleans, MA: Parnassus Imprints, 1992.

Lepore, Jill. *The Name of War: King Philip's War and the Origins of American Identity*. New York: Knopf, 1998.

Miles, Nelson Appleton

Birth Date: August 8, 1839
Death Date: May 15, 1925

U.S. Army officer. Born near Westminster, Massachusetts, on August 8, 1839, Nelson Appleton Miles attended public school before moving to Boston in 1856, where he worked as a store clerk. Interested in the military, Miles received some instruction from a retired French colonel.

At the outbreak of the American Civil War (1861–1865), Miles recruited some 100 men for a Massachusetts regiment and was commissioned a first lieutenant of volunteers. Considered too young for battlefield command, Miles initially served in a staff position during the 1862 Peninsula Campaign. Demonstrating a natural capacity for leadership, Miles began a meteoric advance in rank. After the Battle of Seven Pines (May 31–June 1, 1862), he was promoted to lieutenant colonel in the 61st New York Infantry. Miles then fought in the Seven Days' Campaign (June 25–July 1, 1862) and the Battle of Antietam (September 17, 1862). Promoted to colonel, he was wounded in the Battle of Fredericksburg (December 11–15, 1862) and again in the Battle of Chancellorsville (May 1–4, 1863). For his actions at Chancellorsville, Miles later (1892) received the Medal of Honor. He commanded a brigade of II Corps during the 1864 Overland Campaign, seeing combat in the Battle of the Wilderness (May 5–7) and the Battle of Spotsylvania Court House (May 8–24), after which he was promoted to brigadier general of volunteers. Miles commanded a division in the Siege of Petersburg and briefly (at age 26) a corps. He suffered his fourth wound of the war in the Battle of Reams' Station (August 25, 1864).

Following the war, Miles was advanced to major general of volunteers in October 1865 and assumed command of II Corps. In the reorganization of the army in 1866, he became colonel of the 40th Infantry Regiment, an African American unit. In 1869, he took command of the 5th Infantry Regiment.

Miles saw extensive service in the American West and became renowned as one of the army's finest commanders in the Indian Wars, fighting in the Red River War (1874–1875), the Great Sioux War (1876–1877), and the Nez Perce War (1877). He personally accepted the surrenders of Sioux war chief Crazy Horse and Nez Perce chief Joseph. Promoted to brigadier general in the regular army in December 1880, Miles commanded the Department of the Columbia (1880–1885) and Department of the Missouri (1885–1886), before replacing Brigadier General George Crook as commander of the Department of Arizona in 1886. Miles discontinued Crook's wise practice of employing Apaches as scouts, choosing instead to rely mostly on U.S. troops. Following several months of failure, Miles reintroduced Apache scouts and oversaw the final surrender of Geronimo and the Chiricahua Apaches in September 1886. Miles then engaged in a public dispute with Crook over the subsequent exile of the Apaches, including the loyal scouts, to Florida. In 1888, Miles took command of the Division of the Pacific. Promoted to major general in April 1890, he directed the suppression of the Sioux Ghost Dance uprising in the Dakota Territory. Angered by the bloodshed at Wounded Knee on December 29, 1890, Miles relieved Colonel James W. Forsyth for his role in that action and wanted to court-martial him, but the War Department reinstated Forsyth.

After being called upon to employ troops in suppressing the Pullman Strike in 1894 and appointed commander of the Department of the East, Miles succeeded Lieutenant General John M. Schofield as commanding general of the army on October 5, 1895. He opposed the Spanish-American War (1898), believing that diplomacy could resolve the differences between Spain and the United States. When the war began, Miles favored using regulars in Cuba rather than volunteer forces, which he believed should remain in the United States to defend against a possible Spanish attack. He convinced President William McKinley to shift the main American land assault from Havana to Santiago de Cuba. Once Santiago was secured, Miles received approval to invade Puerto Rico. His highly successful campaign in Puerto Rico was cut short by the armistice of August 12, which denied him the capture of San Juan.

After the war Miles was the central figure in the notorious Embalmed Beef Scandal. He alleged that the Commissary Department had issued spoiled beef to the troops. He was subsequently reprimanded by the Dodge Commission for making unsubstantiated charges. Despite this controversy, Miles was promoted to lieutenant general in June 1900. President Theodore Roosevelt, who called Miles a "brave peacock" for his love of excessive uniform display, also crossed swords with Miles, as did Secretary of War Elihu Root, who found Miles in sharp opposition to Root's plan to create a General Staff and do away with the position of commanding general of the army, substituting for it the new position of chief of staff.

Miles retired from the army on his 64th birthday in 1903. Combative, vain, and ambitious, Miles was, along with Ranald S. Mackenzie, one of the finest field commanders during the Indian Wars. Despite his leadership qualities in battle, Miles displayed little political sense and did not fit well in the new 20th-century army. In 1917, when the United States entered World War I (1914–1918) Miles offered his service, but it was not accepted. In retirement, he wrote articles and several books, including a two-volume memoir. Miles died at Washington, D.C., on May 15, 1925.

Jerry Keenan and Spencer C. Tucker

Further Reading

DeMontravel, Peter R. *A Hero to His Fighting Men: Nelson A. Miles, 1839–1925*. Kent, OH: Kent State University Press, 1998.

Miles, Nelson A. *Personal Recollections and Observations of General Nelson A. Miles*, 2 vols. Lincoln: University of Nebraska Press, 1992.

Wooster, Robert. *Nelson A. Miles and the Twilight of the Frontier Army*. Lincoln: University of Nebraska Press, 1993.

Minnesota Sioux Uprising

Start Date: August 17, 1862
End Date: September 23, 1862

Armed clash between the Minnesota Sioux (also known as the Santee Sioux) and U.S. Volunteer forces in August and September 1862. The Minnesota Sioux Uprising began on August 17, 1862, along the Minnesota River in Meeker County in southwestern Minnesota. The uprising ended on September 23, 1862, with the defeat of the Sioux. One of the bloodiest Indian wars in U.S.

history, the conflict claimed the lives of 500–800 settlers. Native American casualties are unknown.

In 1851, the United States and the Dakotas signed the Treaty of Traverse des Sioux and the Treaty of Mendota, whereby Dakota lands in Minnesota became open to white settlers. In return, the Dakotas were to receive monetary compensation and a stretch of land 20 miles wide and 150 miles long along the upper Minnesota River, where a reservation would be created. However, during the ratification process in the U.S. Senate, Article 3 of each treaty that guaranteed compensation to the Indians for their land was deleted. This along with rampant corruption in the Bureau of Indian Affairs ensured that the Dakotas never received the promised compensation.

When Minnesota entered the Union in 1858, its borders shifted from the Missouri River to the Red River. Despite appeals by Sioux chief Little Crow (also known as Taoyateduta) to Washington, the northern half of the reservation was ceded for white settlement. Little Crow lost much of his standing within the tribe as the Dakota were ultimately driven out of the state, while those who remained were confined to the remaining small reservation.

White settlement in the region had adverse effects on Native American lifestyles. Clearing timber to make room for farmlands interrupted the natural cycle of farming, hunting, and fishing practiced by the Sioux. Also, wildlife populations of bison, elk, whitetail deer, and bear decreased steadily because of excessive hunting by white settlers. Dwindling lands, lack of game, and crop failures brought starvation, and the Sioux began attacking white settlers in search of food.

On August 4, 1862, representatives of the Minnesota Sioux approached the Upper Sioux Agency to plead for food. After successful negotiations, they returned on August 15 to receive promised supplies. Minnesota state senator and Indian agent Thomas Galbraith refused to distribute the supplies without payment, however. At a subsequent meeting of the Sioux, U.S. government officials, and local traders, the Sioux pleaded with the lead trader, Andrew Myrick, for his support, but he essentially replied that they should go away and eat grass.

This offensive and dehumanizing comment enraged the Sioux. With the U.S. Army occupied by the American Civil War (1861–1865), the Dakota chiefs seized the opportunity for an armed uprising. On August 17, 1862, four Sioux warriors, stealing food from a settlement in Meeker County, killed five white settlers. Although Chief Little Crow initially opposed a violent solution to the problem, the other chiefs convinced him to lead further attacks. At the council of war, the chiefs decided to attack without warning.

Myrick was one of the first to die in the subsequent attacks. He was found dead with grass stuffed in his mouth, a macabre allusion to his earlier comment. Captain John March then led a force of 44–46 men from Fort Ridgely, but the Sioux attacked them as they were attempting to cross the Minnesota River on the Redwood Ferry on August 18. Either 24 or 25 soldiers died in the ensuing Battle of Redwood Ferry. Sioux casualties are unknown.

Over the next week, the Sioux attacked scores of settlements and farms, killing many white settlers in the process. The Sioux also attacked military installations, including Fort Ridgely and Fort Abercrombie. Fort Ridgely, defended by about 175 men and perhaps 300 settlers who had managed to take refuge there, came under attack by as many as 800 Sioux warriors on August 20. In two days of fighting, the defenders managed to drive off the attacking Sioux, thanks in large part to the assistance of three howitzers. The Sioux also attacked the town of New Ulm on August 19 and 23. Although both assaults were repulsed, much of the town was destroyed in the second attack, forcing inhabitants to evacuate the settlement on August 26.

Minnesota governor Alexander Ramsey ordered Colonel Henry Hastings Sibley to lead a force of 1,500 militiamen to relieve the settlers. Sibley detached part of his force as a burial detail, and it came under attack at Birch Coulee on September 2, 1862. Although 20 soldiers died and 60 more were wounded, the survivors managed to hold out until Sibley arrived with a relief column the next day. Sibley then went looking for the hostiles and on September 23, 1862, at the Battle of Wood Lake soundly defeated the Sioux. During the next several days, many of the Sioux defected from Little Crow and began releasing captives.

By the end of November, a military tribunal had convicted 303 Sioux of murder and rape and sentenced them to death. At the trials, some of which lasted just five minutes, the Sioux had no representation. Bishop Henry Whipple pleaded with the president for clemency for the Dakotas. After a review of the records, President Abraham Lincoln upheld the convictions of 38 Sioux accused of rape and murder and commuted the death sentences of the others. Those sentenced to death were hanged on December 26, 1862, at Mankato, Minnesota. It was the largest public execution in U.S. history.

In 1863, 1,300–1,700 Minnesota Sioux were sent to the Nebraska and Dakota territories. Four years later, the surviving imprisoned Sioux were released—30 percent had died of disease while in prison. The Sioux were sent to Nebraska and Dakota with their families in an attempt to expel the Sioux from

Minnesota for good. After that, a bounty of $25 was paid for the scalp of any Sioux found within Minnesota borders. The U.S. government also abolished the reservation and voided all previous treaties with the Dakotas. Little Crow and his son, who had returned to Minnesota, were shot and killed by two farmers in the summer of 1863.

Anna Rulska

Further Reading

Carley, Kenneth. *The Sioux Uprising of 1862*. 2nd ed. St. Paul: Minnesota Historical Society, 1976.

Keenan, Jerry. *The Great Sioux Uprising: Rebellion on the Plains, August–September, 1862*. Cambridge, MA: Da Capo, 2003.

Modoc War

Start Date: November 1872
End Date: June 1873

Seven-month-long conflict between the Modoc tribe and U.S. Army forces that exposed the inefficiencies of army tactics against the Native Americans and strained President Ulysses S. Grant's peace policy. From November 1872 through June 1873, a small faction of Modocs held off a much larger U.S. Army force using the rugged lava beds of northeastern California as a natural redoubt.

Occupying the border area between Oregon and California, the Modocs, although small in number, were fierce warriors who had wrought havoc against white settlers for decades. Despite their hostility toward whites, they did establish relationships with white miners at Yreka, California. Thus, many of the Modocs were given white nicknames; one in particular was Kintpuash, leader of one of the more militant factions and known to whites as Captain Jack.

Captain Jack refused to honor the Treaty of 1864 in which most of his traditional tribal land had been ceded to white settlers. He and a group of Modocs left the reservation in southwestern Oregon, which they shared with the Klamaths, and moved back to the Lost River basin, where whites demanded their removal. Brigadier General Edward R. S. Canby warned his subordinates that when the time came to attack, they should use overwhelming force. Superintendent of Indian affairs Thomas B. Ordeneal, however, pressured Major John Green, commander of the 1st Cavalry Regiment, to strike quickly, which prevented him from bringing preponderant force to bear.

On November 29, 1872, Captain James Jackson, along with 3 officers and 40 enlisted personnel, approached Captain Jack's camp of 17 families along the Lost River and demanded their arms. A melee ensued, and the Modocs fled. Ranchers then attempted to overtake a second encampment of Modocs on the opposite bank but were repulsed. The two Modoc camps then joined forces, killing 14 civilians along the way, and withdrew across Tule Lake. At the southern tip of the lake, the Modocs—a mere 60 warriors—occupied a treacherous region of jagged black volcanic rocks and caverns, which the soldiers would dub Captain Jack's Stronghold.

Army reinforcements poured into the area, and on January 16, 1873, two contingents of soldiers approached under cover of darkness, attempting to surround the lava beds. Two mountain howitzers were positioned for support, but a thick fog rendered them ineffective. Unable to surround the beds entirely, the two companies fell back and tried to join flanks. By early afternoon, the fog had lifted, exposing the troops to gunfire from the entrenched Modocs. Snipers pinned down the attackers until nightfall, when they were able to retreat. In this engagement, soldiers suffered 9 dead and 28 wounded.

Although events unfolding in the Pacific Northwest did not bode well for Grant's conciliatory policy toward Native Americans, Washington pressed for peace negotiations. When a civilian commission failed to make any headway, Canby was ordered to take direct control of the talks. On April 11, the commission was attacked at the peace table. Canby was shot in the face by Captain Jack, stabbed, and stripped, becoming the sole regular army general officer killed during the Indian Wars. Two civilian commissioners were also attacked, and one of them was slain. This act of treachery brought demands for harsher treatment of the Modocs, and the army renewed its offensive.

Army forces moved against Captain Jack's stronghold again during April 15–17, 1873, employing the same two-pronged attack that had failed earlier in the campaign. A slow methodical battle ensued, with the Modocs firing from protected positions and retreating farther into the lava beds. On April 26, a patrol led by Captain Evan Thomas was ambushed, leaving 5 officers and 20 enlisted men dead with another 16 wounded. Colonel Jefferson C. Davis took command in early May, but by then the Modocs had fled.

As it turned out, it was not the army that had driven the hostile Modocs out but rather internal dissension. Another Modoc leader, known as Hooker Jim, had decided to retreat. He was later caught and offered to help find Captain Jack, who was captured on June 3, 1873. Ultimately, six Modocs were tried for the murders of Canby and the other peace commissioner. Four including Captain Jack were hanged, while two had their sentences commuted. The Modocs were then dispersed to reservations throughout Indian Territory (Oklahoma).

The U.S. Army's inability to deal effectively with a small number of Modocs revealed a lack of training, poor tactical planning, and overall ineptitude. On the other hand, the Modocs' cold-blooded murder of a high-ranking army officer and a civilian commissioner helped sway public opinion against Grant's Peace Policy, bringing a much harsher policy toward them.

William Whyte

Further Reading

Cothran, Boyd. *Remembering the Modoc War: Redemptive Violence and the Making of American Innocence*. 1st ed. First Peoples: New Directions in Indigenous Studies. Chapel Hill: University of North Carolina Press, 2014.

Murray, Keith A. *The Modocs and Their War*. 1959; reprint, Norman: University of Oklahoma Press, 2001.

Quinn, Arthur. *Hell with the Fire Out: A History of the Modoc War*. Boston: Faber and Faber, 1997.

Muscle Shoals, Grand Council on

Event Date: May 1776

Council between northern and southern Native American tribes held in May 1776 at Muscle Shoals on the Tennessee River near present-day Florence, Alabama. The principal impetus for the meeting was the commencement of the American Revolutionary War (1775–1783) that had led many Native Americans to take sides in the imperial struggle. The British sought to organize the Trans-Appalachian tribes to fight on their behalf against the American colonists.

Although the British had previously fought many of these tribes, most recently in the French and Indian War (1754–1763) and Pontiac's Rebellion (1763), Native Americans clearly understood that American settlers from the 13 colonies presented the greatest threat to their survival as a people. Indeed, in 1774 Virginians had launched a campaign against the Shawnees in what became known as Lord Dunmore's War. Consequently, Henry Hamilton, the British governor at Fort Detroit, found a receptive audience when he urged Shawnee chief Cornstalk and tribal leaders from the Delawares (Lenni Lenapes), Iroquois, and Ottawas to forge an alliance with southern tribes (the Cherokees, Chickasaws, Creeks, and Choctaws).

In May 1776, Cornstalk and the other northern leaders met with their southern counterparts at Muscle Shoals. Although Cornstalk had been an advocate for neutrality after his defeat in the Battle of Point Pleasant in 1774, the bellicosity of other tribes at the council led him to offer his war belt to Cherokee chief Dragging Canoe (although some sources contradict this). Ottawa and Iroquois warriors likewise offered their war belts to Dragging Canoe, and the Delawares offered their war belt to Savanukah, the leader of the Cherokee town of Chota. Before the conference ended, Dragging Canoe led a raid into Kentucky and returned with four white scalps, symbolizing his acceptance of the alliance.

The Grand Council on Muscle Shoals led directly to the Cherokee War of 1776 (sometimes known as the Second Cherokee War) during which Dragging Canoe and his southern allies launched raids all along the southern frontier from Virginia to Georgia. Unfortunately for the Cherokees, the British at this time had no military presence in the South outside of Florida. Consequently, North Carolina, South Carolina, and Georgia mobilized approximately 4,400 militiamen against the Cherokees in northern Georgia and the western Carolinas, while the Virginia militia attacked Cherokees in Tennessee.

Within a year, a Cherokee peace party led by Oconostota and Attakullakulla agreed to peace with Georgia and South Carolina in the Treaty of Dewitt's Corner and with Virginia and North Carolina in the Treaty of Fort Henry. Meanwhile, Cornstalk reverted to a policy of peace upon his return to Ohio. When other members of the tribe appeared determined to go to war, Cornstalk and his son traveled to Point Pleasant to warn the American garrison, only to be arrested and then killed in retaliation for the murder of white settlers by other Shawnees. The murder of Cornstalk made the Shawnees the most implacable Native American foe the Americans would face for the next 40 years.

Justin D. Murphy

Further Reading

Calloway, Colin G. *The American Revolution in Indian Country: Crisis and Diversity in Native American Communities.* Cambridge: Cambridge University Press, 1995.

Calloway, Colin G. *The Shawnees and the War for America.* New York: Viking, 2007.

N

Narragansetts

Powerful Native American group inhabiting southeastern New England. The Narragansetts lived in present-day Rhode Island, although their authority frequently extended south to Long Island and Block Island. Other area tribes that fell under Narragansett control were the Pawtuxets, the Niantics, the Manisseans, the Cowesets, and the Shawomets. Some Nipmucks and Montauks were also beholden to the Narragansett sachems (chiefs). The Narragansetts came to be known by Europeans through their relationship with Rhode Island founder Roger Williams, who was banished from Massachusetts Bay because of his unconventional ideas, especially in regard to religion. His relationship with the Narragansetts helped him pen *A Key into the Language of America*, written in 1643. It is from this account that much of the knowledge of the Narragansetts is derived.

The Narragansetts spoke an eastern Algonquian language and were governed politically by two sachems, usually an uncle and a nephew. In addition to cultivating maize, squash, beans, and similar crops, the Narragansetts fished and hunted. Because wampum was usually made of shells, the abundance of quahogs (a large clam indigenous to the Northeast) and whelks ensured that the Narragansetts dominated the wampum trade. By the mid-1620s, the tribe had grown quite wealthy as wampum was used as currency for trade, gifts, and even diplomacy, allowing the Narragansetts to develop strong trading ties and tributary relationships with other tribes in New England. When English settlement developed in the 1620s, the Narragansetts were quite powerful. Fortunately for them, they had avoided the devastating epidemics of 1616–1619 that had diminished many Native American nations.

During the Pequot War (1636–1638), the Narragansetts allied with Massachusetts Bay. Accompanying the English to Mystic Fort in 1637, Narragansett warriors were appalled by the behavior of the English, who burned the entire village. Most Pequot adult males were away preparing for war, so primarily women and children remained. As the village burned, fleeing survivors were shot outside the walls. The Mystic Fort Fight killed as many as 700 Pequots and essentially annihilated the tribe. During the fighting, the English had attacked some 20 Narragansetts in the mistaken belief that they were Pequots.

In the 1640s, the colonies of Massachusetts, Connecticut, and Plymouth formed the New England Confederation, a loose union for a military alliance. In 1643, when Narragansett sachem Miantonomo sold a large parcel of land to an enemy of the Puritans, the confederation-allied Mohegans murdered him. Threatened with war, the Narragansetts agreed to a treaty in 1644 that placed them in a subordinate position, and they continued to lose ancestral lands to the colonists.

As New England colonists encroached on native lands into the 1670s, Wampanoag leader Metacom, also known as King Philip, attacked outlying settlements of Plymouth Colony in July 1675, sparking King Philip's

War (1675–1676). Following Metacom's initial success, other tribes joined in the attacks against remote colonial towns. Although the Narragansetts tried to remain neutral, they covertly aided the Wampanoags. In retaliation, the English organized a force of some 1,000 men who attacked the Narragansetts in late 1675. This offensive culminated in the devastating Great Swamp Fight (December 19) that devastated the tribe, with more than 600 Narragansetts killed. At least 300 more became prisoners.

The Great Swamp Fight was one of the bloodiest battles of the war and deeply demoralized the tribe, although afterward the Narragansetts openly assisted Metacom. King Philip's War raged on with sporadic attacks until spring 1676. Hunger and disease drove many warriors from the field, and Metacom was killed during the summer. Afterward, the English sold many of the native captives into slavery and imposed strict regulations on those who remained.

After King Philip's War, the Narragansetts ceased to exist as an independent entity as they joined together with the Niantics, Abenakis, and Mahicans. During the next two centuries, the Narragansetts assimilated into American society as the only way to survive. The language and the last full-blooded Narragansetts died in the 1800s. Although the Narragansetts were detribalized in 1880, activists were able to gain recognition of the tribe in 1983.

Sarah E. Miller

Further Reading

Calloway, Colin G., ed. *After King Philip's War: Presence and Persistence in Indian New England.* Hanover, NH: University Press of New England, 1997.

Drake, James D. *King Philip's War: Civil War in New England, 1675–1676.* Amherst: University of Massachusetts Press, 1999.

Simmons, William S. *The Narragansett.* New York: Chelsea House, 1989.

Natchez War

Start Date: December 1729
End Date: 1733

The last of three conflicts between the French and the Natchez tribe that escalated into a regional struggle including the British and numerous southern and northern tribes. The Natchez, who lived along the Mississippi River near present-day Natchez, Mississippi, were devastated and ceased to function as an independent people after the conflict. The Natchez War also eroded French authority and influence in Louisiana.

The French routinely disregarded Natchez culture and had fought the Natchez previously during 1715–1716 and again in 1722 without reaching any substantial accommodation. British efforts to antagonize tribes within the French sphere of influence added to this volatile political and military environment. The Chickasaws, trading partners of the British, goaded the Natchez people by insinuating that they were merely minions of the French. A flash point occurred in 1729 when Captain Étienne de Chépart, the commandant of Fort Rosalie, demanded that the Natchez vacate a village containing a sacred burial mound to make room for his plantation. On November 28, 1729, Natchez warriors rose in a general revolt targeting the entire French population within their reach. Roughly 550 French citizens and slaves were killed or captured. Some slaves were freed and encouraged to join the fight.

The French assembled an army in Louisiana dominated by 1,500 Choctaw warriors and proceeded into the Natchez heartland. Ensconced within a fort strong enough to resist cannon fire, Natchez warriors taunted their attackers with promises that the Chickasaws and the British would soon come to their rescue. This only heightened French suspicions that outside agitation had prompted the Natchez rebellion. While negotiations were being conducted for the release of women and children, the Natchez quietly left the fort and scattered. One group was captured by Choctaw and Chackchiuma warriors while trying to reach the Chickasaws in early 1730. Some 150 warriors were executed, whereas women, children, and slaves were freed. The main Natchez body was discovered later in 1730 on an island in the Mississippi. Following a French artillery bombardment, the defenders were largely wiped out. Another sizable contingent was captured by the French and their Caddo allies near Natchitoches, Louisiana, and subjected to wholesale slaughter. Some Natchez escaped to live among the British, the Creeks, and the Cherokees, but approximately 1,000 Natchez, including 200 warriors, settled among the Chickasaws.

Believing that the Chickasaws were responsible for the war, the French recruited among northern tribes for mercenaries to launch a retaliatory strike. The Wyandots (Hurons) and the Illinois responded in the greatest numbers. The French, hoping to deal with the remaining Natchez elements first, did not officially declare war on the Chickasaws. A raid in September 1730 by northern warriors killed or captured some 50 Chickasaw men, but the French feigned ignorance when queried about the attack. Chickasaw counterattacks on northern villages, combined with gifts and peace messages, dissuaded these distant foes from further attacks.

Emboldened by their virtual genocide of the Fox tribe in the Illinois Country in 1730, the French intensified their efforts to eradicate the Natchez by demanding that the Chickasaws turn over refugees and cease trade with the British. When the Chickasaws refused, French authorities arranged for the Choctaws to burn three Chickasaw prisoners at the stake. By February 1731, many Choctaws clamored for war, in part because of a rumor that the British had poisoned some cloth acquired through trade. Initially, Red Shoe, an ambitious chief, urged neutrality as part of an effort to play the European powers against one another. The existence of heavily fortified Chickasaw towns further discouraged the Choctaws. Meanwhile, the Chickasaws were increasingly divided over the utility of harboring Natchez refugees. As the pro-Natchez faction gradually prevailed, Red Shoes settled on war, and in July 1731, the Choctaws assaulted a Chickasaw hunting party to secure scalps and prisoners.

As the conflict widened, the Choctaws grew adept at using decoys to lure away major Chickasaw forces before raiding their camps. Suffering heavy casualties, the Chickasaws sought peace with the Choctaws to isolate the French. But French officials demanded the surrender of the Natchez as a condition for peace. By the end of 1732, the French-Choctaw alliance was deteriorating over the French refusal to provide troops for native offensives. On the fringes of New France, Louisiana ranked low among priorities in asserting French authority.

By 1733, the Chickasaws were weakening in their resolve to stand by the Natchez. A Chickasaw chief known as Courcerai parleyed with the French that spring to secure peace in exchange for handing over all Natchez refugees. The French governor of Louisiana, Jean-Baptiste Le Moyne de Bienville, incarcerated Courcerai in retaliation for the capture of two Frenchmen, and Courcerai was never heard from again. Meanwhile, the French desperately appealed to the Choctaws for assistance. French officials often assumed cowardice when faced with Choctaw timidity.

But Choctaw warriors readied themselves for combat through a series of elaborate rituals deeply rooted in their culture. Expeditions hastily contrived by the French clashed with Choctaw norms. In 1733, the Chickasaws concluded a peace with the northern Choctaws that encouraged an abatement of hostilities. When the Chickasaws closed the Mississippi River to French commerce in 1734, the stage was set for another conflict. Only then would the French mount an expedition of their own against the Chickasaws, one that failed in 1736.

Jeffrey D. Bass

Further Reading

Atkinson, James R. *Splendid Land, Splendid People: The Chickasaw Indians to Removal.* Tuscaloosa: University of Alabama Press, 2004.

Axtell, James. *The Indians' New South: Cultural Change in the Colonial Southeast.* Baton Rouge: Louisiana State University Press, 1997.

Milne, George Edward. *Natchez Country: Indians, Colonists, and the Landscapes of Race in French Louisiana.* Athens: University of Georgia Press, 2015.

Navajos

Native American tribe of the American Southwest. The Navajos, or Dinés (meaning "the People"), are the largest reservation tribe in the United States with a population of more than 200,000 people. The Navajo Nation comprises 25,000 square miles in New Mexico, Arizona, and southern Utah in an area known as Dinétah. Navajo lineage can be traced to the Athabascan tribes of northwestern Canada and Alaska that migrated southward and arrived in the American Southwest by the early 1500s. Their language, Navajo, is derived from their Athabascan heritage. Navajo culture is matrilineal, based on clan kinship, and their religion is polytheistic. The center of Navajo life is the home (hogan).

Early Navajo subsistence, predicated upon trade, demanded the creation of trading agreements with neighboring tribes. Navajo and Pueblo trade existed for generations, as did commerce with the Utes, Hopis, and Comanches. Tribal interaction was mostly positive, but issues such as land control, horse stealing, and human slave trafficking led to bloodshed. Intertribal conflict and the Navajos' desire to expand their territory led to them being considered warlike, a reputation they carried into the 20th century.

During the Spanish occupation of the Southwest, the Navajos remained nomadic traders and expansionists. These ideals eventually brought the Navajos and Pueblos into conflict. Navajo and Spanish trade was extensive, as were land disputes and horse theft. Fighting between the two was sporadic throughout the Spanish colonial period. Contact with Spanish settlers brought the introduction of domestic livestock, especially sheep, and sheepherding became an integral part of Navajo life, as did seasonal farming. Whereas early Navajo units were wanderers and without a singular identity, herding tied them to the land and acted as a strong tribal unifier. The protection of their land would eventually bring them into direct conflict with a westward-bound United States.

During the Mexican-American War (1846–1848), the United States sought control of the Southwest. Newly commissioned governor of the New Mexico Territory Brigadier General Stephen Watts Kearny quickly declared the Navajos as enemies. Occupation of Dinétah by an outside power was unacceptable to the Navajos and resulted in a series of raids by both sides. One such raid occurred on August 31, 1849, and resulted in the killing of the elderly Navajo leader

Narbona. Narbona was replaced by his son-in-law Manuelito, who witnessed the killing and was particularly outraged. The following September the U.S. Congress ratified the Navajo Treaty of 1849, which allowed the United States to establish posts and agencies and set restrictions on Navajo boundaries.

Many Navajos, including Manuelito, who was not a party to its signing, despised the treaty. In 1851, the United States constructed Fort Defiance, situated on ancestral Navajo land. On April 30, 1860, Manuelito and Barboncito led an unsuccessful attack on the fort in an attempt to reclaim lost territory, but the attack resulted only in the strengthening of anti-Navajo sentiment.

With the outbreak of the American Civil War (1861–1865), the control of the territory soon fell to Brigadier General James H. Carleton. He decided on a plan of removal for the Navajos to end conflict and thus encourage white settlement in the western interior. The plan involved forcibly removing the Navajos from Dinétah to an area on the Pecos River in eastern New Mexico known as Bosque Redondo. Colonel Christopher "Kit" Carson, a Mexican-American War veteran and frontiersman, was appointed to oversee the removal. He decided that a mixed force of U.S. volunteers working with neighboring tribes could force the Navajos into exile.

Beginning in 1863, attacks on Diné settlements were overwhelmingly destructive and brutal and culminated in a showdown in the Navajo stronghold of Canyon de Chelly in January 1864. Those Navajos not killed faced starvation and exposure during a freezing winter. With few options left, some 9,000 Dinés began their southeastern migration, known as the Long Walk, to Fort Sumner in the Bosque Redondo. Hundreds died en route.

Known to the Navajo as Hweeldi, Fort Sumner was inadequately provisioned to provide for the 7,300 Navajos who had survived the harrowing journey. Timber for building hogans was scarce, food supplies were limited, and the water was polluted. Diseases and attacks by other Native American groups resulted in the deaths of one-third of the Dinés.

After four years of incarceration, peace negotiations began between American representatives and Navajo leaders, including Manuelito and Barboncito. On June 1, 1868, the Treaty of Bosque Redondo ended the Navajos' exile. The return of the Navajos to Dinétah was contingent upon their acceptance of a land reduction equal to less than 10 percent of their original territory or 3.5 million acres. By 1886, more land was returned to the Navajos. Today the Diné Bikéyah, or Navajo Country, is a semiautonomous homeland covering some 26,000 square miles (17 million acres) and occupying all of northeastern Arizona, the southeastern portion of Utah, and northwestern New Mexico. These territorial holdings represent the largest land area assigned primarily to a Native American jurisdiction within the United States. The 2000 census reported 298,215 Navajo people in the United States, of which 173,987 were within the Navajo Nation boundaries.

Jason Lutz and Jim Piecuch

Further Reading

Iverson, Peter. *Diné: A History of the Navajos.* Albuquerque: University of New Mexico Press, 2002.

Simonelli, Jeanne M. *Crossing between Worlds: The Navajos of Canyon de Chelly.* Santa Fe, NM: School of American Research Press, 1997.

White, Richard. *The Roots of Dependency: Subsistence, Environment, and Social Change among the Choctaws, Pawnees, and Navajos.* Lincoln: University of Nebraska Press, 1983.

Nez Perce War

Event Date: 1877

Military conflict between the Nez Perces and the U.S. Army. In 1855, most Nez Perce bands signed a treaty with the United States accepting a reservation in present-day Idaho. Some bands, however, refused to sign and did not agree to a second treaty in 1863 that greatly reduced the size of the Nez Perce Reservation. For more than a decade, no action was taken against the Nez Perces who had not signed the treaties, but under mounting pressure from white settlers in northeastern Oregon and southeastern Washington in 1877, the government sent Brigadier General Oliver O. Howard to remove those recalcitrant bands to the reservation. Howard met several times with Nez Perce leaders Joseph and Ollokot of the Wallowa band, White Bird of the Salmon River band, and Looking Glass of the Asotins before issuing them an ultimatum on May 14, 1877, to move to the reservation within 30 days or face military action.

The Nez Perce leaders reluctantly began moving their people, but during the journey, three young Nez Perce warriors killed four white settlers. Howard then sent troops in pursuit, and Joseph moved to White Bird Canyon. Still hoping to preserve peace, Joseph sent a truce party to meet with U.S. soldiers on June 17, but the troops opened fire, sparking a battle in which they were badly defeated by the Nez Perces.

Joseph tried to escape, while Howard called out troops across the Northwest to pursue and capture the Nez Perces. Some of these soldiers attacked Looking Glass's village on July 1, and he and his people joined the other fleeing Nez Perces, bringing their numbers to about 700, including 200 fighting men.

Sporadic fighting ensued as the fleeing Nez Perces encountered army detachments. Howard's troops defeated the Nez Perces in a battle at the Clearwater River during July 11–12, although the surviving Nez Perces managed to escape.

On the night of July 15, Looking Glass proposed crossing the Bitterroot Mountains into Montana, where the Nez Perces could take refuge with their Crow allies or, if that failed, escape north to Canada. They set out the next day and reached the Big Hole River on August 7, where they stopped to rest. The halt allowed Colonel John Gibbon's column to catch up and attack them on August 9. Recovering from the surprise assault, the disciplined Nez Perce warriors drove back the soldiers and held them off while the noncombatant Nez Perces escaped. Nevertheless, 90 Nez Perces had been killed.

The Nez Perces eluded several army units as they moved across Montana. Having encountered Crow scouts assisting the soldiers, the Nez Perces realized that they would get no assistance from their ally and directed their march toward Canada, where Sitting Bull established his followers after the Great Sioux War (1876–1877).

Howard now ordered Colonel Nelson A. Miles at Fort Keough, Montana, to block their escape. While the Nez Perces were taking advantage of another rest break suggested by Looking Glass, on September 30, Miles caught them in the Bear Paw Mountains less than 40 miles from sanctuary in Canada. In the five-day siege that followed, during which Howard arrived with his command, about 300 Nez Perces escaped to Canada, but Joseph, with most of his fighting men killed or wounded, surrendered the remainder of his force to Miles on October 5. Looking Glass was killed in a final exchange. During the course of this remarkable campaign, the Nez Perces covered some 1,500 miles and defeated or eluded several quality army units in the process. Despite Miles's promise to Joseph that the Nez Perces would be sent to the Idaho reservation, the government exiled them to the Indian Territory (present-day Oklahoma), where many died.

Jim Piecuch

Further Reading

Brown, Mark H. *The Flight of the Nez Perce*. Lincoln: University of Nebraska Press, 1967.

Greene, Jerome A. *Nez Perce Summer, 1877: The U.S. Army and the Nee-Me-Poo Crisis*. Helena: Montana Historical Society Press, 2000.

Nerburn, Kent. *Chief Joseph and the Flight of the Nez Perce: The Untold Story of an American Tragedy*. New York: HarperCollins, 2005.

Nez Perces

Native American people whose traditional lands ranged from the Pacific Northwest to the Great Plains until the close of the 19th century. This territory included much of present-day Washington, Oregon, and Idaho. The Nez Perces aided the Lewis and Clark expedition in 1805, and after a series of failed treaties with the federal government, some bands fought the U.S. Army during the Nez Perce War (1877).

The name "Nez Perce" means "pierced nose," a misnomer attributed to a French interpreter with Lewis and Clark. The tribe refers to itself as Ni Mii Puu ("Real people") and never practiced nose piercing as a regular part of the culture, although native groups farther south did. The Nez Perces traditionally relied on salmon and camas (a versatile edible root) for their food staples. The introduction of horses in the early 18th century greatly expanded their ability to hunt, and they soon ranged onto the Great Plains for buffalo. Therefore, the Nez Perces can be said to have been seminomadic, following herds for hunting but also engaging in some agriculture. They also engaged in trade with whites and other friendly native tribes. Territorial expansion led to frequent conflict with other Plains peoples, particularly the Blackfeet and the Shoshones, and the Nez Perces developed leadership structures and tactics that made them successful warriors.

The Nez Perces traveled in autonomous bands that occasionally joined together for hunting or war. These large groups would temporarily form a supreme council that included leaders from each band, who selected a war chief to direct military operations and a camp chief to oversee travel and maintain harmony. Diplomatic skills, negotiation, and oral argument were as important to this structure as was military prowess.

Through the late 18th century, the horse also played a significant role in the Nez Perces' military and economic success. Using selective breeding, they created the foundation for the Appaloosa horse, developing a line of animals remarkable for their temperament, soundness, and color. The Nez Perces amassed large herds, becoming both wealthy and highly mobile. They also refined techniques and procedures for hunting and fighting on horseback, making them formidable raiders.

The Nez Perces first encountered white Americans in September 1805, when they extended traditional hospitality to the Lewis and Clark expedition. They fed the starving strangers, furnishing them with supplies and information on both their westward and homeward journeys.

The 1815 Treaty of Ghent that ended the War of 1812 opened the unorganized Oregon Territory to both white American and British settlement. Thus, Nez Perce lands were at the center of an imperial dispute that lasted until 1846, when the Oregon

Treaty ceded the territory to the United States and established the 49th Parallel as the border with Canada. These events ultimately led to the Nez Perce War and the subsequent Nez Perce diaspora.

The Nez Perces were divided into two chief factions. The more sedentary Christianized bands farmed and raised cattle, advocating interracial tolerance, while many traditionalist bands adhered to the Dreamer religion and rejected white culture altogether. During the treaty period, from 1855 to 1877, these factions became more polarized. Hallalhotsoot, or Lawyer, aided missionaries and advocated cooperation with whites, while Old Joseph of the Wallowas spoke adamantly of retaining rights to all the land.

Expansion and white settlement led the United States to negotiate the Treaty of Camp Stevens, signed on June 11, 1855. This treaty reduced Nez Perce lands to less than one-third what they had been but allowed the natives to retain a reservation of about five million acres on their homeland. Congress failed to ratify the treaty for four years, and the Nez Perces received none of the promised goods or services even though settlers began claiming the ceded lands. Gold was discovered in Nez Perce territory in 1860, so hundreds of miners flooded the reservation in violation of the 1855 treaty.

The 1863 Lapwai Treaty and the Third Nez Perce Treaty of 1868 contributed to further discontent on both sides. Most non-Christian bands rejected these negotiations, while Lawyer and his people agreed to live on a drastically reduced reservation. Consequently, the 784,996-acre reservation preserved the property of Christian Nez Perces while ceding lands occupied by the more traditional Nez Perces. The nontreaty Nez Perces refused to recognize the boundaries and continued horse herding and hunting throughout the region.

When Old Joseph died in 1871, his son, Young Joseph, became camp chief of the Wallowa band. Friction between settlers and the Nez Perces prompted Brigadier General Oliver Otis Howard to meet with the chiefs in July 1876. Chief Joseph and his brother Ollokot represented the nontreaty Nez Perces, testifying about crimes committed against their people by white settlers. A series of meetings failed to resolve the situation, and in January 1877, Howard sent an ultimatum to Joseph demanding that his band move to the reservation in Idaho by April 1. When Joseph refused, Howard promptly sent two companies of the 1st Cavalry from Fort Walla Walla to the mouth of the Wallowa Valley. Joseph sought peace and counseled his people against violence. When Joseph and Howard met at Fort Lapwai in early May, Howard issued a new ultimatum, and under threat of military action, Joseph finally agreed to move his people to the reservation.

On June 14, 1877, three Nez Perce warriors killed four white men, sparking the Nez Perce War. A small war party attacked white settlements during June 14–15, while others fled. Joseph decided that he would not take the Wallowas to the reservation and embarked on a running tactical retreat of more than 1,500 miles in an attempt to reach Canada. U.S. forces ultimately chased Joseph to the Bear Paw Mountains in northern Montana, less than 40 miles from sanctuary in Canada. With most of his men killed or wounded and hopelessly outnumbered, Joseph surrendered to Colonel Nelson A. Miles on October 5, 1877.

Although some Nez Perces reached Canada, most of the nontreaty natives were transported to Indian Territory. Many eventually made their way back to Oregon but were never allowed to return to their traditional homelands. Today the Nez Perces live on the Colville Reservation (Washington) and the Nez Perce Reservation (Idaho).

Dawn Ottevaere Nickeson

Further Reading

Greene, Jerome A. *Nez Perce Summer, 1877: The U. S. Army and the Nee-Me-Poo Crisis.* Helena: Montana Historical Society Press, 2000.

Josephy, Alvin M. *The Nez Perce Indians and the Opening of the Northwest.* New Haven, CT: Yale University Press, 1965.

Moulton, Candy. *Chief Joseph: Guardian of the People.* New York: Tom Doherty, 2005.

O

Opechancanough

Birth Date: 1575
Death Date: 1646

Pamunkey chief and paramount leader of the Powhatan Confederacy (1618–1646) in Virginia's Chesapeake region. Opechancanough was sometimes referred to as the "King of the Pamunkeys," a name given to him by Jamestown leader Captain John Smith. Opechancanough was born sometime in 1575, probably in the eastern part of present-day Virginia. Nothing is known of his early life, but Opechancanough's half-brother was the powerful Chief Powhatan, leader of a confederacy of local natives. In 1617, Powhatan migrated north toward the Potomac River, leaving Opechancanough in charge of the Chesapeake region. When Powhatan died in 1618, Opechancanough succeeded him as the werowance ("chieftain") of the confederacy.

Unlike Powhatan, Opechancanough saw English settlers as interlopers who had to be driven away or destroyed. In March 1622, he staged a daring attack against English settlements around Jamestown. Only weeks before, Opechancanough had given English leaders the impression that he advocated peace and tranquility. Settlers thus had little reason to prepare against a potential attack. Opechancanough's offensive killed 347 colonists, or some 25 percent of the English population.

The stunned but furious survivors sought a hasty retribution. Although Opechancanough escaped capture, many of his subjects fell to blistering attacks and starvation at the hands of the English. Within a year, Opechancanough sued for peace. In 1644, a frail and failing Opechancanough authorized yet another broad offensive against English settlements, allegedly to avenge the murder of a Pamunkey leader. His decision launched the Third Anglo-Powhatan War (1644–1646) in which roughly 500 of Virginia's 8,000 white inhabitants died. The natives, however, again suffered disproportionately. In 1645, Virginians managed to track down Opechancanough and took him captive. He died in 1646 in Jamestown, murdered by a militiaman.

Jaime Ramón Olivares

Further Reading

Axtell, James. *The Rise and Fall of the Powhatan Empire: Indians in Seventeenth-Century Virginia.* Williamsburg, VA: Colonial Williamsburg Foundation, 1995.

McCary, Ben C. *Indians in Seventeenth-Century Virginia.* Charlottesville: University Press of Virginia, 1957.

Osceola

Birth Date: ca. 1804
Death Date: January 31, 1838

Native leader in the Second Seminole War (1835–1842). Born near the Tallapoosa River in present-day Alabama circa 1804, Osceola was the son of a mixed-blood Creek mother. His father was probably the Scottish trader William Powell. Osceola in his youth was called Billy Powell, although he later asserted that he had been born before his mother's relationship with Powell and that his father was Creek. Following the Creek War (1813–1814), Osceola and his mother moved to Spanish Florida and settled in a Seminole town at Peas Creek. There Osceola's hunting and leadership skills gained him prominence.

When Major General Andrew Jackson invaded Florida in 1818, Osceola and his mother were captured but soon released. They eventually moved to a Seminole reservation in central Florida, where Osceola worked for the U.S. government in the 1820s, policing the Seminole boundaries against intruders.

In 1834, the Seminoles became divided over acquiescence to the Treaty of Payne's Landing in which many members of the tribe accepted removal to the west. Osceola's denunciation of the treaty earned him a leadership position among Seminoles who opposed removal. Wiley Thompson, U.S. agent to the Seminoles, tried to convince Osceola to sign the treaty on April 22, 1835, but Osceola refused. Some accounts say that Osceola thrust a knife into the document in an act of defiance. Fearing Osceola's influence, Thompson had him arrested. After five days' imprisonment, Osceola signed the treaty. Upon his release, Osceola immediately fled to the swamps and began preparing for war.

Osceola and his followers began their campaign by killing Charley Emathla, a chief who had favored removal, and attacking his supporters. On December 28, 1835, Osceola attacked Fort King, killing Thompson and an army officer. The same day, the Seminoles ambushed an army baggage train and killed all but 3 of 110 soldiers. At the Withlacoochee River on December 31, Osceola turned on a force of 600 regulars

and militia sent to attack him. Catching them as they crossed the river, he mauled 250 men on one side while the remainder watched. Osceola was, however, wounded in the battle.

Osceola's offensive ignited the Second Seminole War. U.S. officials and Florida governor Richard K. Call recognized Osceola's importance as the leader of Seminole resistance and targeted him for death or capture. Eventually 8,000 troops were in the field pursuing Osceola, but for two years, he evaded them while launching hit-and-run raids against vulnerable detachments and posts. In one such operation in June 1837, Osceola freed several hundred Seminoles held in a detention compound.

Throughout the campaign, army officers made overtures to the Seminoles, urging them to meet and negotiate peace. Osceola accepted Brigadier General Joseph M. Hernandez's offer of a parley on October 22, 1837. On the orders of his superior, Major General Thomas S. Jesup, Hernandez violated the truce and arrested Osceola and 80–100 of his followers.

Osceola was imprisoned in St. Augustine until December 31, 1837, when he was transferred to Fort Moultrie in Charleston, South Carolina. He became ill but refused treatment because he distrusted the fort's doctor, Frederick Weedon, who was the brother-in-law of Wiley Thompson. Osceola died in Charleston on January 31, 1838.

Jim Piecuch

Further Reading

Bland, Celia. *Osceola: Seminole Rebel*. New York: Chelsea House, 1994.

Oppenheim, Joanne. *Osceola: Seminole Warrior*. Mahwah, NJ: Troll Associates, 1979.

P

Pequot War

Start Date: July 1636
End Date: September 21, 1638

Conflict between the Pequot people of the lower Connecticut River Valley and the English colonies of Massachusetts Bay and Connecticut, resulting in the near destruction of the Pequots. The Pequot War grew out of a series of confrontations and growing tensions between the Pequots and English settlers in Connecticut and Massachusetts Bay in the early 1630s. The Pequots were growing as a regional trading power just as English settlers extended trading posts and settlements into the Connecticut River Valley. While the Pequots were interested in trading with the English, a few violent incidents quickly changed the tone of interaction.

In spring 1634, a Virginia merchant, John Stone, was exploring the Connecticut River while returning from a trading voyage to Massachusetts. Stone apparently provoked the Pequots, and they or a subordinate tribe killed Stone and his crew. Because the Pequots were then embroiled in conflict with the Narragansetts in Rhode Island and eastern Connecticut and the Dutch in New Netherland, they quickly made a treaty with the English. Pequot sachems (chiefs) claimed that Stone had provoked the incident by kidnapping two Pequots to serve as guides up the Connecticut River. During a Pequot rescue attempt, some powder on board the ship had ignited, destroying the ship. The sachems also claimed that most of the murderers had since died of smallpox, but they agreed to hand over two who remained.

They also agreed to pay a large indemnity of wampum and pelts. The failure of Pequot sachems to ratify the treaty confirmed Puritan notions that the Pequots were not to be trusted. Only a portion of the tribute was ever paid, but Massachusetts did not pursue the issue.

The negative attitude of Puritan settlers in Massachusetts Bay toward the Pequots was fueled by charges brought by Uncas, sachem of the rival Mohegans, that the murderers of Stone and his crew continued to live among the Pequots. Uncas also reported that the Pequots were planning a preemptive war against the English.

In this increasingly charged atmosphere in July 1636, a ship captained by John Gallop discovered Captain John Oldham's pinnace adrift off Block Island. Seeing only natives on deck, Gallop assumed that they had taken the vessel. Gallop and his crew attacked the pinnace and retook it at a cost of 10–11 Native American dead and discovered Oldham's body. Because of the proximity of the vessel to Block Island, Massachusetts Bay held the natives there as well as the Narragansetts responsible because the Massachusetts leaders believed that the Block Islanders paid tribute to the Narragansetts. The Narragansett sachem, Canonicus, agreed to return both property and captives taken from Oldham's vessel, but to deflect English anger, he claimed that Oldham's murderers had fled to the Pequots. Canonicus subsequently signed a peace treaty with Massachusetts and agreed to help avenge the murders.

The Narragansetts' claims, Uncas's efforts to discredit his rivals, Puritan preconceptions about Native Americans, and the murders of Stone and Oldham all combined to produce a violent response. In August 1636, Massachusetts dispatched captains John Endicott and John Underhill and some 90 militiamen with orders to seize Block Island, kill the men, and capture the women and children. As the colonial force moved ashore, it was immediately assaulted by warriors concealed in the brush. Scattering the natives with a volley, the Massachusetts volunteers searched the island but failed to come to grips with the warriors, who had taken refuge in a swamp.

Following two days of pillaging and burning villages, the English expedition marched into Pequot territory, where Endicott demanded the extradition of Oldham's murderers, payment of 1,000 wampum, and hostages. Meanwhile, the Pequots quietly evacuated their women and children. Misunderstanding or refusing the English demands, the Pequots then refused battle. The English destroyed the Pequot village, burning wigwams and corn. Having suffered no casualties, the expedition then returned to Massachusetts Bay.

The Pequots responded to this Massachusetts attack by raiding colonial settlements in the Connecticut River Valley. Pequots attacked soldiers gathering corn outside of Fort Saybrook, at the mouth of the Connecticut River, capturing and subsequently torturing to death two men. On February 22, 1637, Fort Saybrook itself came under attack. Lieutenant Lion Gardiner and nine men were clearing a wooded area to provide better fields of fire when several hundred Pequots attacked, killing three of the soldiers. The Pequots also struck undefended settlements along the river. Most notable was the attack on Wethersfield, Connecticut, on April 23, 1637, in which nine English inhabitants died and two young women were taken captive.

Fearing English reprisal, the Pequots attempted to enlist the support of neighboring native nations. The Mohegans under Uncas spurned overtures of alliance, while the timely intervention of Roger Williams, the banished Puritan minister, prevented the more powerful Narragansetts from siding with the Pequots.

The Pequots had been right to fear retribution as both Massachusetts Bay and Connecticut raised troops for expeditions against the Pequots. Assuming command of Connecticut forces, Captain John Mason led a force of 80 soldiers and 80 Mohegans under Uncas. When the expedition stopped at Fort Saybrook, Gardiner questioned Uncas's loyalty. To prove their allegiance, the Mohegans killed four Pequots seen lurking in the fort's vicinity and captured another.

At this point, Captain John Underhill and 20 Massachusetts militiamen joined Mason at Fort Saybrook, and the two discussed the expedition's goals. The Connecticut General Court had ordered Mason to attack the Pequots at the mouth of the Pequot River (today the Thames River). Mason was certain that the Pequots would be watching the river and would repel any frontal assault. He thus proposed sailing farther east and then marching overland through Narragansett territory, flanking the Pequots. Several officers opposed the plan, but after the expedition's chaplain averred that God was in agreement with it, the expedition proceeded.

Sailing past Pequot Harbor, Mason and his force arrived in Narragansett Bay, where Mason convinced the Narragansett sachems Miantonomo and Canonicus to support his efforts. They supplied both guides and warriors, most of whom deserted before the battle, however. On May 25, 1637, Mason's force approached the smaller of two Pequot forts on the Mystic River. At daybreak on May 26, Mason moved in, positioning his men in a circle around Mystic village, with his Mohegan and Narragansett allies in a second outer ring. Detected by dogs, the Englishmen acted quickly, firing through the palisade and storming the village's two entrances. As the Pequots responded, Mason feared being overwhelmed and ordered a retreat. His men blocked the two gates and, with the aid of gunpowder, torched the wigwams. The two rings of soldiers and warriors prevented most Pequots from escaping. Of an estimated population of 400–700 Pequots, only 7 were captured alive, and a reported 7 escaped. The rest were slaughtered.

Despite this overwhelming victory, Mason was deep in hostile territory, and 20 of his own men were wounded. He was also perilously close to a larger Pequot village. Indeed, some 500 Pequots converged on Mason's men as they marched toward their boats, seven miles distant. Although the warriors harried the English for most of this distance, frequent volleys of musket fire prevented them from overrunning the small English force.

The so-called Mystic Fort Fight largely broke Pequot resistance. Massachusetts forces led by Captain Israel Stoughton, assisted by Narragansetts, pursued the surviving Pequots during summer 1637. These forces ultimately captured more than 100 Pequot women and children and executed more than 20 warriors. The fighting effectively ended in July, when numerous Pequots were surrounded in a swamp near present-day New Haven.

The Treaty of Hartford, signed on September 21, 1638, officially ended the Pequot War. With it the Pequots ceased to exist as an independent people. The Mohegans, the Narragansetts, and the Eastern Niantics absorbed the surviving Pequots in return for an annual tribute to the English. The destruction of the Pequots shifted the balance of power in New England to the English. The war also demonstrated to the English not only the importance of Native American allies but also that European methods of warfare, particularly encirclement, could be successful in America.

David M. Corlett

Further Reading

Cave, Alfred A. *The Pequot War*. Amherst: University of Massachusetts Press, 1996.

Hauptman, Laurence M., and James D Wherry, eds. *The Pequots in Southern New England: The Rise and Fall of an American Indian Nation*. Norman: University of Oklahoma Press, 1990.

Pequots

Algonquian-speaking tribe that inhabited southeastern Connecticut, centered around present-day New London, between the Pawcatuck River and Niantic Bay. At the height of Pequot dominance, the tribe's territory encompassed nearly 2,000 square miles.

The Pequots were recent arrivals who had established their military dominance over many tribes in the Connecticut River Valley in the century before European settlement. This is illustrated by their Algonquian name, which translates as "destroyer." Not surprisingly, tribes forced to pay tribute to the Pequots welcomed the English as allies. Only five years after their first sustained contact with whites, the Pequots were nearly exterminated by disease and the Pequot War (1636–1638) at the hands of the English and their Native American allies.

Pequot livelihood centered on agriculture, foraging, trade, hunting, and fishing. The Pequots lived in small dispersed familial villages of 10–20 dwellings each. These villages were not stationary but instead were relocated throughout the year, allowing the Pequots to follow seasonal changes that affected the availability of game, fish, and crop cultivation. In the summer, the Pequots lived near the coast and planted, hunted, and fished. In the winter, they moved inland, taking with them as much food as possible gathered in the summer. For subsistence in the winter, the tribe depended on hunting and stores from its summer and autumn plantings.

A sachem (sagamore or chief) headed the tribe. The position was patrilineal in that the office was held by men who were related. However, female sachems were not unknown. A council of elders composed of prominent warriors and other notables within the tribe advised the sachem, who ruled through persuasion and the granting and receiving of gifts.

The arrival of Europeans in the region and their eventual penetration into the Connecticut Valley presented the Pequots with new rivals to their dominance in the region. Unfortunately for the Pequots, the high tide of European confrontation came as they, like most Native American tribes, were devastated by disease. Two outbreaks of European diseases in 1616–1619 and 1633 occurred just as the Pequots confronted European incursions onto their lands.

The Puritans chose to regard the Pequots as little more than bloodthirsty savages. This view helped precipitate the tragic Pequot War in 1636. The English allied with the Pequots' enemies, the Narragansett and Mohegans, to destroy the Pequots and nearly succeeded in their aim.

According to some estimates, the Pequot population numbered 13,000 people just before European contact but had fallen to just 3,000 by 1636. With the conclusion of the Pequot War, fewer than 1,500 Pequots remained. The great majority were sold into slavery or took refuge with neighboring tribes. The Pequots all but disappeared, as the English refused to allow them to use their tribal name. Today the tribe survives on small reservations in eastern Connecticut.

Rick Dyson

Further Reading

Cave, Alfred A. *The Pequot War*. Amherst: University of Massachusetts Press, 1996.

Hauptman, Laurence M., and James D Wherry, eds. *The Pequots in Southern New England: The Rise and Fall of an American Indian Nation*. Norman: University of Oklahoma Press, 1990.

Vaughan, Alden T. *New England Frontier: Puritans and Indians, 1620–1675*. 3rd ed. Norman: University of Oklahoma Press, 1995.

Point Pleasant, Battle of

Event Date: October 10, 1774

The only major battle of Lord Dunmore's War of 1774. This war began in April 1774 when frontiersmen attacked native settlements in the Ohio River Valley. Subsequent retaliatory raids by natives prompted Virginia governor John Murray, Fourth Earl of Dunmore, to send 2,000 militiamen into the area. The desire of many in Virginia and Pennsylvania to expand colonial settlement beyond the boundary delineated by the Proclamation of 1763 had much to do with the war.

Two major militia columns—one headed by Dunmore and the other by Colonel Andrew Lewis—moved into Indian country. On July 12, 1774, Dunmore ordered Lewis to proceed from Camp Union (present-day Lewisburg, West Virginia) to the mouth of the Kanawha River, where Dunmore was to link up with Lewis from Fort Pitt. Lewis arrived at the rendezvous point with 1,100 men on October 6, 1774, and camped at Point Pleasant, a triangle of land at the confluence of the Kanawha and Ohio rivers and site of present-day Point Pleasant, West Virginia. Dunmore changed his plans, however, ordering Lewis to join him in attacks on Shawnee settlements along the Scioto River. Before Lewis could depart Point Pleasant, he came under a fierce Indian attack.

Shawnee scouts had located Lewis's force on October 6, and the warriors sought an immediate attack. Chief Cornstalk, an advocate of peace negotiations, insisted on a council to discuss the issue. When the council voted for an attack, at dawn on October 10 Cornstalk led a force variously estimated at 300–1,000 Shawnee, Mingo, Delaware, Wyandot, and Ottawa warriors against the unsuspecting militiamen.

The battle was hard fought and lasted all day. Lewis sent some of his men around to outflank the attackers, who were finally driven off at nightfall. In the Battle of Point Pleasant (also known as the Battle of Kanawha), the militiamen sustained some 75 killed and 150 wounded, while the Shawnees and their allies are reported to have lost only 33 dead. Nonetheless, the battle is counted as a militia victory because the militiamen held the field and because Cornstalk now entered into negotiations with Lord Dunmore, securing peace on October 19, 1774, with the Shawnees surrendering all claims to lands south and east of the Ohio River. Eventually the other tribes also agreed, bringing the war to an end.

Spencer C. Tucker

Further Reading

Brand, Irene. "Dunmore's War." *West Virginia History* 40 (Fall 1978): 28–46.

Holton, Woody. "The Ohio Indians and the Coming of the American Revolution in Virginia." *Journal of Southern History* 60 (August 1994): 453–478.

Sosin, Jack M. "The British Indian Department and Dunmore's War." *Virginia Magazine of History and Biography* 74 (1966): 34–50.

Thomas, William H. B., and Howard McKnight Wilson. "The Battle of Point Pleasant." *Virginia Calvacade* 24 (Winter 1975): 100–107.

Pontiac's Rebellion

Event Date: 1763

Conflict between Native Americans and British troops and colonists following the French and Indian War (1754–1763). Pontiac's Rebellion, also known as Pontiac's War or Pontiac's Uprising, was named for its principal leader, Ottawa war chief Pontiac (c. 1720–1769).

During the colonial period, the French enjoyed great success in building long-standing and mutually beneficial alliances with Native American tribes. Many Frenchmen lived among the natives and married native women. French policies toward the natives were far more benign than were those of the British, because the French, vastly outnumbered by the British, desperately needed Native American support in times of war. That the arrangement worked is demonstrated by the fact that most Native Americans repeatedly fought on the French side in its wars against the British. It was therefore most disquieting to Native Americans of the Great Lakes and Ohio Valley region to have their long-standing friends depart and be replaced by their long-standing enemies. As early as 1761, the Senecas had circulated a wampum belt calling for the formation of a confederation to continue the armed struggle against the British. Although this Seneca appeal elicited little response, it nonetheless indicated widespread native discontent.

Following their victory in the war, Great Britain's Native American policy fell to Major General Jeffrey Amherst, the commander in chief in North America. Amherst thought little of natives and did not understand the need for policies to allay their fears and win their friendship. Although George Croghan and Sir William Johnson, two men with wide knowledge of native affairs, sought to dissuade him, Amherst proceeded to raise the price of trade goods and end the long-standing French practice of gift giving as part of diplomatic negotiations. These decisions outraged and deeply offended many native people and increased their desire to resist the British. By spring 1763, tribes from western New York to the Illinois River were prepared to go to war.

Two Native Americans had a decided influence on subsequent events. The first was the Delaware mystic Neolin, known as the Delaware Prophet. Influenced partly by Christianity, Neolin preached a nativist message that called on his people to reform their habits, sever relations with the Europeans, and return to the ways of their forefathers. Neolin had an immense influence on the people of the Great Lakes. The second individual was Ottawa war chief Pontiac. Deeply upset over the British victory and determined to oust them from the region, Pontiac issued a call for a meeting of Great Lakes nations.

Responding to Pontiac's appeal, in April 1763 representatives from numerous tribes arrived near Detroit on the Ecorse River. For about a month, they discussed the course of action to be followed. Pontiac added his impassioned oratory to the Prophet's teachings and assured the representatives that it was time to act. For practical reasons, Pontiac assured his listeners that the Delaware Prophet's teachings regarding Europeans did not include the French, who were to be left alone. Instead, the British and the few natives allied with them were to be attacked and annihilated. After the native representatives agreed to go to war, each native group was assigned certain military objectives, and delegates returned to their villages to organize the effort.

The British military presence in the Great Lakes area was concentrated at Fort Detroit and at Fort Pitt in the Ohio Valley. Another dozen smaller British posts were scattered throughout the region. Pontiac himself took responsibility for the reduction of Detroit, while warriors of various nations launched semi-coordinated assaults on British forts all along the frontier. On May 7, Pontiac and a large party of warriors entered Fort Detroit after arranging with its commander, Major Henry Gladwin, to hold a ceremonial dance there. According to the plan, natives were to carry concealed weapons, and they were to attack the unsuspecting British once the dance had begun. Either because he had been forewarned or was naturally skeptical, Gladwin had his men fully armed and prepared, leading Pontiac to call off the attack.

After he and his men had departed the fort, Pontiac found himself the object of heavy criticism from many of his warriors and therefore allowed them to attack settlers who remained outside the fort. On May 10, Pontiac called for a parley with Gladwin, who refused. Captain Donald Campbell then offered to meet with Pontiac. Gladwin sought to dissuade him but allowed Campbell to depart. When the British captain reached the designated meeting place outside the fort, the natives immediately took him hostage. Pontiac then demanded that Gladwin surrender the fort. Gladwin refused, whereupon Pontiac initiated what would become the longest Native American siege of a fortified position.

While the siege of Detroit went forward without result, natives enjoyed great success in operations elsewhere. On May 16, warriors secured entrance to Fort Sandusky by pretending to call a council. They then killed or captured all the men at the fort, both soldiers and traders, and secured the trade goods there. At Fort Miami (near present-day Fort Wayne, Indiana) on May 27, the native mistress of fort commander Robert Holmes asked his assistance in bleeding her sick sister. As Holmes exited the fort, he was killed. A second soldier responded to the gunfire and was captured. The remaining nine men of the garrison then surrendered to an overwhelming number of warriors. On June 2 at Fort Michilimackinac, the largest of the forts taken by the natives, Ojibwas and Sauks staged a game of bag'gat'iway, similar to lacrosse, outside the fort. Native women and other spectators watched with guns and other weapons hidden under blankets. After several hours of play, the ball was launched into the fort. Securing weapons from the spectators, the players then entered the fort, supposedly to retrieve the ball, and seized the post.

In a two-week span, eight forts had fallen to the natives. The British forts lost also included St. Joseph (Niles, Michigan), Ouiatenon (Lafayette, Indiana), Venango (Franklin, Pennsylvania), Le Boeuf (Waterford, Pennsylvania), and Presque Isle (Erie, Pennsylvania), all of which had been held by fewer than 30 men each. The British abandoned Fort Burd and Fort Edward Augustus. Fort Pitt, Fort Ligonier, and Fort Bedford were all attacked but held out, as did Fort Detroit.

On May 28, a British force of 96 men in 10 bateaux under Lieutenant Abraham Cuyler put in to Point Pelee on the western end of Lake Erie on their way from Fort Niagara to Fort Detroit with supplies. After making camp, they came under surprise native attack. Cuyler and only a handful of his men managed to escape in two bateaux.

Attacks after mid-June 1763 confronted a now-alert British military. Various Native Americans, including but not limited to the Senecas, Mingos, Shawnees, Delawares, and Wyandots, assaulted the string of forts leading to Fort Detroit and the roads that supplied it.

The key was Fort Detroit, and victory there eluded the natives. Pontiac led a coalition of Ojibwas, Pottawatomis, Wyandots, and Ottawas in a loose siege. Although the natives could block access to the fort by land, they could not do so on the water. Two ships, the schooner *Huron* and the sloop *Michigan*, successfully resupplied Fort Detroit. Pontiac ordered fire rafts to be floated down the Detroit River into the anchored ships, but the latter were moved in time to avoid destruction. A native attempt to board the ships and take them by storm was discovered and beaten back. In November, a frustrated Pontiac ended the siege and withdrew his forces to the Maumee River.

The British were not idle, and soon reinforcements were on their way to the northwest. British colonel Henry Bouquet led 400 men from Fort Niagara to relieve Fort Pitt, which had been under considerable pressure since the beginning of the fighting. Its commander, Simeon Ecuyer, refused to yield to Delaware demands for surrender and reportedly sent smallpox-infected clothing among the natives that led to an epidemic.

About 30 miles from Fort Pitt, Bouquet's relief column came under heavy attack by a large force of Delawares, Wyandots, Mingos, and Shawnees. In the Battle of Bushy Run (August 5–6, 1763), Bouquet's men drove off the attackers and marched on to Fort Pitt, relieving it.

The Battle of Bushy Run proved to be the turning point in the struggle. Although sporadic warfare continued for another two years, isolated native groups began to conclude peace with the British. In July 1766, Pontiac and other chiefs met with Johnson, the British superintendent of Indian affairs in the North, at Fort Ontario to negotiate a formal peace treaty. Pontiac alienated many of the natives by attempting to speak for all the tribes of the Northwest. On April 20, 1769, in the village of Cahokia, across the Mississippi River from present-day St. Louis, Missouri, Pontiac was stabbed in the back by a Peoria Native American and left to die in the open.

Sarah E. Miller and Spencer C. Tucker

Further Reading

Dixon, David. *Never Come to Peace Again: Pontiac's Uprising and the Fate of the British Empire in North America.* Norman: University of Oklahoma Press, 2005.

Dowd, Gregory Evans. *War under Heaven: Pontiac, the Indian Nations, and the British Empire.* Baltimore: Johns Hopkins University Press, 2002.

Nester, William R. *"Haughty Conquerers": Amherst and the Great Indian Uprising of 1763.* Westport, CT: Praeger, 2000.

Powder River Expedition

Start Date: November 1876
End Date: December 1876

U.S. military campaign that took place in autumn 1876 during the Great Sioux War (1876–1877) and essentially ended any further resistance from the Northern Cheyennes, who were allied with the Sioux. The successful Powder River Expedition was overshadowed by defeats earlier in the year, including Brigadier General George Crook's defeat at the Battle of the Rosebud (June 17,

1876) and Lieutenant Colonel George Armstrong Custer's debacle at the Battle of the Little Bighorn (June 25–26, 1876).

The Great Sioux War had been a direct consequence of the July 1874 discovery of gold in the Black Hills of South Dakota, which attracted a large influx of white prospectors. The Black Hills was sacred Sioux territory and contained some of their best hunting grounds, so the Sioux were outraged at the escalating white encroachment. When the U.S. government decided not to stop whites from entering the region in violation of the 1868 Fort Laramie Treaty, the Sioux went to war and gathered many Northern Plains tribes as allies. After a series of army blunders throughout spring and summer 1876, U.S. forces regrouped, were reinforced, and again took the offensive.

At Fort Fetterman in the Wyoming Territory, Crook assembled a formidable force of 11 cavalry troops, 15 infantry companies, 400 Native American scouts, and more than 300 civilians to man the supply train. His objective was to destroy the Lakota-Cheyenne coalition by capturing Crazy Horse, the audacious Lakota chief. Crook's force departed on November 14, 1876, and marched north up the Bozeman Trail toward Rosebud, Montana, the scene of his defeat that prior June. A blizzard stalled the column for four days when word came that a large Cheyenne village of Chief Dull Knife (Morning Star) was nearby.

Crook ordered Colonel Ranald S. Mackenzie to take 10 troops of cavalry and the Indian scouts to seek out and destroy the village. The Cheyennes were encamped in a canyon along the Powder River. Mackenzie attacked at dawn on November 25, driving the sleepy Cheyennes from their lodges into the high bluffs above the village. There they made their stand, and a bloody close-quarter battle ensued. The village was seized later that day and burned. Among the items looted by the soldiers were items belonging to Custer's 7th Cavalry Regiment. The army suffered 1 officer and 5 enlisted men killed, with 24 wounded. The Cheyennes lost 40 dead, but the loss of their housing, horses, and supplies that late in the year proved devastating. Many Cheyennes froze during a three-week trek to unite with Crazy Horse on the upper Tongue River.

Harsh winter weather forced Crook to call off his expedition in December and return to the fort. The campaign was successful in that Mackenzie's destruction of Dull Knife's village rendered any future Cheyenne resistance futile. Crook's campaign coincided with similar efforts by other army elements in the region that largely subdued the Sioux by early 1877, making the Great Sioux War a significant success for the army.

William Whyte

Further Reading

Greene, Jerome A. *Morning Star Dawn: The Powder River Expedition and the Northern Cheyennes, 1876*. Norman: University of Oklahoma Press, 2003.

Robinson, Charles M., III. *A Good Year to Die: The Story of the Great Sioux War*. New York: Random House, 1995.

Powhatan

Birth Date: ca. 1547
Death Date: 1618

Paramount chief over a loose confederacy of Algonquian-speaking nations on the coastal plain of Virginia when the English established Jamestown in 1607. Powhatan (his throne name) inherited leadership of at least five native nations, whose territory adjoined the fall lines of three rivers: the James, the Pamunkey, and the Mattaponi. The rest were brought under his control through a combination of force, persuasion, and intimidation in the decades preceding English settlement. By 1618, Powhatan presided over roughly 30 Native American groups.

Powhatan's powers as paramount chief were limited. He usually ruled by prestige rather than force, with his ceremonial powers outweighing his real political or legal authority. He did not control much of the day-to-day lives of his people, and ordinary natives had considerable personal freedom.

Powhatan's success in building his paramount chiefdom was based in part on his personal qualities. The English described the chief as tall, kingly, and charismatic. However, these qualities do not explain why he created the Powhatan Confederacy. He might have wanted to rebuild a population ravaged by disease or monopolize the European seaborne trade for copper, firearms, and other high-status goods. He may also have been reacting to other unknown internal native issues.

Powhatan initially welcomed the English outpost at Jamestown, for a permanent English presence meant easy access to trade goods. The English might also have become useful allies in his wars with the Siouan-speaking Monacans to the west. His goal was to maintain an English presence while not allowing the English to become too powerful or to make contact with his enemies.

Powhatan's relations with the English quickly soured. The newcomers' insistence on exploring beyond Powhatan's territory and expanding onto Powhatan lands greatly agitated the Powhatans. The situation was made worse when English colonists stole supplies of corn from the Powhatan settlements near Jamestown.

These tensions ultimately resulted in the First Anglo-Powhatan War (1610–1614), which ended when the English captured

Powhatan's favorite daughter, Pocahontas. Following this event, Powhatan's power waned. The conflict seemed to have had a profound effect on Powhatan. He lost the will to fight white encroachments and instead chose to live a life of quiet solitude. Although he remained paramount chief until his death sometime in 1618, his younger brother and successor Opechancanough and others with great antipathy toward the English dominated Powhatan foreign policy in the 1610s.

Jennifer Bridges Oast

Further Reading

Rountree, Helen C. *Pocahontas, Powhatan, Opechancanough: Three Indian Lives Changed by Jamestown.* Charlottesville: University of Virginia Press, 2005.

Rountree, Helen C., ed. *Powhatan Foreign Relations, 1500–1722.* Charlottesville: University Press of Virginia, 1993.

Rountree, Helen C., and E. Randolph Turner III. *Before and After Jamestown: Virginia's Powhatans and Their Predecessors.* Gainesville: University Press of Florida, 2002.

Powhatan Confederacy

Confederation of Native American tribes in eastern Virginia. Powhatan, a powerful chief, created the Powhatan Confederacy in the late 16th century as a loose collection of approximately 30 Algonquian-speaking tribes along the Virginia coastal plain. Tsenacomoco, as the Powhatans referred to this area, contained about 13,000 native inhabitants when the English arrived at Jamestown in 1607. Powhatan inherited control over several nations, including the Powhatans, Arrohatecks, Appomattocks, Pamunkeys, Youghtanunds, and Mattaponis. He may also have inherited control

of the Werowocomocos, Chiskiacks, and Orapaks, according to contemporary English sources. Powhatan brought the other neighboring tribes into his chiefdom through a combination of warfare, intimidation, and personal persuasion.

Sometimes referred to as a miniempire, the Powhatan Confederacy might best be viewed as a paramount chiefdom in which Powhatan received tribute and homage from local chieftains of individual tribes. Powhatan usually ruled through prestige rather than by force, as his ceremonial powers outweighed his real legal and political authority. He in fact had little control over the day-to-day lives of his people.

Following Powhatan's death in 1618, the paramount chieftaincy fell to his younger brothers, Opitchapam (Otiotan) and Opechancanough. It was Opechancanough who held the real power in the Powhatan Confederacy from the last years of Powhatan's reign until his own death in 1646. Opechancanough organized two massive assaults against the English, in 1622 and 1644. His capture by the English in 1646 ended Powhatan resistance. After 1646, the Powhatans were subject people of the English. In 1649, the paramount chiefdom was dismantled, and after that time, local chiefs negotiated with the English independently.

Jennifer Bridges Oast

Further Reading

Gleach, Frederic W. *Powhatan's World and Colonial Virginia.* Lincoln: University of Nebraska Press, 1997.

Rountree, Helen C. *The Powhatan Indians of Virginia: Their Traditional Culture.* Norman: University of Oklahoma Press, 1989.

Rountree, Helen C., and E. Randolph Turner III. *Before and After Jamestown: Virginia's Powhatans and Their Predecessors.* Gainesville: University Press of Florida, 2002.

Pueblo Revolt

Start Date: August 10, 1680
End Date: August 21, 1680

Revolt of the Pueblo Native Americans against the Spaniards in New Mexico. The Spanish conquest of New Mexico began with Francisco Vásquez de Coronado's 1540–1542 quest for the mythical Seven Golden Cities of Cíbola. Intermittent Spanish forays into New Mexico occurred thereafter, although permanent European settlements were not begun until Don Juan de Oñate y Salazar formally established New Mexico in 1598. Franciscan missionaries, eager to convert the sedentary horticulturalists they called Indios de los pueblos (village Indians), soon took up residence in the scattered pueblos.

Relations between the Spanish and the Pueblos took a turn for the worse in 1675 when Governor Juan Francisco Treviño imprisoned 47 Native Americans whom he termed "sorcerers." These men were shamans who were perpetuating their sacred ceremonies. Three of the detainees were executed. Another committed suicide before angry Pueblo warriors forced the zealous governor to release the remaining prisoners.

Nearly a century of colonial encroachments, smallpox outbreaks, prolonged drought, forced conversions, demands for tribute, and the suppression of traditional practices led most Pueblos to long for an end to Spanish oppression. Popé, a Tewa shaman from San Juan Pueblo, made this wish reality after experiencing a powerful vision that had followed his 1675 detention.

The Pueblos' plot to drive out the Spanish unfolded on August 9, 1680, when runners carried knotted cords and instructions to two dozen villages as far south as Isleta in New Mexico, a distance of some 400 miles. Tribal leaders receiving the knotted yucca cords were instructed to untie one knot each day until none remained. After the last knot was untied, the warriors would attack the Spanish.

Governor Don Antonio de Otermín downplayed the seriousness of the planned uprising on learning about it from native informants. The rebellion, Otermín had learned, was to begin during the night of the new moon. In addition, the attacks would coincide with the arrival of the triennial Spanish supply caravan dispatched from Mexico City. The governor then ordered the torture of Nicolás Catua and Pedro Omtua, captured runners from Tesuque, for further details. Confident that the uprising would not commence until August 13, 1680, Otermín adopted a strategy of watchful waiting.

Pueblo raiders, however, attacked unsuspecting Spanish outposts on August 10, 1680, after learning that the Spaniards had captured the two runners. The stunned Otermín responded by dispatching soldiers to subdue the warriors. In addition, he ordered all Spanish colonists to gather within the safe confines of Santa Fe's defenses.

Spanish settlements in northern New Mexico as far west as the Hopi mesas in present-day Arizona felt the fury of war. The uprising claimed the lives of 19 Franciscan friars and 2 assistants. In all, some 380 Spaniards, including women and children, perished. Alonso García, New Mexico's lieutenant governor residing in Ro Abajo, learned about the devastation on August 11. On the receipt of false reports that all Spanish settlements had been destroyed in the attack and that no colonists had survived, García organized a withdrawal of all remaining Spaniards in the region to El Paso del Norte (present-day Juárez) instead of marching north to the settlers' relief.

Governor Otermín, waiting at Santa Fe for reinforcements that never arrived, prepared for a long siege. Nearly 500 Pueblo warriors attacked the capital on August 15,

1680. Within two days more than 2,500 Pueblos had joined the fight. Otermín, severely wounded in a desperate counterattack designed to drive off the attackers, abandoned Santa Fe on August 21 after the attackers cut off the city's water supply. The Spaniards then withdrew down the Rio Grande Valley.

After the Spanish departed, Popé and other leaders of the rebellion launched a purification campaign, destroying Catholic churches, statues, and relics. All Pueblos who had received the sacraments were ordered to cleanse themselves by scrubbing their bodies with yucca fibers while bathing in the Rio Grande. Pueblo traditionalists constructed kivas (partially subterranean ceremonial chambers) to replace those that the Spanish had earlier destroyed.

Otermín attempted to reclaim New Mexico in November 1681, but Pueblo warriors repelled his invading forces. Spain's interest in New Mexico waned until French explorers visited the lower Mississippi River Delta. Eager to secure the Southwest lest it fall to France, Spanish officials dispatched soldiers there in 1688 and 1689. Although unsuccessful, these expeditions revealed fissures in Pueblo civilization. Officials also learned that Ute, Apache, and Navajo raids, combined with drought and famine, had created severe hardship for the Pueblos.

On August 10, 1692, 12 years to the day of the Pueblo Revolt, Governor Diego José de Vargas vowed to retake New Mexico. By September 13, 1692, a force of 40 Spanish soldiers, 50 Mexican natives, and 2 missionaries reached Santa Fe. Vargas, anxious to assure the defenders that he meant them no harm, pardoned Tewa leaders for their past transgressions. Amazingly, the governor eventually entered the city without having to fire a shot. Maintaining constant vigilance, Vargas also visited the outlying pueblos to assure villagers of his desire for peace.

Despite the governor's efforts, violence erupted in 1693 when hostile Pueblos recaptured Santa Fe. A furious Vargas retook the city on December 29, 1693, after cutting off the defenders' water supply. The governor's reconquest of New Mexico ended in December 1696, when Vargas secured a lasting peace.

Although Spanish colonizers and missionaries returned, they had learned an important lesson. After 1696, the villages were allowed to govern themselves, and the missionaries tolerated residents' traditional practices. The Pueblo Revolt of 1680 had thus succeeded in ensuring the perpetuation of cherished tribal languages, dances, and ceremonies for centuries to come.

Jon L. Brudvig

Further Reading

Bowden, Henry Warner. "Spanish Missions, Cultural Conflict, and the Pueblo Revolt of 1680." *Church History* 44 (June 1975): 217–228.

Knaut, Andrew L. *The Pueblo Revolt of 1680: Conquest and Resistance in Seventeenth-Century New Mexico.* Norman: University of Oklahoma Press, 1995.

Roberts, David. *The Pueblo Revolt: The Secret Rebellion That Drove the Spanish out of the Southwest.* New York: Simon and Schuster, 2004.

Pueblos

Native American groups that lived along the upper reaches of the Rio Grande Valley in the American Southwest (principally in present-day New Mexico and parts of Arizona). The Pueblos had prospered for thousands of years prior to European contact. Population estimates vary, but their numbers probably reached as high as 60,000, divided into 80 towns, by the end of the 16th century. With sufficient water to sustain agriculture, the Pueblos cultivated maize, beans, and squash and used artificial means to irrigate their crops. They dwelled in terraced apartment-like buildings built of adobe and stone, which were usually two to three stories high. Towns were often situated on elevated terrain (cliffs and mesas), offering security for the community. The people were called Pueblos because they resided in permanent settlements, or pueblos in Spanish.

Pueblo government was theocratic, and ceremonial life dominated community affairs. Each pueblo was politically autonomous, with leadership originating from the community's priesthood. This along with the presence of multiple languages and dialects (Keresan or the Tanoan tongues: Tano, Tewa, Tiwa, or Towa) made collaboration between pueblos very rare.

In the early 16th century, the viceroy of New Spain authorized expeditions north of Mexico in hopes of discovering riches rumored to be found among the adobe towns scattered across the landscape. Francisco Vásquez de Coronado, governor of the province of New Galicia in northern Mexico, led the largest of these expeditions from 1540 to 1542. With approximately 300 Spanish cavalry and infantry and more than 1,000 Tlaxcalan warriors, Coronado journeyed up the Rio Grande into the land of the Pueblos. He found none of the anticipated opulent cities. Instead, Spanish conquistadors discovered desert towns of stone and mud-plastered dwellings whose stores of maize and beans offered inviting targets for raids and consumption.

Despite the efforts of the Pueblos to welcome the strangers, conflict was commonplace. Resistance to Spanish incursions proved futile at Zuni Pueblo, where Spanish horses, lances, and guns overwhelmed attempts by the Zunis to protect their foodstuffs. At the Tiwa Pueblos, the approaching winter led Coronado to commandeer buildings, clothing, and food supplies for the benefit of his soldiers. Tiwa resistance to these demands instigated three months of merciless Spanish reprisals. When Coronado's expedition returned to Mexico in 1542 after venturing all the way to present-day Kansas, it left behind a wide swath of devastation among the Pueblos.

Coronado's accounts of his profitless expedition dissuaded further forays into Pueblo country for more than half a century. In 1595, Don Juan de Oñate, the son of a wealthy silver mine owner, was charged by the Spanish court with leading an expedition up the Rio Grande to spread the Catholic faith, pacify the natives, and establish a permanent colony in the northern provinces of New Spain. In 1598, Oñate and 500 men, women, and children entered New Mexico near present-day El Paso, Texas, and claimed dominion over the land and its people. By late May 1598, Oñate had reached the upper Rio Grande and encountered the first of many pueblos he would formally claim for Spain. Despite the expedition's habit of requisitioning food from the Pueblos it encountered, the indigenous population generally welcomed the newcomers, choosing to suppress the memory of Coronado and any desire for retribution.

In July 1598, Oñate arrived at the confluence of the Chama River and the Rio Grande and established his headquarters at Ohke Pueblo, which he renamed San Juan, the capital of the new colony. From San Juan, Oñate inaugurated his missionary program by dispersing friars to the pueblos while he personally conducted a reconnaissance of the province. Native hospitality turned to resistance at Acoma Pueblo in January 1599, leaving 11 Spanish soldiers dead. In retaliation, Oñate sent a punitive expedition against the town that killed 800 men, women, and children and took another 580 captive. Adolescents were sentenced to 20 years of servitude, while adult men were subjected to public mutilation to be conducted in the plazas of pueblos along the Rio Grande. In 1601, Oñate moved the capital across the Rio Grande to Yunque Ouinge Pueblo and renamed it San Gabriel. Nine years later, the capital was moved again, this time to its permanent location in Santa Fe.

By 1610, the realization that there were few riches to be found among the pueblos led many colonists to return to Mexico. There was little incentive for new colonists to venture northward. Those who remained in New Mexico lived in scattered settlements along the Rio Grande and profited from the exploitation of native labor.

For the Pueblo people, the 70 years following the establishment of the Spanish capital at Santa Fe proved intolerable. Spanish labor demands on native people were burdensome. Native children were placed into permanent servitude, Franciscan friars strove to abolish Pueblo religious icons and ceremonies, epidemic diseases became rampant, and to make matters worse, Apache, Ute, and Navajo raiding parties preyed on Pueblo livestock. Sporadic revolts against the Spanish materialized on occasion in isolated pueblos but were easily put down, mostly because of the lack of cooperation between the native towns.

All of this dramatically changed in 1680 when Popé, a spiritual leader from San Juan Pueblo, led one of the most effective native revolts in American history. Popé successfully overcame obstacles created by distance and language barriers to unify at least 24 pueblos in a coordinated revolt against the Spanish in early August 1680. His 8,000 followers killed more than 400 Spanish colonists and 21 of the 33 Franciscan friars. Those Spaniards who were not killed or wounded fled back to Mexico, and the victors destroyed the vestiges of Spanish rule.

The success of the Pueblo Revolt kept the upper reaches of the Rio Grande free from Spanish control for 12 years. The Pueblo alliance was short-lived, however, as native towns soon returned to their familiar practice of autonomy. When the Spanish under Diego de Vargas returned to New Mexico in 1692, the Pueblos responded with minimal resistance. What opposition the Spanish did encounter was quickly suppressed. Effective Spanish control of the province resumed in 1694 but with a decidedly different approach toward the Pueblos.

Natives were now allowed to retain their religious icons and ceremonies. Labor and food requisitions were moderated. Spanish officials went so far as to arm the Pueblos to help them ward off raiding tribes. Throughout the remainder of the colonial period, the land of the Pueblos was spared the repressive policies of the pre-1680 colonists and quickly evolved into a military buffer zone protecting Mexico's northern provinces from native and European incursions. Ironically, what emerged in effect was a Pueblo-Spanish alliance that helped to preserve Pueblo culture for generations to come. In 1820, Pueblo lands came under Mexican control, and in 1848 after the Mexican land cession to the United States following the Mexican-American War (1846–1848), they came under American control. There were few instances of violence between the Pueblos and Americans. Today Pueblo natives continue to thrive in various pueblos, mainly in New Mexico.

Alan C. Downs

Further Reading

Dozier, Edward P. *The Pueblo Indians of North America*. Prospect Heights, IL: Waveland Press, 1983.

Knaut, Andrew L. *The Pueblo Revolt of 1680: Conquest and Resistance in Seventeenth-Century New Mexico*. Norman: University of Oklahoma Press, 1995.

Minge, Ward Alan. *Acoma: Pueblo in the Sky*. Albuquerque: University of New Mexico Press, 1976.

Q

Quanah Parker

Birth Date: ca. 1845
Death Date: February 23, 1911

Comanche chief known for his tenacious-ness and skills as a guerrilla leader in an effort to keep the Quahada (Antelope) band of Comanche free on the Llano Estacado (Staked Plains) of western Texas and also known for his white mother, Cynthia Ann Parker. Natives had seized Cynthia Ann in 1836 when she was nine years old during a raid on Parker's Fort in Central Texas. Adopted into a family of the Noconi (Wan-derer) band of Comanches, she received the name Naudah. Quanah, born in western Texas as early as 1845, was the eldest child of her marriage to Peta Nocona.

Historians dispute whether Quanah was a chief before the Quahadas surrendered in 1875. Quanah spoke openly in the councils of the Quahadas, a mark of high standing and respect. He was also among those who denounced the Medicine Lodge Treaty Coun-cil of 1867, which the Quahadas refused to attend. He was designated in 1871 to lead his village away from advancing U.S. troops and provided leadership in the attack against buf-falo hunters during the Second Battle of Adobe Walls in the Texas Panhandle on June 28, 1874. Quanah was a respected leader dur-ing the Red River War (1874–1875).

No record indicates when Quanah learned that his mother had been adopted. His father may have told him only after Naudah was captured in 1860 during a raid led by Texas Rangers under Captain Lawrence S. "Sul" Ross against Comanches camped on Pease River. Quanah did not see his mother again, as she was returned to her Texas relatives. She never renounced her Comanche ways. Quanah was known as Quanah Parker to Colonel (later Brigadier General) Ranald S. Mackenzie, who pursued the Quahada from 1871 to 1875. Mackenzie's troops weakened but never captured the band.

In 1875, following the disastrous Red River War, the Quahadas agreed to go to Fort Sill (Oklahoma) and settle on the reser-vation. Mackenzie's emissary, Dr. Jacob J. Sturm, reported that Quanah had spoken positively of relocating to the area. Quanah was also among a small group sent ahead to Fort Sill as messengers to inform Macken-zie of the success of Sturm's mission.

Mackenzie very much respected the Qua-hadas. He knew their skill and determina-tion as warriors, and he also knew that they had never lived a lifestyle such as that which would be required on a reservation. Qua-nah's band was allowed to keep many of its horses, and no one was imprisoned in the Fort Sill guardhouse or the uncompleted icehouse stockade.

By late 1875, Quanah had been appointed by reservation agent James M. Haworth as one of 30 band leaders for distributing beef and other supplies owed to the Comanches. Qua-nah sometimes undertook assignments from Mackenzie to locate runaways, returning them to the reservation while insisting that they not be imprisoned. In 1878 when the U.S. govern-ment insisted on a single chief for all the Comanches, Mackenzie named Quanah as the designated leader. This came with the agree-ment of many, though not all, Comanches and the support of Indian agent P. B. Hunt. From 1886 to 1901, Quanah also served as one of three judges on the Court of Indian Offenses.

As chief, Quanah encouraged his people to develop cattle herds to replace the bison, which were then all but extinct. He also took the lead in leasing unused reservation land to American cattle owners to generate income from the large herds of Texas cattle already being grazed on the reservation. From 1892 to 1901, Quanah worked diligently to delay the allotment of Native American lands, which would open reservation space for settlement by American farmers.

A leading practitioner of traditional peyote rituals, Quanah defended the ancient ceremonies against agents and missionaries who sought to stamp them out. He also advised the Comanches to stay away from the Ghost Dance religion in the 1890s. Quanah became friends with missionaries such as the Reverend A. E. Butterfield (whose father Quanah had captured in 1865) but never formally became a Christian.

Quanah's polygamous family, a traditional prerogative of leading Comanches, was controversial. He had at least three wives when he arrived in Fort Sill in 1875. Later he had as many as seven wives. Quanah died on February 23, 1911, at Cache, Oklahoma.

Charles Rosenberg

Further Reading

Gwynne, S. C. *Empire of the Summer Moon: Quanah Parker and the Rise and Fall of the Comanches, the Most Powerful Indian Tribe in American History.* New York: Scribner, 2010.

Hagan, William T. *Quanah Parker, Comanche Chief.* Norman: University of Oklahoma Press, 1993.

Neeley, Bill. *The Last Comanche Chief: The Life and Times of Quanah Parker.* New York: Wiley, 1995.

Queen Anne's War

Start Date: May 1702
End Date: April 1713

A series of engagements fought in North America and tied to the greater European conflict known as the War of the Spanish Succession (1702–1713). Carlos II (1661–1700), the Habsburg king of Spain, was childless. Since Louis XIV of France had married Carlos's sister, Marie-Thérèse, French diplomats worked successfully to secure the Spanish inheritance for Louis's grandson, Philippe, Duc d'Anjou. On his death in November 1700, Carlos left his considerable European and overseas possessions to Philippe on the condition that they not be divided. European leaders had long dreaded the Spanish succession and held discussions over possible partition plans (along the lines of the eventual settlement in 1713). A diplomatic solution would have averted a long and costly war, but Louis rejected any such arrangement.

The union of France with Spain and its possessions would be a formidable power bloc. To prevent this, the threatened powers assembled a coalition, and fighting in Europe began in March 1701. The war has sometimes been called the first world war, for the fighting took place around the globe in Europe, India, and North America. England became a leading player in the coalition to stymie French ambitions, allying itself with Austria, the Netherlands, Prussia, and most of the other German states against France, Spain, and Bavaria. In May 1702, England formally declared war, and John Churchill, Earl of Marlborough, arrived in Holland as captain general of English and Dutch forces.

In North America, the war became the second of four conflicts fought for control of the continent. English colonists called it Queen Anne's War for the English ruler Queen Anne (1702–1714). They saw the war as an opportunity to break the ring of French and Spanish settlements extending in a great arc from Canada (New France) to the Gulf of Mexico.

The first fighting in the New World occurred in 1702, when the English moved against French and Spanish holdings in the Caribbean. English forces moved from their possessions in the Leeward Islands to occupy the French portion of the island of Saint Kitts. This early success led to the unsuccessful siege of French Guadeloupe in spring 1703.

British North American colonists saw the war as an opportunity to raid and plunder French and Spanish colonial holdings. South Carolina raised a force of militia and native warriors. Under the command of Governor James Moore Jr., this force moved southward against Spanish Florida in October 1702. Moore destroyed several outposts along the St. Johns River and then moved on St. Augustine. The Spanish abandoned the town and withdrew to the Castillo de San Marcos. Moore's forces burned the town and returned to their ships on the approach of Spanish warships. Moore later mounted another expedition to strike at the Spanish outposts in western Florida. He used the promise of plunder to enlist native allies for attacks against Spanish missions. This expedition proved a success, capturing all but 1 of the 14 missions and taking nearly 1,000 mission natives as slaves. The Carolinians were unable to push through the Choctaws, however, to get at the French settlements on the Gulf of Mexico.

In June 1703, the French colonial government enlisted the help of the Abenaki Native Americans for a series of raids along the northern frontier of New England that sought to prevent the expansion of the British colonists into the interior near New France. With French assistance and leadership, nearly 500 warriors swept into English settlements in Maine (then part of Massachusetts). Towns such as Wells and Saco were destroyed, and numerous inhabitants were either killed or carried off into captivity.

During these attacks, New England colonies were left to their own devices because Britain was heavily committed to fighting on the European continent, and the New York colony had made a separate peace with the natives and was not subject to native raids. New England colonies therefore continued to suffer severe losses amid increasing rumors regarding New Yorkers' trade with natives.

During the night of February 29, 1704, a force numbering 48 Frenchmen and Canadians and 200–250 native allies attacked Deerfield, Massachusetts. They achieved complete surprise. The raid resulted in the deaths of 50 English colonists and the capture of 112 more. Twenty-one of the captives died during the 300-mile trek back to Montreal. Eventually 62 survivors were ransomed and returned to Deerfield, while the others chose to remain in Canada.

In response to the French and native raids on New England, Massachusetts raised troops to carry the war to the French in spring 1704. In June 1704, Colonel Benjamin Church led 500 New Englanders north to destroy Abenaki supplies and to take control of the Acadian fisheries. Church destroyed Abenaki villages at Minas and Beaubassin in July and then besieged the French Acadian fortress of Port Royal. Unable to take it, the troops then voted to return home. In Newfoundland, a force of French and Native Americans mounted a raid from Placentia against an English settlement at Bonavista during August 18–29, 1704.

In 1705, there was a lull in the fighting in North America, and the French governor proposed a prisoner exchange with the New England colonies. Both sides had taken large numbers of captives over the previous two years in raids along the frontier, but the negotiations yielded only a small number of exchanges. The governments of New France and Massachusetts considered a separate peace, but the negotiations failed.

In 1706, a commissioner from Massachusetts, Samuel Vetch, sailed for Britain to obtain military assistance from the Board of Trade to settle the conflict. That same year, the French and Spanish combined their forces to strike at the British in the American South and in the Caribbean. A combined force of Spanish troops and French privateers sailed from Havana, Cuba, and St. Augustine, Florida, to raid Charles Town (present-day Charleston), South Carolina. South Carolinians defeated the poorly led landing force and then raised a naval force to defeat the French ships. South Carolina then attempted to enlist native allies to attack Spanish holdings around Pensacola and Mobile. Although an attack was mounted on Pensacola in 1707, it was not successful.

In spring and summer 1707, New Englanders again attempted to attack the seat of the French colonial government in Acadia by attacking Port Royal. Colonel John March led a force of roughly 1,500 men funded by the government of Massachusetts. The force landed and drove the French back into their defensive works. A lack of discipline and poor colonial leadership, however, enabled the French to reinforce the garrison. By August, the attempt to take Port Royal had failed, and the troops returned to Massachusetts.

In summer 1708, the French took the initiative by launching raids along the New England frontier. A large force of 400 French Canadians and their native allies set out, but a significant number of Native Americans left the expedition. On August 29, 1708, the now-reduced force attempted to strike at Haverhill, Massachusetts. The raiders faced a spirited defense and were forced to withdraw on the arrival of Massachusetts reinforcements. The French did succeed in capturing St. John's on January 2, 1709, bringing all of the eastern shore of Newfoundland under their control.

Throughout 1706–1709, colonial representatives sought military assistance from the Board of Trade in Britain. In 1709, Queen Anne granted approval for a military force to be sent to New England to move in concert with a colonial military force commanded by Colonel Francis Nicholson. Provincial troops gathered in Albany, New York, in preparation for an advance on Montreal to support the planned British advance on Quebec and Port Royal. In October, however, word was received that European demands had led the British to cancel their participation and send the forces to Portugal instead, whereupon the entire operation was called off. Colonial representatives then dispatched another team of delegates to plead their case before the Board of Trade.

Representatives of Massachusetts, New Hampshire, Connecticut, and Rhode Island petitioned Queen Anne for a new British military operation against the French in 1710. The representatives also voted to assemble their own expedition to take Port Royal as soon as possible. Toward that end, in September 1710 a colonial force of 3,500 men under the command of Nicholson sailed from Boston for Port Royal. This time the British supplied a naval contingent of 36 vessels, including a bomb ketch. Captain George Martin had command. The British also contributed a regiment of Royal Marines. The siege of Port Royal opened on September 24, 1710, and the badly outnumbered French surrendered the citadel on October 1. The British renamed the town Annapolis Royal.

In 1711, the British government approved plans to send a military force to New England for an invasion of New France. Colonial representatives agreed to raise provincial troops to assist in this invasion. The British force of more than 60 ships and 5,000 men arrived in June 1711, but a fractured British command structure prevented rapid movement northward. By August 1711, the force sailed for the Saint Lawrence River. At the mouth of the Saint Lawrence, an incompetent pilot led some of the British ships onto the rocks, with the loss of 8 transports and more than 700 soldiers and 200 sailors. British admiral Sir Hovenden Walker abandoned the operation and returned with his remaining ships to England. With the loss of British military assistance, the colonial forces again disbanded.

A new Tory government in London opened negotiations for peace with the French in December 1711, and in April 1713, the warring parties agreed to peace in the Treaty of Utrecht. Philippe, Duc d'Anjou, became King Philip V of Spain, with the proviso that the French Crown and the Spanish Crown could never be united in one person. Spain was forced to cede territory in Europe to the Austrian Habsburgs and grant Britain the right to sell African slaves (*Asiento de Negros*) to Spanish colonies in the New World. In the New World, the English received recognition of their claim to Hudson Bay and control of both Acadia and Newfoundland. The French retained Cape Breton Island and the islands of the Saint Lawrence. The French then moved to build Fortress Louisbourg, an even stronger fortification than Port Royal, on Cape Breton Island.

Although many New England colonists were unhappy with the settlement, it considerably advanced British fishing, fur trading, and commercial interests in North America and opened new lands for British settlement. The failure to define the frontiers precisely, however, led to renewed conflicts in North America.

William H. Brown and Spencer C. Tucker

Further Reading

Eccles, William J. *France in America*. New American Nation Series. New York: Harper and Row, 1972.

Haefeli, Evan, and Kevin Sweeney. *Captors and Captives: The 1704 French and Indian Raid on Deerfield*. Amherst: University of Massachusetts Press, 2003.

Peckham, Howard Henry. *The Colonial Wars, 1689–1762*. Chicago: University of Chicago Press, 1964.

R

Red Cloud

Birth Date: ca. 1821–1822
Death Date: December 10, 1909

Oglala Sioux war leader. Red Cloud (Makhpyia-luta) was born in 1821 or 1822 possibly near the forks of the Platte River in present-day Nebraska. In conflicts against the Pawnees, Crows, and other rival tribes, Red Cloud demonstrated great courage and earned the position of war leader for the Teton Lakota Sioux, which included his Oglala band. The discovery of gold in Montana drew numerous white immigrants to the Bozeman Trail that passed through the Powder River region of Wyoming and Montana, territory claimed by the Sioux, Arapahos, and Northern Cheyennes. The influx began in 1864, and by early 1865, the Sioux, at Red Cloud's urging, had begun to attack these interlopers.

American peace commissioner E. B. Taylor invited the Sioux to Fort Laramie in Wyoming Territory for talks. Red Cloud along with Man-Afraid-of-His-Horses and other leaders arrived in June 1866. During the negotiations, Colonel Henry Carrington arrived with troops to build forts along the Bozeman Trail. Red Cloud denounced this as treachery, promised to fight anyone who intruded onto Sioux lands, and promptly left the conference.

Throughout summer and autumn 1866, Sioux, Cheyenne, and Arapaho warriors under Red Cloud and other leaders attacked travelers and the soldiers building three forts along the trail. The raids culminated in the Fetterman Massacre of December 21, 1866. Lured from Fort Phil Kearny by a Sioux decoy party, Captain William Fetterman and his 80 men were ambushed and annihilated.

Native raids continued during 1867, including an unsuccessful assault against woodcutters from Fort Phil Kearny that Red Cloud led in person. Meanwhile, after much debate the U.S. government agreed to a conciliatory approach to Native Americans in the Powder River region.

Red Cloud, on the advice of Man-Afraid-of-His-Horses, rejected an invitation to a peace conference in November 1867. When Red Cloud received a second invitation the following spring, he agreed to attend on the condition that the soldiers first evacuate the forts on the Bozeman Trail. American officials complied, and the forts were evacuated in July and August 1868. Red Cloud and his followers then burned the abandoned forts.

In November, Red Cloud arrived at Fort Laramie for negotiations. The resulting treaty ended the war, recognized Sioux claims to a vast tract of land in Montana and Wyoming, and set aside most of present-day western South Dakota as the Great Sioux Reservation.

Red Cloud chose to ignore the terms of the treaty by remaining near Fort Laramie, regardless of government efforts to have him move to the reservation. In 1870, he visited Washington, D.C., and met with President Ulysses S. Grant. In 1873, the government created the Red Cloud Agency in northwestern Nebraska for Red Cloud and his followers, but in 1878, the agency was relocated within the confines of the old Great Sioux Reservation in the Dakota Territory and redesignated the Pine Ridge Agency. There Red Cloud feuded with the Indian agent, Dr. Valentine T. McGillycuddy, who wanted the Sioux to abandon hunting and take up farming.

Despite his conflict with McGillycuddy, repeated violations of the Fort Laramie Treaty by the U.S. government, and pressure from Sioux militants to join them in armed resistance, Red Cloud played no role in the Great Sioux War (1876–1877) or the Ghost Dance movement that ended with the tragedy at Wounded Knee. For the remainder of his life Red Cloud honored his commitment to remain at peace. He died on December 10, 1909, at Pine Ridge.

Jim Piecuch

Further Reading

Larson, Robert W. *Red Cloud: Warrior-Statesman of the Lakota Sioux*. Norman: University of Oklahoma Press, 1997.

Olson, James C. *Red Cloud and the Sioux Problem*. Lincoln: University of Nebraska Press, 1965.

Red Cloud's War

Start Date: 1866
End Date: 1868

Conflict between Native Americans and the U.S. government over control of the Powder River Country, through which passed the Bozeman Trail leading to the Montana goldfields. Fought from 1866 to 1868, and also known as the Powder River War, the conflict is named after Red Cloud, an Oglala Sioux war leader, who led the most successful war Native Americans had ever waged against the U.S. Army. Red Cloud's determined resistance led to the abandonment of the Bozeman Trail and three U.S. Army forts in the summer of 1868.

The discovery of gold in 1862 and 1863 in Idaho and Montana opened a new front in the ongoing conflict between white settlers and the Plains Indian tribes. Although the American Civil War (1861–1865) was still in progress, thousands of adventurers and fortune seekers flocked to the area, and pressure mounted to establish more direct lines of access to the Virginia City goldfields. To respond to these challenges, army officials finally adopted the route pioneered by John Bozeman that extended from Fort Laramie on the North Platte River and the Oregon Trail northwestward along the eastern base and around the northern shoulder of the Bighorn Mountains and on to Virginia City. Although the Bozeman Trail was nearly 400 miles shorter than other routes to the region, it also cut through hunting grounds reserved for the Sioux, Northern Cheyennes, and Arapahos by the Harney-Sanborn Treaties of 1865.

In 1866, U.S. government representatives, under considerable public pressure and also lured by the gold in the region that might relieve the financial stress left by the Civil War, engaged tribes in new negotiations to gain passage through their lands. Although a few chiefs signed new treaties at Fort Laramie, others led by Red Cloud quit the discussions when Colonel Henry B. Carrington marched in with a battalion from the 18th Infantry on his way to establish posts along the Bozeman Trail. This occurred well before agreements with all the tribes had been reached.

On June 17, 1866, Carrington's battalion of about 700 men, plus several cavalry units and hundreds of mule teams hauling large quantities of equipment and supplies, departed Fort Laramie and headed toward the Bighorn Mountains. At Fort Reno, located on the

Powder River many miles from the nearest telegraph station, Carrington relieved two companies of the 5th U.S. Volunteers, comprising former Confederate prisoners who had agreed to frontier service with the Union in exchange for their freedom. Farther to the northwest some 225 miles from Fort Laramie, Carrington constructed his headquarters on the Piney tributary of the Powder River, which he named Fort Phil Kearny. Five companies stayed at Fort Phil Kearny, while the remaining two marched another 90 miles to establish Fort C. F. Smith on a bluff some 500 yards from the Bighorn River.

Fort Phil Kearny almost immediately came under Native American attack and, during its brief existence, remained in an almost continual state of siege. On December 21, 1866, Red Cloud's warriors attacked a wagon train six miles from the fort. Captain William Fetterman, who had boasted that he could ride through the whole Sioux Nation with just 80 men, asked to lead a relief column. Native decoys lured Fetterman from the fort, and against Carrington's orders, Fetterman crossed the ridge toward hundreds of waiting warriors. In a carefully executed ambush, the Sioux annihilated Fetterman's entire force, including two civilians who had accompanied the soldiers to test their new Henry repeating rifles.

The army was more successful in two other notable actions on the Bozeman Trail. In August 1867, Cheyenne and Sioux warriors launched separate but seemingly coordinated attacks known as the Hayfield Fight (August 1) and the Wagon Box Fight (August 2). In the Hayfield Fight, 19 soldiers and 6 civilians from Fort C. F. Smith under Lieutenant Sigismund Sternberg, equipped with converted breech-loading Springfields and several repeating rifles, held off a superior force with the loss of three killed and three wounded. In the Wagon Box Fight near Fort Phil Kearny, Captain James Powell and 31 men positioned themselves behind wagons that had their running gear removed. There they managed to hold at bay a force of several hundred warriors for four hours with only three killed and two wounded.

Despite these small victories, the days of the Bozeman Trail were numbered. After eight months of negotiations, the majority of tribal leaders finally agreed to a new treaty, but it was not until November 6, 1868, that Red Cloud signed the document at Fort Laramie, officially ending Red Cloud's War. The 1868 treaty met almost all Sioux demands, including the abandonment of Fort Reno, Fort Phil Kearny, and Fort C. F. Smith and the closing of the Bozeman Trail. The treaty also recognized Native American dominion over the Powder River Country and vast hunting grounds in Wyoming and Montana and set aside most of the Dakota Territory west of the Missouri River as the Great Sioux Reservation. For the first time in its history, the U.S. government had negotiated a peace that had conceded everything demanded by the opposing party and that had extracted nothing in return.

Brett F. Woods

Further Reading

Larson, Robert W. *Red Cloud: Warrior-Statesman of the Lakota Sioux.* Norman: University of Oklahoma Press, 1997.

Olson, James C. *Red Cloud and the Sioux Problem.* Lincoln: University of Nebraska Press, 1965.

Red River War

Start Date: June 27, 1874
End Date: June 2, 1875

Major conflict on the southern Plains. The Red River War began on June 27, 1874, and officially ended on June 2, 1875. The

Medicine Lodge Treaty of 1867 created two new reservations in Indian Territory (Oklahoma): one for the Comanches, Kiowas, and Kiowa Apaches and another for the southern Cheyennes and Arapahos. The treaty provided that the American government would supply the tribes with food, clothing, and other goods in return for which the tribal leaders agreed to prevent warriors from launching raids on settlers. The tribes were also given permission to hunt buffalo on any lands south of the Arkansas River.

However, the activities of commercial buffalo hunters were not curbed, and by 1874, the number of buffalo had plummeted. Also, many of the U.S. officials providing the tribes with the goods specified in the treaty were either inefficient or corrupt, the quality of the items delivered to the tribes was poor, and the quantity was insufficient. Thus, many warriors chose to leave the reservations for the freedom of the Texas plains. Rising tensions as whites pastured cattle on the reservations in violation of the treaty and stole Native American horses also compelled Native Americans to leave. These factors led to a major Native American uprising.

By 1874, Isa-tai, a Comanche shaman, rose to prominence on the Comanche reservation. He claimed to have talked with the Great Spirit, who had granted him supernatural powers. Having convinced many Comanches of his spiritual power, Isa-tai began to urge war on the white settlers. He had a personal reason for doing so, as his uncle had been killed in battle with U.S. forces. Isa-tai convinced many tribal leaders that conflict with the Americans was inevitable and that it would be better if the Comanches struck first.

Isa-tai brought the Comanches together for a sun dance in May 1874. Small numbers of Kiowas and Southern Cheyennes also joined the gathering. Initially tribal leaders wanted to attack the Tonkawas, who provided scouts for the U.S. Army. However, they later decided that the attack should be focused on the buffalo hunters at a trading post known as Adobe Walls, located in the Texas Panhandle.

On June 27, 1874, a war party numbering several hundred Cheyenne and Comanche warriors attacked Adobe Walls. Among the leaders was the Comanche Quanah Parker, son of an influential Comanche chief and his captured settler wife. Isa-tai did not join in the attack but watched from a nearby hill. Native Americans were held at bay by long-range rifle fire and were unable to close in on a small group of buildings defended by 28 men and 1 woman. Fifteen warriors died in the failed attack.

Isa-tai claimed that the attack failed because a warrior violated a sacred taboo. Several Cheyenne warriors refused to accept this explanation, however, and publicly beat Isa-tai, who was now disgraced. Most of the Kiowas had not joined in the attack, but on July 12, a small party of 50 warriors under Lone Wolf attacked a force of Texas Rangers near Jacksboro, killing 2.

General William Tecumseh Sherman, commanding general of the U.S. Army, ordered Lieutenant General Philip Sheridan, commander of the Military Division of the Missouri, to end the uprising. Both Sherman and Sheridan advocated total war, and neither was well disposed toward the Native Americans. Sheridan's plan called for five independent army columns to converge on the Native Americans of the Texas Panhandle and exact such retribution that there would not be another uprising. The five columns consisted of those under Colonel Nelson A. Miles from Fort Dodge, Kansas; Colonel Ranald S. Mackenzie from Fort Concho, Texas; Major William R. Price from Fort Bascom, New Mexico; Lieutenant Colonel John W. Davidson from Fort Sill in Indian Territory (Oklahoma); and Lieutenant Colonel George P. Buell from Fort Griffin, Texas. Altogether the force numbered more than 2,000 soldiers and Native American scouts.

Beginning in August 1874, the army units moved onto the reservations to separate the hostile from the peaceful Native Americans. Most of the Arapahos were judged to be friendly, while the majority of the Cheyennes were considered hostile. At Fort Sill, a confrontation occurred between Davidson's cavalrymen and Comanches supported by Kiowas under Lone Wolf. Altogether the army estimated that there were some 5,000 hostile Native Americans, including 1,200 warriors.

The first column in action was that of Miles. He departed Fort Dodge on August 11, 1874, with eight companies of cavalry and four of infantry, all supported by Gatling guns and artillery. During August 27–31, Miles fought a series of running battles near Palo Duro Canyon with Cheyenne warriors, who were then joined by Kiowas. Although the soldiers drove off the Native Americans in these engagements, Miles was short of supplies and was forced to halt and await them. On September 7, his column joined Price's cavalry squadron. Two days later, Miles's supply train under the command of Captain Wyllys Lyman came under attack and was besieged for three days until the Native Americans broke off their effort.

Miles sent out scouting parties to learn what had happened to his supply train. One of these groups, composed of six men, was attacked on September 12 and sought refuge in a buffalo wallow. One man was killed, and the remainder were wounded. On the same day, Price reached the beleaguered wagon train.

By now a third column was in the field. Mackenzie's eight cavalry troops and five infantry companies advanced from Fort Concho. Mackenzie fought a skirmish in Tule Canyon on September 26, frustrating a Comanche attack. Two days later, on September 28, his men located a large group of Native Americans in the upper Palo Duro Canyon. After a harrowing descent into the canyon, Mackenzie's 4th Cavalry attacked at dawn, forcing dozens of Native Americans to surrender. The troops then destroyed the camp, lodges, supplies, and food stores for the coming winter. They also captured some 1,500 ponies, 1,000 of which Mackenzie ordered slaughtered. The Battle of Palo Duro Canyon and the loss of the horses had a major impact on the fighting capacity of the Comanches, and by October, many began to move back toward the reservations. The weather had now turned cold and treacherous, but the soldiers nonetheless continued to tighten their grip. On November 8, 1874, Lieutenant Frank Baldwin from Miles's command destroyed a large Cheyenne camp. The other columns were then reinforced with the additional two columns under Davidson and Buell.

Throughout winter and spring 1875, the number of Native American surrenders increased. In late February 1875, Lone Wolf came in with some 500 Kiowas. On March 6, some 800 Cheyennes under Gray Beard surrendered. On June 2, Quanah Parker and some 400 Comanches surrendered at Fort Sill.

The Red River War ended the Native American threat on the southern Plains and was certainly among the most successful U.S. campaigns against Native Americans in the history of North America and confirmed the total war approach and the effectiveness of winter campaigning.

Ralph Martin Baker and Spencer C. Tucker

Further Reading

Hayley, James L. *The Buffalo War: The History of the Red River Indian Uprising of 1874.* Sacramento, CA: State House Press, 1998.

Jauken, Arlene F. *The Moccasin Speaks: Living as Captives of the Dog Soldier Warriors, Red River War, 1874–1875.* Lincoln, NE: Dageforde Publishing, 1998.

Leckie, William, ed. *Indian Wars of the Red River Valley.* Newcastle, CA: Sierra Oaks Publishing, 1987.

Roman Nose

Birth Date: ca. 1830
Death Date: September 17, 1868

Southern Cheyenne war leader. Also known as Wakini (Hook Nose), Roman Nose was born around 1830. Little is known of his early life, but by the 1860s, he had emerged as a leader of the Cheyennes' Crooked Lance Society and had closely aligned the group with another Cheyenne society, the Dog Soldiers. In summer 1864, he led many Cheyennes to the Powder River area to hunt and thus escaped the Sand Creek Massacre in November.

In January 1865, Roman Nose learned of the events at Sand Creek. He and his warriors, yearning for vengeance, joined Red Cloud's Sioux, who had decided to drive out white intruders on the Bozeman Trail. On July 26, while the Sioux attacked a cavalry detachment on the North Platte River, Roman Nose led an attack on a nearby army wagon train. Wearing a special headdress of eagle feathers made for him by a shaman and believing that this medicine bonnet rendered him immune to bullets and arrows, Roman Nose drew the soldiers' fire, and the Cheyenne followed him in a charge that overran the circled wagons and annihilated the soldiers.

On September 1, Roman Nose led a force of Cheyenne, Sioux, and Arapaho warriors in an attack on a detachment of soldiers along the Powder River. Protected by his medicine bonnet, he rode several times along the full length of the soldiers' line to expend their ammunition before the Native Americans attacked. His horse was killed, but Roman Nose remained unscathed. The soldiers, however, withstood the assault.

By 1866, Roman Nose and his followers had returned to their home territory. At a council at Fort Ellsworth, Kansas, Roman Nose protested against the Union Pacific Railroad's encroachment into Cheyenne hunting grounds. When railroad construction continued and growing numbers of settlers began moving westward along the Smoky Hill Road, the more militant among the Cheyennes resolved to attack the stagecoach stations. In the autumn, Roman Nose visited Fort Wallace to announce that he would commence attacks in 15 days if travel on the road was not halted. A harsh winter limited Cheyenne operations to a few raids.

In April 1867, Major General Winfield Scott Hancock arrived at Fort Larned with 1,400 men, intending to force the Cheyennes to allow settlers unimpeded passage on the roads and railways. Hancock presented his demands at a council with Cheyenne chiefs and insisted on meeting Roman Nose, who had not attended the meeting because he was not a chief. Hancock then marched his force toward the Cheyenne camp at Pawnee Fork. The Cheyennes believed that Hancock intended to attack their camp. While they gathered their possessions and fled, Roman Nose, at the head of 300 warriors, met Hancock on April 14. Roman Nose wanted to kill Hancock but was restrained by one of the Cheyenne leader's lieutenants. After Hancock insisted that Roman Nose instruct the fleeing Cheyennes to return to their camp, the meeting broke up. Hancock's troops then destroyed the abandoned village.

Once the Cheyenne women and children were safe, Roman Nose and his followers unleashed the offensive they had planned earlier, attacking wagon trains, railroad work crews, and settlers in western Kansas. Roman Nose refused to attend the Medicine Lodge Council in October 1867 at which Kiowa, Comanche, Arapaho, and some Cheyenne leaders signed a treaty that restricted the tribes to a joint reservation and accepted construction of the railroad.

Roman Nose and his 300 warriors, assisted by some Sioux and a few Arapahos, continued their raids into autumn 1868. On September 16, a Sioux party discovered a company of 53 army scouts under Major George Forsyth. The Sioux sent a message to Roman Nose urging an immediate attack. When the message arrived, Roman Nose was in his lodge undergoing a purification ritual; several days earlier, he had inadvertently eaten food prepared with metal utensils, which supposedly rendered his medicine bonnet ineffective. Native Americans attacked the scouts' camp the next morning in what became known as the Battle of Beecher's Island. Roman Nose joined them in the afternoon without properly completing the ritual. While leading an unsuccessful charge on the scouts' position, he was mortally wounded and died later that night.

Robert W. Malick and Jim Piecuch

Further Reading

Grinnell, George Bird. *The Fighting Cheyenne*. 1915; reprint, Norman: University of Oklahoma Press, 1989.

Nye, Wilber S. *Plains Indian Raiders: The Final Phase of Warfare from the Arkansas to the Red River*. Norman: University of Oklahoma Press, 1968.

S

Sand Creek Massacre

Event Date: November 29, 1864

Infamous attack by Colorado militia on a peaceful Cheyenne village. Located in southeastern Colorado 50 miles from present-day Lamar, Sand Creek was the site of a deliberate and unprovoked 1864 attack on a peaceful Southern Cheyenne village by Colorado volunteers. In just more than an hour, 148 Native Americans lay dead, many of their bodies mutilated for souvenirs.

Included in the land guaranteed to the Cheyennes and the Arapahos in Article V of the Fort Laramie Treaty of 1851 was eastern Colorado, from its border with Kansas and Nebraska westward to the Rocky Mountains and south to the Arkansas River. The discovery of gold at the confluence of the South Platte River and Cherry Creek, however, drew a multitude of prospective miners into Cheyenne territory during the latter half of the 1850s. New trails traversed Cheyenne hunting grounds, opening the way for immigrants who constructed settlements on land promised to the Native Americans. Soon buffalo and other wildlife grew scarce. Tensions mounted as hunger and disease spread through Native American bands.

The U.S. government sought to relieve the friction by further reducing Native American lands. Believing that obstinacy and delay would result in a less favorable settlement, Cheyenne leaders Black Kettle and White Antelope, along with an Arapaho delegation led by Little Raven and Left Hand, met with government agents on February 8, 1861, and placed their "X" on the Treaty of Fort Wise. The document ceded to the United States the vast territory granted to the Native Americans in the 1851 Fort Laramie agreement in exchange for annuity payments and a small reservation of 600 square miles in southeastern Colorado between the Big Sandy and Arkansas rivers.

The reservation was unable to sustain Native Americans compelled to live there. Unsuitable for agriculture, the desolate, gameless terrain proved to be a breeding ground for epidemic diseases. With the nearest buffalo herd more than 200 miles away, young Cheyenne men left the reservation in search of food. Raids on livestock and passing wagon trains became more and more frequent. Between 1861 and 1864, sporadic violence spread across eastern Colorado and the plains of Kansas and Nebraska as Cheyenne and Arapaho warriors clashed with soldiers and volunteer militia units. Fear and panic swept among white homesteaders, who were fully aware of the incidents associated with the Minnesota Sioux Uprising of 1862.

In June 1864, John Evans, who had become the second governor of Colorado Territory two years earlier, issued a proclamation inviting all "friendly Indians" to certain designated forts, where they would be fed and allowed to camp under the protection of the military. Those who chose not to comply with this directive would be considered hostile and subject to punitive raids. With most of the territory's regular troops away fighting Confederates in the American Civil War (1861–1865), Evans called for civilians to join the new 3rd Colorado Cavalry for 100 days, stressing that "any man who kills a hostile Indian is a patriot . . . and no one has been or will be restrained from this."

Colonel John M. Chivington, a 43-year-old Methodist minister turned soldier and politician, commanded the Colorado volunteers. In 1862, Chivington replaced his clerical attire with a major's uniform in the 1st Colorado Volunteer Regiment and won acclaim for his role in defeating Confederate troops at the battle of Glorieta Pass in eastern New Mexico (March 26–28, 1862). Now he was to lead an expedition against the Native Americans.

Black Kettle and six other chiefs decided to accept the governor's invitation and traveled with Major Edward Wynkoop, the commander of Fort Lyon, to Denver to meet with Evans and Chivington. Meeting at Camp Weld on September 28, 1864, the Native Americans were told to submit to military authority as represented by the garrison at Fort Lyon. Black Kettle believed that he had secured peace and safety for his band and others. Unbeknownst to the Native Americans, Chivington received an order that same day from Major General Samuel R. Curtis, commanding officer of the Department of Kansas, instructing him not to make peace. Chivington readily assented, with the blessing of Governor Evans.

On November 4, 1864, Major Scott Anthony relieved Wynkoop of command of Fort Lyon. Anthony proceeded to disperse Native Americans, sending them away from the fort toward Sand Creek. Chivington meanwhile moved his column of nearly 600 men down the Arkansas River toward Fort Lyon, arriving at the post on November 28. The enlistment of his 100-day volunteers was about to expire, and the men were already disappointed at not having experienced a battle. Also, Chivington had been ridiculed in the press for his inactivity.

Accompanied by 125 men of 1st Colorado Cavalry under Major Anthony and four mountain howitzers, the volunteers started for Black Kettle's camp at 8:00 p.m. Having covered the 40 miles to the village that night, Chivington's men were in position to attack as dawn broke on November 29.

Black Kettle's camp along Sand Creek was composed of approximately 450 Southern Cheyennes and 40 Arapahos split into separate groups of lodges, each headed by a chief. While a few women were up starting fires for cooking, most of the village was still asleep when the volunteers struck. Anthony drove away the herd of Native American ponies and then approached the village from the west. Three companies of the 1st Colorado Cavalry crossed the mostly dry creek bed and attacked from the east and north, while the 3rd Colorado Cavalry under Colonel George L. Shoup charged straight into the center of the encampment. Cheyenne oral history is replete with accounts of confusion and chaos as the Colorado volunteers swept through the village, firing indiscriminately into the lodges. The mountain howitzers positioned on the south bank of the creek began to rain grapeshot down on the fleeing Native Americans. Black Kettle tied an American flag that he had received in Denver, along with a white flag of truce, to one of his lodge poles in an unsuccessful effort to halt the slaughter. Black Kettle and Left Hand were left with no choice but to try to escape. White Antelope chose to remain and was shot in front of his lodge.

The bloodletting continued as Chivington's men chased the remaining Cheyennes and Arapahos for miles up Sand Creek, overtaking and killing as many men, women, and children as they could find. Some of the refugees, including Black Kettle, managed to escape by digging into the sandy soil or hiding under the embankments of the creek. Returning to the village, the Colorado volunteers proceeded to kill all the remaining wounded and mutilate the bodies. Chivington did nothing to halt the carnage. On December 1, the remains of the village and its inhabitants were set on fire, and the Colorado volunteers departed for Denver. Chivington's casualties were 9 killed and 38 wounded. The Cheyenne and Arapaho dead numbered 148, only 60 of them men.

At first Chivington and his volunteers were wildly praised and rewarded for their actions. Soon, however, rumors and testimonials about what really happened at Sand Creek convinced the U.S. Congress to order a formal investigation of the affair. Although never formally punished for his actions, Chivington nevertheless resigned from military service and withdrew from political life. Black Kettle, having miraculously escaped the carnage, returned to his efforts to bring peace on the plains. On October 14, 1865, Cheyenne and Arapaho representatives agreed to a treaty that called for giving up the Sand Creek Reservation in Colorado in exchange for a reservation in southwestern Kansas and Indian Territory.

Alan C. Downs

Further Reading

Hoig, Stan. *The Sand Creek Massacre.* Norman: University of Oklahoma Press, 1961.

Josephy, Alvin M., Jr. *The Civil War in the American West.* New York: Knopf, 1991.

Utley, Robert M. *Frontiersmen in Blue: The United States and the Indian, 1848–1865.* Lincoln: University of Nebraska Press, 1967.

Satanta

Birth Date: ca. 1820
Death Date: September 11, 1878

Prominent Kiowa warrior. Born in present-day northern New Mexico or Oklahoma around 1820 into the Onde (prominent warriors) caste, which comprised about 10 percent of the Kiowa tribe, Satanta emerged as a leading warrior and spokesman for his people while in his early twenties. Accustomed to leading raids into Texas, New Mexico, and Mexico to capture horses and obtain captives to augment their numbers, the Kiowas began to face pressure to stop their raids after Texas entered the United States in 1845. Despite increased warnings from U.S. Indian agents and military officers, Satanta and other Kiowa leaders considered these threats to be mere bluffs. The outbreak of the American Civil War (1861–1865) served to reinforce this attitude because whites were virtually powerless to prevent the Kiowas from raiding.

In November 1864, Brigadier General James H. Carleton, commanding in the Department of New Mexico, dispatched a volunteer force of 350 men under Colonel Christopher "Kit" Carson to attack the Kiowas and Comanches along the South Canadian River in the Texas Panhandle. The ease with which the Kiowas and Comanches defeated Carson's volunteers at Adobe Walls further convinced Satanta that the Kiowas could remain masters of the southern Plains.

Despite their victory, not all Kiowas shared Satanta's bellicose outlook toward the whites. Kicking Bird and Stumbling Bear in particular believed that tribal survival required peace. In 1865, they and other Kiowa leaders signed a peace treaty in which the Kiowas agreed to remain between the Red and Arkansas rivers and surrender claims to land in Colorado, Kansas, and New Mexico. Satanta, Lone Wolf, and Satank, however, ignored the treaty and continued to raid into Texas.

In April 1867, Satanta was the leading voice against concessions at a meeting between Kiowa leaders and Major General Winfield Scott Hancock at Fort Dodge,

Kansas. In October 1867, Satanta was among the many leaders of southern Plains tribes who attended the peace commission at Medicine Lodge Creek in Kansas. Once again, he eloquently rejected demands that the Kiowas confine themselves to a reservation in Indian Territory (Oklahoma) and adopt white culture. In an effort to conciliate Satanta, the U.S. government recognized the right of the Kiowas to leave the reservation to hunt buffalo on the southern Plains.

Although Satanta joined the Kiowas on the reservation, the failure of the government to provide sufficient rations and the decline of the buffalo herds led him to return to the time-honored pattern of raiding, first against the nearby Caddos and Wichitas and then into Texas. Following Lieutenant Colonel George Armstrong Custer's attack on Cheyenne chief Black Kettle's village along the Washita River on November 27, 1868, Satanta and Lone Wolf went under a flag of truce to meet with Major General Philip Sheridan, who promptly had them arrested and taken to Fort Cobb, where they were held for three months. Angered at their captivity, Satanta and other Kiowa leaders launched raids into Texas during the next three years.

On May 18, 1871, Satanta took a leading role in an attack on a civilian wagon train owned by Henry Warren as it crossed the Salt Creek Prairie near Fort Richardson in northern Texas. The raiders tortured and killed a number of teamsters and drove off some 40 mules. Satanta and other leaders then returned to the Fort Sill Reservation, where they boasted of their participation in the raid. U.S. Army commander General William Tecumseh Sherman, who had narrowly missed the attack that struck the wagon train and who too had moved on to Fort Sill, had Satanta, Satank, and Big Tree arrested and sent to Jacksboro, Texas, to be tried. Satank, an aged warrior chief,

was killed when he tried to escape, but Satanta and Big Tree were convicted and sentenced to death. Governor Edmund J. Davis succumbed to federal pressure and commuted the sentences to life imprisonment at the state penitentiary in Huntsville.

In an effort to conciliate the Kiowas, federal authorities pressured Davis to parole Satanta and Big Tree to Fort Sill in 1873 on the promise that they refrain from further raids. Although Satanta remained at peace, he was nevertheless held responsible for Kiowas who attacked buffalo hunters in the Second Battle of Adobe Walls (June 27, 1874) and carried out raids in Texas in 1874. Even though Indian agents at the Kiowa Reservation confirmed that Satanta had not participated in either the battle or the raids, Sheridan ordered that Satanta be arrested and returned to Huntsville. After four years' captivity, Satanta took his own life by leaping from the second floor of the prison on September 11, 1878.

Justin D. Murphy

Further Reading

Mayhall, Mildred P. *The Kiowas*. Civilization of the American Indian Series. 1971; reprint, Norman: University of Oklahoma Press, 1984.

Robinson, Charles M., III. *Satanta: The Life and Death of a War Chief*. Austin, TX: State House Press, 1997.

Worcester, Donald. "Satanta." In *Studies in Diversity: American Indian Leaders*, edited by R. David Edmunds, 107–130. Lincoln: University of Nebraska Press, 1980.

Scouts, Native American

Native American allies or auxiliaries in European or American military organizations. These groups frequently depended on Native Americans because of their familiarity with relevant terrain and the indigenous populations or simply because they were an additional source of military manpower.

The use of native scouts dates to the initial stages of European contact with the indigenous populations of the Americas. Meso-Americans helped the Spaniards topple the Aztecs, for example, while the Dutch, French, and English all relied on Native American allies to maintain their tenuous footholds in North America and to challenge the hegemony of their European rivals. These allies provided not only scouts but also sizable contingents of warriors who often operated in concert with, but usually independently of, European forces.

As sovereign powers, Native Americans entered into alliances with European nations to obtain military advantage over their Native American enemies, to gain access to European manufactured goods, and to seek revenge on a European enemy. Individual warriors relished the opportunity to distinguish themselves in battle and reap the spoils of war. Given the diffuse nature of political authority among most Native American societies, Europeans allied with groups as small as individual villages or as large as multi-tribal confederacies. Competition between colonial powers often worked to the advantage of Native Americans, who offered their military service to competing suitors and thus played them against one another. The demise of New France in the French and Indian War (1754–1763) and Great Britain's successive losses in the American Revolutionary War (1775–1783) and the War of 1812, however, gradually eliminated this advantage. From 1815 onward, few Native American groups retained the power to treat with the United States as sovereign entities.

Some eastern tribes, devastated by disease and subsumed by the advance of the English colonial frontier, had been reduced to subject status as early as the 17th century. As a means of sustaining their people in the face of wrenching change, they offered military service not as allies but instead as auxiliaries. This form of cooperation between Americans and Native Americans predominated in the Trans-Mississippi West during the 19th century and is most commonly associated with the term "Indian scout."

Native American motivations for allying with Europeans and Americans are relatively easy to discern, but understanding their auxiliary service is more complicated. Often regarded as mercenaries or race traitors by other natives, Native American auxiliaries have endured the scorn of some scholars and even their own descendants. Almost invariably, however, auxiliary service permitted Native Americans to provide for their communities in accordance with their cultural and societal values. Intending to "civilize" Native Americans, U.S. officials forbade intertribal warfare and encouraged Native American men to abandon hunting in favor of intensive sedentary agriculture. As most Native American societies regarded farming as women's work and held accomplished warriors in the highest esteem, federal officials were, in effect, requiring Native American men to surrender their manhood. Auxiliary service thus provided some men an attractive opportunity to distinguish themselves, provide for their families, and perhaps exact revenge against Native American antagonists.

For their part, Europeans and Americans were often ambivalent about the employment of Native American allies and auxiliaries. Military necessity demanded the practice initially, but English colonists feared that it advertised weakness to potential enemies. These colonists and their American descendants relied on Native American allies only as an expedient of last resort and regularly punished their allies as harshly as their enemies. These concerns diminished by the mid-19th century, however, with the erosion of Native American sovereignty east of the Mississippi River.

In the sparsely populated West, army commanders found ready Native American auxiliaries among sedentary tribes that had long been victimized by their horse-mounted aggressive neighbors. During the American Civil War (1861–1865), local commanders increasingly turned to auxiliaries. Congress regularized the practice on August 1, 1866, when it authorized a force of 1,000 Native American auxiliaries, who were to receive the same pay as regular U.S. Army cavalrymen.

Some officers opposed the enlistment of Native American auxiliaries because it offended their sense of military professionalism or seemed to retard the process of "civilization." Others simply doubted Native American loyalty. With the exception of a single mutiny among Apache scouts at Cibecue Creek in 1881, however, Native American troops provided loyal and invaluable service to the U.S. Army in the West.

Indian scouts contributed meaningfully to most of the major campaigns of the post–Civil War era. The more prominent and numerous Native American scouts hailed from among the Pawnees, Apaches, Navajos, Crows, Seminoles, and Arikaras. The most forceful advocate for the use of Indian scouts was Brigadier General George Crook, who employed them widely in his many campaigns, most notably against Geronimo. Apache scouts accompanying Lieutenant Charles Gatewood located Geronimo and helped to secure his surrender. Black Seminole (Seminole Negro) scouts played a conspicuous role in campaigns along the Texas-Mexico border, including Colonel Ranald S. Mackenzie's cross-border incursions. Many Indian scouts rode to their deaths

with Lieutenant Colonel George Armstrong Custer's 7th Cavalry in the Battle of the Little Bighorn (June 25–26, 1876). Surveyors, explorers, pioneers, and railroad companies also employed Native American scouts. The Shoshone Sacagawea, who accompanied the Lewis and Clark expedition of 1803–1806, is perhaps the most famous example.

Undeniably, scouts' and auxiliaries' service facilitated American conquest of the West, yielding a historical legacy as ambiguous as it was important.

John W. Hall

Further Reading

Downey, Fairfax, and J. N. Jacobsen. *The Red-Bluecoats: The Indian Scouts.* Fort Collins, CO: Old Army, 1973.

Dunlay, Thomas W. *Wolves for the Blue Soldiers: Indian Scouts and Auxiliaries with the United States Army, 1860–90.* Lincoln: University of Nebraska Press, 1982.

Innis, Ben. *Bloody Knife: Custer's Favorite Scout.* Bismarck, ND: Smoky Water, 1994.

Seminole Wars

Start Date: 1816
End Date: 1858

Three wars between Seminoles and the United States. The Seminoles inhabited southern Georgia and much of Spanish Florida and had once been part of the Creek Confederacy. In the early 19th century, the Seminoles came into conflict with Americans encroaching onto their lands and retaliated with occasional raids on frontier settlements. The Seminoles' practice of harboring fugitive slaves from Georgia and Alabama increased tensions. American desires to acquire Spanish Florida also contributed to conflict with the Seminoles.

In March 1812, a group of Georgians invaded northern Florida, hoping to convince the inhabitants there to declare independence from Spain. They were later joined by regular U.S. Army troops and militiamen from Georgia. Concerned that the Americans would seize their land, the Seminoles joined forces with Blacks who feared being returned to slavery and on July 25, 1812, attacked pro-American planters along the St. Johns River. On September 12, another force of African Americans and Seminoles ambushed a supply train escorted by U.S. marines and Georgia militia at Twelve Mile Swamp. The ambush sparked an extended period of fighting that culminated in an American expedition that destroyed several Seminole towns. Although American troops withdrew from Florida in May 1813, the Seminoles continued to launch occasional raids into southern Georgia and Alabama while also continuing to provide refuge to fugitive slaves. When fugitives fortified a former British post on the Apalachicola River after the War of 1812, creating a magnet for runaway slaves, Brigadier General Edmund P. Gaines dispatched an expedition that destroyed the so-called Negro Fort on July 27, 1816. Angered at this attack on their allies, the Seminoles retaliated with new raids into the United States, beginning the First Seminole War (1816–1818).

In 1817, Gaines insisted that Neamathla, chief of Fowltown on the Flint River in Georgia, turn over Seminoles who had killed whites. Neamathla rejected the demand, and Gaines ordered Major David Twiggs and 250 men to arrest him. Although Twiggs burned Fowltown on November 12, Neamathla and most of his people successfully fled and took refuge with their fellow Seminoles in Florida. From there, the Seminoles and their African American allies launched a series of raids into the United States. On November 30, they attacked a boat on the Apalachicola River, killing 36 soldiers and 10 women and children. In response, President James Monroe ordered Major General Andrew Jackson to defeat the Seminoles.

Assembling more than 3,000 troops and about 1,500 Creeks, Jackson invaded Florida in March 1818. After establishing a post at the site of the demolished Negro Fort, Jackson moved against Spanish Fort San Marcos, which surrendered on April 7. Jackson then set out eastward through Seminole territory, overcoming sporadic opposition from parties of Seminoles and Blacks. Jackson's force occupied the town inhabited by Peter McQueen and his Red Stick Creek followers on April 12 and then pushed toward the predominantly Black settlement headed by Nero, where on April 16 some of the inhabitants fought a rearguard action that allowed most of the people to escape. Nero's defense also enabled the Seminoles in nearby Billy Bowlegs's town to flee before Jackson arrived that evening. Jackson burned the abandoned towns and then marched on Pensacola, forcing the Spanish garrison to surrender on May 24. Jackson also ordered the execution of four prisoners who had been captured by his supporting naval force: Hillis Hadjo, a Seminole leader also known as Francis or the Prophet, and Himollemico, an elderly Red Stick Creek chief, were sentenced to death on charges that they had instigated the war; Scottish trader Alexander Arbuthnot was hanged for inciting the Seminoles to war against the United States; and Robert Armbrister, a former British marine, was shot for arming, training, and leading Seminoles and Blacks against American forces.

Having ended the First Seminole War, Jackson began his withdrawal from Florida on May 30, 1818. His invasion and the executions had outraged Spain and Great Britain. Monroe distanced himself from Jackson's actions by noting that the general had not been ordered to attack the Spanish, although the government's instructions to Jackson had been deliberately vague. American officials blamed Spain for the incidents, accusing the Spanish of failing to control the Seminoles and Blacks in Florida. The most important consequence of Jackson's invasion was that it convinced the Spanish government that it could no longer hold on to Florida. Under the terms of the Adams-Onís Treaty of 1819, Spain sold Florida to the United States.

Jackson's election as President in 1828 and policy of forced Native American relocation through the Indian Removal Act of 1830 would produce the Second Seminole War (1835–1842). In 1832, many Seminoles, either willingly or under pressure, signed the Treaty of Payne's Landing, agreeing to remove to present-day Oklahoma in exchange for the surrender of their territory in Florida. Others refused to leave their lands, as Seminole leader Osceola organized opposition to removal. In November 1835, the U.S. Army hastened to move the Seminoles gathered at Fort Brooke on Tampa Bay to the west because officers feared that poor conditions at the post would drive many to join Osceola. Before the army could remove the Seminoles, Osceola confronted Charley Emathla, a leader of the faction favoring removal, and killed him on November 26, 1835. Osceola then attacked a detachment of Florida militia on December 18, and other Seminole parties launched raids in the area south of St. Augustine as the Second Seminole War erupted.

On December 28, 108 regular army troops commanded by Major Francis Dade were ambushed and virtually annihilated while marching to Fort King. Brigadier General Duncan Clinch, commander of U.S. troops in Florida, retaliated by trying to strike a Seminole stronghold on the Withlacoochee River.

Clinch's force suffered heavy casualties in inconclusive fighting on December 31.

President Jackson appointed Brigadier General Winfield Scott to replace Clinch in January 1836, but Scott did not arrive until March. Meanwhile, Gaines, who commanded the army's Western Division, learned of the trouble in Florida and sailed from New Orleans with regular troops and volunteers. He landed in Tampa and on February 13 advanced into the Florida interior with 1,100 men. Gaines reached the Withlacoochee River but was prevented from crossing by heavy fire from Osceola's warriors. The troops constructed makeshift fortifications and, although surrounded, withstood Seminole attacks until forces under Clinch forced Osceola to withdraw on March 5.

Shortly afterward, Scott mounted his own offensive at the head of 2,000 regular troops. He reached the Withlacoochee in late March, came under constant harassment from small parties of Seminoles, became bogged down in the swamps, and withdrew. A supporting column of 1,200 Louisiana and Alabama volunteers withstood two Seminole attacks, but its commander decided to turn back. Jackson then replaced Scott with Brigadier General Thomas Jesup, who sent expeditions into the Florida in the autumn that destroyed Seminole crops but accomplished little else.

In spring 1837, Jesup dispatched new expeditions and succeeded in preventing the Seminoles from planting crops. Osceola, suffering from an unknown illness, was unable to lead the Seminole opposition. Jesup also used flags of truce to lure Seminole parties into the open and then took them prisoner; Osceola was captured on October 27. Imprisoned at Fort Moultrie, Sullivan's Island, South Carolina, he died in captivity on January 30, 1838. Despite these successes, U.S. battlefield victories remained elusive. A detachment of 1,000 troops under Colonel Zachary Taylor attacked 400 Seminoles near Lake Okeechobee on December 25, 1837, and drove them off, but Taylor lost 150 men—six times more than the Seminoles.

In 1838, Jesup tried a new strategy, offering African Americans fighting alongside the Seminoles freedom in exchange for military service against the warring tribe. This appeal compelled some 400 Blacks to switch sides. Jesup resigned shortly afterward, having been harshly criticized for using a flag of truce to capture Osceola. Taylor assumed command in May 1838, and with the war seemingly over, the government ordered him to end the campaign even though Seminole raids continued. Taylor soon asked to be relieved, and in April 1839, Major General Alexander Macomb replaced him. By that time, the war had settled into a pattern of army forays into the interior that suffered from Seminole harassment as well as Seminole retaliatory raids that likewise achieved little.

The government continued to change the army's commanders, sending Brevet Brigadier General Walker Armistead to succeed Macomb and then Colonel William Worth as Armistead's replacement. Worth's aggressive forays drove the Seminoles into the Everglades, where he continued to assail them with help from the navy. With the cost of the war approaching $20 million, in 1842 American officials decided to make concessions to achieve peace. An August 1842 agreement granted the 600 Seminole survivors (those captured had already been sent west) a reservation in southern Florida and officially ended hostilities, although sporadic fighting continued into 1843.

In the aftermath of the Second Seminole War, leadership of the Seminoles remaining in Florida fell primarily to Alachua leader Billy Bowlegs. When five Seminoles attacked a white-owned farm east of Fort Pierce on July 12, 1849, and a trading post at Charlotte Harbor on July 17, 1849, Bowlegs ordered the capture of the renegades to avoid retribution by the U.S. Army. Three were eventually captured and turned over to the U.S. military, while another of the outlaws was killed. Although Bowlegs's quick action calmed the immediate situation, the government's desire to settle southern Florida undermined his efforts. In 1850, Congress passed the Swamp and Overflowed Land Act, which provided that all federal lands at least half covered with water and that might be drained be turned over to the states. In Florida, this amounted to about 20 million acres. Developers and land speculators soon rushed to southern Florida, while various plans for draining the Everglades were proposed to the state legislature. All that stood in the way, it appeared, were the few remaining Seminoles.

Efforts to persuade the Seminoles to relocate west of the Mississippi now increased, as several old forts were reactivated to intimidate the tribe. Seminole chiefs who had moved west were brought back in an effort to convince Bowlegs and his followers to leave Florida. When this failed, Bowlegs and other Seminole leaders were invited to tour Washington, D.C., Baltimore, and New York City to impress upon them the power of the United States. The government offered thousands of dollars to every Seminole who peacefully relocated west, but Bowlegs and most of the Seminoles still refused to go. The federal government then proceeded to construct more forts, including one on the edge of the Big Cypress Swamp. Soldiers and survey parties continued to move throughout southern Florida, marking the location of Seminole villages and trails. On December 20, 1855, a survey detachment of 11 men was ambushed by 40 Seminole warriors. Four of the party died, while another four were wounded. The Third Seminole War (1855–1858) had begun.

Fighting primarily a guerrilla war, the Seminoles appeared to strike at will. On January 7, 1856, warriors attacked a flour mill near Fort Dallas. In February, two oystermen were killed on their boats in Charlotte Harbor. No one in southern Florida appeared safe. By late March, the Sarasota home of state senate president H. V. Snell was attacked by a dozen Seminoles. State militia and volunteers offered feeble resistance, and there was little desire to invade the Everglades, a massive swampy jungle-like wetland that occupied much of southern Florida. Many people preferred to remain near their homes and crops. As fear of Seminole raids grew, many settlers fled southern Florida, and pressure began to mount on the government for its handling of the war.

The Battle of Tillis Farm on June 14, 1856, marked the turning point in the conflict. It was initially a successful Seminole raid against a white homestead, but the natives were forced to retreat when militia was dispatched from nearby Fort Meade. Reinforced, they discovered a Seminole camp and killed the war chief Oscen Tustenuggee and several of his warriors. The death of their chief and the realization that they did not possess the manpower to carry the battle to the whites resulted in the Seminoles' withdrawal into their territory. They then conducted only minor raids.

With the Seminoles on the defensive, the federal government prepared to go on the offensive. Regular army and militia forces gathered near Fort Meade and Fort Dallas under the command of Brevet Brigadier General William S. Harney, a veteran of the Second Seminole War. Realizing that the only way to defeat the Seminoles was to drive them from their territory, Harney began his offensive in January 1857. Outnumbered and with families to protect, the Seminoles were forced from one hiding place to another as Harney's forces moved deeper into Seminole territory. Those Seminoles and their families who were captured were taken to Egmont Key off Tampa Bay to await removal west.

In April 1857, Harney was transferred to Utah, and the command of southern Florida fell to Colonel Gustavus Loomis. Loomis continued the offensive into Seminole territory and developed the use of alligator boats. Flat-bottomed and more than 30 feet long, they could operate efficiently in shallow water and could transport up to 16 soldiers each. In them, companies of soldiers traveled throughout the Everglades and the Kissimmee River harassing Seminole camps.

As the war progressed, efforts continued to convince Bowlegs and the Seminoles to surrender and voluntarily move west. Western Seminoles were again brought in to persuade them. It was also decided that the Seminoles would be allowed their own territory in Oklahoma, separate from the hated Creeks. The government also agreed to establish a $500,000 trust for Seminoles whenever Bowlegs and his followers relocated. Exhausted, Bowlegs finally accepted the arrangement on March 27, 1858. On May 4, 38 men and 85 women and children, including Bowlegs, boarded a ship for the West. About 300 Seminoles refused to go and were allowed to remain. On May 8, 1858, Loomis announced an end to all hostilities. The Third Seminole War marked the end of effective native resistance in Florida.

Jim Piecuch and Robert W. Malick

Further Reading

Covington, James W. *The Billy Bowlegs War, 1855–1858: The Final Stand of the Seminoles against the Whites.* Chuluota, FL: Mickler House, 1982.

Knetsch, Joe. *Florida's Seminole Wars, 1817–1858.* Charleston, SC: Arcadia Publishing, 2003.

Mahon, John K. *History of the Second Seminole War, 1835–1842*. Rev. ed. Gainesville: University Press of Florida, 1991.

Missall, John, and Mary Lou Missall. *The Seminole Wars: America's Longest Indian Conflict*. Gainesville: University Press of Florida, 2004.

Seminoles

Native American group whose traditional territory was located chiefly in Florida. The name "Seminole" means "pioneer" or "runaway" and is possibly derived from the Spanish cimarrón ("wild"). The Seminoles formed in the 18th century from members of other Native American peoples, mainly Creeks but also Oconees, Yamasees, and others. The Seminoles spoke two mutually unintelligible Muskogean languages: Hitchiti, spoken by the Oconees and today mostly by the Miccosukees (Mikasukis), and Muskogee. The Creeks, Choctaws, Chickasaws, Cherokees, and Seminoles were known by non–Native Americans in the 19th century as the Five Civilized Tribes.

Before the First Seminole War (1816–1818), Seminole towns had chiefs and councils of elders. After the Third Seminole War (1855–1858), there were three bands (two Miccosukee bands and one Creek band), based on language. Each band had its own chief and council of elders. Matrilineal clans helped provide cultural continuity among widely scattered bands after the wars. There was also a dual division among the people. Particularly after 1817, the Seminoles lived in small extended families.

Owing to a fairly mobile and decentralized existence, the early towns were much less organized than were those of the Creeks. Seminole women grew corn, beans, squash, and tobacco. They made hominy and flour from corn and the coontie plant. They also grew such nonnative crops as sweet potatoes, bananas, peanuts, lemons, melons, and oranges. They gathered wild rice; cabbage palmetto; various roots and wild foods, such as persimmon, plum, honey, and sugarcane; and nuts, such as hickory and acorns. Men hunted alligators, bears, opossums, rabbits, squirrels, wild fowl, manatees, and turkeys. The Seminoles ate fish, turtles, and shellfish in abundance.

Traditional trade items included alligator hides, otter pelts, bird plumes, and foods. Bird plumes and alligator hides were in high demand in the late 19th century. The Seminoles were also known for their fine patchwork clothing and their baskets. Their geometric designs were often in the pattern of a snake. Ribbon appliqué, previously consisting mainly of bands of triangles along borders, became much more elaborate during the late 19th century.

The Apalachees and Timucuas had been the original inhabitants of northern Florida, but by 1700, most had been killed by disease and raids by more northerly tribes. Non-Muskogee Oconee people from southern Georgia, who moved south during the early 18th century, formed the kernel of the Seminole people. They were joined by Yamasee refugees from the Yamasee War (1715–1717) as well as by some Apalachicolas, Calusas, Hitchitis, and Chiahas and escaped slaves. The Chiahas were known as Miccosukees by the late 18th century. Several small Muskogean groups joined the nascent Seminole Nation in the late 18th century.

Seminoles considered themselves Creeks. They supported the Creeks in war and often attended their councils. By the outbreak of the American Revolutionary War (1775–1783), the Seminoles' ties to the Creeks were diminishing. Under the leadership of Cowkeeper (Ahaya of Cuscowilla), the

Seminoles allied with the British but saw little action, given their homeland's distance from the main theaters of combat. When Spain resumed control of the Florida peninsula in 1785, the Seminoles generally enjoyed good relations with the Spanish.

The Seminoles experienced considerable population growth after the Creek War (1813–1814), mainly from Muskogean immigrants from Upper Creek towns. From this time on, the dominant language among the Seminoles was Muskogee, or Creek. Seminole settlements, mainly between the Apalachicola and Suwannee rivers, were too scattered to permit the reestablishment of Creek towns and clan structures.

Prior to the American Civil War (1861–1865), some Seminoles owned slaves, but the slaves' obligations were minimal, and the Seminoles welcomed escaped slaves into their communities. Until 1821, U.S. slaves could flee across an international boundary to Florida. Even after that year, the region remained a haven for escaped slaves because of the presence of free African American and mixed African American and Seminole communities.

The First Seminole War (1816–1818) began with state militias chasing runaway slaves and resulted in the Spanish cession of Florida. In the Treaty of Moultrie Creek (1823), the Seminole traded their north Florida land for a reservation in central Florida. The 1832 Treaty of Payne's Landing, which was signed by unrepresentative chiefs and was not supported by most Seminoles, called for the tribe to relocate west to Indian Territory (Oklahoma). By 1838, up to 1,500 Seminoles had been rounded up and penned in concentration camps. They were forcibly marched west, during which time as many as 1,000 died from disease, starvation, fatigue, or attacks from whites. The Seminoles consistently refused to give up the

considerable number of African Americans among them. In 1856, the Seminoles in Indian Territory, who wished to remain free of Creek domination, were given approximately two million acres west of the Creeks.

Resistance to relocation and to white slave-capturing raids led to the Second Seminole War (1835–1842). Under Osceola, Jumper, and other leaders, the Seminoles waged a guerrilla war against the United States, retreating deep into the southern swamps. Although Osceola was captured at a peace conference and soon died in captivity and although at war's end most Seminoles (about 4,500 people) were forced to move to Indian Territory, the Seminoles were not militarily defeated. The war ended because the United States decided not to spend more than the $20 million it had already spent or to lose more than the 1,500 soldiers who had already been killed.

The Third Seminole War took place during 1855–1858. From their redoubt in the Everglades, the Seminoles attacked surveyors and settlers. The army, through its own attacks and by bringing in some Oklahoma Seminoles, succeeded in persuading another 100 or so Seminoles to relocate, but about 300 remained, undefeated, in Florida. There was never a formal peace treaty.

In the 1870s as the first nonnatives began moving south of Lake Okeechobee, there was another call for Seminole removal, but the government decided against an attempt. In the late 19th century, a great demand for Seminole trade items led to close trade relationships being formed.

The Western Seminoles settled in present-day Seminole County, Oklahoma. By the 1890s, they had formed 14 bands, including 2 composed of freedmen, or Black Seminoles. Each band was self-governing and had representation on the tribal council. Most of the Western Seminole Reservation, almost 350,000 acres, was allotted in the early 20th century. Through fraud and other questionable and illegal means, by 1920 nonnatives had acquired about 80 percent of the land originally deeded to the Seminoles. Tribal governments were unilaterally dissolved when Oklahoma became a state in 1907.

Most Seminoles still in Florida relocated to reservations during the 1930s and 1940s. There they quickly acculturated, adopting cattle herding, wage labor, schools, and Christianity. With the help of Florida's congressional delegation, the tribe avoided termination in the 1950s. The tribe adopted an Indian Reorganization Act–style corporate charter and received formal federal recognition in 1957. By the 1950s, a group of more traditional Miccosukee-speaking Seminoles, mostly living deep in the Everglades, moved to separate themselves from the Seminoles, whom they regarded as having largely renounced their native traditions. The Miccosukees won recognition as a separate nation in 1962.

Barry M. Pritzker

Further Reading

Covington, James W. *The Seminoles of Florida*. Gainesville: University Press of Florida, 1993.

Knetsch, Joe. *Florida's Seminole Wars, 1817–1858*. Charleston, SC: Arcadia Publishing, 2003.

Mulroy, Kevin. *Freedom on the Border: The Seminole Maroons in Florida, the Indian Territory, Coahuila, and Texas*. Lubbock: Texas Tech University Press, 1993.

Shawnees

An Algonquian-speaking people whose name, chawunagi, means "southerners" in Algonquian. The name originated from the Shawnees living south of other Algonquians. While the Shawnees are generally classified as natives of the Northeast Woodlands, their migrations taught them to adopt the lifeways of other Native Americans, especially those of the Southeast.

Although nomadic, the Shawnees in the warm months inhabited villages, around which they grew crops. Winter brought more scattered habitation patterns as small groups went out to hunt. The Shawnees moved many times throughout their history. Their original homeland was in present-day southern Ohio, West Virginia, and western Pennsylvania. In the mid-1600s, the Iroquois drove them out of these areas, and they were scattered to South Carolina, Tennessee's Cumberland River basin, and southern Illinois. By the 1730s, most Shawnees had returned to their original lands. In the following decades, they fought hard against encroaching white settlements in Ohio and Pennsylvania.

As the several Shawnee bands moved, they also changed their alliances between the French and the English. Many of the Shawnees sided with the French in the period from 1689 until the end of the French and Indian War (1754–1763). Some did ally with the British because they believed that British trade goods were better than those of the French. As a result, the British were able to establish an important trading post at Pickawillany in Shawnee territory in Ohio. Most of the Shawnees, however, fought the British along with other natives, including the Ottawas, in Pontiac's Rebellion (1763).

Although King George III's Proclamation of 1763 had all but promised Native Americans the lands west of the Appalachian Mountains, the governor of Virginia, John Murray, Fourth Earl of Dunmore, began parceling out western lands to veterans of the French and Indian War. Thus, Shawnee chief Cornstalk led Shawnee warriors in an armed attempt to drive the settlers out of trans-Appalachian lands, sparking Lord Dunmore's War in 1774.

After a series of bloody raids and counter-raids, on October 6, 1774, Colonel Andrew Lewis, commanding 1,100 militiamen, defeated chiefs Cornstalk and Logan (of the Mingos) in a fierce battle at Point Pleasant in present-day West Virginia. Cornstalk subsequently signed a peace treaty that punished the Shawnees with forfeiture of some of their lands.

During the American Revolutionary War (1775–1783), the Shawnees sided with the British. In 1778, the Shawnees even managed to capture famed frontiersman Daniel Boone. He was held prisoner at Chillicothe, Ohio, but subsequently escaped. From 1783 to 1790, a Shawnee-led coalition killed perhaps as many as 1,000 white settlers in the Old Northwest Territory. By 1794, the Shawnees and other natives in the Northwest Territory had fought several pitched engagements with forces dispatched by the U.S. government. Tecumseh and his brother Tenskwatawa (also known as the Prophet) tried to unite the natives of the Mississippi Valley against the Americans. Tenskwatawa's defeat at the Battle of Tippecanoe (November 7, 1811) combined with the death of Tecumseh in Canada at the Battle of the Thames (October 5, 1813) during the War of 1812 effectively ended Shawnee resistance.

Tecumseh's alliance splintered after his death, and soon the Shawnees began to divide into factions, largely a result of nearly constant warfare that badly weakened the Shawnee Nation. In the years after the War of 1812, some Shawnees moved to Missouri; others migrated as far west as Texas. By the early 1830s, most Shawnees had settled in northeastern Kansas. In 1870, they were forced to move to Indian Territory (Oklahoma), where they resided near the Cherokees. One Shawnee band, however, remained in the Ohio area and still has small landholdings there.

Andrew J. Waskey

Further Reading

Clark, Jerry E. *The Shawnee*. Lexington: University Press of Kentucky, 2007.

Noe, Randolph. *The Shawnee Indians: An Annotated Bibliography*. Lanham, MD: Scarecrow, 2001.

Sheridan, Philip Henry

Birth Date: March 6, 1831
Death Date: August 5, 1888

U.S. Army general. Born in Albany, New York, to Irish immigrants on March 6, 1831, Philip Henry Sheridan grew up in Somerset, Ohio. Too young to serve in the Mexican-American War (1846–1848), he attended the U.S. Military Academy at West Point. Suspended for one year for disciplinary reasons, he graduated in 1853 and was commissioned a second lieutenant in the infantry. Sheridan then served with the 1st Infantry Regiment in Texas and with the 4th Infantry Regiment in Oregon, being promoted to first lieutenant in March 1861 on the eve of the American Civil War (1861–1865).

Assigned to the western theater, Sheridan won rapid advancement. Promoted to captain in May 1861, he served in the 13th Infantry Regiment in southwestern Missouri and then as quartermaster for the Department of the Missouri under Major General Henry W. Halleck during Halleck's Corinth Campaign (May–June 1862). Sheridan intensely disliked staff duty and secured transfer to the volunteer establishment as colonel of the 2nd Michigan Cavalry in May. His subsequent victory at Booneville, Mississippi (July 1, 1862), earned him promotion to brigadier general of volunteers that September. Sheridan commanded an infantry division and distinguished himself in Kentucky in the Battle of Perryville and especially at Stones River, where he perhaps saved Major General

William S. Rosecrans's Army of the Cumberland from defeat. For this action, Sheridan was promoted to major general of volunteers in March 1863. In the Battle of Chickamauga that September, Sheridan gained laurels for his division's tenacious fighting. His men played a key role in the Union victory in the Battle of Chattanooga that November.

When Ulysses S. Grant was promoted to lieutenant general and became the army's general in chief, he selected Sheridan to command the Army of the Potomac's three-division cavalry corps. During the spring and summer of 1864, Sheridan's men won several victories against the Confederate cavalry. His forces took part in Grant's Overland Campaign and disrupted Confederate lines of communication. Sheridan was victorious in the Battle of Yellow Tavern (May 1864) in Virginia, although his forces suffered defeat at Trevilian Station the next month.

Grant gave Sheridan command of the Army of the Shenandoah in August 1864 and instructed him to drive the Confederates south and destroy any supplies that might be of use to the Confederate Army. Sheridan defeated Confederate forces under Lieutenant General Jubal Early in the Shenandoah Valley in the Third Battle of Winchester (September 19) and at Fisher's Hill (September 21–22). This accomplishment led to Sheridan's advancement to brigadier general in the regular army. Although caught off guard by Early's attack at Cedar Creek (October 19), Sheridan helped to rally his army to victory. Sheridan then laid waste to the Shenandoah Valley, depriving the Confederates of much-needed supplies. The extent of this destruction is seen in his boast that "a crow couldn't fly from Winchester to Staunton without taking its rations along."

Promoted to major general in the regular army in November 1864, Sheridan raided from Winchester to Petersburg, where he joined Grant. Sheridan played a major role in the final defeat of General Robert E. Lee's Army of Northern Virginia in April 1865, besting the Confederates at Five Forks and Sayler's Creek before trapping Lee's army near Appomattox Court House.

Sheridan was then ordered to Texas with a large force to encourage the French to quit Mexico. He remained in Texas as commander of the Military Division of the Gulf from May 1865 to March 1867, when he was named to command the Fifth Military District of Louisiana and Texas, but his harsh policies brought his removal that September.

Sheridan took over the Department of the Missouri in September 1867 and as such was responsible for the federal effort against hostile western Native Americans. In his new position, he aggressively prosecuted a winter campaign in the Washita Valley in Indian Territory (Oklahoma) and on the southern Plains during 1868–1869, attacking the Cheyennes, Kiowas, and Comanches and destroying their livestock and supplies. Units from his department also fought in Colorado in the Battle of Beecher's Island (September 17, 1868) and the Battle of the Washita River (November 27, 1868).

When Grant became president and William Tecumseh Sherman moved up to command the army as a full general, Sheridan was promoted to lieutenant general in March 1869 and assumed command of the Military Division of the Missouri. Sheridan then traveled to Europe, where he was an official observer attached to the Prussian Army during the Franco-Prussian War (1870–1871).

Returning to the United States, Sheridan planned the campaign of three converging columns against the Sioux that resulted in the Battle of the Little Bighorn (June 25–26, 1876) and directed the punitive effort that followed. He also directed the final operations that prevented Chief Joseph and most of his

Nez Perces from reaching Canada in 1877. Under Sheridan's direction, the army fought the Ute War of 1879. Sheridan succeeded Sherman as commanding general of the U.S. Army in 1884 and was promoted to general in June 1888. As commanding general, Sheridan oversaw the final operations of the army against the Apaches under Geronimo. Sheridan was also a prime mover behind the creation of Yellowstone National Park. He died at Nonquitt, Massachusetts, on August 5, 1888. Known as "Little Phil," Sheridan was blunt and outspoken. He was also industrious, offensive-minded, and aggressive and was a superb tactical commander.

Spencer C. Tucker

Further Reading

Hutton, Paul Andrew. *Phil Sheridan and His Army.* Lincoln: University of Nebraska Press, 1985.

Morris, Roy, Jr. *Sheridan: The Life and Wars of General Phil Sheridan.* New York: Crown, 1992.

O'Connor, Richard. *Sheridan the Inevitable.* Indianapolis: Bobbs-Merrill, 1953.

Shoshone War

Event Date: 1863

Key conflict fought for control of the Great Basin of the West (centered on the present-day state of Utah) involving the Shoshone (Shoshoni) tribe and federal volunteer troops from January to October 1863. The culmination of a quarter century of raids and skirmishes, the Shoshone War compelled the U.S. government to recognize those Native Americans occupying the territory through which the western trails passed and to make a concerted attempt at peace through treaties combined with the threat of overwhelming military force.

The primary cause of the Shoshone War was the steady encroachment of white settlers onto the traditional homelands of three distinct Shoshone populations: the Eastern Shoshones, the Northern Shoshones, and the Western Shoshones. Major developments that had placed increased pressure on Shoshone lands and resources included the influx of Mormon settlers beginning in 1847; the California Gold Rush (1848–1849); the mail route running through Deep Creek, completed in 1854; the creation of the Overland Stage Route in 1858; the 1859 Comstock Lode Silver Rush; the Oregon Gold Rush of 1860; the establishment of the Pony Express (1860); and the Grasshopper Creek Gold Rush of 1862. The establishment of farms, ranches, and mail stations near the best springs and the most productive lands provoked frustrated and starving Shoshone bands to raid for horses and food supplies.

The late summer of 1862 found the Shoshones particularly desperate and aggressive when Colonel Patrick Edward Connor and his California Volunteers (the 3rd California Infantry) arrived in the Great Basin to protect the overland route between Carson City and Fort Bridger. Worried about California's vulnerability to Confederate forces during the American Civil War (1861–1865), the U.S. government ordered Connor to secure lines of communication and sources of gold and silver vital to the Union war effort. Numerous attacks by separate Native American bands along the trails, including the Western Shoshones' killing of 12 whites at Gravelly Ford in September 1862, spurred Connor to dispatch Major Edward McGarry and two companies to the Humboldt River to kill all Shoshones they encountered. This order resulted in 25 Native American deaths. Connor continued to batter the Shoshones, while Utah superintendent of Indian affairs James Doty postponed assistance and treaties until May 1863 when he could also negotiate with the Bannocks and Utes. The delay proved disastrous, as hunger led Native American bands to increase the frequency and ferocity of their attacks.

Chief Bear Hunter of the Northern Shoshones concentrated his attacks on the mail and stage lines, and he and his followers became the primary target of Connor's military campaign. In November 1862, Connor sent McGarry to rescue a boy taken by the Shoshones some two years earlier. McGarry proceeded to attack Bear Hunter's camp, chasing him and others into a canyon where three more Indians died. Bear Hunter surrendered and was held hostage until the boy was returned. In retaliation, the Shoshones killed two miners within a half mile of their winter camp at Bear River.

When raids on white settlements continued, Connor sent McGarry to retrieve the stolen stock. At Bear River Crossing on December 6, McGarry executed four Shoshones for their failure to cooperate. A flurry of Shoshone attacks ensued through January 1863, prompting Utah Territory Supreme Court chief justice John F. Kinney to issue arrest warrants for chiefs Bear Hunter, Sagwitch, and Sanpitch.

Connor decided that a massive assault on the Shoshones' winter camp was the most effective approach. Sending Captain Samuel Hoyt with 69 infantrymen, 13 wagons, and 2 howitzers toward Cache Valley on January 22, 1863, Connor waited two days before he and McGarry led 220 cavalrymen to a rendezvous point in hopes of misleading Shoshone scouts as to his intentions. At Bear River on January 29, 1863, Connor's four-hour attack killed at least 224 Shoshones and wounded 70 men, women, and children while capturing 170 horses and destroying the tribe's winter provisions and supplies. The California Volunteers lost 17 men.

This attack is often referred to as a massacre by historians. The number of Shoshone killed was likely closer to 300. Bear Hunter died. Sanpitch and Sagwitch escaped, as did Chief Pocatello of the Fort Hall Shoshones days before the attack.

The battle was an important victory for the government, removing one of its most troublesome opponents and convincing the Shoshones of the military's superior firepower. The engagement would stand as perhaps the single greatest loss of Native American lives in Western battles with whites and precipitated major unrest among bands.

Eluding U.S. troops for months, the hostile Shoshones could manage little more than small raids. Attacks were met with military counterattacks, none larger than Captain Samuel Smith's killing of 53 Goshutes in early May 1863. Connor strengthened the area around Fort Ruby to the west and Fort Bridger to the east and established Camp Connor near Soda Springs to the north. By the summer, Doty negotiated five treaties with the Shoshones: the Treaty of Fort Bridger with the Eastern Shoshones (July 2), the Treaty of Box-Elder with the Northwestern Shoshones (July 30), the Treaty of Ruby Valley with the Western Shoshones (October 1), the Treaty of Tooele Valley with the Goshutes (October 12), and the Treaty of Soda Springs with the Fort Hall Bannock-Shoshones (October 14). The treaties contained nearly identical terms, promising 20 years of annuity payments in exchange for guarantees of safe passage and settlement. Thus, by October 1863, the Shoshone War had been brought to a close. The conflict and the agreements concluding it demilitarized the Shoshones and demonstrated the fundamental role of U.S. troops in safeguarding the western trails.

Michael F. Dove

Further Reading

Christensen, Scott R. *Sagwitch: Shoshone Chieftain, Mormon Elder, 1822–1887.* Logan: Utah State University Press, 1999.

Madsen, Brigham D. *Glory Hunter: A Biography of Patrick Edward Connor.* Salt Lake City: University of Utah Press, 1990.

Madsen, Brigham D. *The Shoshoni Frontier and the Bear River Massacre.* Salt Lake City: University of Utah Press, 1985.

Shoshones

Native American group of the Great Plains, Great Basin, and West divided into the Eastern, Northern, and Western Shoshones. The Eastern Shoshones, sometimes referred to as the Wind River Shoshones, lived in present-day western Wyoming since at least the 16th century. Thereafter they moved into the northern Great Plains and by the late 18th century inhabited areas of Wyoming, northern Colorado, and Montana. The Comanches separated from the Shoshones around 1700, moving toward Texas.

Buffalo hunting and fur trading provided the bulk of the Eastern Shoshones' food, clothing, shelter, and economic activity. Buffalo hunts were augmented by small-scale seasonal agriculture and the use of wild plants and trees. Because of the centrality of the buffalo hunt, the Eastern Shoshones were seminomadic. As with many Native American tribes, the Eastern Shoshones were decimated by European-introduced diseases; by 1840, the tribe had dwindled to as few as 3,000 people.

The Eastern Shoshones divided themselves into three to five bands during the winter, setting up camp principally in the Wind River Valley. Each band had its own chief, military society, and warriors. Warfare with enemy tribes was highly destructive to the Shoshones and from the early to mid-18th century onward proceeded nearly uninterrupted. In the 19th century, the Eastern Shoshones frequently allied themselves with white Americans and, as a result, underwent a renaissance, enhancing themselves both demographically and materially.

From 1810 to about 1840, the Eastern Shoshones were major players in the buffalo hide trade. When settlers began arriving on their lands in the 1850s, they tried to coexist under the leadership of their chief, Washakie. The Eastern Shoshones often allied with the U.S. Army to fight the Lakota Sioux. The Eastern Shoshones became disenchanted in 1878 when the U.S. government forced the Arapahos, one of their perennial enemies, to join them on their reservation. Destruction of the buffalo herds essentially ended the traditional Shoshone cultural and economic ways by the 1880s. Until well into the 20th century, the surviving Eastern Shoshones lived a hard-scrabble existence as their numbers continued to decline.

The Northern Shoshones demonstrated more of a cultural delineation than an ethnic or even geographic orientation. They shared some cultural traits with the Bannock, Ute, and Paiute tribes as well as the Eastern Shoshones. As such, the Northern Shoshone culture blended features of tribes found in the Great Plains, the Northwest Plateau, and the Great Basin. By the early 19th century, the Northern Shoshones inhabited eastern Idaho, western Wyoming, and northeastern Utah. They numbered some 30,000 people prior to European contact but by the 1850s numbered just 3,000 or so. Seminomadic, the Northern Shoshones divided themselves into impermanent bands that often lacked long-term leadership; indeed, some bands had no discernible leadership. Like the Eastern Shoshones, the Northern Shoshones relied on buffalo for their economic activity and daily subsistence. They augmented this by hunting elk, deer, and mountain sheep and employing local flora that they used for food and medicinal purposes. Salmon also formed a key part of their diet.

After they integrated horses into their culture in the late 17th century, the Northern Shoshones, along with the Bannocks, adopted some of the Great Plains cultural traits, including warrior societies and tepees. By the mid-19th century, the Northern Shoshones had come in conflict with the Blackfeet and were prevented from moving farther west. As whites moved into Northern Shoshone lands, competition for resources was keen, and by the 1860s, most of the beaver and buffalo had been hunted to near extinction, forcing radical lifestyle and cultural changes. This led to raids against American settlements and wagon trains. After increased conflict with whites, the Northern Shoshones were placed on reservations by the mid- to late 1870s. Perhaps the most famous Northern Shoshone was Sacagawea, who served as a guide during the 1804–1806 Lewis and Clark expedition.

The Western Shoshones' territory ranged from south-central Idaho, northwestern Utah, and central Nevada south and west to California's Death Valley. From as many as 10,000 people before European contact, the Western Shoshones dwindled to perhaps only 2,000 by 1820. The group lived in loosely organized bands, the membership of which was quite fluid. Chiefs had few powers other than directing hunting and gathering and allocating resources. Because of the harsh climate and terrain within their territory, buffalo were not prevalent. Thus, the seminomadic Western Shoshones relied primarily on native plants and small game for sustenance.

The influx of Mormons into the Great Salt Lake region beginning in the 1840s placed much pressure on the Western Shoshones.

The discovery of the Comstock Lode in Nevada in 1857 attracted a flood of new white settlers, which further disrupted the Shoshones' way of life. Falling victim to disease and near starvation, the Western Shoshone sometimes resorted to raids on white settlements. After 1860 when the Pony Express routinely traversed their lands, the Western Shoshones began staging raids, which almost always brought retaliation by local or U.S. military forces. During the 1870s, some Western Shoshones joined the Bannocks and Northern Paiutes in their struggle against white encroachment. Many refused to be relocated to reservations, and they tried their best to retain as much of their original culture as they could.

Paul G. Pierpaoli Jr.

Further Reading

Bial, Raymond. *The Shoshone*. Tarrytown, NY: Benchmark Books, 2001.

Dramer, Kim. *Shoshone*. New York: Chelsea House, 1996.

Stamm, Henry E., IV. *People of the Wind River: The Eastern Shoshones, 1825–1900*. Norman: University of Oklahoma Press, 1999.

Sioux

A northern Plains nation made up of three major tribes: the Eastern Sioux or Dakotas, the Middle Sioux or Yanktonai-Yanktons, and the Western Sioux or Lakotas. The Sioux speak mutually intelligible dialects of the same Siouan language. The groups were closely aligned at the time French explorer Pierre Radisson found them located in western Wisconsin and northeastern Minnesota. They lived in a woodlands pattern, subsisting on a mixture of farming, gathering, and hunting. Their principal crops were maize, beans, and squash in the southern region and wild rice in the northern region. They also frequently ventured out onto the prairies in search of bison.

Under pressure from the better-armed Ojibwas, the Sioux moved west and south. By 1804, the Sioux were situated on the prairies between the Mississippi and Missouri rivers and moving westward. The Dakotas were in southern Minnesota, while the Yanktonai-Yanktons were in what would become the eastern Dakotas. The Lakotas migrated onto the Great Plains and were west of the Missouri River when they encountered the Lewis and Clark expedition (1804–1806). The Lakotas drove the Kiowas from the Black Hills and pushed against the Crows in the Powder River Country of Wyoming and Montana. The Dakotas and the Yanktonai-Yanktons were now sedentary, relying on farming and hunting for subsistence. The Lakotas, however, adopted the nomadic Great Plains culture of horses, bison, and tepees. The Lakotas become the prototypical Indians of the Plains, although they adopted the horse later than their neighbors.

The U.S. government tried to maintain peace between the Dakotas and Ojibwas with some success. The Dakotas lived in peace with the whites of Minnesota, northern Iowa, and the eastern Dakotas until the 1862 Minnesota Sioux Uprising. During the uprising, which lasted six weeks, the Dakotas raided the Minnesota River Valley, killing 500 whites while losing many of their own people to volunteer troops and civilians. The uprising ended with the dispersion of the Dakotas as far as Canada and out to their Yankton and Yanktonai cousins. In addition, 303 warriors were sentenced to be hanged, but President Abraham Lincoln pardoned all but 38, who were known to have committed murder and rape. They were hanged in Mankato, Minnesota, in early 1863 in the largest public execution in

U.S. history. By 1870, fewer than 100 Sioux remained in Minnesota, although many subsequently moved back onto reservations established in the state. The Yankton-Yanktonais attempted to resist settler pressure in central South Dakota but succumbed to the inevitable, signing a treaty in 1858 that restricted them to small reservations there.

Moving west, the Lakotas made many tribal enemies. By holding their territory against all comers, they made more. As the Lakotas moved onto the Plains, war became an integral part of their culture. Manhood and social respect for men were determined by their abilities and bravery in warfare; in this way, young men acquired respect and obtained wealth in horses. Women and children captives were integrated into the tribe, building its population further.

The Lakotas were often at war with their neighbors. To the west, the Crows were their most constant opponents. The Lakotas finally pushed the Crows out of the Powder River region of Wyoming and Montana. To the north, the Lakotas warred with the Blackfeet and the Assiniboines. To their east, the Lakotas raided the Mandan, Arikara, and Hidatsa tribes. To the south, the Lakotas fought with the Pawnees of Nebraska and Kansas. The Lakotas were also capable of making allies among their neighbors, however. Although the Lakotas had pushed the Cheyennes from the Black Hills region, as the two moved farther west, they became close allies, often traveling together along with the Arapahos. By 1800, the three tribes had an alliance, and Lakota war parties often included Cheyenne and Arapaho warriors.

The Lakotas had little contact with whites until the 1850s as more settlers traversed the southern edges of Lakota territory. The first significant conflict, known as the Grattan Massacre of 1854, resulted from the overconfidence of U.S. Army lieutenant John Grattan.

Ordered to arrest a Lakota warrior accused of killing cattle near Fort Laramie in Wyoming, Grattan's escort of 30 men attacked the suspected Lakota village and was quickly wiped out. The U.S. government responded by sending a 600-man expedition under Brevet Brigadier General William Harney. Harney's force advanced into Nebraska and attacked a village, killing and capturing many Lakotas. Sporadic conflict continued throughout the late 1850s as more settlers moved west and plans unfolded to begin building railroads through the Plains.

The Lakotas were not easily subdued. Between the mid-1850s and 1877, they actively resisted white encroachment. Under Chief Red Cloud, they drove whites out of the Powder River Country and from the Bozeman Trail after Red Cloud's War (1866–1868), which witnessed the siege of Fort Phil Kearny and the Fetterman Massacre. The great Sioux war chief Crazy Horse rose to prominence during this war, but it was only later in the 1870s that he became an iconic figure both to the Lakotas and whites.

By 1870, the Lakotas and their allies numbered more than 20,000 people, about a quarter of whom were warriors. War parties could number 500–1,000 warriors, numbers unheard of in earlier times. The climax of warfare came with the government decision to push Native Americans onto reservations. By restricting the Plains Indians to reservations, millions of acres opened for white settlement, the huge bison herds disappeared, and railroad construction expanded.

In 1874, Lieutenant Colonel George Armstrong Custer led an expedition into the Black Hills. This exploratory endeavor discovered gold, which brought more pressure on the Lakotas and led to the final campaigns of the Plains Indian wars, including the Great Sioux War (1876–1877). In the process, Custer and 267 troopers of the 7th Cavalry were killed in the Battle of the Little Bighorn (June 25–26, 1876) by the Lakota alliance led by Sitting Bull, Crazy Horse, Spotted Tail, and the Cheyenne and Arapaho warriors, led by Dull Knife and Black Bear. This was the largest defeat and loss of life by the U.S. Army in the Plains wars.

A concerted effort by the U.S. Army under colonels Ranald S. Mackenzie, Wesley Merritt, and Nelson A. Miles resulted in the pursuit and capture of many of the Lakotas, with Crazy Horse surrendering in May 1877; he was later killed in a scuffle with an arresting soldier. Sitting Bull fled to Canada with many of his people, remaining there until 1881, when he returned and surrendered himself and his people to the army.

The Lakotas were placed on reservations in the western Dakotas, where they remained. In 1890, the Ghost Dance movement, promising the return of the buffalo and, in the Lakota version, the disappearance of whites, swept across the northern Plains. Standing Rock Reservation agent James McLaughlin ordered the arrest of Sitting Bull, who was killed by a native policeman in the scuffle. Chief Big Foot and his band then fled from the Cheyenne River Agency, pursued by soldiers of the 7th Cavalry. The troops soon caught up with Big Foot's followers. Something triggered an outbreak of gunfire. When the smoke had cleared on Wounded Knee Creek, more than 150 Lakotas lay dead, including women and children, and another 50 wounded. The December 29, 1890, Battle of Wounded Knee (Wounded Knee Massacre) is regarded as the final event of the Indian Wars.

Stefan M. Brooks

Further Reading

Gibbon, Guy. *The Sioux: The Dakota and Lakota Nations.* Malden, MA: Blackwell, 2003.

Hassrick, Royal B. *The Sioux: The Life and Customs of a Warrior Nation*. Norman: University of Oklahoma Press, 1964.

Hedren, Paul L., ed. *The Great Sioux War, 1876–77*. Helena: Montana Historical Society Press, 1991.

Sitting Bull

Birth Date: ca. 1831
Death Date: December 15, 1890

Hunkpapa Lakota chief and holy man under whom the Lakota tribes in the mid-1870s united in their struggle against encroaching white settlement on the northern Plains. Sitting Bull (Tatanka-Iyotanka) was born around 1831 at a place the Lakota called Many Caches on the Grand River in present-day South Dakota. He received the name Tatanka-Iyotanka, which describes a buffalo bull sitting on its hind legs. At 14 years old, he experienced his first battle in a raid against the Crow Nation. He first encountered American soldiers in June 1863 during a campaign in retaliation for the Minnesota Sioux Uprising in which the Lakotas had not participated. The next year Sitting Bull fought U.S. volunteers at the Battle of Killdeer Mountain, and in 1865, he led a siege against Fort Rice in present-day North Dakota. Widely respected for his bravery and insight, he became head chief of the Lakota Nation around 1868.

In 1874, Lieutenant Colonel George Armstrong Custer led an army expedition that confirmed the presence of gold in the Black Hills of the Dakota Territory, an area sacred to many native tribes and placed off-limits to whites by the 1868 Fort Laramie Treaty. Despite this ban, white prospectors moved into the Black Hills and provoked the Lakotas into defending their land. The U.S. government tried to purchase the Black Hills, but the tribes refused to sell. The government then abrogated the Fort Laramie Treaty, and the commissioner of Indian affairs decreed that all Lakotas must return to their reservation by January 31, 1876, or be considered hostile. Sitting Bull and his people refused to return to the reservation.

In March 1876, brigadier generals George Crook and Alfred Terry and Colonel John Gibbon led separate army columns into the Yellowstone Valley. At his camp on Rosebud Creek in Montana Territory, Sitting Bull led the Lakota, Cheyenne, and Arapaho nations in the sun dance ritual, offering prayers to Wakan Tanka, their Great Spirit. During this ceremony, Sitting Bull had a vision in which he saw soldiers falling into the Lakota camp like grasshoppers falling from the sky.

Inspired by Sitting Bull's vision, the Oglala Lakota war chief Crazy Horse, with 500 warriors, surprised Crook's troops on June 17, forcing them to retreat at the Battle of the Rosebud. The Lakotas then moved their camp to the valley of the Little Bighorn River, where 3,000 more Native Americans who had left the reservations joined them. On June 25 in the Battle of the Little Bighorn, the badly outnumbered troops of the 7th Cavalry, commanded by Custer, attacked the camp but were overwhelmed. Custer and 267 soldiers of the regiment were annihilated.

After this disaster, the army sent thousands of troops into the Yellowstone Valley and the Black Hills and over the next year relentlessly pursued the Lakotas. Because the Lakotas had split up after the Battle of the Little Bighorn, the army was able to defeat them piecemeal. However, the defiant Sitting Bull led his band into Canada in May 1877. There he refused a pardon offered by Terry, who had traveled to Canada for that purpose, in exchange for settling on a reservation.

After three years, Sitting Bull, unable to feed his people, returned to the United States and surrendered to the commanding officer of Fort Buford in Montana on July 19, 1881. The army sent him to the Standing Rock Reservation and soon afterward farther down the Missouri River to Fort Randall because of fears that he might inspire a new uprising. Sitting Bull and his followers remained there as prisoners of war for almost two years.

On May 10, 1883, Sitting Bull rejoined his tribe at Standing Rock. James McLaughlin, the Indian agent in charge of the reservation, was determined not to give Sitting Bull any special privileges and even forced him to work in the fields. However, Sitting Bull still knew his own authority and spoke forcefully, although futilely, to a delegation of U.S. senators who presented him with a plan to open a part of the reservation to white settlers.

In 1885, Sitting Bull joined Buffalo Bill Cody's Wild West Show and earned $50 a week for riding once around the arena in addition to any fees that he obtained for his autograph and picture. During that time, Sitting Bull shook hands with President Grover Cleveland, a sign to Sitting Bull that he was still regarded as a great chief. Unable to tolerate white society, he left the show after only four months. He returned to Standing Rock and lived in a cabin on the Grand River near where he had been born. He maintained his traditional ways despite the rules of the reservation, living with his two wives and rejecting Christianity. Sitting Bull did send his children to a nearby Christian school so they could learn to read and write.

Soon after his return, Sitting Bull had another vision in which a meadowlark sat beside him on a hill and said to him that a Lakota would kill him. In autumn 1890, a Miniconjou Lakota named Kicking Bear told Sitting Bull about the Ghost Dance, a ceremony that promised to rid the land of white people and restore the Native Americans' way of life. Because many Lakotas at the Pine Ridge and Rosebud reservations had already adopted the ceremony, U.S. Indian agents had called for troops to control the growing movement. Some authorities at Standing Rock, fearing that Sitting Bull would join the Ghost Dancers, sent 43 Lakota policemen to apprehend him. Before dawn on December 15, 1890, the policemen forced their way into Sitting Bull's cabin and dragged him outside. During an ensuing gunfight between Sitting Bull's supporters and the Lakota policemen, one of the policemen shot Sitting Bull in the head. Sitting Bull was buried at Fort Yates in North Dakota, but in 1953, his remains were moved to Mobridge, South Dakota, where a granite shaft marks his grave.

Robert B. Kane

Further Reading

Bernotas, Bob. *Sitting Bull: Chief of the Sioux.* North American Indians of Achievement. New York: Chelsea House, 1992.

Utley, Robert M. *The Lance and the Shield: The Life and Times of Sitting Bull.* New York: Ballantine, 1993.

Skulking Way of War

A form of warfare in which attackers used stealth to surprise their enemies. Employed largely by Native Americans and later adopted by Europeans in North America, the skulking way of war involved ambushes and raids on small, isolated garrisons or settlements. Skulking tactics relied on detailed knowledge of local terrain and the cover of darkness to conceal movements and acquire positions from which to waylay foes. Attackers also exercised individual initiative, advancing or retreating in open order. Many times, individual combatants aimed and fired at specific targets on their own volition. Combatants usually did not press attacks against enemies who were well prepared to receive an assault, avoided pitched battles, and retreated if they were themselves ambushed.

Native Americans pursued skulking warfare throughout the era of the Indian Wars. Over time, Native American combatants also replaced indigenous arms (bow and arrows, edged weapons, etc.) with firearms of European and later American manufacture as their primary weapon.

In contrast to the skulking way of war, conventional European warfare of the colonial period emphasized the role of prescribed orderly battle. Infantry moved in unison in compact close order formations, handling and discharging weapons together in volleys fired under the direction of officers. Europeans and their colonial descendants varied in their abilities to adapt to or cope with skulking warfare. Militiamen from New France were largely successful in employing these tactics. In fact, they often joined with their American Indian allies in raiding the English colonial frontier during wars between the two countries.

English forces often had more difficulty coping with skulking foes, particularly in conflicts such as King Philip's War (1675–1676), in which effective military responses emphasized direct assaults on American Indian communities or employed native allies against aboriginal foes. By the mid-18th century, some British colonial units such as Rogers' Rangers were primarily employing skulking tactics. Skulking tactics saw widespread use among both Native American and U.S. forces in most of the Indian Wars that transpired from the 1790s to the 1890s.

Matthew S. Muehlbauer

Further Reading

Malone, Patrick M. *The Skulking Way of War: Technology and Tactics among the New England Indians.* Lanham, MD: Madison Books, 2000.

Starkey, Armstrong. *European and Native American Warfare, 1675–1815.* Norman: University of Oklahoma Press, 1998.

St. Clair's Campaign

Start Date: September 6, 1791
End Date: November 4, 1791

U.S. Army campaign during Little Turtle's War (1785–1795) in the Northwest Territory marked by the Battle of the Wabash (November 4, 1791), the worst defeat ever inflicted upon the U.S. Army by Native American forces. When Brigadier General Josiah Harmar's attack on Miami villages in the Northwest Territory failed in October 1790, President George Washington blamed undisciplined militia as the cause of the failure rather than the skill of Native American warriors commanded by Miami chief Little Turtle. In March 1791, Secretary of War Henry Knox secured the appointment of Arthur St. Clair, governor of the Northwest Territory, as a major general and ranking officer in the U.S. Army to command a new expedition into Native American country. St. Clair hoped to raise a force of about 3,000 men and to establish a fort near the Miami villages to secure the territory for white settlers and deter further Native American attacks.

During the late summer of 1791, St. Clair tried to organize his force but faced numerous delays because of inadequate logistics, including poor-quality gunpowder and a limited number of horses. Recruiting for the army was slow, many men suffered from smallpox, and others were lost to accidents and attempted desertion. St. Clair himself was ill much of the time and did little to train his men. Beyond that, he had never served on the frontier and knew little of American Indian warfare. To make matters worse, he ignored advice proffered by knowledgeable subordinates. Eventually his force consisted of the 1st and 2nd regular army regiments, two Kentucky Militia regiments, a battery of 6 cannon, and about 400 noncombatant civilian camp followers, including women and children. On September 6, 1791, some three months behind schedule, St. Clair's army departed its base at Fort Washington (Cincinnati, Ohio) for the movement into the Northwest Territory.

The lack of roads required the army to carve one out of the wilderness and establish a series of fortifications to guard their line of communication and supply back to Fort Washington. Inclement late autumn weather hampered operations, and in two months, the expedition had advanced little more than 100 miles. By the beginning of November, St. Clair's force had been reduced by illness and desertion to only 1,400 effectives.

On November 3, 1791, St. Clair's army encamped in a clearing near a tributary of the Wabash River (near the border of present-day Ohio and Indiana). The clearing was too small for the whole army, so the militia was forced to encamp a few hundred yards on the other side of the river. Believing that he was still 15–20 miles from the main Indian villages, St. Clair posted sentries but made no attempt to fortify the camp or send out patrols to ensure that hostile warriors were not nearby. In fact, the Americans were less than a mile from about 1,200 Miami, Wyandot, Ottawa, Delaware, and Shawnee warriors led by Little Turtle and Blue Jacket.

At dawn on November 4, Little Turtle's warriors attacked just as the Americans were arousing in camp. They hit the militia first, forcing them to flee into the main camp and spreading panic among the rest of the army. After several hours of fighting, the American perimeter had been constricted to a point where men huddled together in a bewildered crowd. By 9:30 a.m., the Battle of the Wabash (also known as St. Clair's Defeat) was over. St. Clair had lost 632 killed and 264 wounded, a 64 percent casualty rate. More significantly, Little Turtle had effectively destroyed almost the entire existing U.S. Army.

Two years later, Major General Anthony Wayne would avenge St. Clair's defeat by organizing and training a new army, the Legion of the United States, which decisively defeated the Native Americans at the Battle of Fallen Timbers (August 20, 1794).

Steven J. Rauch

Further Reading

Guthman, William H. *March to Massacre: A History of the First Seven Years of the United States Army 1784–1791*. New York: McGraw-Hill, 1970.

Lytle, Richard. *The Soldiers of America's First Army, 1791*. Lanham, MD: Scarecrow, 2004.

Sword, Wiley. *President Washington's Indian War: The Struggle for the Old Northwest, 1790–1795*. Norman: University of Oklahoma Press, 1985.

Susquehannock War

Start Date: 1675
End Date: 1676

Frontier war between backcountry settlers in Virginia and Maryland and Susquehannock Native Americans in the upper Potomac River region. The Susquehannock War began in 1675 when a dispute over stolen hogs escalated into a full-scale war. Virginia frontiersmen killed a group of Doeg natives who were trying to confiscate a farmer's hogs as payment for goods they had sold him. The killings set off a series of raids and counterraids. These quickly expanded to involve both Maryland residents and the Susquehannocks.

The Susquehannocks were relative newcomers to the upper Potomac River area. They had only recently accepted an invitation from Governor Charles Calvert of Maryland to settle closer to their principal trading partners. Early in the conflict, Susquehannock leaders sought to negotiate a peaceful resolution. Nearly 1,000 Virginians and Marylanders led by John Washington, however, surrounded a principal Susquehannock town and murdered several Susquehannock headmen.

Outnumbered by the Virginians, the enraged Susquehannocks nonetheless wrought devastation across the Potomac frontier region, raiding and pillaging the isolated farms. Hard pressed by the natives, the frontier populace sought aid from the Virginia government. Colonial officials, fearful of potential disruptions in the profitable Native American trade, responded only with a bland and ineffective defensive strategy. Incensed, frontier settlers rallied around the leadership of Nathaniel Bacon, a young but out-of-favor Virginia aristocrat. Under Bacon's leadership, settlers began indiscriminately killing Native Americans, not only the hostile Susquehannocks but also friendly Algonquian-speaking groups such as the Pamunkeys and the Appomattocks.

Bacon's attacks greatly troubled Virginia lawmakers, who sought to avoid a general war with the natives. In early 1676, Governor William Berkeley of Virginia declared Bacon an outlaw. That move touched off the brief but violent uprising known as Bacon's Rebellion (June 1676–January 1677). Disaffected and disenfranchised frontier residents quickly rallied to Bacon. In September 1676, his makeshift army chased Berkeley from Jamestown and then burned the town. Bacon died of dysentery only a month later, however, and the rebellion quickly collapsed.

The Susquehannock War ended in 1676 as well. Reluctantly the Susquehannocks migrated back into Pennsylvania, where they soon dispersed. Some joined the Delawares (Lenni Lenapes) in southeastern Pennsylvania, whereas others were forcefully assimilated into the Iroquois Confederacy, and still others returned to their old home in the Susquehanna River Valley, where they became known as the Conestogas. After the war, the Susquehannocks in essence ceased to exist, reduced instead to a small constituency in other tribes or reconfigured as only a shadow of their former selves.

Daniel P. Barr

Further Reading

Sheehan, Bernard W. *Savagism and Civility: Indians and Englishmen in Colonial Virginia*. Cambridge: Cambridge University Press, 1980.

Washburn, Wilcomb E. *The Governor and the Rebel: A History of Bacon's Rebellion in Virginia*. Chapel Hill: University of North Carolina Press, 1957.

Susquehannocks

Native American group concentrated in the Susquehanna River Valley. Among the most powerful tribes of the Mid-Atlantic region at the time of the European arrival in North America, the Susquehannocks were exterminated in 1763.

The Susquehannocks, who spoke a dialect of the Iroquois language, lived in about two dozen fortified villages along the Susquehanna River and its tributaries in Maryland, central Pennsylvania, and southern New York. Their villages, the largest of which was located near present-day Lancaster, Pennsylvania, were vast stockades that surrounded longhouses. The longhouses were framed with logs and had a rectangular shape and vaulted roofs. They were 50–100 feet long and 18–25 feet wide, were covered with bark, and had vent holes in the roof to allow smoke from fires to escape. Families slept together on raised platforms on either side of the structure and used animal furs for covers. Because the Susquehannocks were matrilineal, the oldest female was the head of the longhouse.

The Susquehannocks arrived from the north and occupied the Susquehanna Valley from at least 1150. Their earliest known village dates to 1550. At the height of their power during the early 17th century, they numbered some 7,000 people.

The Susquehannocks were farmers, fishermen, and hunters. They planted corn, beans, and squash in the spring and then went south to the Chesapeake Bay area to fish. They returned in the fall to harvest and hunt. Their first recorded European contact was with Captain John Smith in 1608 near Chesapeake Bay.

"Susquehannock" was a descriptive term used by Smith's Algonquian-speaking guide to describe the tall Susquehannocks he met. "Susquehannock" is an Algonquian word meaning "people of the muddy river," a reference to the Susquehanna River.

The Susquehannocks frequently fought with their neighbors, such as the Delawares (Lenni Lenapes) to the east and the Powhatan Confederacy to the south. Although linguistically and culturally related to the Iroquois, the Susquehannocks were allies of the Hurons and bitter enemies of the Iroquois. During the first half of the 17th century, the Susquehannocks were the only natives in the region to become major trading partners with the French, the English, the Dutch, and the Swedes. As such, the Susquehannocks made huge profits from the fur trade.

In their search for greater supplies of furs, the Susquehannocks became involved in increased intertribal rivalry between 1630 and 1700. As the Susquehannocks expanded their search for furs westward, they were drawn into the Beaver Wars (1641–1701), a period of intense native rivalry in the Great Lakes and Ohio River Valley region. Although the Beaver Wars were primarily a competition between the Hurons and the Iroquois, the Susquehannocks contributed to the escalation of the conflict.

Because of their multiple alliances with European colonial powers, the Susquehannocks had more European weapons than any other natives in the region. They even possessed a cannon, a weapon not held by any other natives at the time. The Susquehannocks were placed in jeopardy when the Iroquois Confederacy overwhelmed the Hurons during 1648–1649. The Iroquois had also been strengthened when they absorbed many of the defeated Hurons into their ranks. In 1651, the Mohawks attacked the Susquehannocks and fought a war with them that lasted until 1656. During the course of that conflict, the Susquehannocks were pushed farther south along the banks of the Susquehanna River.

In return for assistance from the English in Maryland, the Susquehannocks ceded much of their Maryland territory to the English in 1652. In 1654, a smallpox epidemic hit the Susquehannocks, which further weakened their ability to resist the Mohawks. The Susquehannocks also lost their major arms supplier when the Dutch seized the Swedish colony in Delaware in 1655. Another smallpox epidemic struck the Susquehannocks in 1661, further inhibiting their ability to withstand Iroquois attack. In 1663, Maryland settlers, fearful of the Iroquois, provided the Susquehannocks with weapons. In 1664, however, the English took New Netherland (New York) from the Dutch and formed an alliance with the Iroquois. Weakened by war and disease, the Susquehannocks were defeated by the Iroquois in 1675 and were also driven out of Pennsylvania.

Governor Charles Calvert of Maryland then offered the Susquehannocks refuge on the upper bank of the Potomac River, much to the chagrin of English colonists living there. The English colonists subsequently attacked the Susquehannocks, sparking the Susquehannock War (1675–1676). The Susquehannocks responded with retaliatory raids on colonial settlements but in 1676 were forced to flee north. Ultimately the Susquehannocks either surrendered to the Iroquois or were dispersed among other regional tribes.

The Iroquois resettled what was left of the Susquehannocks among the Mohawks and the Oneidas in New York. The Susquehannocks thus became part of the so-called Covenant Chain. In 1706, the Iroquois allowed 300 Susquehannocks to return to the Susquehanna Valley and establish the village of Conestoga. Quaker missionaries converted many of the Susquehannocks there to Christianity. In protest, the traditional Susquehannocks left to join the Mingos in Ohio. By 1763, there were only 20 Susquehannocks remaining in Conestoga.

Although these 20 natives were living peacefully and causing no harm, the Paxton Boys, enraged by Pontiac's Rebellion (1763), which did not involve the Susquehannocks, decided that all natives in the region were a threat and should be exterminated. Local officials arrested 14 members of the Conestoga community and placed them in a jail in Lancaster for their own protection. Meanwhile, the Paxton Boys killed the six Susquehannock Christians remaining in Conestoga. The Paxton Boys then proceeded to the Lancaster jail, where they murdered the remaining Susquehannocks. By the end of 1763, the Susquehannocks ceased to exist as a separate tribe; thereafter, individual families joined other neighboring tribes. A few Susquehannock descendants currently live in Oklahoma among the Cayugas and Senecas.

Michael R. Hall

Further Reading

Chadwick, Joseph L. *Susquehannock: The Rogue Iroquois Nation and Its Descendants.* Mechanicsburg, PA: Stackpole, 2001.

Eshleman, H. Frank. *Annals of the Susquehannocks and Other Indian Tribes of Pennsylvania, 1500–1763.* Philadelphia: Pennsylvania Historical Society, 2000.

Wallace, Paul A. W. *Indians in Pennsylvania.* Harrisburg: Pennsylvania Historical and Museum Commission, 2000.

T

Tecumseh

Birth Date: ca. March 1768
Death Date: October 5, 1813

Shawnee chief and organizer of a Pan-Indian resistance movement. Little is known with certainty about Tecumseh's early life. He was born around March 1768 in a Shawnee village along the Scioto River in Ohio near present-day Piqua. His father was a war chief of the Kispoko band. At the time of Tecumseh's birth, the Shawnees were trying to resist white settlers flooding into the Ohio Country. The result was Lord Dunmore's War (1774). When the American Revolutionary War (1775–1783) broke out, the Shawnees sided with the British in an attempt to retain their land. In 1777, Tecumseh's people were forced to flee westward to a village on the Mad River and then moved farther west in 1780. These experiences instilled in Tecumseh a hatred for whites in general and for Americans in particular.

Beginning at age 16, Tecumseh participated in war parties that raided white settlements, but the advance by white settlers continued. In 1786, Kentucky militia burned Tecumseh's village, forcing his people to flee to a new location on the Maumee River. Under the leadership of his older brother Cheeseekau, Tecumseh earned a reputation as a brave and skillful warrior. Cheeseekau was killed in 1792 in an attack on Nashville, and Tecumseh succeeded him as war chief of the Kispoko band.

Tecumseh supported a loose confederacy of tribes organized by Blue Jacket and Little Turtle in 1790. When American armies under brigadier generals Josiah Harmar in 1790 and Arthur St. Clair in 1791 marched against the tribes in Ohio, Tecumseh was among those who ambushed and defeated them. On August 20, 1794, Tecumseh participated in the Battle of Fallen Timbers in which Major General Anthony "Mad Anthony" Wayne decisively defeated Blue Jacket and broke the Pan-Indian confederacy.

Tecumseh refused to attend the signing of the Treaty of Greenville in 1795 in which Native Americans ceded most of Ohio to the United States. Instead, he led his followers into Indiana Territory to get away from white influence. In 1797, the band settled near present-day Anderson, Indiana. Meanwhile, Native American settlements continued to decline because of alcoholism and renewed attempts by whites to take their lands. During this time, Tecumseh joined his younger brother, the prophet Tenskwatawa, in calling for a return to traditional values and a rejection of all white influences. In 1805, Tecumseh moved his band back to Ohio, settling at the site of Fort Greenville, which the U.S. Army had abandoned in 1796. Soon Tecumseh and Tenskwatawa began to exert growing influence among other tribes. Delegations visited Tecumseh and listened to his ideas of an Indian confederacy against white encroachment.

While Tecumseh's message found favor among younger warriors, older leaders opposed him. Whites were also uncomfortable with Tecumseh's presence so close to the border. Although he was careful to give no pretext for attacks by whites, Tecumseh realized that he was in danger in Ohio. The most damaging and dangerous charges against Tecumseh were that he was plotting with the British in Canada and receiving arms from them. To avoid possible conflict before he was ready, Tecumseh moved his band back to Indiana in spring 1808, settling along the Wabash River, just below the mouth of the Tippecanoe River. Tecumseh now became more outspoken in his criticism of American expansionism.

In 1809 in the Treaty of Fort Wayne, Indiana territorial governor William Henry Harrison secured the cession of three million acres from tribes in Indiana. The outraged Tecumseh denounced these land cessions, believing that the land belonged to all tribes and that none could be sold or given away without the consent of all. At a meeting with Harrison, the two nearly came to blows. Realizing that only strength could stop American settlements, Tecumseh began traveling widely to recruit followers for his confederacy. Although many favored his message, only the nativist Red Stick faction of the Creeks was willing to commit to joining his confederacy. While Tecumseh was away in 1811, Harrison brought an American army to attack Tecumseh's village at Prophetstown. Tenskwatawa launched an unsuccessful surprise attack on Harrison but was decisively defeated at the Battle of Tippecanoe (November 7, 1811). This defeat diminished Tecumseh's power and following among Native Americans.

Tecumseh was now forced to turn to the British for aid. When word reached Tecumseh in July 1812 that the United States had declared war against Great Britain, he gathered a band of followers and led them into Canada, joining British major general Isaac Brock in defending Fort Malden against an invasion by Brigadier General William Hull from Detroit. There is a tradition that

Tecumseh was commissioned a brigadier general in the British Army, the only Indian to be so recognized. While Hull proved to be an indecisive leader, on August 5, Tecumseh ambushed and destroyed an American supply column in Michigan. He continued to harass American forces around Detroit, helping to convince Hull to retreat from Canada and later to surrender Detroit.

His victory over Hull caused large numbers of warriors to join Tecumseh and Brock in a combined British and Native American advance into Ohio. They fought a series of battles against American columns under Harrison, who sought to recapture Detroit. Tecumseh was in Indiana in January 1813 when an American force was destroyed on the Raisin River and the wounded were massacred. Tecumseh returned in time to join Brigadier General Henry Procter in the siege of Fort Meigs from April 28 to May 9. Tecumseh's warriors destroyed an American relief column on May 5 before the allies gave up the siege. A second attempt to capture Fort Meigs in July also failed, and many of the warriors began to lose confidence in the British.

When Procter, now a major general, retreated to Canada after the American victory in the Battle of Lake Erie, Tecumseh was outraged. He did not understand how the naval defeat would prevent the British from resupplying the army and the thousands of Native American families massed around Fort Malden. Nevertheless, Tecumseh and a small group of warriors joined the British in their retreat eastward from Fort Malden. To pacify Tecumseh, Procter agreed to make a stand on the Thames River on October 5, 1813. Tecumseh was killed in the battle. After Tecumseh's death and the British defeat, the Native Americans lost heart and dispersed.

Tim J. Watts

Further Reading

Edmunds, R. David. *Tecumseh and the Quest for Indian Leadership*. Boston: Little, Brown, 1984.

Sugden, John. *Tecumseh: A Life*. New York: Holt, 1997.

Tenskwatawa

Birth Date: ca. 1775
Death Date: November 1836

Shawnee religious prophet and political leader in the Old Northwest during the early 19th century. Tenskwatawa (known as the Shawnee Prophet or simply the Prophet) was born around 1775 at Old Piqua, Ohio, as one of triplets into a family of at least six older brothers and sisters. Just prior to Tenskwatawa's birth, his father, Shawnee war chief Puckeshinwa, died in the 1774 Battle of Point Pleasant in present-day West Virginia. Their Creek mother, Methoataske, left the Ohio Valley in 1779 and entrusted her children—Tenskwatawa, Tecumseh (who would become one of the most famous Native American military leaders of all time), and another child—to an older sister, Tecumapease.

Tenskwatawa's childhood name was Lalawethika. In 1804, he assumed the role of community shaman when the renowned shaman Penagashea died. Lalawethika had been studying with him since 1795. After a series of visions in 1805, Lalawethika changed his name to Tenskwatawa, meaning "The Open Door." In the visions, Tenskwatawa met the Master of Life, who showed him heaven and hell and gave him instructions on how to avoid the latter while gaining admission to the former. Tenskwatawa preached that Native Americans must give up alcohol, reject Christianity, destroy their medicine bags, and respect all life. If the Master of Life's teachings were followed,

Tenskwatawa claimed, the dead would be brought back to life, and wildlife populations would be restored. Adherents were given prayer sticks inscribed with prayers for the Master of Life. Tenskwatawa also claimed that Americans were products of the evil Great Serpent who, assisted by witches, spread death and destruction. Tenskwatawa nonetheless sanctioned trade with the Americans but only on terms set by the Native Americans until trade was no longer needed. Finally, the nativist vision of Tenskwatawa and Tecumseh included a call for Pan-Indian unity to resist white encroachments on ancestral lands. Of the brothers, Tenskwatawa's approach was more spiritual, while Tecumseh's was more pragmatic, but both were very persuasive.

Immediately following his vision and explanations, Tenskwatawa and Tecumseh established a village in Ohio near the site of Fort Greenville, which the U.S. Army had abandoned in 1796, and called for all Native American peoples to settle there. This settlement was a direct challenge to the 1795 Treaty of Greenville. In 1806, Tenskwatawa participated in witchcraft trials among the Delawares and Wyandots; the accused were individuals who appeared to be acculturated to white ways. As Tenskwatawa's prestige and popularity grew, the settlement of Greenville proved to be inadequate, resulting in the establishment of Prophetstown in 1808 at the mouth of the Tippecanoe River.

The brothers' influence was interpreted as a threat by Indiana governor William Henry Harrison. In 1811, when Tecumseh was in the South recruiting tribes to his Pan-Indian coalition, Harrison led a force of 970 men against Prophetstown. Tenskwatawa promised to meet with Harrison and suggested that he camp for the night at a location some two miles distant from Prophetstown. Tecumseh had warned his brother not to give battle, but that night, Tenskwatawa incited some 500–700 of his followers to strike first, promising them that the white men's bullets could not harm them, as their powder had already turned to sand and their bullets to soft mud.

Early on the morning of November 7, the Native Americans struck. During the battle, Tenskwatawa stood on a high rock and chanted war songs to encourage his followers. Informed early that some of his warriors had been slain, he insisted that his followers fight on, promising an easy victory. Although Harrison lost up to a quarter of his force in casualties, the Battle of Tippecanoe ended in a Native American defeat, and the next day Harrison went on to destroy Prophetstown.

Tenskwatawa's followers almost killed him in their fury over the outcome of the Battle of Tippecanoe. It was clearly the nadir of his influence among the Great Lakes nations. The battle was significant because it drove many Native Americans of the Old Northwest to side with the British in the War of 1812. The British also decided to assist Native Americans there against the United States.

Although Tenskwatawa participated in the major events of the War of 1812, he did not take part in any of the actual fighting. In the Battle of the Thames on October 5, 1813, Tenskwatawa fled with the British, leaving Tecumseh and dozens of other warriors to die protecting their retreat. The American victory in this battle effectively ended British and Native American power in the Old Northwest.

Denied admission to the United States in 1815, Tenskwatawa and a few Shawnee followers remained in Upper Canada until 1824. In 1826, Tenskwatawa and the Shawnees were removed from the Ohio Valley. They traveled to Kaskaskia and western Missouri, eventually reaching the Shawnee Reservation in Kansas in 1828. Tenskwatawa sat for an iconic portrait by American artist George Catlin in 1832 and died in November 1836 in present-day Kansas City, Kansas.

Karl S. Hele

Further Reading

Dowd, Gregory Evans. *A Spirited Resistance: The North American Indian Struggle for Unity, 1745–1815*. Baltimore: Johns Hopkins University Press, 1992.

Dowd, Gregory Evans. "Thinking and Believing: Nativism and Unity in the Ages of Pontiac and Tecumseh." *American Indian Quarterly* 16, no. 3 (Summer 1992): 309–335.

Edmunds, R. David. *The Shawnee Prophet*. Lincoln: University of Nebraska Press, 1983.

Terry, Alfred Howe

Birth Date: November 10, 1827
Death Date: December 16, 1890

U.S. Army officer. Alfred Howe Terry was born into a wealthy New England family on November 10, 1827, in Hartford, Connecticut. After briefly attending Yale University Law School from 1848 to 1849, he served as a law clerk for the New Haven County Superior Court from 1854 until the beginning of the American Civil War (1861–1865).

At the onset of the Civil War, Terry raised the 2nd Connecticut Regiment, was commissioned its colonel, and led it in the First Battle of Bull Run (Manassas) in Virginia (July 21, 1861). He subsequently recruited and led the 7th Connecticut Regiment in helping to secure Port Royal, South Carolina, on November 7, 1861. Terry's role in the capture of Fort Pulaski at the mouth of the strategic Savannah River (April 11, 1862) led to his promotion to brigadier general of volunteers on April 26, 1862. He then commanded a division of X Corps and took part in operations against Charleston, including the capture of Fort Wagner in September 1863. In 1864, X Corps was assigned to Major General Benjamin Butler's Army of the James in Virginia, and Terry saw extensive action in the Bermuda Hundred Campaign. Terry's greatest recognition came when he received command of a provisional corps for an attack on Fort Fisher. He and Rear Admiral David D. Porter worked well together, and Fort Fisher fell to Union forces on January 13, 1865. For this achievement, Terry received an official thanks from the U.S. Congress, a brigadier general's commission in the regular army, and a major general's commission in the volunteer army. His promotion to brigadier general in the regular army was a rare accomplishment for someone who had not graduated from the U.S. Military Academy. Terry finished the war in the Carolinas as part of Major General John M. Schofield's Army of the Ohio, which was operating under Major General William Tecumseh Sherman.

After the Civil War, Terry commanded the Department of Dakota from 1866 to 1868 and again from 1873 to 1886. He was a key architect of the 1867 Medicine Lodge Treaty that temporarily ended the fighting on the southern Plains with the Comanches, Kiowas, Kiowa-Apaches, Cheyennes, and Arapahoes. Terry also participated in the 1868 Treaty of Fort Laramie negotiations, which brought an end to Red Cloud's War (1866–1868).

In 1873, Terry returned to command the Department of Dakota and participated in the Great Sioux War (Black Hills War) of 1876–1877. He commanded one of the three converging columns designed to locate and destroy the hostile Native Americans. This led to the disastrous Battle of the Little Bighorn (June 25–26, 1876) in which the 7th Cavalry Regiment, commanded by Lieutenant Colonel George Armstrong Custer, spearheading Terry's column, attacked without waiting for the supporting columns and suffered a devastating defeat, including the annihilation of Custer and 267 men under him. Afterward, Terry refused to say anything that might tarnish Custer's reputation.

In October 1877, Terry went to Canada to negotiate the surrender of the Sioux leader Sitting Bull. These talks were not successful, but in 1881, Terry was the man to whom Sitting Bull surrendered. Still commander of the Department of Dakota during the Nez Perce War of 1877, Terry sent troops to help intercept Chief Joseph and his people. In 1878, Terry joined Major General John Schofield and Colonel George W. Getty on the so-called Schofield Commission, a board charged with reexamining the Civil War court-martial of Major General Fitz John Porter.

In 1886, Terry was promoted to major general, one of only three men to hold that rank in the army at the time. He was also the first Civil War volunteer officer to attain that rank in the regular army. Terry received command of the Division of the Missouri, with headquarters in Chicago. He retired from the army in 1888 and died on December 16, 1890, in New Haven, Connecticut.

Alan K. Lamm

Further Reading

Bailey, John W. *Pacifying the Plains: General Alfred Terry and the Decline of the Sioux, 1866–1890.* Westport, CT: Greenwood, 1979.

Hutton, Paul Andrew. *Phil Sheridan and His Army.* Lincoln: University of Nebraska Press, 1985.

Thames, Battle of the

Event Date: October 5, 1813

Climactic battle of the War of 1812 in the Old Northwest. Also known as the Battle of Moraviantown, the Battle of the Thames marked the end of British and Native American influence on the Great Lakes frontier. The engagement occurred near present-day Chatham, Ontario, along the Thames River. Throughout 1813, the British and their Native American allies, commanded by Major General Henry Procter and Shawnee war chief Tecumseh, had frustrated efforts by Major General William Henry Harrison to regain U.S. control over the region. When U.S. Navy master commandant Oliver Hazard Perry defeated the British in the Battle of Lake Erie on September 10, 1813, the Americans regained control of Lake Erie. This naval victory enabled Harrison to undertake an offensive to recapture Detroit, farther west, and to invade Canada.

With his logistical support now all but cut off, Procter hoped to withdraw from Detroit by moving through Upper Canada along the Thames River. Tecumseh strongly opposed Procter's decision, viewing it as evidence of abandonment by the British, who had promised Native Americans their own lands. Eventually the allies reached a compromise to retreat but to make a stand somewhere along the route. The march from Sandwich began on September 24 with about 880 British troops and perhaps 500 Native American warriors and their families. The withdrawal was not well organized and proceeded slowly, encumbered with considerable personal baggage. Soon the men were on half rations. Morale was low, and the officers were reportedly dissatisfied with Procter's leadership, although Lieutenant Colonel Augustus Warburton, second in command, resisted calls that he intervene to remove Procter.

On September 27, Harrison's army landed in Canada. He had almost 5,000 U.S. regulars and Kentucky militia. Harrison left Sandwich on October 2, the speed of his advance greatly enhanced by mounted Kentucky riflemen led by Colonel Richard M. Johnson. On October 4, the American column reached the third and unfordable branch of the Thames. Tecumseh and his warriors had dismantled the bridge there and were on the opposite side. Harrison used two 6-pounders to drive away the Native Americans and then ordered his men to repair the bridge. In just two hours, Harrison was again on the move. Johnson's Kentuckians caught up with Procter a few miles from Moraviantown along the Thames River, the British having already set fire to the craft they were using to transport some of their baggage and supplies on the river.

By the morning of October 5, it was clear to Procter that he would have to stand and fight. He deployed his regulars in a wedge-shaped clearing in a beech forest. The left flank rested on the river beside which ran the road to Moraviantown some three and a half miles to the east. The line ran about 250 yards to the north, ending at a small swamp, and then extended another 250 yards, where it ended at a large swamp. The left portion of the British line was held by 540 men of the 41st Regiment of Foot and 290 men of the Royal Newfoundland Regiment. Procter positioned a 6-pounder on the road to provide some support. The portion to the right of the small swamp was held by Tecumseh's 500 Native Americans. The British had not erected any sort of earthworks or abatis.

The Americans arrived before the British position at about 8:00 a.m. The American force numbered 140 regulars, 1,000 Kentuckians in Johnson's regiment, and another 2,300 Kentucky volunteers. There were also perhaps 160 allied Native Americans. As

Harrison was making his dispositions prior to an attack, Johnson learned that the British left was only thinly held by men standing about three feet apart. The situation seemed tailor-made for Johnson's mounted men, and he asked permission from Harrison to make an immediate charge. Harrison agreed. With many of the attackers screaming "Remember the Raisin!" (a reference to the Raisin River Massacre), the Kentuckians in only a few minutes drove through the British line—the British 6-pounder having failed to fire—and then dismounted and used their rifles to attack the British from the rear. Under attack from both front and rear, the British line quickly crumbled, and most of the British troops surrendered.

The Native Americans, protected somewhat by the swamp, held their ground and halted Johnson's horsemen with musket fire, killing or wounding 15 of them. Johnson himself was wounded several times. Tecumseh, who had a premonition of his own death, was slain. His body was never recovered (the Native Americans said it had been lifted up to heaven), but Johnson claimed to have killed him and was generally so credited. With the sizable American force converging on their position, most of the Native Americans fled.

The Battle of the Thames lasted less than an hour, with the British suffering 12 killed, 22 wounded, and some 600 captured. Thirty-three Native Americans were also slain. American casualties were 7 killed and 22 wounded. Procter, who escaped, was widely blamed for the defeat. He blamed his men, saying that they had not carried out his orders. Procter demanded a court of inquiry, and when this was not held, he wrote directly to the British commander, Frederick, Duke of York. This led to a court-martial and a finding that Procter was guilty of failing to prepare properly for the retreat and of exercising

poor tactical judgment. The court recommended that he be reprimanded and suspended from duty for six months. In the end he was only reprimanded, in July 1815.

Although a relatively minor action, the Battle of the Thames proved decisive and provided a rare victory for the United States in the War of 1812. The victory was received with great enthusiasm in Kentucky and helped renew public support for the war. The battle destroyed the British position west of the head of Lake Erie and broke forever Native American power in the Old Northwest. This opened that territory for white settlement west to the Mississippi River. After their victory, the American troops burned Moraviantown, a peaceful Native American settlement. Then, lacking naval support that was needed elsewhere, they departed Canada for Detroit.

Steven J. Rauch and Spencer C. Tucker

Further Reading

Antal, Sandy. *A Wampum Denied: Procter's War of 1812.* Ottawa: Carleton University Press, 1997.

Latimer, Jon. *1812: War with America.* Cambridge: Belknap Press of Harvard University Press, 2007.

Sugden, John. *Tecumseh's Last Stand.* Norman: University of Oklahoma Press, 1985.

Tippecanoe, Battle of

Event Date: November 7, 1811

Battle between American forces and Native American warriors that occurred on the banks of the Wabash River near Prophetstown (near present-day Lafayette, Indiana) on November 7, 1811. The Battle of Tippecanoe served to blunt Shawnee leader Tecumseh's efforts to forge a native confederation for resisting American expansion in the Old Northwest.

Tecumseh and his half-brother Tenskwatawa, known as the Prophet, had founded Prophetstown in May 1808 as the capital of their growing native confederacy. The town was not only the center for diplomatic activities among the tribes but also a training ground for warriors. At its peak, more than 1,000 people resided there.

In November 1811, while Tecumseh was recruiting other Native American groups in the southern states for his confederation, Tenskwatawa was in charge of Prophetstown. At the same time, Indiana Territorial Governor William Henry Harrison sought to destroy Prophetstown. Harrison had aggressively pursued land cession treaties with the Native Americans, often playing one tribe or individual against another or plying native leaders with alcohol to get them to sign away their lands. Tecumseh's growing Native American confederation was a threat to this process. To western whites, Prophetstown had become a symbol of British influence, although the native raids on American frontier settlements almost certainly did not originate with them. Governors Ninian Edwards of the Illinois Territory and Benjamin Howard of the newly formed Missouri Territory both approved Harrison's proposed plan for a march up the Wabash River to the limits of the purchase of 1809. Harrison so informed Secretary of War William Eustis, who responded that he favored approaching the Prophet, asking him to disperse his followers, and, should he refuse, attacking him. Eustis also authorized Harrison to establish a new frontier post, but in no circumstances was he to antagonize the British.

The most important element of Harrison's expeditionary force, Colonel John Boyd's 4th U.S. Infantry Regiment, arrived at Vincennes, Indiana, from Philadelphia on September 19, 1811, having covered the 1,300 miles on foot and in boats. Six days later on September 25, Harrison gave the order to move out. A total of 970 men responded: 350 members of the 4th Regiment, 400 Indiana militiamen, 84 mounted Indiana riflemen, 123 Kentucky dragoons, and 13 scouts and guides. The march order, adopted from Major General Anthony Wayne's practice in the Fallen Timbers Campaign of 1794, consisted of a company of riflemen leading, followed 100 yards behind by a mounted troop and 50 yards behind it the infantry in column. Another mounted troop took up the rear 100 yards behind the infantry. Detached troops protected the flanks of the column 100 yards on either side. Each night, the men prepared a fortified camp to protect against possible native attack.

Because of these precautions, it took Harrison more than two weeks to cover the 65 miles from Vincennes to the bend in the Wabash River at present-day Terre Haute. There the men completed Fort Harrison on October 27 before moving to the mouth of the Vermillion River. Harrison now ordered the construction of a blockhouse, later called Fort Boyd, at the site.

Harrison had warned that whether he advanced farther would depend on Native American conduct, so when some natives stole horses from the camp and someone fired into the camp, wounding a man on October 10, Harrison took these incidences as justification to cross the Vermillion into Native American territory. More shots were fired into Harrison's advancing forces but without casualties. Harrison was now determined to destroy Prophetstown, and his officers urged that he attack without delay. On November 6, however, a native delegation requested talks, and Harrison, against the advice of his subordinate commanders, accepted, with the parley scheduled for the next day.

The native delegation then suggested the campsite for Harrison's force. Harrison's enemies later claimed that the natives had selected an ideal ambush position, but in fact it was the best site in the area for defensive purposes. Located some two miles west of Prophetstown on an oak-covered knoll, it was a wedge-shaped area covering about 10 acres, bordered by wet prairie land and by Burnet's Creek on its west side. On its east the knoll rose about 10 feet above the prairie and on its west about 20 feet before the creek.

Harrison ordered his men to bed down for the night fully clothed, with their weapons loaded and bayonets fixed. It was a cold night, and Harrison allowed fires to help the men stay warm. In case of native attack, Harrison instructed that the men rise, advance a pace or two, and form a line of battle and return fire. Harrison was confident that he could hold during a night attack and then take the offensive when it was light. The horses were kept within the camp, and to warn of any attack, Harrison ordered the posting of a sizable night guard of 108 men. He did not, however, order the construction of breastworks, nor was he concerned about the possibility of fires illuminating the American positions.

Although Tecumseh had warned his brother against fighting until the confederation was stronger and fully unified, Tenskwatawa ignored the advice. On the night of November 6, the natives discussed their options. Later Shabonee, a Pottawatomi chief, testified that two Englishmen were present during the deliberations and had urged an attack. A captured African American wagon driver informed Tenskwatawa that Harrison had no artillery with him and that he planned to attack Prophetstown after his discussions with the natives the next day.

That night some 550–700 natives, largely Kickapoos, Pottawatomies, and Winnebagos but also including Ojibwas, Wyandots, Mucos, Ottawas, Piankashaws, and Shawnees, worked themselves into a frenzy.

Using fiery speeches, Tenskwatawa urged action. He claimed that the white man's bullets could not harm them, that the whites' powder had already turned to sand and their bullets to soft mud.

The warriors left Prophetstown during the night, and by 4:00 a.m. on November 7, they surrounded Harrison's camp. One of the American sentinels, Stephen Mars, heard movement in the darkness and fired a shot or two before fleeing for the safety of the camp. He was killed before he could reach it, but his shot alerted Harrison's men. The Indians then let out war whoops and opened fire. The battle opened first on the northwest side of the camp. Unfortunately for Harrison's men, when they rose many were silhouetted against their campfires, making them easy targets. Harrison himself mounted and rode to the sound of the firing. His own white horse had broken its tether during the night, and he rode a dark one. This probably saved his life, for the natives were looking for him on a white horse. (Harrison's aide Colonel Abraham Owen, who found and rode Harrison's white horse, was shot and killed.) Firing then broke out on the east side of the camp, and the battle became general. During the battle, Tenskwatawa stationed himself on a high rock to the east and chanted war songs to encourage his followers. Informed early that some of his warriors had been slain, he insisted that his followers fight on, promising an easy victory.

After two hours of fighting and when it was sufficiently light, Harrison sent out mounted men to attack the natives on their flanks. Soon the natives were in retreat. In the battle, Harrison lost 68 men killed and 126 wounded, a significant casualty rate of up to a quarter of his force. The number of Native American dead is not known for certain. Thirty-seven bodies were found at the battle site, but this did not account for those who were carried off or died later from their wounds. Native American losses are estimated at no fewer than 50 killed and 70 or more wounded.

Worried by a false report that Tecumseh was nearby with a larger native force, Harrison ordered his men to fortify their position. A reconnaissance the next day revealed, however, that Prophetstown had been abandoned, and Harrison then advanced on it. Among supplies that the natives abandoned in their hasty withdrawal was some new British equipment. Harrison ordered the men to take what supplies they could and destroy the rest. Prophetstown, its supplies, and its food stocks were soon ablaze. In order to move swiftly and provide for his wounded in carts, Harrison also ordered much of the expedition's private property, including his own, destroyed. His force then set out for Vincennes, 150 miles distant. The return march was an agony for the wounded who, tossed about in the carts, died at the rate of two or three per day.

The native warriors came close to killing Tenskwatawa for his false predictions. Certainly the Battle of Tippecanoe also badly damaged Tecumseh's vision of building a confederation to stave off white settlement. Tecumseh returned to Prophetstown several weeks later to find only ruins. Although Prophetstown was rebuilt, Tecumseh never recovered the momentum behind his confederation movement after the battle.

In the end, the battle only hardened positions on both sides. Frontiersmen were convinced that the British had been behind native aggression, while the battle drove many natives to side with the British during the War of 1812. The British were also convinced of the need to aid the natives. In effect, Tippecanoe served to cement the British–Native American alliance. For all these reasons, many have called it the opening battle of the War of 1812. For Harrison, the Battle of Tippecanoe had mixed results. Although he described the battle as "a complete and decisive victory," his political enemies charged that he had been guilty of poor leadership and undue aggressiveness. Harrison's friends, however, claimed that he had saved the Old Northwest from the natives. Certainly the battle helped establish his national reputation and clearly assisted him in securing the presidency in the election of 1840, during which the slogan "Tippecanoe and Tyler Too" was used.

Daniel W. Kuthy and Spencer C. Tucker

Further Reading

Cave, Alfred. "The Shawnee Prophet, Tecumseh, and Tippecanoe." *Journal of the Early Republic* 22, no. 4 (Winter 2002): 637–673.

Edmunds, R. David. *The Shawnee Prophet.* Lincoln: University of Nebraska Press, 1983.

Edmunds, R. David. *Tecumseh and the Quest for Indian Leadership.* Boston: Little, Brown, 1984.

Jortner, Adam Joseph. *The Gods of Prophetstown: The Battle of Tippecanoe and the Holy War for the American Frontier.* New York: Oxford University Press, 2012.

Trail of Tears

Event Date: 1838

Name given to the forced movement of the Cherokee tribe from their homelands in the Southeast to Indian Territory by the U.S. Army. This movement, which consisted of a series of brutal forced marches, began on May 26, 1838, and was part of the U.S. government's Indian Removal Policy. Some 17,000 Cherokees were gathered together, mostly in Georgia and Tennessee, and were then forced to travel nearly 1,200 miles to Indian Territory (Oklahoma). In the Cherokee language, the removal was referred to as "the trail where we cried," a name that has described the grim event ever since.

Tensions between the Cherokee Nation and white settlers reached new heights in 1829, when gold was discovered in Dahlonega in northwestern Georgia. The Cherokees considered this area their tribal land and insisted on exercising sole sovereignty over it. In 1830, the State of Georgia sought legal clarification of the land dispute in a case that ultimately went to the U.S. Supreme Court as *Cherokee Nation v. Georgia* (1831). The Supreme Court refused to hear the case because it did not consider the Cherokee Nation a sovereign state. However, in *Worcester v. Georgia* (1832), the U.S. Supreme Court ruled that state governments could not invoke sovereignty over the Cherokees, arguing that this was the prerogative of the federal government. After his landslide 1832 reelection to the presidency, Andrew Jackson was more determined than ever to pursue with vigor the removal of the Cherokees and other eastern tribes, which had been made easier by the 1830 Indian Removal Act.

Soon thereafter, a splinter faction of the Cherokees, called the Ridge Party or the Treaty Party, was formed, led by Cherokees Major Ridge, Elias Boudinot, and Stand Watie. Believing that removal was inevitable, they began negotiations with the Jackson administration to secure equitable treatment but acted without the support of the elected Cherokee Council, headed by Chief John Ross, and firmly opposed to any kind of removal. This created a split among the Cherokees, with the Ridge contingent forming its own ruling council and becoming known as the Western Cherokees. Those loyal to Ross were then known as the Eastern Cherokees.

In 1835, Jackson appointed Reverend John Schermerhorn as a treaty commissioner to negotiate with the Cherokees.

That same year, the U.S. government proposed to pay $4.5 million to the Cherokees as compensation for their land. In return, they were to vacate the area voluntarily. Schermerhorn then organized a meeting with a small number of Cherokee Council members who were prepared to accept removal. Although no more than 500 Cherokees (out of many thousands) parleyed with the commissioner, on December 30, 1835, 20 Cherokees—including Ridge—signed the Treaty of New Echota. It was signed later by Ridge's son John and Stand Watie. No members of the main Cherokee Council signed the document.

The treaty ceded all Cherokee lands east of the Mississippi River. Naturally, Ross rejected the treaty out of hand. The U.S. Senate nevertheless ratified it—just barely—on May 23, 1836, and set the date of May 23, 1838, as the deadline for the removal of the Cherokees. Although Ross presented a 15,000-signature petition to Congress against the treaty, this appeal fell on deaf ears. Meanwhile, Cherokees who had supported the removal policy began to migrate from Georgia to Indian Territory. By the end of 1836, at least 6,000 Cherokees had voluntarily left their ancestral lands, but some 17,000 remained.

In May 1838 with the removal deadline looming, President Martin Van Buren appointed Brigadier General Winfield Scott to oversee the forcible removal of the recalcitrant Cherokees. By May 17, Scott had reached New Echota, Georgia, the heart of Cherokee country, with 7,000 troops. They began to round up the Cherokees in Georgia beginning on May 26. Operations in Tennessee, North Carolina, and Alabama began on June 5. Systematically the Cherokees were forced from their homes at gunpoint and marched to a series of camps. They were allowed to take no belongings with them, and they offered little resistance.

Thirty-one forts—basically makeshift detention camps—had been built to aid in the removal. Thirteen of them were in Georgia. The Cherokees were then moved from these temporary encampments to 11 fortified camps, of which all but 1 was in Tennessee. By late July 1838, some 17,000 Cherokees and an additional 2,000 Black slaves owned by wealthy Native Americans were in the camps. Conditions in the camps were appalling, and diseases including dysentery were rife. As a result, there was a high mortality rate. The Cherokees were then gradually removed to three transfer points: Ross's Landing (Chattanooga, Tennessee), Gunter's Landing (Guntersville, Alabama), and the Cherokee Agency (Calhoun, Tennessee).

Three groups of Cherokees, totaling 2,800 people, were moved from Ross's Landing by steamboat along the Tennessee, Ohio, Mississippi, and Arkansas rivers to Sallisaw Creek in Indian Territory by June 19. However, the majority of the Cherokees were moved in groups of between 700 and 1,500 people, along with guides appointed by Ross, on overland routes. Ross had received the contract to oversee the relocation under Cherokee supervision despite resistance from within his own nation and members of Congress who resented the extra cost. In the end, the army was to be used only to oversee the removal and to prevent outbreaks of violence. There was one exception to this mass removal, which was the small group of Cherokees who had signed the Treaty of New Echota. They were escorted by Lieutenant Edward Deas of the army, mainly for their own protection.

The movement of detachments began on August 28, 1838. It was customary for the detachments to be accompanied by a physician and a clergyman. For most Cherokees, the journey was about 1,200 miles. Although there were three distinct overland routes, the majority took the northern route through central Tennessee, southwestern Kentucky, and southern Illinois. These groups crossed the Mississippi at Cape Girardeau, Missouri, and trekked across Missouri to northern Arkansas. They then entered present-day Oklahoma near Westville, having met troops from Fort Gibson.

The conditions on the march varied. The first groups to undertake the journey experienced high temperatures, and many suffered from heat exhaustion. In the winter, many Cherokees suffered from frostbite and hypothermia while waiting to cross frozen rivers. Most Cherokees marched on foot, but some were loaded into overcrowded wagons. Many died on the way. The official government total was 424, but the most widely cited number is 4,000, half of them in the camps and half on the march. A recent scholarly study, however, estimates a much higher figure of 8,000 dead.

Many of the Cherokees settled around Tahlequah (Oklahoma) which became the center for the tribal government. Local districts were established that in turn elected officials to serve on the new National Council. Bilingual schools were created, and missionaries from the American Board of Commissioners for Foreign Missions built churches on the reservations. There was great resentment on the part of many Cherokees against Ridge, Boudinot, Watie, and the signatories of the Treaty of Echota Treaty. Ridge and his son John were killed on June 22, 1839, in separate incidents, and Boudinot was also murdered.

It should be noted that other eastern tribes—the Choctaws, Chickasaws, Creeks, and Seminoles in particular—experienced their own "trail of tears" with losses similar to those of the Cherokees. The Trail of Tears is generally considered to be one of the most deplorable eras in American history.

Ralph Martin Baker and
Paul G. Pierpaoli Jr.

Further Reading

Carter, Samuel, III. *Cherokee Sunset: A Nation Betrayed: A Narrative of Travail and Triumph, Persecution and Exile.* Garden City, NY: Doubleday, 1976.

Ehle, John. *Trail of Tears: The Rise and Fall of the Cherokee Nation.* New York: Doubleday, 1988.

Foreman, Grant. *Indian Removal: The Emigration of the Five Civilized Tribes of Indians.* Norman: University of Oklahoma Press, 1989.

Remini, Robert Vincenti. *Andrew Jackson and His Indian Wars.* New York: Penguin, 2001.

Tuscarora War

Start Date: September 22, 1711
End Date: April 14, 1713

Major war between Native Americans and colonists in North Carolina. The Tuscarora War began on September 22, 1711, when Tuscarora and allied Algonquian militants attacked colonial settlements on the Neuse and Pamlico rivers. The uprising, proprietary North Carolina's largest and costliest Native American war, was the result of the colonists' fraudulent trading practices, land seizures, and forced enslavement of Native Americans. When peace returned in 1713, political, religious, and economic reforms fueled North Carolina's growth. The defeat of the Tuscaroras also removed the last obstacle blocking European expansion in the colony.

The Iroquoian-speaking Tuscaroras, the largest tribe in North Carolina's central coastal plain, occupied several towns along the Pamlico, Neuse, and Trent rivers. Resentment toward Europeans began when Baron Christoph von Graffenried founded New Bern at the site of a vacated Tuscarora town. Other colonists followed suit, establishing communities on or abutting tribal lands. Although colonial expansion increased trade between Native Americans and Europeans, mistreatment, cultural prejudice, and fraud engendered hard feelings. The prohibition of hunting in newly settled areas also enraged the Tuscaroras.

The enslavement of children, however, produced the greatest outcry. Although the colony's lord proprietors forbade the practice, Native American slavery flourished throughout the Carolinas. The Tuscaroras discovered, however, that their children, entrusted to neighboring colonists for apprenticeships, were in fact often enslaved.

By 1710, the Tuscaroras sought to escape the abuses and encroachments by moving north. Pennsylvania's leaders, however, rejected the tribal diplomats' petition to relocate there. Hancock, chief of the southern Tuscaroras, responded with force.

On September 22, 1711, some 250 Bear River, Pamlico, Neusiok, Coree, Machapunga, and Tuscarora warriors visited the homes of unsuspecting white settlers. Once welcomed into the colonists' abodes, the warriors brandished weapons and killed the inhabitants. Nearly 130 men, women, and children perished during the attacks. Many others, including Graffenried, were captured. News of the onslaught shocked colonial leaders. Political instability, civil unrest, disease, and drought initially prevented Governor Edward Hyde from organizing a military response or providing relief to those in need.

Thomas Pollock, president of the provincial council, immediately marched militia to the war zone. Problems resulted, however, when soldiers from Bath Town refused to cross the Pamlico River to join troops from New Bern. As a result, New Bern's forces were stranded without reinforcements in hostile territory.

Governor Hyde meanwhile appealed to neighboring colonies for assistance. Lieutenant Governor Alexander Spotswood of

Virginia responded by securing the neutrality of several tribes with promises of trade, bounties for enemies, recognition of tribal boundaries, and protection. He also dispatched Peter Poythres, a veteran scout and interpreter, to neutral Tuscarora settlements. Poythres's diplomacy produced treaties with the eight upper towns, thereby halving the Tuscaroras' fighting power and diminishing the hostiles' chance of victory. Spotswood also secured the safe release of Graffenried and other prisoners while ratifying treaties with the Nottoways, the Saponis, and the Meherrins, thereby further isolating the militant Tuscaroras.

In 1712, Spotswood sent blankets and clothing to help ease the plight of war refugees. He also readied Virginia's militia, bolstered by 100 Native American allies, to march against the hostiles. Plans for the expedition fell through, however, when North Carolina's leaders failed to provide provisions for Spotswood's force.

South Carolina officials responded to Hyde's pleas by recruiting Catawba and Yamasee warriors to march against their traditional enemies. Many volunteers saw the campaign as an opportunity to secure Native American slaves, a line of reasoning encouraged by Hyde.

Colonel John Barnwell, a South Carolina trader and experienced soldier, commanded an army of 495 Native Americans and 30 colonists. On reaching New Bern in February 1712, Barnwell's force encountered fierce resistance. A short time later, Barnwell learned that two-thirds of his force had deserted, taking a large supply of slaves and goods with them. Sixty-seven locals bolstered what remained of Barnwell's force in a campaign against Fort Hancock, a fortified Tuscarora town along the Neuse River. Although Barnwell's first assault was unsuccessful, his use of cannon ultimately produced a negotiated settlement.

The truce did not last long. Shortly after negotiating the agreement, Barnwell enslaved those who had accepted his terms. Not surprisingly, his treachery sparked a series of Tuscarora raids during summer 1712, a situation exacerbated by food shortages, Quaker politicians' refusal to support the war, and Hyde's death in September 1712.

Once again, South Carolinians responded with military force. In March 1713, Colonel James Moore Jr. led 50 colonists and 1,000 Native American allies against Nehucke, a Tuscarora town protected by palisades, blockhouses, and escape tunnels. Moore achieved victory only after setting fire to the town's palisades. He subsequently estimated that 558 Native Americans perished in the fight. Nearly 400 others were taken prisoner. Following the victory, all but 180 of Moore's soldiers deserted, taking their slaves and plunder with them back to South Carolina.

Moore's campaign signaled the end of the Tuscarora War. By 1713, both the Native Americans and North Carolina officials lacked the resources needed to prolong the conflict. News of Nehucke's destruction also prompted residents of other lower Tuscarora settlements to escape a similar fate by fleeing west to the headwaters of the Roanoke River.

On April 14, 1713, Thomas Pollock concluded peace with the remaining Tuscaroras. Tom Blunt, declared "king" of all Tuscaroras, accepted a reservation established for the tribe between the Neuse and the Pamlico. Although the treaty did not end hostilities, it marked the end of Tuscarora dominance.

Peaceful Tuscaroras, now the targets of frequent enemy raids, depended on their colonial neighbors for supplies and protection. North Carolina officials approved relocation to a new reservation along the

Roanoke River following Catawba attacks during the 1720s. Later removals to New York to join the Iroquois Confederacy, which had adopted the Tuscaroras around 1722, finally brought the promise of revitalization to a defeated people.

Jon L. Brudvig

Further Reading

La Vere, David. *The Tuscarora War: Indians, Settlers, and the Fight for the Carolina Colonies.* Chapel Hill: The University of North Carolina Press, 2013.

Richter, Daniel K., and James H. Merrell, eds. *Beyond the Covenant Chain: The Iroquois and Their Neighbors in Indian North America, 1600–1800.* Syracuse, NY: Syracuse University Press, 1987.

Robinson, W. Stitt. *The Southern Colonial Frontier, 1607–1763.* Albuquerque: University of New Mexico Press, 1979.

Tuscaroras

Iroquoian-speaking Native Americans whose territory included most of eastern North Carolina during the colonial period. The Tuscaroras were a loose confederacy of three tribes with an estimated population of around 25,000 people prior to European contact. The Tuscarora Nation was the most powerful in a vast region running from Virginia in the north to South Carolina in the south. The Tuscaroras later became the sixth nation to join the Iroquois Confederacy in 1722.

The Tuscaroras were farmers, hunters, gatherers, and saltwater fishers along the lower Neuse, Tar, Pamlico, and Roanoke rivers. Many Tuscarora towns featured oblong and oval houses, each serving several families. The longhouse was more typical in the Tuscarora-Iroquoian tradition. Structural frames of pine, cedar, and hickory were secured with bark and

moss to form the shell of the longhouses. Cedar and cypress bark covered quadrangular arched roofs, which had smoke holes in the centers. Animal skins covered mats of reed sprawled over bed benches skirting the inner structure. Windowless granary structures and houses encircled the villages' council meeting area. Often situated on slopes along waterways, some strategic villages were heavily fortified and palisaded.

Weapons and dress were tied to regional tribes and climate, but Tuscarora adornment was elaborate. Tattooing displayed tribal symbols, usually on the right shoulder. Regalia included pendants of bone and teeth; wampum ear pendants; necklaces; and beads of bone, copper, and colored stones. Chieftain adornments included pearls.

By 1650, the Tuscaroras were fully involved in the fur trade and slave trade with Europeans. The Tuscaroras' primary town of Kentenuaka came to be regarded as a center for Native American commerce by 1670. Described in 1701 as the largest tribe in the region, their population was greatly diminished by 1707. Both disease and slave traders exacerbated the population decline.

The Tuscaroras' relationship with English colonists deteriorated in the early 18th century. In 1710, Baron Christoph von Graffenried founded the German and Swiss colony of New Bern, North Carolina, at the site of a vacated Tuscarora town. Not content to stay there, he continued surveying along the Trent and Neuse rivers, the heart of Tuscarora country. Graffenried's bold encroachments, combined with abuses by colonial traders in South Carolina, North Carolina, and Virginia, forced the Tuscaroras to war in 1711.

In what became known as the Tuscarora War (1711–1713), the Tuscaroras raided white settlements, killing some 200 Europeans. The war had two phases. The first was a conflict between the Tuscaroras and English settlers, and the second witnessed the Tuscaroras fighting Europeans and rival tribes, including their northern Tuscarora kin, the Creeks, and the Yamasees.

The war ended in March 1713 with a Tuscarora capitulation. After that, in 1715 numerous Tuscaroras were forced onto a small North Carolina reservation. Some 2,000 others fled northward to live among tribes of the Iroquois Confederacy. The Tuscaroras were officially recognized as the confederation's sixth nation in 1722. The Tuscaroras tried to remain neutral during the American Revolutionary War (1775–1783), but most ended up siding with the Patriots.

Alongside the Oneidas, many Tuscaroras warriors fought the British at the Battle of Oriskany (August 6, 1777). The Tuscaroras then helped to defeat the British campaign down the Hudson River from Canada. After the war, New York confiscated land that the Tuscaroras shared with the Oneidas and forcibly removed the Tuscaroras to the Seneca Reservation near present-day Lewiston, New York. There the Tuscaroras eventually purchased land in 1796 and in 1804 where their descendants live today. The Tuscaroras who sided with the British eventually moved to the Six Nations Reserve in Ontario, Canada.

Raeschelle Potter-Deimel

Further Reading

Gallay, Alan. *The Indian Slave Trade: The Rise of the English Empire in the American South, 1670–1717*. New Haven, CT: Yale University Press, 2002.

La Vere, David. *The Tuscarora War: Indians, Settlers, and the Fight for the Carolina Colonies*. Chapel Hill: The University of North Carolina Press, 2013.

Wallace, Anthony F. C. *Tuscarora: A History*. Tribal Worlds: Critical Studies in American Indian Nation Building Series. Albany: State University of New York Press, 2012.

U

Ute War

Start Date: September 1879
End Date: October 1879

Little more than a minor skirmish, the Ute War of late September and early October 1879 reflected the frustrations of the Ute tribe with attempts by the U.S. government to transform the Utes into yeoman farmers. The war also set the stage for the final removal of most of the tribe from Colorado.

Originally the Utes were divided into 11 independent bands. After contact with Europeans, decimation by European-introduced diseases, and U.S. government efforts to put the Utes on reservations, the Ute population diminished significantly. The eastern Ute bands had encountered the Spanish as early as 1600. After acquiring horses, the Utes raided the Spanish and other natives in the Southwest and on the southern Great Plains. Until 1850, most Utes had little contact with Americans. By the 1870s, however, the remaining Ute bands lived on reservation land located along the Colorado, San Juan, and White rivers in western Colorado and eastern Utah. The U.S. government administered these reservations, and until 1879, the Utes had a long history of peaceful relations with settlers.

Because of silver strikes on Ute reservations during the early and mid-1870s, Coloradans began to demand that the Utes be removed to Indian Territory in Oklahoma. The federal government exacerbated the situation by appointing Nathan C. Meeker as the Indian agent to the White River Agency in spring 1878. Uniquely unqualified as an agent and with no experience dealing with Native Americans, Meeker attempted to force the Utes to plow their meadows used for pasturage to grow crops. This threatened the Utes' large pony herds, on which they depended heavily for their survival. Meeker's insistence upon initiating this policy and his assertion that the Utes had too many horses, some of which should be killed, compelled a Ute chief to throw Meeker out the front door of the agency. In response, U.S. Army troops were dispatched to the area from Fort Fred Steele, Wyoming.

Major Thomas T. Thornburgh led this force south to the White River Agency. His command consisted of 175–200 men, most of whom were from the 5th Cavalry, but some soldiers from the 4th Infantry were also present primarily to protect the supply train. Upon his arrival, Thornburgh agreed to a council with the Utes to resolve the conflict but then decided to advance with his cavalry to Milk Creek. On September 29, 100 Ute warriors confronted Thornburgh's command there. Although it appeared at first that conflict might be avoided, a single gunshot from an undetermined rifle sparked the Battle of Milk Creek (September 29–October 5, 1879).

After the initial exchange, the soldiers fell back to their wagon train. During the retreat, Thornburgh was killed by a shot to the head. The Utes kept the soldiers pinned down for six days, but a detachment of buffalo soldiers from the 9th Cavalry reinforced the besieged soldiers on October 2. Eventually, Colonel Wesley Merritt arrived with a larger number of reinforcements, which forced the Utes to leave the battle-field on October 5.

During the Battle of Milk Creek, Ute warriors also attacked and burned the White River Agency, killing most of the men there, including Meeker. The Utes took the women and children captive. Eventually Charles Adams, a former agent to the Utes, and Ouray, the chief of the Uncompahgre band, negotiated an end to hostilities. As part of the terms, the Utes gave up their captives. Although the government planned to prosecute 12 Ute warriors for the massacre of Meeker and his subordinates, none ever stood trial. However, the Ute War led even more Coloradans to take part of the land held in reserve for the Utes. Eventually, the tribe lost most of its land in Colorado and was forced to settle on small reservations in southwestern Colorado and eastern Utah.

Dixie Ray Haggard

Further Reading

Dawson, Thomas Fulton. *The Ute War*. New York: Garland, 1976.

Decker, Peter R. *"The Utes Must Go!" American Expansion and the Removal of a People*. Golden, CO: Fulcrum, 2004.

Miller, Mark E. *Hollow Victory: The White River Expedition of 1879 and the Battle of Milk Creek*. Niwot: The University Press of Colorado, 1997.

Utes

Uto-Aztecan speaking Native American people who initially occupied western Colorado and eastern Utah. The Utes were divided into 11 bands, with the eastern bands living in Colorado and the western bands residing primarily in Utah. The eastern bands were the Capotes, Muaches, Uncompahgres, Parusanuchs, Weeminuches, and Yampas. The western bands were the Moanunts, Pahvant Sanpits, Timpanogots, and Uintahs.

The Ute economic system centered on hunting, gathering, and raiding. The Utes traditionally raided the Apaches, Hopis, Navajos, Pueblos, and Shoshones, and once the Spanish arrived in New Mexico, the Utes began raiding them as well. However, hostilities with these groups were sporadic.

The Eastern Utes encountered Europeans sooner than their western counterparts and, as a result, acquired horses sooner. By the early 17th century, the Eastern Utes began participating in the horse culture that had developed on the Great Plains. Therefore, they began to spend more time on the Plains hunting buffalo. The Western Utes did not gain horses until the turn of the 18th century. In the 17th and early 18th centuries, the Utes used their horses to expand their raiding to Paiute communities in western Utah and Nevada in order to enslave women and children and sell them to the Spanish in New Mexico.

As the Utes began to spend more time on the Plains and in the eastern valleys of the Rocky Mountains, they began to encounter hostile groups of people. These included the Arapahos, Cheyennes, Comanches, and Lakota Sioux. The Comanches had previously been Ute allies living in the Colorado and Nevada areas before they acquired horses and moved to the Plains. Because of the tense relations with these groups, the Utes began to participate in a larger network of captive exchanges that extended from the upper Mississippi River Valley westward to Arizona and Nevada.

When Americans first began moving into the Southwest, the Utes maintained good relations with them but over time ceded land to the U.S. government. In treaties signed in 1855, 1863, 1868, and 1873, the Utes saw their landholdings reduced to fewer than 12 million acres. Utes living on the White River Agency briefly rebelled in 1879 against federal control. This incident, known as the Ute War, occurred after the local agent, Nathan C. Meeker, tried to force the Utes to plow up their pastureland to plant crops. The failure of this uprising forced the Utes to give up most of their land in Colorado and move to the southwestern part of the state or to a new reservation in Utah in 1882.

In 1887, the U.S. Congress passed the Dawes Severalty Act to end communal control of native land by the tribe and divide it among individual members. Excess land was to be given to whites for settlement. The implementation of the Dawes Act diminished the Utes' landholdings to just 40,600 acres.

Fortunately for the Utes, the passage of the Indian Reorganization Act in 1933 aided their reacquisition of some former tribal land, and by the end of the 1960s, the Utes controlled 304,700 acres of land.

Dixie Ray Haggard

Further Reading

Decker, Peter R. *"The Utes Must Go!" American Expansion and the Removal of a People*. Golden, CO: Fulcrum, 2004.

Miller, Mark E. *Hollow Victory: The White River Expedition of 1879 and the Battle of Milk Creek*. Niwot: The University Press of Colorado, 1997.

Simmons, Virginia McConnell. *The Ute Indians of Utah, Colorado, and New Mexico*. Niwot: University Press of Colorado, 2000.

V

Victorio

Birth Date: ca. 1825
Death Date: October 15, 1880

Mimbres (Mimbreño) Apache chief, one of the greatest guerilla fighters and military strategists of the 19th-century Indian Wars. Victorio was born about 1825 in southwestern New Mexico. Legends about his origins persist, most holding that he was a captured Mexican boy raised among the Apaches. Biduyé, as he was called by tribal members, was renamed by his enemies when he became a respected war leader, even though he tried very hard to find a course other than war.

The Mimbres Apaches initially lived near present-day Monticello, New Mexico. Their most notable early leader was Mangas Coloradas. At about age 16, Victorio, as an apprentice, rode along on the first of four raids during which the older warriors acted as his teachers and tested his skills in the many aspects of warfare. By 1850, U.S. military leaders had begun to take note of Victorio's military prowess. In 1855, Victorio conducted a successful raid into the Mexican states of Sonora and Chihuahua and brought back large numbers of captives and livestock. In July 1862, he took part in the Battle of Apache Pass near Tucson, Arizona, and continued to participate in numerous skirmishes and raids against white settlers and the U.S. military.

After the death of Mangas Coloradas in 1863, Victorio assumed leadership of the Mimbres Apaches. In 1869, he settled near Fort Craig, New Mexico, where he and his followers awaited completion of a reservation near Ojo Caliente, New Mexico. Victorio and his band remained quiescent until after April 20, 1877, when the U.S. government ordered them removed to the San Carlos Reservation. In September 1879, he and 60 warriors raided a U.S. cavalry unit camped near a small settlement in southwestern New Mexico. The Apaches killed 5 soldiers and 3 civilians and made off with 68 horses and mules. The attack signaled the start of what is sometimes known as the Victorio War.

By January 1880, Victorio had led his people in battles across three states. He fought Anglo and Mexican settlers, Mexican regulars, Texas Rangers, and the Black troops of the 9th U.S. Cavalry Regiment in New Mexico, Texas, and Mexico, winning almost every engagement. On April 6, 1880, 71 members of the 9th Cavalry, led by Captain Henry Carroll, cautiously approached Victorio's camp in the Hembrillo Basin, a natural stronghold, in south-central New Mexico. They were immediately surrounded by a larger force of about 150 Apaches under Victorio. The Apaches fired volley after volley from behind stacked breastworks erected on the surrounding ridge tops. However, a relief column sent by 9th Cavalry commander Colonel Edward Hatch drove off Victorio's warriors from their positions. Undeterred, Victorio raided extensively throughout May and June before slipping into Mexico, in the process wearing out the buffalo soldiers of the 9th Cavalry.

In July, anticipating Victorio's return through western Texas, Colonel Benjamin Grierson of the 10th Cavalry Regiment posted his command at the few essential water holes that the Apaches would need and waited. Grierson himself, with 2 officers and 21 Black troopers, held a position in Quitman Canyon when Victorio and some 150 warriors attacked on July 30. The soldiers held out until relieved, while Victorio's band, denied water, fell back into Mexico. On August 2, Victorio attacked again only to be turned back by Grierson's troops at Rattlesnake Springs four days later.

Driven back into Mexico, Victorio became the target of both U.S. and Mexican forces. Although a large U.S. force entered Mexico for the proposed campaign, the Americans were soon ordered out, leaving Victorio to the Mexicans. Victorio eventually took his people to a site on the plains, three rocky peaks called Tres Castillos, where they were attacked by a group of Mexican irregulars and Tarahumara auxiliaries. Fighting continued for hours until dawn on October 15, 1880, when Victorio was killed, possibly by his own hand but most likely by a bullet fired by an Indian auxiliary. Sixty warriors and 18 women and children also lay dead. Sixty-eight other women and children were taken captive, along with 180 animals. After the prisoners were gathered, the adolescent boys were taken to a nearby arroyo and shot, while the remaining women and children were enslaved.

H. Henrietta Stockel

Further Reading

Thrapp, Dan L. *The Conquest of Apacheria.* Norman: University of Oklahoma Press, 1967.

Thrapp, Dan L. *Victorio and the Mimbres Apaches.* Norman: University of Oklahoma Press, 1974.

W

Wampanoags

Algonquian speaking Native American group that once inhabited a region ranging from the eastern shore of Narragansett Bay to the tip of Cape Cod, including the islands of Martha's Vineyard and Nantucket. The Wampanoags, or "People of the Morning Light," were farmers, fishermen, hunters, and gatherers. At the time of European contact, there were approximately 12,000 Wampanoags divided among 40 villages. The term "Pokanoket," the name of one of the principal Wampanoag villages and home to Ousa Mequin (Massasoit), the grand sachem (chief) who treated with the Pilgrims, was often mistakenly used in the early 17th century to identify the Wampanoags.

Epidemic diseases introduced by European fishermen and slave traders in the late 16th and early 17th centuries devastated the indigenous population of New England. The coastal Wampanoags were especially affected. By the establishment of the Plymouth colony in 1620, there were perhaps no more than 2,000 Wampanoags left on the mainland. Some villages, such as Patuxet (site of Plymouth Colony), were entirely wiped out. Island Wampanoag populations fared slightly better owing to their relative isolation.

In addition to the devastation wrought by disease, the Wampanoag Confederacy was weakened in the early 17th century by raids from Micmac war parties to the north and encroaching Pequots to the south. The formidable Narragansetts, essentially untouched by the epidemics because of their isolation on the islands of Narragansett Bay, grew in power and prestige during this period, ultimately forcing the Wampanoags to pay them tribute.

Seeing his power diminish, Massasoit skillfully concluded an alliance with Plymouth in 1621. The treaty provided security for the vulnerable Englishmen in exchange for aid to the Wampanoag Confederacy in case of hostilities with their rivals. The alliance also served to keep the Wampanoags out of the Pequot War (1636–1638) and enabled Massasoit to resist Puritan efforts to Christianize his people.

The death of Massasoit in 1661 or 1662 ushered in a dramatic change in the relationship between the Wampanoags and English colonists. Massasoit's eldest son, Wamsutta, succeeded his father as grand sachem and began selling land to colonies other than Plymouth. Seized at gunpoint by Plymouth colonists who interpreted his land deals as a threat, Wamsutta was taken to the Plymouth court in 1662 and forced to defend his actions. Before he could do so, the grand sachem fell ill and died. His untimely death—there is some circumstantial evidence that he was poisoned by the English—shifted power to Wamsutta's younger brother Metacom, known to the English as King Philip.

During the next decade, Metacom grew increasingly distrustful of the colonists. English encroachments onto Wampanoag land, interference in native political affairs, and establishment of Christian missions and praying towns of converted natives ultimately drove Metacom to the breaking point. The resulting conflict, known as King Philip's War (1675–1676), proved devastating to the Wampanoags as well as to the indigenous population of southern New England. One-fourth of the estimated 3,000 natives killed in the war were Wampanoags, and many Wampanoags who surrendered or were captured were subsequently sold into slavery. The survivors (possibly as few as 400 people) were relocated, along with remnants of other native communities, onto Cape Cod or into praying towns. Their descendants can be found today around Gay Head on Martha's Vineyard and at Mashpee on the mainland.

Alan C. Downs

Further Reading

Philbrick, Nathaniel. *Mayflower: A Story of Courage, Community, and War.* New York: Viking, 2006.

Vaughan, Alden T. *New England Frontier: Puritans and Indians, 1620–1675.* 3rd ed. Norman: University of Oklahoma Press, 1995.

Washita, Battle of the

Event Date: November 27, 1868

U.S. Army attack on a Southern Cheyenne village in western Indian Territory (Oklahoma) two miles from present-day Cheyenne. A tranquil bend in the Washita River was the site of a surprise winter attack on November 27, 1868, by the U.S. 7th Cavalry Regiment under the command of Lieutenant Colonel George Armstrong Custer on Chief Black Kettle's peaceful band of Southern Cheyennes. Black Kettle, a survivor of the Sand Creek Massacre four years earlier, died along with his wife and 101 other men, women, and children.

Custer's attack was the result of the U.S. Army's evolving strategy for imposing the government's reservation policy on noncompliant Indians of the Great Plains. In October 1867, peace commissioners from the U.S. government met with representatives of the Arapahos, Comanches, Kiowas, Kiowa Apaches, and Southern Cheyennes in a grove of trees along Medicine Lodge Creek, 60 miles south of Fort Larned, Kansas. There the principal leaders of the southern Plains tribes signed treaties promising to move onto two reservations in western Indian Territory and to take no action to impede the construction of nearby railroads, wagon roads, and government facilities. In exchange for their compliance, signatory tribes were promised agricultural implements, clothing, education for their children, annuity payments, and the prohibition of white settlement on reservation land.

Of the five nations represented at the Medicine Lodge Council, the Southern Cheyennes were the least united in support of the treaty. Black Kettle was reluctant to sign the document until the militant Cheyenne Dog Soldiers agreed to its terms. Unable to convince war chief Roman Nose and his band of the merits of peace under the terms of the treaty, Black Kettle nevertheless affixed his mark to the paper. Despite the lack of a unified following, the Cheyenne chief settled peaceably into reservation life below the Arkansas River.

Throughout winter 1867–1868, food stores from the autumn buffalo hunts sustained the reservation Cheyennes. As spring approached and supplies dwindled, the promised government support materialized in insufficient quantities. Most disconcerting for the Cheyennes was the absence of the promised guns and ammunition needed for hunting. Notwithstanding the best efforts of Agent Edward W. Wynkoop to reassure the disaffected, some young Cheyenne men, angered by the duplicity of the white peace commissioners, ventured northward away from the reservation to join

Roman Nose and the leaders of other resistant factions.

In response to the growing defiance of the government's reservation policy among Native American peoples on the southern Plains, Major General Philip Sheridan, commander of the Department of the Missouri, with the support of Lieutenant General William Tecumseh Sherman, commander of the Military Division of the Missouri, orchestrated a strategy to force submission. Sheridan envisioned a winter operation utilizing converging columns of cavalry and infantry to round up warriors whose limited supplies and grass-fed ponies would make them virtually immobile and susceptible to capture. Accordingly, on November 18, 1868, Major Andrew W. Evans left Fort Bascom, New Mexico, with 563 men and marched eastward down the South Canadian River. Two weeks later, Major Eugene Carr and 650 men left Fort Lyon, Colorado, and moved southward (guided by Buffalo Bill Cody) toward Antelope Hills in Indian Territory. The third and largest column, comprising 800 troopers of the 7th U.S. Cavalry under the command of Custer, departed Camp Supply, a depot on the North Canadian River 100 miles south of Fort Dodge, Kansas, on November 23 and headed south toward the Washita River. Sheridan instructed Custer to follow a fresh trail in the snow, suspecting its creators to be a Cheyenne raiding party returning from Kansas.

That same autumn as Sheridan put the finishing touches on his planned winter campaign, Black Kettle and his followers set up an encampment on a bend in the Washita River 40 miles east of the Antelope Hills. Consisting of 51 lodges, the village was populated by Cheyenne women, children, and elders as well as recently returned young warriors who were now more willing to accept the peaceful ways of Black Kettle

after Roman Nose's death on September 17 at the Battle of Beecher's Island. Downriver, Arapaho, Kiowa, and additional Cheyenne camps dotted the landscape. Learning that U.S. troops were on the move, Black Kettle and other Cheyenne and Arapaho leaders traveled 100 miles down the Washita River Valley to Fort Cobb to meet with the garrison's commander, Brigadier General William B. Hazen, to seek protection for their people. To their dismay, the heretofore convivial Hazen maintained that he lacked authority to allow the Cheyenne and Arapaho bands to move closer to the fort and instructed Black Kettle to return to his camp.

On November 26, Custer's undetected column drew near the bend in the Washita River occupied by Black Kettle's band. The trail that Custer's column followed led directly to the encampment. Without bothering to determine the size and strength of his foe, Custer ordered an attack for the following day. Just before daybreak on November 27, troops from the 7th Cavalry, with the regimental band playing "Garryowen," charged into Black Kettle's sleeping village from four directions. The shaken and surprised Cheyennes could do nothing except run for safety. A few warriors vainly fought back. Black Kettle and his wife attempted to escape across a ford in the river, only to be gunned down in the mud. Within 10 minutes, the 7th Cavalry troops controlled the village.

Estimates vary, but it is probable that 103 Cheyenne men, women, and children died in the attack, while 53 women and children were taken captive. Custer lost 2 officers and 19 enlisted men, most of whom were under the command of Major Joel H. Elliott. Attempting to corral a group of Indians fleeing downriver, Elliot and his men were themselves surrounded and killed by members of the nearby Arapaho and Cheyenne camps who were coming to Black Kettle's aid.

As more mounted warriors arrived at the scene, Custer's troops set up a defensive perimeter and then systematically set fire to the lodges, destroying the Cheyennes' winter supply of food and clothing. The cavalry likewise slaughtered more than 800 Cheyenne ponies and mules. To remove his command from an increasingly foreboding environment, Custer abandoned efforts to locate Major Elliott, feigned an attack in the late afternoon against Indian encampments farther downriver, and then escaped back across the river after dark. The 7th Cavalry returned triumphantly to Camp Supply on December 2, much to the satisfaction of Sheridan.

More of a massacre than a battle, Washita proved to be a debilitating blow to the Southern Cheyennes. With their winter supplies and herd of mules and ponies destroyed, the majority of the Cheyenne had little choice but to submit to reservation life. Perhaps of equal consequence, the Battle of the Washita demonstrated to the noncompliant tribes of the Plains that winter no longer provided the element of security that it once had.

Alan C. Downs

Further Reading

Greene, Jerome A. *Washita: The U.S. Army and the Southern Cheyennes, 1867–1869*. Norman: University of Oklahoma Press, 2004.

Hatch, Thom. *Black Kettle: The Cheyenne Chief Who Sought Peace but Found War*. Hoboken, NJ: Wiley, 2004.

Wayne, Anthony

Birth Date: January 1, 1745
Death Date: December 16, 1796

Continental Army officer and commander of the Legion of the United States. Born on January 1, 1745, in Waynesborough, Chester County, Pennsylvania, Anthony Wayne was educated at the Academy in Philadelphia but left school to become a surveyor. He was then a tanner in his father's business.

Elected to the Pennsylvania colonial assembly in 1774, Wayne resigned upon the outbreak of the American Revolutionary War (1775–1783) to raise a regiment of volunteers. Although he had no formal military training, in January 1776 Wayne was commissioned a colonel in the 4th Pennsylvania Regiment. He was wounded in the Battle of Trois Rivières (June 8, 1776), and his action in covering the retreat of U.S. forces from Canada won him promotion to brigadier general in February 1777.

Wayne again distinguished himself in the Battle of Brandywine Creek (September 11, 1777) but was caught by surprise in a British night attack on his camp at Paoli (September 21, 1777). He requested a court-martial, which cleared him of any negligence. He earned praise for his conduct in the Battle of Germantown (October 4, 1777) and performed well in the Battle of Monmouth (June 28, 1778), leading the initial attack and then defending against the British counterattack. He then led a bayonet attack that carried the British position at Stony Point, New York, on July 16, 1779, an action that won him the nickname "Mad Anthony." In January 1781, he ably defused a mutiny of the Pennsylvania line. During the latter stages of the Revolution, Wayne participated in the Yorktown Campaign (May–October 19, 1781) and then campaigned with Major General Nathanael Greene in Georgia until the British evacuated Savannah in July 1782. Wayne was brevetted a major general in September 1783.

After the war, Wayne retired to his farm in Pennsylvania. He was a member of the Pennsylvania State Assembly in 1785 and was elected to the state convention that ratified the U.S. Constitution. He then relocated to Georgia to manage landholdings that the state had awarded him for his services as Continental Army commander there in 1782. Unsuccessful in securing election to the U.S. Senate from Georgia, he did win election to the U.S. House of Representatives from that state in 1791, but the election was subsequently declared invalid because of voting irregularities.

In April 1792, following two disastrous expeditions against the Native Americans during Little Turtle's War (1785–1895) in the Northwest Territory by Brigadier General Josiah Harmar and Northwest Territory governor Arthur St. Clair, President George Washington recalled Wayne as a major general to command the newly authorized 5,000-man Legion of the United States.

Wayne took advantage of extended negotiations with the Native Americans to establish a camp at Legionville in western Pennsylvania and properly train the army. He stressed drill, proper sanitation, field fortifications, and marksmanship. Finally in the summer, Wayne led the army, supported by Kentucky militia, west into the Ohio Country. In the Battle of Fallen Timbers (August 20, 1794), he defeated Native American forces led by Shawnee chief Blue Jacket. This victory broke the power of the Native Americans in the eastern part of the Old Northwest and did much to restore the prestige of the U.S. Army, which had been so badly tarnished during the earlier Harmar and St. Clair expeditions. As a result, Wayne is often called the father of the new U.S. regular army. A year later, Wayne concluded the Treaty of Greenville with the Native Americans.

In 1796, Wayne secured the relinquishment to the United States of British forts in the Great Lakes area. While on a military excursion from Fort Detroit to Pennsylvania,

Wayne died suddenly at Presque Isle (Erie), Pennsylvania, on December 16, 1796.

Paul G. Pierpaoli Jr. and
Spencer C. Tucker

Further Reading

Fox, Joseph L. *Anthony Wayne: Washington's Reliable General*. Chicago: Adams, 1988.

Gaff, Alan D. *Bayonets in the Wilderness: Anthony Wayne's Legion in the Old Northwest*. Norman: University of Oklahoma Press, 2004.

Nelson, Paul David. *Anthony Wayne: Soldier of the Early Republic*. Bloomington: Indiana University Press, 1985.

Winnebago War

Event Date: Summer 1827

A short conflict in summer 1827 between the U.S. Army and local militiamen and members of the Winnebago tribe. The Winnebago tribe (Ho-chunk-gra, or "People with a Big Voice") resided in the western Great Lakes region (present-day Wisconsin and Illinois). During the 1820s, numerous lead miners began settling on Winnebago lands along the Galena River, located near the present-day Illinois-Wisconsin border. At the time, lead prices were steadily rising, and the Winnebagos began digging and selling lead to white traders. Government officials were afraid, however, that the Winnebago practice of selling lead would mean that they would not want to give up their profitable lands in the future. Consequently, officials ordered local Indian agents to prevent the sale of lead by Native Americans.

In March 1826, several members of a white family were attacked and murdered by warriors in their maple sugar camp near Prairie du Chien (in present-day southwestern Wisconsin). Two warriors were arrested and charged with the crime in 1827, and Dakota Sioux militants subsequently spread a false rumor that the captives had been sent to Fort Snelling, Minnesota, for execution. When news reached the Winnebagos in Prairie La Crosse, the tribal council selected Red Bird to uphold the tribe's honor. Based on the frustration and tension caused by widespread white intrusions on Native American land and the prohibition of lead sales, Red Bird believed that other tribes would support them in taking action.

In June 1827, Red Bird, Wekau, and Chickhonsic scalped and murdered a white farmer, Registre Gagnier, and a hired hand, Solomon Lipcap. They also scalped Gagnier's 18-month-old daughter, who miraculously survived. Red Bird returned to his tribe with the scalps, proclaiming that "there are my trophies, now you do the rest." The deed ignited both anxiety and passion among the Winnebagos.

Local settlers and miners in the area feared the Winnebagos and pressured officials to increase the number of garrisons for their protection. Also in June 1827, two Mississippi keelboats stopped in Prairie du Chien at a Winnebago village after making a delivery at Fort Snelling. Several boatmen drank rum with the Native Americans and then kidnapped and raped several Native American women. The tribe was enraged by the incident and took revenge on the *General Ashby* and *O. H. Perry* keelboats in the Fever River, which were mistakenly thought to be the same keelboats encountered earlier. In the resultant attack, 4 whites and 12 Winnebagos were killed. This action on June 27, 1827, is considered the only actual engagement of the Winnebago War.

Troops were finally dispatched to deal with the Winnebago militants. The troops included regular forces under Brigadier General Henry Atkinson, volunteers under Illinois governor Ninian Edwards, regulars under Colonel Josiah Snelling from Fort Snelling, and various miner volunteers. Meanwhile, Governor Lewis Cass of Michigan and U.S. superintendent Thomas McKenney attempted to negotiate with several Wisconsin tribes to isolate the Winnebago rebels. About 125 Menominee, Oneida, and Stockbridge warriors joined the troops, and they converged from different directions to meet the Winnebagos near Portage, Wisconsin.

In an attempt to prevent bloodshed at Butte de Morts, negotiations occurred during the first two weeks of August 1827 between military officials and the Winnebago peace faction led by Four Legs and Nawkaw. Recognizing the military strength arrayed against him and the lack of support received from the other Winnebago bands, Red Bird decided to surrender to save his people. Consequently, Red Bird and six warriors involved in the attack on Gagnier's farm and the keelboats were arrested and sent to Fort Crawford at Prairie du Chien, Wisconsin. Red Bird sang his death song while leaving Portage, knowing that he would be executed. He died of dysentery in January 1828 while waiting for his trial. The others who had been arrested were convicted and sentenced to death but were soon thereafter pardoned.

In August 1829, the Winnebago chiefs were forced to sign their first cession treaty. The Treaty of Prairie du Chien relinquished Winnebago land claims in Illinois and Wisconsin south of the Wisconsin and Fox rivers. Many Winnebagos were angered by the treaty and continued white settlement. This played a part in the decision by the prophet White Cloud to enter the Black Hawk War in 1832 and in the consequent loss of more land to the government in their defeat.

Justin D. Murphy and Lorin Lowrie Scott

Further Reading

Radin, Paul. *The Winnebago Tribe*. Lincoln: University of Nebraska Press, 1970.

Wyman, Mark. *The Wisconsin Frontier*. Bloomington: Indiana University Press, 1998.

Wounded Knee, Battle of

Event Date: December 29, 1890

Last battle of the Indian Wars. Despite having been deprived of their traditional lifestyles and forced onto reservations, many Native Americans remained defiant and resisted the U.S. government's attempts to assimilate them into white civilization. In this atmosphere of despair, many sought solace and hope in religious movements promising deliverance from reservations and a return to traditional lifestyles.

The late 19th century saw many such movements, which were similar to Tenskwatawa's religious revival in the Old Northwest at the beginning of the 19th century. The most important of these was the Ghost Dance message preached by Wovoka, a Paiute shaman in Nevada who attracted attention from many western tribes. Influenced by Christian teachings, Wovoka emphasized a strict moral code and promised a future world in which Native Americans would be reunited with the dead and would live a life free from sickness, death, and whites. By dancing the Ghost Dance, believers would be able to glimpse this future world.

Although Wovoka's message specifically warned against fighting, when the Ghost Dance was introduced to the Sioux by Short Bull and Kicking Bear, it morphed into a message of defiance and resistance that sought to hasten the arrival of the new millennium by eliminating whites. Short Bull and Kicking Bear preached that dancing the Ghost Dance and wearing ghost shirts would protect the Sioux against the white man's bullets.

By November 1890, the spread of the Ghost Dance among the Oglalas on the Pine Ridge Reservation and the Brulés on the Rosebud Reservation, where the Sioux defied agents' efforts to stop the dance, so alarmed Pine Ridge Indian agent Daniel F. Royer and nearby white settlers that they called for military intervention. On November 13, President Benjamin Harrison ordered the War Department to restore order on the reservations. By November 20, 600 soldiers from the 2nd and 8th Infantry Regiments and the 9th Cavalry Regiment had occupied the Pine Ridge and Rosebud agencies, and Brigadier General John R. Brooke, commander of the Department of the Platte, moved his headquarters to Pine Ridge. The arrival of troops split the Sioux asunder, as those who feared war flocked to the agency headquarters while hostile Sioux moved to remote corners of the reservations, where they continued to dance. By early December, the Brulé and Oglala hostiles had joined together in a village of 600 lodges on a high plateau between the Cheyenne and White rivers in the northwest corner of the Pine Ridge Reservation.

Meanwhile, Division of the Missouri commander Major General Nelson A. Miles moved to suppress the Ghost Dance movement at other Sioux reservations before it became as powerful as it had become on the Pine Ridge and Rosebud reservations. Toward that end, he ordered the arrest of Sitting Bull at the Standing Rock Reservation and Big Foot at the Cheyenne River Reservation. When Native American police arrested Sitting Bull on December 15, his Ghost Dance followers attempted to rescue him, resulting in a firefight that left six policemen and five Ghost Dancers, along with Sitting Bull, dead.

News of Sitting Bull's death produced great outrage among the Ghost Dancers, leading 38 Hunkpapa dancers to seek refuge with Chief Big Foot's Miniconjous. Ironically, Big Foot had by this time begun to lose faith in the Ghost Dance movement. More important, Oglala chiefs had invited him to the Pine Ridge Reservation to make peace among the different factions. On the night of December 23, Big Foot's village—a total of 350 people, including the Hunkpapas who had fled after Sitting Bull's death—headed south toward the Pine Ridge Reservation.

Unaware of Big Foot's intentions and fearful that a concentration of Ghost Dancers on the Pine Ridge Reservation would spark a war, Miles, who had taken personal command of the campaign after relocating to Rapid City, ordered units of the 6th and 9th Cavalry Regiments to prevent Big Foot from reaching the Ghost Dance village on the Pine Ridge Reservation, while Major Samuel M. Whitside led four troops of the 7th Cavalry Regiment to scout eastward from the Pine Ridge Agency. On December 28, 1890, Whitside confronted Big Foot's party and convinced Big Foot, who was now ill with pneumonia, to accept a military escort to the Pine Ridge Agency. During the night of December 28, as Big Foot's people camped with the soldiers along Wounded Knee Creek approximately 20 miles from the agency, Colonel James W. Forsyth arrived with the remainder of the 7th Cavalry and Light Battery E of the First Artillery. Ordered to arrest Big Foot, disarm his people, and march them to the railroad so they could be moved to Omaha, Forsyth recognized that force might be necessary to ensure compliance.

When the Sioux awoke on the morning of December 29, they found themselves surrounded by 500 soldiers who were supported by four Hotchkiss cannons located on a nearby hilltop and pointed directly at the village. After assembling the 120 Sioux men and ordering the 230 women and children to begin packing for the march, Forsyth demanded that the warriors turn over their repeating rifles. When they refused, Forsyth's soldiers began searching through the lodges and underneath the blankets of the men and women.

As the search continued, Yellow Bird, a medicine man, began performing the Ghost Dance and calling on warriors to resist. When a scuffle between a warrior and a soldier resulted in a rifle discharging, soldiers and warriors instinctively opened fire on each other at close range. The artillery then opened fire with the Hotchkiss guns, sending exploding shells into the middle of the camp, hitting both soldiers and Native Americans, and a ravine where the Sioux had fled to find shelter. By the time the smoke cleared, more than 150 Sioux, including Big Foot, lay dead, and another 50 were wounded. At least 62 of the Sioux dead were women and children. Army casualties totaled 25 dead and 39 wounded, many from friendly fire. More significantly, news of the tragedy at Wounded Knee galvanized the Ghost Dance movement on the Pine Ridge Agency, where Brooke was beginning to enjoy success in negotiating an end to the crisis. Indeed, Kicking Bear and Short Bull were in the process of leading their followers back to the Pine Ridge Agency. Now they halted approximately 15 miles from the agency in a massive village along White Clay Creek. Other Sioux quickly joined them.

In the aftermath of the Battle of Wounded Knee, Miles moved to the Pine Ridge Agency and concentrated his forces against the Ghost Dance village on White Clay Creek. Although the village contained perhaps 1,000 warriors and 3,000 women and children, the Ghost Dancers had no real chance at resistance, as Miles surrounded the village with approximately 2,500 troops with another 2,000 in reserve. Seeking to avoid another Wounded Knee, Miles relied upon gentle pressure and negotiations to finally convince the Ghost Dancers to submit on January 15, 1891. With their surrender, the crisis came to an end, but controversy over the Battle of Wounded Knee persisted. The large number of women and children killed at Wounded Knee led many eastern newspapers to condemn the action as a massacre, although it should be noted that this was no deliberate action, as had been the case at Sand Creek in 1864. Nevertheless, Miles relieved Forsyth of his command and ordered a military inquiry, which eventually cleared Forsyth and resulted in him being restored to command. In reality, the chief cause of the tragedy was the order to disarm Big Foot's people. Had they been allowed to continue on the march to the agency under military escort, the confrontation of December 29 would have been avoided. In any event, the Battle of Wounded Knee crushed the Ghost Dance movement and ended Indian resistance once and for all.

Justin D. Murphy

Further Reading

Coleman, William S. E. *Voices of Wounded Knee*. Lincoln: University of Nebraska Press, 2000.

Greene, Jerome A. *American Carnage: Wounded Knee, 1890*. Norman, Oklahoma: University of Oklahoma Press, 2014.

Utley, Robert M. *The Last Days of the Sioux Nation*. 2nd ed. New Haven, CT: Yale University Press, 2004.

Wovoka

Birth Date: ca. 1856
Death Date: September 20, 1932

Native American spiritual leader. A member of the Northern Paiute tribe, Wovoka was born around 1856 in present-day Esmeralda County, Nevada. When Wovoka was about 14 years old, his father died, and Wovoka was raised in the household of David Wilson, a white rancher, where he was exposed to Christian beliefs. Wovoka took the name Jack Wilson and worked for the Wilsons at least until he reached adulthood. At some point, he left the Wilson ranch and lived among the Paiutes, perhaps because other Native Americans criticized him for having adopted white ways.

In about 1870, a Northern Paiute prophet named Tavibo began proclaiming that the earth would soon swallow the whites and that dead Native Americans would rise to reclaim their land. Tavibo taught his followers to worship by performing the traditional Paiute Round Dance. He briefly found a following among Native Americans in Nevada, Oregon, and California but was discredited when the events that he had prophesied failed to occur. Nonetheless, Tavibo's teachings evidently influenced Wovoka, and many people later claimed that Tavibo was his father. Other sources indicate that Wovoka's father was probably Numuraivo'o, who was also said to have been a prophet.

On January 1, 1889, Wovoka underwent a profound religious experience. Accounts vary regarding the details of what occurred, but believers agreed that during a total solar eclipse, Wovoka was taken up to heaven. There he spoke with God, who told him to teach Native Americans to live a moral life, refrain from fighting, work for the whites, and perform the Round Dance as an act of worship. Following these commands would lead to the resurrection of dead Native Americans, an end to illness, and the return of wild game.

Wovoka began preaching this message to the Paiutes, reinforcing his prophetic authority with his apparent ability to predict and control the weather. His accurate forecasts of rain during a drought and his alleged power to produce ice in hot weather convinced many Native Americans that his religious authority was legitimate. Wovoka also claimed to be invulnerable to gunpowder and to be able to return to heaven while in a trance. He preached that Jesus was back on earth and would be revealed when the dead arose. Because this resurrection would result from faithful performance of the ritual dances, Wovoka's religious blend of Christianity and Tavibo's teachings was commonly called the Ghost Dance movement.

News of Wovoka's teachings quickly spread eastward to Native Americans of the Great Plains. Several made the long journey west to hear him preach and returned to share his revelations. The visitors either misunderstood or embellished what they had learned, as they proclaimed that Wovoka was the Native Americans' Messiah: Christ himself returned to earth as a Native American.

The teachings that they related drew as heavily from Tavibo's message as they did from Wovoka. Kicking Bear, a Lakota who in autumn 1890 told Sitting Bull of his encounter with Wovoka, asserted that the next spring Native Americans who performed the Ghost Dance would ascend into the air while new soil appeared and buried the whites. The natural environment would be restored, the buffalo would return, and then the Native Americans would descend again to be united with their risen ancestors. In the meantime, Native Americans who wore Ghost Dance Shirts would be impervious to bullets.

Although Sitting Bull dismissed this version of Wovoka's teachings, large numbers of Native Americans believed it and faithfully performed the ritual dance. Fearing

that the movement might spark a new round of warfare with Native Americans, U.S. government officials decided to suppress the Ghost Dance among the Lakotas. After Sitting Bull was erroneously identified as a leader of the movement, he was arrested, provoking a confrontation that ended in his murder on December 15, 1890. Two weeks later at Wounded Knee, South Dakota, a battle erupted when U.S. troops tried to disarm a Lakota band whose members were adherents of the Ghost Dance movement, resulting in the deaths of more than 150 Native Americans.

Wovoka had never intended for violence to be a consequence of his teaching. In 1891, the Bureau of American Ethnology sent James Mooney to investigate his movement, and Mooney found that Wovoka had instructed his followers to pursue peace and good works and to dance every six weeks while awaiting the resurrection. Wovoka's boldest statements were promises to send rain.

By 1892, Wovoka, denounced as a fraud by whites and some disappointed Native Americans, ceased preaching. Although some Native Americans continued to consider him a prophet, he was relegated to selling trinkets to earn a living. Wovoka died on September 20, 1932, near Yerington, Nevada.

Jim Piecuch

Further Reading

Hittman, Michael. *Wovoka and the Ghost Dance.* Expanded ed. Edited by Don Lynch. Lincoln: University of Nebraska Press, 1997.

Kehoe, Alice Beck. *The Ghost Dance: Ethnohistory and Revitalization.* New York: Holt, Rinehart and Winston, 1989.

Miller, David Humphreys. *Ghost Dance.* Lincoln: University of Nebraska Press, 1985.

Y

Yamasee War

Start Date: April 15, 1715
End Date: November 1717

A costly frontier conflict that devastated the colony of South Carolina and led to the near extinction of the Yamasee tribe. The Yamasees, a Muskogean-speaking people inhabiting the southern reaches of Georgia at the time the Spanish were occupying nearby Florida, enjoyed cordial relations initially and received Franciscan missionaries until 1680, when the Spanish attempted to deport tribal members to the Caribbean to work as slaves. A war ensued, and the Yamasees migrated northward to the vicinity of St. Helena Island and present-day Hilton Head Island, where the English colony of South Carolina was developing.

Initially the Yamasees and the English were amicably disposed. The Yamasees performed useful services, not the least of which was to act as a buffer between South Carolina and the Spanish. The Yamasees also played a prominent role in the essential deerskin trade and fought on behalf of the British during the Tuscarora War (1711–1713).

Around this time, however, poorly regulated British traders and agents engaged in unscrupulous practices with the Yamasees, including appropriating land without payment, wholesale cheating in trade, and demanding immediate payment for tribal debts estimated at £50,000. When the Yamasees proved unable to comply, the British usually resorted to seizing women and children for the slave market. Such systematic abuse propelled the Yamasees to violence, and they began plotting with neighboring tribes such as the Catawbas, the Apalachees, and the Creeks to initiate military action.

The ensuing Yamasee War began on April 15, 1715 (Good Friday), when native warriors staged carefully orchestrated attacks against British outposts along the South Carolina frontier. Traders and agents were especially targeted for revenge, and 90 colonists were slaughtered at Pocotaligo. Other war bands struck at the settlement of St. Bartholomew, between the Edisto and Combahee rivers, burning it and scattering the inhabitants. The ensuing crush of white refugees toward Charles Town (present-day Charleston, South Carolina) greatly swelled the population of that region, which gave it the ability to muster sufficient manpower for defense.

Governor Charles Craven proved exceptionally able and energetic, and in late April, he mounted a limited offensive with 240 men. Near Salkehatchie Craven's force engaged and defeated 500 warriors. Meanwhile, a second column under Colonel Alexander Mackay stormed the occupied village of Pocotaligo, dispersing a larger force of Yamasees. In another action fought on July 19, 1715, 120 militiamen under Captain George Chicken pursued a band of warriors into a swamp, surrounded them, and then attacked, killing 40 and freeing several white captives.

Warfare by this time had broken down into large-scale raiding by both sides, with notable actions at New London and Daufuskie Island (adjacent to Hilton Head Island and the Savannah River). The

Yamasees and their coalition were unable to withstand the colonial resurgence and began appealing to other tribes for assistance.

Their Creek neighbors agreed to help, providing additional war bands to supplement their original contingent. Thus augmented, the Native Americans were able to resume their destructive raids and in an action near Port Royal on August 1, 1716, killed several defenders. After being reinforced by militiamen from North Carolina and Virginia, South Carolinians successfully withstood this new round of attacks and soon began to drive the Creeks and the Yamasees back into the nearby swamps of Georgia.

By January 1716, the Creeks felt sufficiently threatened to appeal to their traditional enemy, the Cherokees, who constituted the largest tribe in the Southeast. The Cherokees proved coy initially but, in light of their good relations with the British, announced their decision by slaughtering the Creek emissaries. This combination of colonial militia under Craven's effective leadership, now backed by ample Cherokee manpower, proved too much for the Creeks and the remnants of the Yamasee coalition. Both were soon driven from the colony, the Creeks moving deeper into Georgia and the Yamasees withdrawing completely into Florida, where they were welcomed by the Spanish as allies. It was not until November 1717 that the Creeks and the British formally concluded a peace treaty. The Yamasees were never a party to this agreement, and from their Florida enclave, they launched sporadic raids for more than a decade.

Despite its relatively brief duration, the Yamasee War was one of the costliest conflicts waged by a European colony. South Carolina, with a population of only 5,500 settlers, took proportionately heavier losses than those incurred by New Englanders during King Philip's War (1675–1676). Many frontier communities lay gutted, and the lucrative deerskin trade, heretofore a staple of the local economy, was severely disrupted for many years. Despite Craven's able leadership, the proprietary government's response to the crisis was perceived as sluggish. In 1719, it was overthrown by the colonists and replaced by royal governance.

The Creeks also drew important lessons from the conflict, realizing that they lacked the power to openly confront both the British and the Cherokees and, moreover, that they could not readily rely on assistance from either France or Spain. The Creeks thereafter embarked on a course of cautious neutrality, partly to offset half a century of enmity toward the Cherokees, which had arisen from this war. But the most negatively impacted were the Yamasees. Driven from their homeland and subject to periodic raids from the new British colony of Georgia, they grew progressively weaker in numbers and were gradually absorbed by their Creek and Seminole neighbors. This once proud and influential tribe had disappeared as an identifiable culture by the end of the 18th century.

John C. Fredriksen

Further Reading

Haan, Richard L. "'The Trade Does Not Flourish as Formerly': The Ecological Origins of the Yamasee War of 1715." *Ethnohistory* 28 (1982): 341–358.

Oatis, Steven J. *A Colonial Complex: South Carolina's Frontiers in the Era of the Yamasee War, 1680–1730*. Lincoln: University of Nebraska Press, 2004.

Primary Source Documents

I. Powhatan, Remarks to John Smith, 1609 [Excerpts]

Introduction

Captain John Smith (1580–1631) was part of the first expedition to colonize Virginia in 1607. Smith spent much of his time in Virginia exploring the countryside, forging a relationship with the native peoples, and mapping the coastal waterways. The native peoples consisted of the Algonquian inhabitants of some 30 villages who accepted the leadership of their chieftain, Powhatan. Ongoing power struggles propelled Smith to the presidency of the colony after the first two presidents were discredited. Unlike the previous leaders, Smith imposed discipline and forced settlers to work for the survival of the colony. Nevertheless, they faced months of starvation, and many fell ill and died. Smith maintained a tenuous peace with Powhatan, who provided the colony with food, saving it from complete failure. Smith left Virginia in 1609 and returned home to recuperate from an injury. He wrote an account of his adventures in which he described early relations with Powhatan and his people. In the remarks reproduced here, Powhatan explains to Smith his suspicions regarding the colonists and his desire for peace. Powhatan died in 1618 and was succeeded by his brother Opechancanough, who was far less tolerant of the colonists and ordered the devastating Massacre of 1622 in which one-fourth of the white population died at the hands of Indians.

Primary Source

Captain Smith, some doubt I have of your coming hither . . . for many do inform me, your coming is not for trade, but to invade my people and possess my country. . . . I am now grown old, and must soon die; and the succession must descend, in order, to my brothers, Opitchapan, Opekankanough, and Catataugh, and then to my two sisters, and their two daughters. I wish their experience was equal to mine; and that your love to us might not be less than ours to you. Why should you take by force that from us which you can have by love? Why should you destroy us, who have provided you with food? What can you get by war? We can hide our provisions, and fly into the woods; and then you must consequently famish by wronging your friends. What is the cause of your jealousy? You see us unarmed, and willing to supply your wants, if you will come in a friendly manner, and not with swords and guns, as to invade an enemy. I am not so simple, as not to know it is better to eat good meat, lie well, and sleep quietly with my women and children; to laugh and be merry with the English; and, being their friend, to have copper, hatchets, and whatever else I want, than to fly from all, to lie cold in the woods, feed upon acorns, roots, and such trash, and to be so hunted, that I cannot rest, eat, or sleep. In such circumstances, my men must watch, and if a twig should break, all would cry out, "Here comes capt. Smith": and so, in this miserable manner, to end my miserable life; and, capt. Smith, this might be soon your fate too, through your rashness and unadvisedness. I, therefore, exhort you to peaceable councils; and, above all, I insist that the guns and swords, the cause of all our jealousy and uneasiness, be removed and sent away.

Source: Samuel Drake, *Biography and History of the Indians of North America*, 11th ed. (Boston: Benjamin B. Mussey & Company, 1841), 353.

2. Massasoit Peace Treaty, 1621

Introduction
Wampanoag chief Massasoit was the first Indian leader to deal with English colonists shortly after the Pilgrims' arrival at Plymouth, Massachusetts, in late 1620. At the Pilgrims' request, Massasoit agreed to this treaty in March 1621. After the separatist Pilgrims founded the colony, a mix of Puritans and non-Puritans from England founded settlements along the New England coast. By 1635, about 2,000 immigrants were arriving each year, most of them Puritans. The newcomers settled all along the coast from Maine to Long Island. The English and Wampanoags worked hard to maintain peace throughout Massasoit's life, despite bitter conflicts between Indians and colonists in other parts of New England, such as the Pequot War of 1637 in Connecticut. Massasoit died in 1662 and was succeeded by his son Metacom, known to the

English as King Philip, who would launch King Philip's War (1675–1676) in an effort to resist English expansion.

Primary Source
1. That neither he nor any of his should injure or do hurt to any of our people.
2. And if any of his did hurt to any of ours, he should send the offender, that we might punish him.
3. That if any of our tools were taken away when our people were at work, he should cause them to be restored; and if ours did any harm to any of his, we would do the like to them.
4. If any did unjustly war against him, we would aid him; if any did war against us, he should aid us.
5. He should send to his neighbor confederates, to certify them of this, that they might not wrong us, but might be likewise comprised in the conditions of peace.
6. That when their men came to us, they should leave their bows and arrows behind them, as we should do our pieces when we came to them.

Lastly, that doing thus, King James would esteem of him as his friend and ally.

Source: William Bradford, *History of the Plymouth Plantation* (Boston: Little, Brown, 1856), 94.

3. John Gerrard, An Account of the Attack on the Susquehannock Stronghold, 1675

Introduction
The Susquehannocks lived along the Susquehanna River in present-day New York, Pennsylvania, and Maryland. Maryland first declared war on the Susquehannocks in

1642. Ten years later, the Susquehannocks made peace with Maryland and gave the colony large tracts of land. The Susquehannocks had suffered huge losses in their ongoing war with the Iroquois and could no longer fight two wars at once. The peace endured for more than 20 years. In 1674, the Maryland government ordered the Susquehannocks, who were even more weakened by decades of warfare, to move to a settlement on the banks of the Potomac River. The next year, an argument ended in the murder of a Virginian and some 20 Susquehannocks. Fearing reprisals, more than 1,000 Virginia and Maryland militia surrounded the Susquehannock town and murdered 5 Susquehannock chiefs. In this report, a Virginia militiaman attributes the killing to Marylanders. The Susquehannocks fled to southern Virginia and then took revenge by attacking and killing settlers on the frontiers of both colonies. The Susquehannocks remained at war with the English for another 15 years. The Maryland assembly tried and convicted the militia commander for the murders, but he was not punished.

Primary Source
A narrative of the transactions of the Susquehannock Fort. Soe fare as I know concerning the Killing of the five Indians As soone as our Virginia forces were landed in Maryland wee found five Susquehannock Indians, under a guard and inquireing the reason of theire restraint, where [i.e., were] answered they endeavoured an escape and thereof were secured till our comeing in order to a treaty wee informing the Marylanders our businesse was first to treat and require satisfaction for the murder perpetrated before wee declared ourselves open enimies and proceeded to hostile actions[.] Lt. Col. John Washington and Major Isaac Allerton upon this information thought it

convenient to have them stronger guarded and themselves alsoe dureing the treaty which being donne and col. Washington and Major Alerton accordingly treating there first demand was Satisfaction for the murder and spoyles committed on Virginia Shore Major Tilghman in the interim remaining silent: after long debate [word illegible] therein made by Col. Washington and Major Alerton the Indians disowned all that was aledged to them and imputed it all to [the] Senecas[.] Col Washington and Major Alerton urged that severall cannoes loaded with beefe and pork had bin carried into theire fort alleadging that theire enimyes would not be soe kinde as to supply them with provisions and farther that some of their men had a little before been taken on Virginia side who had the cloathes of such as had bin a little before murdered, upon there backes which made it appeare that they had bin the murderers: for these reasons Major Alerton and Col. Washington demanded Satisfaction or else they must proceed against them as enimyes and storme there fort and accordingly commanded the interpreter to bid them defiance[.] Dureing the time of their treaty Major [Thomas] Trewman came and asked the Gentlemen wheather they had finished[,] saying when you have donne I will Say something to them: And when Col. Washington and Major Alerton had ended there treatie he went and commanded his interpreter John Shanks to ask them how theire Indians came to be buried at [Hutsons?] and after a little further discourse caused them to be bound and told them he would carry them to the place and show them theire owne Indians where they lay dead: Major Alerton asked him what he did intend to doe with them afterwards[.] Major Trewman answered he thought they deserved the like to which Major Alerton replyed I doe not thinke soe[.] Noe sooner was this discourse ended between Major Allerton and Major Trewman than the Marylanders carried away those five Indians and before they had got five hundred yards distance from the place of this discourse and treaty spoken of[,] the Marylanders killed them and further saith not

John Gerrard

Sworne before us by virtue of an order to us from the right Honorable the Governor

Nicholas Spencer June the 13th 1677 recorded

Richard Lee

Source: Warren M. Billings, ed., *The Old Dominion in the Seventeenth Century: A Documentary History of Virginia, 1606–1689* (Chapel Hill: University of North Carolina Press, 1975), 291–292.

---

4. Nathaniel Saltonstall, Accounts of King Philip's War, 1675–1676 [Excerpts]

Introduction

These excerpts from a series of letters, sent to London by Boston merchant Nathaniel Saltonstall, recount episodes in King Philip's War (1675–1676). The Wampanoag Indians had lived in peace with the English ever since 1621, when chief Massasoit made a treaty of friendship with the Pilgrims. By Massasoit's death in 1662, thousands of English colonists were arriving in New England annually. His son and successor, Metacom, called King Philip by the English, organized an Indian confederacy to resist English expansion. A June 1675 attack on a village in Plymouth colony set off the war. The United Colonies of New England joined forces against the Narragansetts, Pocumtucs, Nipmucs, and Wampanoags. The Indians destroyed numerous Massachusetts villages, making life on the frontier intolerable for colonists. In December 1675, Plymouth governor Josiah Winslow led his militia into Rhode Island to attack the Narragansetts. Winslow found the Narragansetts camped on high ground in the middle of a vast swamp. The battle inflicted 240 English casualties and more than 900 Narragansett casualties. The war crushed Indian resistance but utterly destroyed parts of New England and killed 1 out of 16 English fighting men. The first excerpt demonstrates how the English treated their Indian allies. The second excerpt describes the Great Swamp Fight.

Primary Source

[. . .]

This Unkus, and all his Subjects professing Christianity, are called Praying Indians. In the first Week in August, the Authority of Boston sent an Express to him, to require him to come in and Surrender himself, Men, and Arms, to the English; Whereupon, he sent along with the Messenger his three Sons, and about Sixty of his Men, with his Arms, to be thus disposed of, viz. His two youngest sons, (about thirty Years old) to remain as Hostages (as now they do at cambridg) and his Eldest Son to go captain of the Men as Assistants to the English against the Heathens, which accordingly they did. And the English not thinking themselves yet secure enough, because they cannot know a Heathen from a Christian by his Visage, nor Apparel: the Authority of Boston, at a council held there the 30th of August, Published this following Order.

At a Council held in Boston, August 30, 1675.

The Council judging it of absolute necessity for the Security of the English, and the Indians that are in Amity with us, that they be Restrained their usual commerce with the English, and Hunting in the Woods, during the time of Hostility with those that are our Enemies.

Do Order, that all those Indians that are desirous to Approve themselves Faithful to the English, be confined to their several Plantations under-written, until the council shall take further Order; and that they so order the setting of their Wigwams, that they may stand compact in some one Part of their Plantations respectively, where it may be best for their own Provision and Defence. And that none of them do presume to travel above one Mile from the center of such their Dwelling, unless in company with some English, or in their Service near their Dwellings; and excepting for gathering and fetching in their corn with one Englishman, on peril of being taken as our Enemies, or their Abettors: And in case that any of them shall be taken without the Limits abovesaid, except as abovesaid, and do lose their Lives, or be otherwise damnified, by English or Indians; the council do hereby Declare, that they shall account themselves wholly Innocent, and their Blood or other Dammage (by them sustained) will be upon their own Heads. Also it shall not be lawful for any Indians that are in Amity with us, to entertain any strange Indians, or receive any of our Enemies Plunder, but shall from time to time make Discovery thereof to some English, that shall be Appointed for that End to sojourn among them, on Penalty of being reputed our Enemies, and of being liable to be proceeded against as such.

Also, whereas it is the Manner of the Heathen that are now in Hostility with us, contrary to the Practice of all civil nations, to Execute their bloody Insolencies by Stealth, and Sculking in small Parties, declining all open Decision of their controversie, either by treaty or by the Sword.

The council do therefore Order, that after the Publication of the Provision aforesaid, It shall be lawful for any Person, whether English or Indian, that shall find any Indians travelling or Sculking in any of our towns or Woods, contrary to the Limits above-named, to command them under their Guard and Examination, or to Kill and destroy them as they best may or can. The council hereby declaring, that it will be most acceptable to them that none be Killed or Wounded that are Willing to surrender themselves into custody.

The Places of the Indians Residencies are, Natick, Punquapaog, Nashoba, Wamesit, and Hassanemesit: And if there be any that belong to any other Plantations, they are to Repair to some one of these.

By the council
EDWARD RAWSON, Secr.
[. . .]

In the Afternoon of that Saturday, some of the Souldiers accidently espied an Indian alone, whom they took and carried to the General, who upon his Refusal to answer to those Questions demanded, was ordered to be Hanged forthwith; Whereupon the Indian to save his Life, told them where the whole Body of the Indians were together, as well King Philip, and all other confederate Sagamores and Sachems with their whole Retinue, as also the whole body of the Narragansets, being joined all in a body in November, about 4500 Indian Men, besides Wives and children: Whereupon, keeping this Indian for their Guide, they having Provisions with them, marched all night, the Indians being then 16 Miles distant from them, and that night there fell a very hard Snow two or three Foot deep, and withal an extream hard Frost, so that some of our Men were frozen in their Hands and Feet, and thereby disabled for Service. The next Day, about noon, they come to a large Swamp, which by Reasons of the Frost all the night before, they were capable of going over (which else they could not have done). They forthwith in one Body entered the said Swamp, and in the Midst thereof was a Piece of firm Land, of about three or four Acres of Ground, whereon the Indians had built a Kind of Fort, being palisado'd round, and within that a clay Wall, as also felled down Abundance of trees to Lay quite round the said Fort, but they had not quite finished the said Work. The General placed Capt. Moseley in the Front, to enter the Fort, and the Rest of the companies were placed according to discretion. In their march they met with three Indians sent out as Scouts, whom they shot dead at Sight thereof: as soon as ever the Indians saw our Army coming, they shot as fast as ever they could, and so our men did the like. Before our men could come up to take Possession of the Fort, the Indians had shot three Bullets through Capt. Davenport, whereupon he bled extreamly, and immediately called for his Lieutenant, Mr. Edward Ting, and committed the charge of the company to him, and desire him to take care of his Gun, and deliver it according to Order, and immediately died in the Place; his company were extreamly grieved at his Death, in Regard he was so courteous to them; for he being commander of that company, belonging to Cambridge and Watertown etc. was a Stranger to most of them; and at the same time that he came to take Possession of his company, he made a very civil Speech to them, and also gave them free Liberty to choose their Serjeants themselves, which pleased them very well, and accordingly did so; and it is very probable the Indians might think that Capt. Davenport was the General, because he had a very good Buff Suit on at that time, and

therefore might shoot at him. In a short time our Forces entered the fort, Captain Moseley being in the Front, the Indians knowing him very well, many directed their shot to him, as he afterwards told the General that he believed he saw 50 aim at him: As soon as he and they had entred the Fort, he espied a Heap of above 50 Indians lay dead in a corner, which the Indians had gathered together; as soon as ever our Men had entred the Fort, the Indians fled, our Men killed many of them, as also of their Wives and children, amongst which an Indian Black-Smith (the only Man amongst them that fitted their Guns and Arrowheads;) and amongst many other Houses burnt his, as also demolished his Forge, and carried away his tools; they fought with the Indians, and pursued them so long as was advantageous to them; then the General gave Order to sound a Retreat, which was done according to Order. The Retreat was no sooner beaten, and the Souldiers were in a Marching Posture, before they were got all out of the Fort, a thousand fresh Indians set on our Men, but in an Hour's time the Indians were forced to Retreat and Flie. Our Men as near as they can judge, may have killed about 600 Indian Men, besides Women and children. Many more Indians were killed which we could have no Account of, by Reason that they would carry away as many dead Indians as they could. Our Men before they had been set on by the fresh Indians, had set fire to most of the Wigwams in and about the Fort (which were near 1000 in all,) how many were burnt down they could not tell positively, only thus; that they marched above three Miles from the Fort by the Light of the Fires.

Source: Charles H. Lincoln, ed., *Narratives of the Indian Wars* (New York: Scribner, 1913), 32–33, 57–59.

5. Count Frontenac, Report on War with the Iroquois, November 2, 1681 [Excerpts]

Introduction

The French and the Iroquois had a long history of hostility dating back to the 1530s, when explorer Jacques Cartier abducted several Iroquois chiefs. During the late 1500s, the five Iroquois nations formed a confederation that featured the most sophisticated native government in North America. New France began with Samuel de Champlain's founding of a settlement at Quebec in 1608. In 1609, Champlain perpetuated French-Iroquois enmity when he attacked the Iroquois on the shore of present-day Lake Champlain. Over the ensuing decades, the Iroquois acquired firearms from Dutch traders and grew more powerful and numerous, extending their influence far beyond their home territory. Iroquois country lay between English New York and New France, and the Iroquois allied themselves with the English. New France and the Iroquois fought a brutal war during the 1650s and 1660s. The comte de Frontenac served as governor of New France from 1672 to 1682 and again from 1689 to 1698. In this letter, he asks the king for a greater military presence to deter the Iroquois from renewing hostilities against New France. However, war resumed in 1683 and continued until 1698. During this period, England and France also went to war against one another.

Primary Source

Frontenac to the King

November 2, 1681

... I have resolved to invite them (the Iroquois) to come next summer to Fort Frontenac to explain their conduct to me.

They have, Sire, become so insolent since this expedition against the Illinois, although they are of no consideration, and they are being so much strengthened in these sentiments in order to induce them to carry on the war, in the belief it will embarrass the explorations of Sieur de la Salle, that it is to be feared that they will push their boldness still further and that, after having seen that we give no support to our allies, will attribute it to a weakness which will give birth to the desire to come to attack us.

[. . .]

I pray you very humbly, to consider that for ten years I alone have kept these Indians in a spirit of obedience, of quiet, and of peace, by a little skill and tact—it is difficult, when one is deprived of everything, to do more, or to anticipate things which could easily be prevented if one had a little help; to consider that the Indians are becoming inured to all I can say to them to hold them in allegiance; and that all these journeys which they see me make almost every year to Fort Frontenac, no longer give them the same cause of amazement as they did at the beginning.

[. . .]

Five or six hundred regular soldiers would soon dispel all these various ideas and it would be necessary only to show them and to march them through their lakes, without any other hostile act, to ensure peace for ten years.

Source: Richard A. Preston, *Royal Fort Frontenac* (Toronto: Champlain Society for the Government of Ontario, University of Toronto Press, 1958), 140. Used with permission.

6. Six Nations, Meeting with Colonial Officials at Albany, August 19, 1746

Introduction

The Iroquois, who had considered the French to be their enemies since French explorers had attacked them in the early

1600s, maintained a strong alliance with the English and cooperated with them in controlling the movements of other Indians in Iroquois territory. Iroquois land in northern New York and Pennsylvania served as a buffer between Canada and the British colonies. The War of the Austrian Succession (1740–1748) spilled over into North America when France entered the war against Great Britain, becoming known to British colonists as King George's War (1744–1748). In 1744, warriors and sachems of the Iroquois Six Nations met colonial officials in Lancaster, Pennsylvania, and reaffirmed their alliance with the English. During a meeting in Albany, New York, two years later, New York officials urged the Iroquois to join them in a major operation against Canada. In his attempt to sway the Iroquois, the speaker cited French and Indian attacks on the frontier, the necessity of avenging one's ancestors, and the opportunity to attain glory.

Primary Source
The King your Father, having been informed of the unmanly Murders committed on the Frontiers of new-England, and of this Province, is resolved to subdue the country of canada, and thereby put an End to all the mischievous Designs of the French in these Parts. And for this purpose, he has ordered his Governors of Virginia, Maryland, Pennsylvania, and new-Jersey, to join their Forces to the Forces of this Province, to attack Canada by Land: they are all now upon their march, and you will soon see them here.

At the same time the Forces of the Massachusets-Bay, Connecticut, Rhode-Island, and New-Hampshire, are to go in Ships to Cape-Breton, and there join with his Majesty's Ships of War, and a great Army of experienc'd Soldiers from Great-Britain.

Many Ships of War are already arrived there, and some thousand of Soldiers; many more Ships and Soldiers are following; and I expect every Hour to hear of their Arrival; after which the Attack upon Canada will be made on all Sides, both by Sea and Land.

You may perceive the King has ordered a Strength sufficient to subdue Canada; but at the same time, the King your Father expects and orders you his children, to join with your whole Force in this Enterprize; and thereby gives the Six nations a glorious Opportunity of establishing their Fame and Renown over all the Indian nations in America, in the conquest of your inveterate Enemies the French; who, however they may dissemble and profess Friendship, can never forget the Slaughter which your Fathers made of them; and for that purpose, caress those nations who have always been your inveterate Enemies, and who desire nothing so much as to see the name of the Six nations become obliterate, and forgot for ever.

[Gave a Belt.]

Brethren, the French, on all Occasions, shew, that they act against your Brethren the English, like Men that know they dare not look them in the Face in Day-Light; and therefore, like thieves, steal upon poor People, who do not expect them, in the night, and consequently are not prepared for them: Your Brethren in their Revenge have acted like Men of courage; they do not attack poor Farmers at their Labour, but boldly attempted the Reduction of Louisburg, the strongest town the French had in America, in the fortifying of which they had spent above twenty Years: It was surrounded with strong Walls and Forts, in which they had planted their largest cannon in every Place, where they thought the English could come near them; notwithstanding of all these Precautions and Advantages, they were forced to submit to the English Valour.

You must have heard from your Fathers, and I doubt not several of your old Men still remember what the French did at Onondaga; how they surprized your countrymen at Cadarackui; how they invaded the Senekas, and what Mischiefs they did to the Mohawks; how many of your countrymen suffered by the Fire at Montreal. Before they entered upon these cruel and mischievous Designs, they sent Priests among you to delude you, and lull you asleep, while they were preparing to knock you on the Head; and I hear they are attempting to do the same now.

[Gave a Belt.]

I need not put you in mind what Revenge your Fathers took for these Injuries, when they put all the Island of Montreal, and a great Part of Canada, to Fire and Sword; can you think that the French forget this? no, they have the Ax privately in their Hands against you, and use these deceitful Arts, by which only they have been able to gain Advantage over you, that by your trusting to them, they may at some time or other, at one Blow, remove from the Face of the Earth, the Remembrance of a People that have so often put them to Shame and Flight.

If your Fathers could now rise out of their Graves, how would their Hearts leap with Joy to see this Day; when so glorious an Opportunity is put into their Hands to revenge all the Injuries their country has received from the French, and be never more exposed to their treachery and Deceit.

I make no doubt you are the true Sons of such renowned and brave Ancestors, animated with the same Spirit for your country's Glory, and in Revenge of the Injuries your Fathers received, uncapable of being deluded by the flattering Speeches of them, who always have been, and always must be, in their Hearts, your Enemies, and who desire nothing more, than the Destruction of your nations.

I therefore invite you, Brethren, by this Belt, to join with us, and to share with us, in the Honour of the conquest of our and your deceitful Enemies; and that you not only join all the Force of the Six nations with us, but likewise invite all the nations depending on you, to take a Share in this glorious Enterprize: And I will furnish your fighting Men with Arms, Ammunition, cloathing, Provisions, and every thing necessary for the War; and in their Absence, take care of their Wives and children.

Source: Cadwallader Colden, *The History of the Five Indian Nations of Canada; Which Are Dependent on the Province of New York, and Are a Barrier between the English and the French in That Part of the World* (New York: Allerton Book Co., 1904), 230–233.

7. Robert Rogers, Journal Account on the Destruction of St. Francis, September 1759 [Excerpts]

Introduction

Rogers's Rangers was the name given to British rangers raised by Major Robert Rogers (1731–1795). A New Hampshire–born frontiersman, Rogers recruited and trained ranger units that operated behind enemy lines during the French and Indian War (1754–1763). He commanded one of the units and served in New York, the Great Lakes region, and Canada. New York was a major battleground in this war. Because few roads existed at this time, the combatants maneuvered by canoes and bateaux along lakes and rivers. French and Indian invasion forces traveled from Canada into New York on Lake Champlain, Lake George, and the Hudson River. Between 1755 and 1760, battles took place along this corridor as well as along the Mohawk River and the shores of

Lake Ontario. These excerpts from Rogers's journal include his secret orders, from General Jeffrey Amherst, to destroy the Abenaki Indian village at St. Francis as well as his report to the general on the results of the predawn surprise attack. St. Francis in Quebec served as a base for Indian attacks into New England. While noting that the Indians had killed many women and children, Amherst ordered Rogers to refrain from doing the same. In fact, Rogers's men killed mostly women and children as they fled the burning village. Rogers claimed to have killed 200, but the actual number was closer to 30. Rogers joined the British forces during the American Revolutionary War.

Primary Source

*You are this night to set out with the detachment as ordered yesterday, viz. of 200 men, which you will take under your command, and proceed to Misisquey Bay, from whence you will march and attack the enemy's settlements on the south-side of the river St. Lawrence, in such a manner as you shall judge most effectual to disgrace the enemy, and for the success and honour of his Majesty's arms.

Remember the barbarities that have been committed by the enemy's Indian scoundrels on every occasion, where they had an opportunity of shewing their infamous cruelties on the King's subjects, which they have done without mercy. Take your revenge, but don't forget that tho' those villains have dastardly and promiscuously murdered the women and children of all ages, it is my orders that no women or children are killed or hurt.

When you have executed your intended service, you will return with your detachment to camp, or to join me wherever the army may be.

Yours, &c.

*That this expedition might be carried on with the utmost secresy after the plan of it was concerted the day before my march, it was put into public orders, that I was to march a different way, at the same time I had private instructions to proceed directly to St. Francis.—Note by the Author.

Camp at Crown Point,
Jeff Amherst
Sept. 13, 1759.
To Major Rogers.

In pursuance of the above orders, I set out the same evening with a detachment; and as to the particulars of my proceedings, and the great difficulties we met with in effecting our design, the reader is referred to the letter I wrote to General Amherst upon my return, and the remarks following it.

Copy of my letter to the General upon my return from St. Francis.

SIR,

The twenty-second day after my departure from crown Point, I came in sight of the Indian town St. Francis in the evening, which I discovered from a tree that I climbed, at about three miles distance. Here I halted my party, which now consisted of 142 men, officers included, being reduced to that number by the unhappy accident which befel capt. Williams*, and several since tiring, whom I was obliged to send back. At eight o'clock this evening I left the detachment, and took with me Lieut. Turner, and Ensign Avery, and went to reconnoitre the town, which I did to my satisfaction, and I found the Indians in a high frolic or dance. I returned to my party at two o'clock, and at three marched it to within five hundred yards of the town, where I lightened the men of their packs, and formed them for the attack.

At half an hour before sun-rise I surprised the town when they were all fast asleep, on the right, left, and center, which was done with so much alacrity by both the officers and men, that the enemy had not time to recover themselves, or take arms for their own defence, till they were chiefly destroyed, except some few of them who took to the water. About forty of my people pursued them, who destroyed such as attempted to make their escape that way, and sunk both them and their boats. A little after sun-rise I set fire to all their houses, except three, in which there was corn, that I reserved for the use of the party.

The fire consumed many of the Indians who had concealed themselves in the cellars and lofts of their houses. About seven o'clock in the morning the affair was completely over, in which time we had killed at least two hundred Indians, and taken twenty of their women and children prisoners,* fifteen of whom I let go their own way, and five I brought with me, viz. Two Indian boys, and three Indian girls.

[. . .]

This nation of Indians was notoriously attached to the French, and had for near a century past harrassed the frontiers of new England, killing people of all ages and sexes in a most barbarous manner, at a time when they did not in the least expect them; and to my own knowledge, in six years' time, carried into captivity, and killed, on the before mentioned frontiers, 400 persons. We found in the town hanging on poles over their doors, &c., about 600 scalps, mostly English.

* Capt. Williams of the Royal Regiment was, the fifth day of our march accidentally burnt with gun-powder, and several men hurt, which, together with some sick, returned back to crown Point, to the number of forty, under the care of Capt. Williams, who returned with great reluctance.—Note by the Author.

Source: Robert Rogers, *Journals of Major Robert Rogers* (Albany, NY: Joel Munsell's Sons, 1883), 140–142, 147.

8. Pontiac, Letter Addressed to the Commander of Detroit, October 30, 1763

Introduction

The end of the French and Indian War (1754–1763) in North America led to British traders replacing French traders on the western frontier. The British also built several permanent frontier forts, and British colonists defied their government's treaties with Native American tribes by crossing the mountains to settle on native lands in the Ohio Valley. Pontiac's Rebellion—named after a chief of the Ottawas—broke out in spring 1763 as western Indians tried to drive British traders and settlers back east. Natives killed or captured some 2,000 frontier settlers and successfully seized all major frontier forts, except for Fort Pitt, Fort Niagara, and Fort Detroit. The British held out at Detroit for five months against the siege mounted by Pontiac and the Ottawas. Running low on ammunition, Pontiac made a peace overture in this letter (the original was in French) to the British commander of the fort. Despite the name given to the uprising by the British, Pontiac did not command the other tribes and villages. The rebellion died down gradually over the course of the next two years, finally ending in 1766 after many native combatants made peace one village at a time.

Primary Source

Detroit, Nov. 1, 1763

Copy of the Letter addressed to the commander of Detroit by Pontiac, the 30th of October, 1763.

My Brother:

The word which my Father sent me to make peace, I have accepted; all my young men have buried their hatchets: I think that you will forget all the evil things which have occurred for some time past. Likewise, I shall forget what you may have done to me, in order to think nothing but good. I, the Saulteurs, the Hurons, we will come to speak when you ask us. Give us a reply. I am sending this council to you in order that you may see it. If you are as good as I, you will send me a reply. I wish you good day.

Signed,

Pontiac

Source: Henry Bouquet, *The Papers of Col. Henry Bouquet*, Ser. 21649, Pt. II (Harrisburg: Department of Public Instruction, Pennsylvania Historical commission, 1942).

9. Anthony Wayne, Letter to Henry Knox on the Victory at Fallen Timbers, August 28, 1794

Introduction

The end of the American Revolutionary War (1775–1783) released pent-up demand for western land. Thousands of settlers headed west. Many of them traveled to Pittsburgh, purchased or built watercraft, and then followed the Ohio River to carve out homes and farms throughout the Ohio River Valley without regard to whether the land had been promised to the Indians. Arthur St. Clair, a veteran Revolutionary War general, served as the first governor of the Northwest Territory (which included the area covered by the present-day states of Ohio, Indiana, Illinois, Michigan, and Wisconsin) from 1789 to 1802. In 1791, St. Clair was also appointed major general in command of the U.S. Army. At first, the army was expected to enforce treaties by driving

illegal settlers off Indian lands. The British remaining in the Northwest Territory encouraged the Indians to step up attacks on settlers. In 1790 and 1791, President George Washington ordered the army to go on campaign against the Miami Indians. The undermanned and poorly organized campaigns led to a costly and humiliating defeat and the replacement of St. Clair with the Revolutionary War hero Anthony Wayne. The more determined and competent Wayne trained his men well and decisively defeated the Indians at Fallen Timbers on August 20, 1794. Wayne's letter to Secretary of War Henry Knox proudly reports on the accomplishment. The victory at Fallen Timbers led to the surrender of many western tribes, including the Miamis, Wyanadots, Chippewas, Shawnees, and Delawares, in 1795.

Primary Source

Head Quarters

Grand Glaize, 28th August, 1794

Sir—It is with infinite pleasure that I now announce to you the brilliant success of the Federal army under my command, in a general action with the combined force of the hostile Indians, and a considerable number of the volunteers and militia of Detroit, on the 20th instant, on the banks of the Miamis, in the vicinity of the British post and garrison, at the foot of the rapids.

The army advanced from this place on the 15th instant, and arrived at Roche de Bout on the 18th; the 19th we were employed in making a temporary post for the reception of our stores and baggage, and in reconnoitering the position of the enemy, who were encamped behind a thick bushy wood and the British fort.

At 8 o'clock, on the morning of the 20th, the army again advanced in columns, agreeably to the standing order of march; the legion on the right flank, covered by the

Miamis,—one brigade of mounted volunteers on the left, under Brigadier-General Todd, and the other in the rear, under Brigadier-General Barbee:—a select battalion of mounted volunteers moved in front of the legion, commanded by Major Price, who was directed to keep sufficiently advanced—so as to give timely notice for the troops to form, in case of action—it being yet undetermined whether the Indians would decide for peace or war. After advancing about five miles, Major Price's corps received so severe a fire from the enemy, who were secreted in the woods, and high grass, as to compel them to retreat.

The legion was immediately formed in two lines, principally in a close, thick wood, which extended for miles on our left; and for a very-considerable distance in front, the ground being covered with old fallen timber, probably occasioned by a tornado, which rendered it impracticable for the cavalry to act with effect; and afforded the enemy the most favorable covert for their savage mode of warfare: they were formed in three lines, within supporting distance of each other, and extending near two miles, at right angles with the river.

I soon discovered, from the weight of the fire, and extent of their lines, that the enemy were in full force in front, in possession of their favorite ground, and endeavoring to turn our left flank. I therefore gave orders for the second line to advance, to support the first, and directed Major-General Scott to gain and turn the right flank of the savages, with the whole of the mounted volunteers, by a circuitous route: at the same time I ordered the front line to advance with trailed arms, and rouse the Indians from their coverts, at the point of the bayonet; and, when up, to deliver a close and well directed fire on their backs, followed by a brisk charge, so as not to give time to load

again. I also ordered Captain Mis Campbell, who commanded the legionary cavalry, to turn the left flank of the enemy next the river, and which afforded a favorable field for that corps to act in.

All those orders were obeyed with spirit and promptitude; but such was the impetuosity of the charge by the first line of infantry, that the Indians and Canadian militia and volunteers were driven from all their coverts in so short a time, that although every exertion was used by the officers of the second line of the legion, and by Generals Scott, Todd, and Barbee, of the mounted volunteers, to gain their proper positions, yet but a part of each could get up in season to participate in the action; the enemy being driven, in the course of one hour, more than two miles, through the thick woods already mentioned, by less than one half their numbers.

From every account, the enemy amounted to 2000 combatants; the troops actually engaged against them, were short of 900. This horde of savages, with their allies, abandoned themselves to flight, and dispersed with terror and dismay; leaving our victorious army in full and quiet possession of the field of battle, which terminated under the influence of the guns of the British garrison, as you will observe by the enclosed correspondence between Major Campbell, the commandant, and myself, upon the occasion.

The bravery and conduct of every officer belonging to the army, from the generals down to the ensigns, merit my highest approbation. There were, however, some whose rank and situation placed their conduct in a very conspicuous point of view, and which I observed with pleasure and the most lively gratitude: among whom I must beg leave to mention Brigadier-General Wilkinson and Colonel Hamtramck, the commandants of the right and left wings of the legion, whose brave example inspired the troops; to these, I must add the names of my faithful and gallant aids-de-camp, Captains De Butts and T. Lewis, and Lieutenant Harrison, who, with the Adjutant-General, Major Mills, rendered the most essential service by communicating my orders in every direction, and by their conduct and bravery exciting the troops to press for victory. Lieutenant Covington, upon whom the command of the cavalry now devolved, cut down two savages with his own hand, and Lieutenant Webb one, in turning the enemy's left flank.

The wounds received by Captains Slough and Prior, and Lieutenants Campbell, Smith, (an extra aid-de-camp to General Wilkinson,) of the legionary infantry, and Captain Van Rensellaer, of the dragoons, and Captain Rawlins, Lieutenant M'Kenney, and Ensign Duncan, of the mounted volunteers, bear honorable testimony of their bravery and conduct.

Captains H. Lewis and Brock, with their companies of light infantry, had to sustain an unequal fire for some time, which they supported with fortitude. In fact, every officer and soldier who had an opportunity to come into action, displayed that true bravery which will always insure success.

And here permit me to declare, that I never discovered more true spirit and anxiety for action, than appeared to pervade the whole of the mounted volunteers; and I am well persuaded that had the enemy maintained their favorite ground but for one half hour longer, they would have most severely felt the prowess of that corps.

But whilst I pay this just tribute to the living, I must not forget the gallant dead; among whom we have to lament the early death of those worthy and brave officers, captain Mis Campbell, of the dragoons, and Lieutenant Towles, of the light infantry of the legion, who fell in the first charge.

Enclosed is a particular return of the killed and wounded. The loss of the enemy was more than double that of the Federal army. The woods were strewed, for a considerable distance, with the dead bodies of Indians and their white auxiliaries; the latter armed with British muskets and bayonets.

We remained three days and nights on the banks of the Miamis, in front of the field of battle; during which time all the houses and corn-fields were consumed and destroyed for a considerable distance, both above and below Fort Miamis, as well as within pistol-shot of that garrison, who were compelled to remain tacit spectators of this general devastation and conflagration; among which were the houses, stores, and property of Colonel M'Kee, the British Indian agent, and principal stimulator of the war now existing between the United States and the savages.

The army returned to this place on the 27th, by easy marches, laying waste the villages and corn-fields for about fifty miles on each side of the Miamis. There remains yet a number of villages, and a great quantity of corn, to be consumed or destroyed upon Au Glaize and the Miamis, above this place, which will be effected in the course of a few days. In the interim, we shall improve Fort Defiance, and as soon as the escort returns with the necessary supplies from Greeneville and Fort Recovery, the army will proceed to the Miami villages, in order to accomplish the object of the campaign.

It is, however, not improbable that the enemy may make one more desperate effort against the army, as it is said that a reinforcement was hourly expected at Fort Miamis, from Niagara, as well as numerous tribes of Indians living on the margins and islands of the lakes. This is a business rather to be wished for than dreaded, whilst the army remains in force. Their numbers will only tend to confuse the savages, and the victory will be the more complete and decisive, and which may eventually insure a permanent and happy peace.

Under these impressions, I have the honor to be your most obedient and very humble servant,

ANTHONY WAYNE

The Hon. Major General Knox,

Secretary of War.

Source: H. N. Moore, *Life and Services of Gen. Anthony Wayne* (Philadelphia: John B. Perry, 1845), 190–197.

10. Tecumseh, Speech to Governor William Henry Harrison, August 12, 1810

Introduction

In 1809, Governor William Henry Harrison of Indiana Territory met with Native American leaders at Fort Wayne and convinced them to cede nearly three million acres to the United States. The great Shawnee leader Tecumseh repeatedly warned Harrison against allowing white settlement of the new territory. The most powerful Native American of his day, Tecumseh forged a Pan-Indian alliance among midwestern tribes with the help of his brother, Tenskwatawa, the Prophet, in the early 1800s. They hoped to prevent American expansion by arguing that by virtue of prior occupancy, Native Americans collectively held rights to the land and that no individual or tribe could sell or barter land without the consent of all. In this 1810 speech to Harrison, Tecumseh set forth the concept of collective land rights and argued that the 1809 Treaty of Fort Wayne was invalid because it

involved only some of the tribes. Harrison became Tecumseh's chief adversary, leading the force that won the Battle of Tippecanoe in 1811. Harrison went on to fight in the War of 1812 and eventually became president of the United States on the strength of his reputation as an Indian fighter. Tecumseh joined the British in fighting the War of 1812 and fell in battle in 1813.

Primary Source

It is true I am a Shawnee. My forefathers were warriors. Their son is a warrior. From them I only take my existence; from my tribe I take nothing. I am the maker of my own fortune; and oh! that I could make that of my red people, and of my country, as great as the conceptions of my mind, when I think of the Spirit that rules the universe. I would not then come to Governor Harrison, to ask him to tear the treaty, and to obliterate the landmark; but I would say to him, Sir, you have liberty to return to your own country. The being within, communing with past ages, tells me, that once, nor until lately, there was no white man on this continent. That it then all belonged to red men, children of the same parents, placed on it by the Great Spirit that made them, to keep it, to traverse it, to enjoy its productions, and to fill it with the same race. Once a happy race. Since made miserable by the white people, who are never contented, but always encroaching. The way, and the only way to check and stop this evil, is, for all the red men to unite in claiming a common and equal right in the land, as it was at first, and should be yet; for it never was divided, but belongs to all, for the use of each. That no part has a right to sell, even to each other, much less to strangers; those who want all, and will not do with less. The white people have no right to take the land from the Indians, because they had it first; it is theirs.

They may sell, but all must join. Any sale not made by all is not valid. The late sale is bad. It was made by a part only. Part do not know how to sell. It requires all to make a bargain for all. All red men have equal rights to the unoccupied land. The right of occupancy is as good in one place as in another. There cannot be two occupations in the same place. The first excludes all others. It is not so in hunting or travelling; for there the same ground will serve many, as they may follow each other all day; but the camp is stationary, and that is occupancy. It belongs to the first who sits down on his blanket or skins, which he has thrown upon the ground, and till he leaves it no other has a right.

Source: Samuel G. Drake, *The Book of the Indians* (Boston: Antiquarian Bookstore, 1841), 121.

II. Black Hawk, Surrender Speech, 1832

Introduction

The end of the War of 1812 and the 1824 completion of the Erie Canal caused settlers to pour into the Midwest. The influx of American settlers forced Native Americans to cede land that had once been promised to them in perpetuity and pushed the Sauk and Fox across the Mississippi River. In 1831, Black Hawk led Sauk warriors, former allies of the British in the War of 1812, across the river into Illinois and burned a number of settlers' houses. Black Hawk returned a year later with some 2,000 men, women, and children to reclaim his people's former territory in western Illinois. The authorities sent regular army troops and militia to eject the Black Hawk's people from Illinois. After a series of battles, the American force decisively defeated Black Hawk on August 2, 1832. The Black Hawk

War lasted only 15 weeks but inflicted hundreds of Indian casualties and brought about the demise of both the Sauk and Fox tribes as political and military forces in the Midwest. Black Hawk delivered this address at the time of his surrender, stating that he was satisfied because he had fulfilled his duty to resist and avenge white encroachment. He spent a year in prison after his capture, and upon his release, he and his fellow captives traveled around the country as something of a public attraction. Black Hawk dictated his autobiography to an interpreter in 1833, and it became a best seller.

Primary Source

Black-Hawk is an Indian. He has done nothing for which an Indian ought to be ashamed. He has fought for his countrymen, the squaws and papooses, against white men, who came, year after year, to cheat them and take away their lands. You know the cause of our making war. It is known to all white men. They ought to be ashamed of it. The white men despise the Indians, and drive them from their homes. But the Indians are not deceitful. The white men speak bad of the Indian, and look at him spitefully. But the Indian does not tell lies; Indians do not steal.

An Indian, who is as bad as the white men, could not live in our nation; he would be put to death, and eat up by the wolves. The white men are bad schoolmasters; they carry false looks, and deal in false actions; they smile in the face of the poor Indian to cheat him; they shake them by the hand to gain their confidence, to make them drunk, to deceive them, and ruin our wives. We told them to let us alone, and keep away from us; but they followed on, and beset our paths, and they coiled themselves among us, like the snake. They poisoned us by their touch. We were not safe. We lived in danger. We were becoming like them, hypocrites and liars, adulterers, lazy drones, all talkers, and no workers.

We looked up to the Great Spirit. We went to our great father. We were encouraged. His great council gave us fair words and big promises; but we got no satisfaction. Things were growing worse. There were no deer in the forest. The opossum and beaver were fled; the springs were drying up, and our squaws and papooses without victuals to keep them from starving; we called a great council, and built a large fire. The spirit of our fathers arose and spoke to us to avenge our wrongs or die. We all spoke before the council fire. It was warm and pleasant. We set up the war-whoop, and dug up the tomahawk; our knives were ready, and the heart of Black-Hawk swelled high in his bosom, when he led his warriors to battle. He is satisfied. He will go to the world of spirits contented. He has done his duty. His father will meet him there, and commend him.

Source: Samuel G. Drake, *The Aboriginal Races of North America* (Philadelphia: Charles Desilver, 1859), 657.

12. John Ross, Letter to Brigadier General Winfield Scott about the Cherokee Removal, August 30, 1838

Introduction

President Andrew Jackson's December 1829 message to Congress set forth his justification for removing the Indians of the southeastern states to what was deemed Indian Territory (present-day Oklahoma). After bitter debates in Congress and in the press, Congress passed the Indian Removal Act in May 1830. The act authorized the government to make treaties with the southeastern tribes and appropriated $500,000 to compensate Native Americans for any houses and other improvements they had made to their land. Tribes were promised perpetual sovereignty over their new territory. When the Cherokees rejected the government's offer, President Jackson ordered the Cherokee Nation off its land in Georgia in 1833. Although the tribe fought against the order in the U.S. Court system, it was eventually forced to comply. Brigadier General Winfield Scott was placed in charge of the massive 1838 removal of some 15,000 Cherokees. In this letter to Scott, Cherokee Chief John Ross reports that on the very eve of their departure, the first contingent of Cherokees has discovered that their property has not yet been valued. The Cherokees feared, with good reason, that their property would not be fairly valued by government agents once the owners departed and that the government would neglect to compensate them at all.

Primary Source

TO WINFIELD SCOTT

Cherokee Agency Aug. 30th 1838

Sir

On the 24th Inst. I had the honor to receive through your aid de camp colo. H. B. Shaw, a communication in reference to the claims of the cherokees presented to you.

In that communication you were pleased to direct, Or "advise, that the claimants should go in person to the commissioners." That course has been taken, by many of Our people in pursuance of your advice, and some difficulties having arisen, I deem it my duty respectfully to present them to you.

In the extract of a letter from the commissioners, with which I am favored, in your communication, it is said, that "All these improvements have been, long since, valued by the Agents of the Government, and placed on the register of payments." But on application made by the cherokees of the first detachment, just on the eve of starting to the West, it was discovered that many of their improvements have not been so valued. The cherokees presented a Statement of their claims accompanyed by ample proof of their correctness, but the commissioners rejected them and said they will send Agents to value the places. It will readily be perceived, that embarrassment and confusion and loss, must result from such a course. The cherokee owners of the improvements being already organized for emigration and just on the eve of starting, with their Detachments, would not feel satisfied that after their departure, agents should go out alone, without any person to point out the property to be valued. nor would they feel satisfied, even were there a prospect that the property could be correctly ascertained; that the amount of valuation, should in accordance with the system heretofore pursued by those Gentlemen, be placed on the registers of payment and left open to the depredations of exparte claims often fictitious against the real owner of the same name: and as was the case affording no security whatever, that the owner would ever receive payment for his property such having been the fact in the cases of several applicants for payment. And if, for the information of the valuing agents, the cherokees were now allowed to go to every part of the country to point our their property, the progress of emigration would be retarded and derangements in the Detachments would in all probability ensue. I beg leave, with submission, to call your attention to the manner in which payments have been made to those who have made application to the commissioners. One half only of the amount has been paid and that, in funds, which will be uncurrent as soon as they pass the limits of tennessee.

I wish also, very respectfully to say, that the cherokee people have claims against the U. States for spoliations of various kinds, the presentation of which for adjudication, has been prevented, by the pressure of their preparatory arrangements for removal.

And with regard to the observation in the commissioners letter, in reference to the valuations made by their Agents, "that those, thus made, are far more liberal than Mr. Ross and his associates have made them," I have only to observe, that we have made no assessments at all but merely described the property, so that the principles of appraisement, recognized by the Govt. might be applied to them.

Source: Gary E. Moulton, ed., *The Papers of Chief John Ross*, Vol. 1 (Norman: University of Oklahoma Press, 1985), 665–666.

13. Little Crow, Speech on the Eve of the Minnesota Sioux Uprising, August 18, 1862

Introduction

In 1851, the Sioux had signed treaties ceding land in exchange for money and goods. Widespread treaty violations, official corruption, and nonpayment of promised annuities led to the Minnesota (Santee) Sioux Uprising of 1862, one of the bloodiest Indian wars in American history. The uprising began at a time when U.S. Army regulars had been withdrawn from the western territories to prosecute the American Civil War (1861–1865) in the East. Multiple bands of Sioux joined forces to attack and kill several hundred white settlers in August 1862. In this speech before the attack, chief Little Crow announces his intention of going to war despite the near certainty of defeat. Noting that whites are fighting among themselves, he predicts that they will nevertheless defeat the Sioux. The task of retaliation for the Sioux attack fell to a volunteer brigade that went on campaign and captured more than 1,000 Sioux in a matter of weeks. In a single day in a series of brief show trials, military tribunals condemned 303 Sioux to death. President Abraham Lincoln commuted most of the sentences: 38 Sioux were hanged in a mass execution on December 26, 1862, while the rest were imprisoned for four years, during which one in three of them died. Minnesota's white population resented Lincoln's intervention. The Sioux reservations were confiscated, and the Sioux were exiled to Nebraska. Little Crow and a small band of his followers escaped to Canada. When Little Crow returned to Minnesota the following summer, a settler shot and killed him.

Primary Source

Taoyateduta is not a coward, and he is not a fool! When did he run away from his enemies? When did he leave his braves behind him on the warpath and turn back to his tepee? When you ran away from your enemies, he walked behind on your trail with his face to the Ojibways and covered your backs as a she-bear covers her cubs! Is Taoyateduta without scalps? Look at his war feathers! Behold the scalp locks of your enemies hanging there on his lodge-poles! Do they call him a coward? Taoyateduta is not a coward, and he is not a fool. Braves, you are like little children: you know not what you are doing.

You are full of the white man's devil water. You are like dogs in the Hot Moon when they run mad and snap at their own shadows. We are only little herds of buffalo left scattered; the great herds that once covered the prairies are no more. See!—the white men are like the locusts when they fly so thick that the whole sky is a snowstorm.

You may kill one—two—ten; yes, as many as the leaves in the forest yonder, and their brothers will not miss them. Kill one—two—ten, and ten times ten will come to kill you. Count your fingers all day long and white men with guns in their hands will come faster than you can count.

Yes, they fight among themselves—away off. Do you hear the thunder of their big guns? no; it would take you two moons to run down to where they are fighting, and all the way your path would be among white soldiers as thick as tamaracks in the swamps of the Ojibways. Yes, they fight among themselves, but if you strike at them they will all turn on you and devour you and your women and little children just as the locusts in their time fall on the trees and devour all the leaves in one day.

You are fools. You cannot see the face of your chief; your eyes are full of smoke. You cannot hear his voice; your ears are full of roaring waters. Braves, you are little children—you are fools. You will die like the rabbits when the hungry wolves hunt them in the Hard Moon.

Taoyateduta is not a coward: he will die with you.

Source: Hanford Lennox Gordon, *Indian Legends and Other Poems* (Salem, MA: Salem Press Company, 1910), 382–383.

14. U.S. Congress, Joint Commission on the Conduct of the War, Report on the Sand Creek Massacre, 1865 [Excerpts]

Introduction

The brutal Sand Creek Massacre of November 29, 1864, saw the murder of approximately 150 Cheyenne and allied Native Americans, most of them women and children. Although some Cheyenne bands still actively resisted American settlement in Colorado, the natives at Sand Creek had previously surrendered their weapons and cooperated with the U.S. government. Local authorities had led them to believe that they were under U.S. protection. Colonel John M. Chivington planned and led the attack, ordering his Colorado volunteers to slaughter every Indian in the Sand Creek village and to take no prisoners. At first Chivington reported victory against a well-armed enemy, but eyewitness accounts of atrocities— including soldiers displaying Indian body parts as trophies—soon surfaced and led to a congressional investigation in 1865. The Joint Committee on the Conduct of the War, whose conclusions are excerpted here, heard testimony about Chivington's calculated cruelty, ruled the attack a massacre, and called for charges against those responsible. No charges were ever brought. The entire history of warfare against Native Americans on the American frontier included indiscriminate slaughter of friendly natives by whites. Such episodes invariably turned friend into foe and prolonged wars. The massacre at Sand Creek prolonged war with the Cheyennes and their allies for years to come.

Primary Source

In the summer of 1864, Governor [John] Evans, of Colorado territory, as acting superintendent of Indian Affairs, sent notice to the various bands and tribes of Indians within his jurisdiction that such as desired to be considered friendly to the whites should at once repair to the nearest military post in order to be protected from the soldiers who were to take the field against the hostile Indians.

About the close of the summer, some Cheyenne Indians, in the neighborhood of the Smoke Hills, sent word to Major [Edward W.] Wynkoop, the commandant of the post of Fort Lyon, that they . . . were willing to deliver up, some white captives they had purchased of other Indians. Major Wynkoop, with a force of over 100 men, visited these Indians and received the white captives. On his return he was accompanied by a number of the chiefs and leading men . . . to visit Denver for the purpose of conferring with the authorities there in regard to keeping peace. Among them were Black Kettle and White Antelope of the Cheyennes, and some chiefs of the Arapahoes. . . . these chiefs stated that they were very friendly to the whites, and always had been, and that they desired peace. Governor Evans and Colonel Chivington, the commander of that military district, advised them to repair to Fort Lyon and submit to whatever terms the military commander there should impose. This was done by the Indians, who were treated somewhat as prisoners of war, receiving rations, and being obliged to remain within certain bounds.

. . .

A northern band of the Cheyennes, known as the Dog Soldiers, had been guilty of acts of hostility; but all the testimony goes to prove that they had no connexion with Black Kettle's band, but acted in spite of his authority and influence. Black Kettle and his band denied all connexion with or responsibility for the Dog Soldiers, and Left Hand and his band of Arapahoes were equally friendly.

These Indians, at the suggestion of Governor Evans and Colonel Chivington, repaired to Fort Lyon and placed themselves under the protection of Major Wynkoop. They were led to believe that they were regarded in the light of friendly Indians, and would be treated as such so long as they conducted themselves quietly.

The treatment extended to those Indians by Major Wynkoop does not seem to have satisfied those in authority there, and for some cause, which does not appear, he was removed, and Major Scott J. Anthony was assigned to the command of Fort Lyon; but even Major Anthony seems to have found it difficult at first to pursue any different course toward the Indians he found there. . . . Major Anthony having demanded their arms, which they surrendered to him, they conducted themselves quietly, and in every way manifested a disposition to remain at peace with the whites. . . . They were called together and told that rations could no longer be issued to them, and they had better go where they could obtain subsistence by hunting. At the suggestion of Major Anthony (and from one in his position a suggestion was the equivalent to a command) these Indians went to a place on Sand Creek, about thirty-five miles from Fort Lyon, and there established their camp, their arms being restored to them. He told them that he then had no authority to make peace with them; but in case he received such authority he would inform them of it. . . .

. . . Everything practicable seems to have been done to remove from the minds of the Indians any fear of approaching danger; and when Colonel Chivington commenced his movement he took all of the precautions in his power to prevent these Indians learning of his approach. For some days all travel on that route was forcibly stopped by him, not even the mail being allowed to pass. On the morning of 28 November he appeared at Fort Lyon with over 700 mounted men and two pieces of artillery. One of his first acts was to throw a guard around the post to prevent any one from leaving it. At this place Major Anthony joined him with 125 men and two pieces of artillery.

That night, the entire party started from Fort Lyon, and, by a forced march, arrived at the Indian camp, on Sand Creek, shortly after daybreak. The Indian camp consisted of about 100 lodges of Cheyennes, under Black Kettle, and from 8 to 10 lodges of Arapahoes under Left Hand. It is estimated that each lodge contained five or more persons, and that more than one-half were women and children.

Upon observing the approach of the soldiers, Black Kettle, the head chief, ran up to the top of his lodge an American flag, which had been presented to him some years before by commissioner [of Indian Affairs Alfred B.] Greenwood, with a small white flag under it, as he had been advised to do in case he met with any troops on the prairies. . . .

And then the scene of murder and barbarity began—men, women, and children were indiscriminately slaughtered. In a few minutes all the Indians were flying over the plain in terror and confusion. A few who endeavored to hide themselves under the bank of the creek were surrounded and shot down in cold blood, offering but feeble resistance. From the sucking babe to the old warrior, all who were overtaken were deliberately murdered. Not content with killing women and children, who were incapable of offering any resistance, the soldiers indulged in acts of barbarity of the most revolting character; such, it is to be hoped, as never before disgraced the acts of men claiming to be civilized. No attempt was made by the officers to restrain the savage cruelty of the men under their command, but they stood by and witnessed these acts without one word of reproof, if they did not incite their commission. For more than two hours the work of murder and barbarity was continued, until more than one hundred dead bodies, three fourths of them women and children, lay on the plain as evidences of the fiendish malignity and cruelty of the officers who had sedulously and carefully plotted the massacre, and of the soldiers who had so faithfully acted out the spirit of their officers.

It is difficult to believe that beings in the form of men, and disgracing the uniform of United States soldiers and officers, could commit or countenance the commission of such acts of cruelty and barbarity as are detailed in the testimony, but which your committee will not specify in the report. . . . the governor in a proclamation calls upon all, "either individually or in such parties as they may organize," "to kill and destroy as enemies of the country, wherever they may be found, all such hostile Indians," authorizing them to "hold to their own private use and benefit all the property of said hostile Indians that they may capture." . . . His testimony before your committee was characterized by such prevarication and shuffling . . . for the evident purpose of avoiding admission that he was fully aware that the Indians massacred so brutally at Sand Creek, were then, and had been, actuated by the most friendly feelings towards the whites . . .

The testimony of Major Anthony . . . is sufficient of itself to show how unprovoked and unwarranted was this massacre. He testifies that he found these Indians in the neighborhood of Fort Lyon when he assumed command of that post; that they professed their friendliness to the whites, and their willingness to do whatever he demanded of them; that they delivered their arms up to him; and they went to and encamped upon the place designated by him; that they gave him information from time to time of acts of hostility which were meditated by other and hostile bands, and in every way conducted themselves properly and peaceably, and yet he says it was fear and not principle which prevented his killing them while they were completely in his power. And when Colonel Chivington appeared at Fort Lyon, on his mission of murder and barbarity, Major Anthony made haste to accompany him with men and artillery . . .

As to Colonel Chivington, your committee can hardly find fitting terms to describe his conduct. Wearing the uniform of the United States, which should be the emblem of justice and humanity; holding the important position of commander of a military district, and therefore having the honor of the government to that extent in his keeping, he deliberately and executed a foul and dastardly massacre which would have disgraced the veriest savage among those who were the victims of his cruelty. Having full knowledge of their friendly character, having himself been instrumental to some extent in placing them in their position of fancied security, he took advantage of their inapprehension and defenceless condition to gratify the worst passions that ever cursed the heart of man. It is thought by some that desire for political preferment prompted him to this cowardly act; that he supposed that by pandering to the inflamed passions of an excited population he could recommend himself to their regard and consideration. Others think it was to avoid being sent where there was more of danger and hard service to be performed; that he was willing to get up a show of hostility on the part of the Indians by committing himself acts which savages themselves would never premeditate. Whatever may have been his motive, it is to be hoped that the authority of this government will never again be disgraced by acts such as he and those acting with him have been guilty of committing.

There were hostile Indians not far distant, against which Colonel Chivington could have led the force under his command. . . . It was not to be expected that they could be surprised as easily as those on Sand Creek;

and the warriors among them were almost, if not quite, as numerous as the soldiers under the control of Colonel Chivington. Whatever influence this may have had upon Colonel Chivington, the truth is that he surprised and murdered in cold blood, the unsuspecting men, women, and children on Sand Creek, who had every reason to believe they were under the protection of the United States authorities, and then returned to Denver and boasted of the brave deeds he and the men under his command had performed.

. . .

In conclusion, your committee are of the opinion that for the purpose of vindicating the cause of justice and upholding the honor of the nation, prompt and energetic measures should be at once taken to remove from office those who have thus disgraced the government by whom they are employed, and to punish, as their crimes deserve, those who have been guilty of these brutal and cowardly acts.

Source: United States Congress, Senate, "Report of the Secretary of War, Sand Creek Massacre," Senate Executive Document no. 26, 39th cong., 2nd Sess., 1867.

15. Ulysses S. Grant, Peace Policy, December 5, 1870

Introduction
After the American Civil War (1861–1865), the U.S. government considered new approaches to pacifying the Indians and making the West safe for white settlement. Ely Parker, a Seneca and an aide to Ulysses S. Grant, emphasized secure boundaries for Indian reservations and prompt payment of promised annuities to encourage Native Americans to take up agriculture. When Grant became president of the United States in 1869, he appointed Parker commissioner of Indian affairs, the first Native American to hold that office. Parker was responsible for designing and implementing Grant's peace policy, which Grant described in this excerpt from his 1870 message to Congress. Many Indian agencies had been staffed by political appointees whose corruption disgraced the government. Their diversion of goods and money intended for Indians had made reservation life one of deprivation and misery, forcing a return to hunting and raiding. Under the new policy, the government appointed Christian missionaries who, it was hoped, would be honest, would look after the Indians' spiritual and physical well-being, and would gently guide them to assimilate into white society. The displaced agents and disgruntled army officers objected to the loss of authority and drove Parker from office with false accusations of corruption. Interdenominational turf battles and overemphasis on religion by missionaries at the expense of material well-being also helped to defeat the peace policy.

Primary Source
Reform in the management of Indian affairs has received the special attention of the Administration from its inauguration to the present day. The experiment of making it a missionary work was tried with a few agencies given to the denomination of Friends, and has been found to work most advantageously. All agencies and superintendencies not so disposed of were given to officers of the Army. The act of congress reducing the Army renders Army officers ineligible for civil positions. Indian agencies being civil offices, I determined to give all the agencies to such religious denominations as had heretofore established missionaries among the Indians, and perhaps to some other denominations who would undertake the work on the same terms; that is, as a

missionary work. The societies selected are allowed to name their own agents, subject to the approval of the Executive, and are expected to watch over them and aid them as missionaries, to christianize and civilize the Indian, and to train him in the arts of peace. The Government watches over the official acts of these agents, and requires of them as strict an accountability as if they were appointed in any other manner. I entertain the confident hope that the policy now pursued will, in a few years, bring all the Indians upon reservations, where they will live in houses, have school-houses and churches, and will be pursuing peaceful and self-sustaining avocations, and where they may be visited by the law abiding white man with the same impunity that he now visits the civilized white settlements. I call your special attention to the report of the commissioner of Indian Affairs for full information on this subject.

Source: Edward McPherson, *A Handbook of Politics for 1872* (Washington, DC: Philp & Solomons, 1872), 21.

16. John G. Bourke, The Use of Apache Scouts, 1873–1886

Introduction

George Crook (1828–1890), a Union general in the American Civil War (1861–1865), earned a reputation as an effective Indian fighter in the postwar decades. He assumed command of the Department of Arizona in 1871. John G. Bourke (1843–1896), author of the memoir excerpted here, was a cavalry captain who served as Crook's aide-de-camp from 1870 to 1886. Bourke describes Crook's employment of Apache scouts, an innovative strategy that brought him victory in the Apache campaign of 1872–1873. Until he recruited Indian scouts in autumn 1872, Crook's troopers had been unsuccessfully pursuing the fast-moving Apaches after their hit-and-run raids. The scouts located the Apaches in two of their strongholds, the troopers surprised them there, and Crook received the surrender of more than 2,000 Apaches in 1873. On Crook's recommendation, 10 of his scouts received the Medal of Honor. In 1875, Crook was transferred to command of the Department of the Platte and fought against the Sioux. He returned to his Arizona command in 1882. Although Crook brought many of the Apaches onto reservations, Geronimo remained at large. Arizona settlers complained that Crook was too sympathetic to Indians. Frustrated by the lack of government support, Crook asked to be reassigned in 1886 and was replaced by General Nelson A. Miles. Crook spent his remaining years advocating for Indian rights.

Primary Source

The presence of the Indian scouts saved the white soldiers a great deal of extra fatigue, for the performance of which the Apaches were better qualified. It was one of the fundamental principles upon which General Crook conducted all his operations, to enlist as many of the Indians as could be induced to serve as scouts, because by this means he not only subtracted a considerable element from those in hostility and received hostages, as it were, for the better behavior of his scouts' kinsmen, but he removed from the shoulders of his men an immense amount of arduous and disagreeable work, and kept them fresh for any emergency that might arise. The Apaches were kept constantly out on the flanks, under the white guides, and swept the country of all hostile bands. The white troops followed upon the heels of the Indians, but at a short distance in the rear, as the native scouts were better acquainted with all the tricks of their calling, and familiar with every square acre of the territory. The longer we knew the Apache scouts, the better we liked them. They were wilder and more suspicious than the Pimas and Maricopas, but far more reliable, and endowed with a greater amount of courage and daring. I have never known an officer whose experience entitled his opinion to the slightest consideration, who did not believe as I do on this subject. On this scout captain Hamilton was compelled to send back his Maricopas as worthless; this was before he joined Brown at MacDowell.

Source: John G. Bourke, *On the Border with Crook* (New York: Scribner, 1902), 202–203.

17. Red Horse, Account of the Battle of the Little Bighorn, 1876 [Excerpts]

Introduction

Angered by white encroachment and starving without promised food rations, Indians of the northern Plains defied government orders and left their reservations. In 1876, Lieutenant General Philip Sheridan ordered three converging columns to move against the Sioux and their allies. On June 25, 1876, Lieutenant Colonel George Armstrong Custer (1839–1876) and his 7th Cavalry discovered the major Sioux encampment on Little Bighorn River. Custer did not realize how large a force he confronted and, without waiting for more troops to arrive, ordered Major Marcus Reno and his detachment to charge. As the outnumbered Reno was fought to a standstill, Custer's force charged from another direction. Custer and his entire force, more than 200 men, died in the ensuing combat. The nation was shocked by the defeat. Custer's judgment and Reno's

actions came under scrutiny, but most important, the army turned its full might against the northern Plains tribes. In 1881, Red Horse, a Sioux war chief, gave this eyewitness account to army physician Charles McChesney. At McChesney's request, Red Horse created 42 illustrations. There is some agreement between Red Horse's account of the battle and the account by army interpreter Frederick Frances Girard. Red Horse's account (translated from sign language) and pictures were eventually published in a congressional document as part of a report on Plains Indian language.

Primary Source

Five springs ago I, with many Sioux Indians, took down and packed up our tipis and moved from Cheyenne River to the Rosebud River, where we camped a few days; then took down and packed up our lodges and moved to the Little Bighorn River and pitched our lodges with the large camp of Sioux.

. . .

I was a Sioux chief in the council lodge. My lodge was pitched in the center of the camp. The day of the attack I and four women were a short distance from the camp digging wild turnips. Suddenly one of the women attracted my attention to a cloud of dust rising a short distance from camp. I soon saw that the soldiers were charging the camp. To the camp I and the women ran. When I arrived a person told me to hurry to the council lodge. The soldiers charged so quickly we could not talk [council]. We came out of the council lodge and talked in all directions. The Sioux mount horses, take guns, and go fight the soldiers. Women and children mount horses and go, meaning to get out of the way.

Among the soldiers was an officer who rode a horse with four white feet. [This officer was evidently Capt. French, Seventh

Cavalry.] The Sioux have for a long time fought many brave men of different people, but the Sioux say this officer was the bravest man they had ever fought. I don't know whether this was Gen. Custer or not. Many of the Sioux men that I hear talking tell me it was. I saw this officer in the fight many times, but did not see his body. It has been told me that he was killed by a Santee Indian, who took his horse. This officer wore a large-brimmed hat and a deerskin coat. This officer saved the lives of many soldiers by turning his horse and covering the retreat. Sioux say this officer was the bravest man they ever fought. I saw two officers looking alike, both having long yellowish hair.

Before the attack the Sioux were camped on the Rosebud river. Sioux moved down a river running into the Little Bighorn river, crossed the Little Bighorn river, and camped on its west bank.

This day [day of attack] a Sioux man started to go to Red Cloud agency, but when he had gone a short distance from camp he saw a cloud of dust rising and turned back and said he thought a herd of buffalo was coming near the village.

The day was hot. In a short time the soldiers charged the camp. [This was Maj. Reno's battalion of the Seventh Cavalry.] The soldiers came on the trail made by the Sioux camp in moving, and crossed the Little Bighorn River above where the Sioux crossed, and attacked the lodges of the Uncpapas, farthest up the river. The women and children ran down the Little Bighorn River a short distance into a ravine. The soldiers set fire to the lodges. All the Sioux now charged the soldiers and drove them in confusion across the Little Bighorn River, which was very rapid, and several soldiers were drowned in it. On a hill the soldiers stopped and the Sioux surrounded them. A Sioux man came and said that a different

party of Soldiers had all the women and children prisoners. Like a whirlwind the word went around, and the Sioux all heard it and left the soldiers on the hill and went quickly to save the women and children.

From the hill that the soldiers were on to the place where the different soldiers [by this term Red-Horse always means the battalion immediately commanded by General Custer, his mode of distinction being that they were a different body from that first encountered] were seen was level ground with the exception of a creek. Sioux thought the soldiers on the hill [i.e., Reno's battalion] would charge them in rear, but when they did not the Sioux thought the soldiers on the hill were out of cartridges. As soon as we had killed all the different soldiers the Sioux all went back to kill the soldiers on the hill. All the Sioux watched around the hill on which were the soldiers until a Sioux man came and said many walking soldiers were coming near. The coming of the walking soldiers was the saving of the soldiers on the hill. Sioux can not fight the walking soldiers [infantry], being afraid of them, so the Sioux hurriedly left.

The soldiers charged the Sioux camp about noon. The soldiers were divided, one party charging right into the camp. After driving these soldiers across the river, the Sioux charged the different soldiers [i.e., Custer's] below, and drive them in confusion; these soldiers became foolish, many throwing away their guns and raising their hands, saying, "Sioux, pity us; take us prisoners." The Sioux did not take a single soldier prisoner, but killed all of them; none were left alive for even a few minutes. these different soldiers discharged their guns but little. I took a gun and two belts off two dead soldiers; out of one belt two cartridges were gone, out of the other five.

The Sioux took the guns and cartridges off the dead soldiers and went to the hill on which the soldiers were, surrounded and fought them with the guns and cartridges of the dead soldiers. Had the soldiers not divided I think they would have killed many Sioux. The different soldiers [i.e., Custer's battalion] that the Sioux killed made five brave stands. Once the Sioux charged right in the midst of the different soldiers and scattered them all, fighting among the soldiers hand to hand.

One band of soldiers was in rear of the Sioux. When this band of soldiers charged, the Sioux fell back, and the Sioux and the soldiers stood facing each other. Then all the Sioux became brave and charged the soldiers. The Sioux went but a short distance before they separated and surrounded the soldiers. I could see the officers riding in front of the soldiers and hear them shooting. Now the Sioux had many killed. The soldiers killed 136 and wounded 160 Sioux. The Sioux killed all these different soldiers in the ravine.

The soldiers charged the Sioux camp farthest up the river. A short time after the different soldiers charged the village below. While the different soldiers and Sioux were fighting together the Sioux chief said, "Sioux men, go watch soldiers on the hill and prevent their joining the different soldiers." The Sioux men took the clothing off the dead and dressed themselves in it. Among the soldiers were white men who were not soldiers. The Sioux dressed in the soldiers' and white men's clothing fought the soldiers on the hill.

The banks of the Little Bighorn River were high, and the Sioux killed many of the soldiers while crossing. The soldiers on the hill dug up the ground [i.e., made earthworks], and the soldiers and Sioux fought at long range, sometimes the Sioux charging close up. The fight continued at long range until a Sioux man saw the walking soldiers coming. When the walking soldiers came near the Sioux became afraid and ran away.

Source: J. W. Powell, *Tenth Annual Report of the Bureau of Ethnology*, 52d Congress, 2d Session, House Doc. 116 (Washington, DC: U.S. Government Printing Office, 1893), 564–566.

18. Chief Joseph, Surrender Speech, October 15, 1877

Introduction

American immigrants began surging into the Pacific Northwest in 1843. Oregon Territory was officially established in 1848, and Washington became a separate territory in 1853. The Indians who lived in the northwestern territories numbered about 42,000 and belonged to several dozen tribes. Many tried to resist the growing population of American settlers, and a state of nearly continuous warfare went on until 1858, when most of the Indians of the northwest were confined to reservations. The Nez Perces, however, maintained friendly relations with the Americans. But in a decision typical of the time, U.S. government authorities decided to remove the Nez Perces from their home reservation in Washington and Oregon to a reservation in Idaho in order to make way for white settlement. While some Nez Perces complied, Chief Joseph and his people refused to move. The army was ordered to remove them by force, which led to war in 1877. The army pursued the band for some 1,500 miles across the mountains. Over the course of four months, Chief Joseph's band of Nez Perces conducted guerrilla warfare, striking and then melting into the wilderness. Their mobility was limited by the presence of women and children. Meanwhile, the army used the telegraph to quickly summon reinforcements. Chief Joseph surrendered in Montana on October 15, 1877, with this brief speech.

Primary Source

At his surrender in the Bear Paw Mountains, 1877

Tell General Howard that I know his heart. What he told me before I have in my heart. I am tired of fighting. Our chiefs are killed. Looking Glass is dead, Tu-hul-hil-sote is dead. The old men are all dead. It is the young men who now say yes or no. He who led the young men is dead. It is cold and we have no blankets. The little children are freezing to death. My people—some of them have run away to the hills and have no blankets and no food. No one knows where they are—perhaps freezing to death. I want to have time to look for my children and see how many of them I can find. Maybe I shall find them among the dead. Hear me, my chiefs, my heart is sick and sad. From where the sun now stands I will fight no more against the white man.

Source: Norman B. Wood, *Lives of Famous Indian Chiefs* (Aurora, IL: American Indian Historical Publishing Company, 1906), 520.

19. Sitting Bull, Speech on Keeping Treaties, 1890

Introduction

Sitting Bull (ca. 1831–1890), a renowned Sioux warrior and chief from the mid-1860s until his death, had led his people and the allied Cheyennes and Arapahos in their steadfast resistance to white encroachment on the northern Plains. Despite military victories, starvation forced his surrender in 1881. This excerpt is taken from a speech he made in 1890 in which he explains that he will not cede any more land to the United States. The Sioux had embraced the rapidly spreading Ghost Dance religion with particular fervor. The religion promised that the white man would disappear, the buffalo would return, dead Indians would be resurrected, and Indians would be restored to their land and their traditional way of life. The U.S. agent at the Pine Ridge Reservation asked for military protection, fearing that the religious fervor would lead to a violent uprising. Concerned about Sitting Bull's influence, the army ordered his arrest. On December 15, 1890, Sitting Bull was shot and killed while his followers tried to prevent his arrest. His people fled the reservation but returned to surrender two weeks later. The confrontation the next day at Wounded Knee marked the end of the Indian Wars.

Primary Source

What treaty that the whites have kept has the red man broken? not one. What treaty that the whites ever made with us red men have they kept? not one. When I was a boy the Sioux owned the world. The sun rose and set in their lands. They sent 10,000 horsemen to battle. Where are the warriors to-day? Who slew them? Where are our lands? Who owns them? What white man can say I ever stole his lands or a penny of his money? Yet they say I am a thief. What white woman, however lonely, was ever when a captive insulted by me? Yet they say I am a bad Indian. What white man has ever seen me drunk? Who has ever come to me hungry and gone unfed? Who has ever seen me beat my wives or abuse my children? What law have I broken? Is it wrong for me to love my own? Is it wicked in me because my skin is red; because I am a Sioux; because I was born where my fathers lived; because I would die for my people and my country?

Source: W. Fletcher Johnson, *The Red Record of the Sioux: Life of Sitting Bull* (Philadelphia, PA: Edgewood Publishing Company, 1891), 201.

Chronology

January 13, 1493

In perhaps the first clash between Europeans and natives in the New World, Christopher Columbus and his ships the *Niña* and *Pinta* are in Samaná Bay in the eastern part of Hispaniola (present-day Dominican Republic) when they encounter a Carib war party. After uneasy negotiations, fighting occurs when more than 50 Caribs attack a Spanish boat party of 7 men. The Spanish weapons intimidate and scatter the Caribs.

April 21, 1513

Having discovered Florida on March 27, 1513, Spanish conquistador Juan Ponce de León comes ashore on April 2, 1513, and, despite his efforts to establish friendly contact with the inhabitants, clashes with a party of Ais natives near the mouth of the Saint Lucie River. Two Spaniards are wounded, but a native is taken prisoner to be trained as an interpreter.

May 30, 1539–September 10, 1543

Spanish conquistador Hernando de Soto, newly named Spanish governor of Cuba, lands in Florida with 513 soldiers and 337 horses to begin its conquest. Frequent clashes occur between the Spaniards and natives as de Soto wanders across much of the present-day southeastern United States.

February 1540–October 1542

Spaniard Francisco Vázquez de Coronado leads an expedition north from Mexico into New Mexico searching for the legendary Seven Cities of Cibola, reportedly rich in gold and other treasures. Coronado reaches the Zuni village of Hawikuh, supposedly one of the Seven Cities, and captures it on July 7, 1540. Hawikuh and the other supposed Cities of Gold turn out to be simple villages devoid of riches. Coronado passes through present-day New Mexico, Texas, and Oklahoma into central Kansas before admitting defeat and returning to Mexico.

January 21–23, 1599

Resentful of harsh treatment by the Spanish, the Indians of Acoma Pueblo in New Mexico revolt. Spanish reinforcements scale the mesa and launch a surprise night attack. The following day, the Spaniards kill approximately 800 natives.

July 1608

French explorer Samuel de Champlain establishes a trading post at Quebec on the Saint Lawrence River. Allying themselves with the Algonquins, the Hurons, and the Montaignais, the French drive the Iroquois from the Saint Lawrence Valley.

August 9, 1610–April 5, 1614
In the First Anglo-Powhatan War, fighting occurs between the English colonists at Jamestown and Native Americans of the Powhatan Confederacy.

March 22, 1622
In widespread coordinated attacks, Native Americans attack the English at Jamestown, Virginia, killing 347 settlers and initiating the Second Anglo-Powhatan War (1622–1632). The colonists retaliate and in 1623, under promise of peace talks, lure 250 natives to their deaths.

July 1636–September 1638
The Pequot War takes place between the Pequots of the lower Connecticut River Valley and the English colonies of Massachusetts Bay and Connecticut. As a result of the fighting, the Pequots are destroyed as an independent people, and most are absorbed by other tribes.

June 1641–1701
The Beaver Wars, also known as the Iroquois Wars and the French and Iroquois Wars, take place. The fighting begins with a skirmish near Trois Rivières in Canada in June 1641. The conflict pits the nations of the Iroquois Confederacy, led by the Mohawks, against the tribes of the Great Lakes area. The French also take part in the fighting against the Iroquois. In the early fighting, the Iroquois greatly expand their territory, destroying several large tribal confederacies that include the Hurons, Eries, and Susquehannocks. The Iroquois also drive other eastern tribes west of the Mississippi River. A series of setbacks follows, and in 1698, the Iroquois seek peace, increasingly seeing themselves as pawns played by the English against the French. For their part, the French are anxious to have the Iroquois as a barrier between New France and the English colonies to the south. In 1701 in Montreal, Native American chiefs, the English, and the French conclude the Grande Paix (Great Peace), bringing an end to a century of nearly continuous warfare. The Iroquois agree to stop their attacks and to allow the remaining refugees from the Great Lakes region to return to their ancestral homes in the east.

1641–1664
Persistent ill will between European settlers in New Netherland and neighboring Algonquian tribes leads to a series of wars: Kieft's War (1639–1645), the Peach War (1655), the First Esopus War (1659–1660), and the Second Esopus War (1663–1664). The outcomes largely favor the Dutch.

April 18, 1644–October 1646
In the Third Anglo-Powhatan War, Opechancanough, chief of the Pamunkeys and leader of the Powhatan Confederacy, leads an effort to drive out English colonists in Virginia. The natives kill some 400–500 colonists, but in the reprisal killings that follow, the natives again suffer disproportionately and are defeated. Opechancanough is captured in late summer 1646 and is brought to Jamestown, where he is murdered by one of his guards. His successor, Necotowance, agrees to a peace treaty in October 1646 in which the Powhatans surrender all their prisoners, firearms, and any runaway servants and agree to cede most of their remaining lands.

June 20, 1675–October 1676
King Philip's War, named for Wampanoag sachem Metacom (known to colonists as King Philip), takes place. Wampanoag warriors attack Swansea in southwestern

Plymouth Colony, and conflict quickly spreads. Metacom is killed on August 12, 1676, and many warriors surrender, although the conflict continues for several years in Maine.

1680–1690
Revolt of Pueblo Native Americans against Spanish authorities in New Mexico. The Spanish retake New Mexico in 1690, although not until 1696 do they secure a lasting peace there.

1711–1713
Encroachments by colonists and abuses by colonial traders in North Carolina lead the Tuscaroras to kill some 200 colonists and fight the English-allied Creeks and the Yamasees. The Tuscaroras surrender in March 1713.

1715–1717
The Yamasees of South Carolina, angered by settler incursions and abusive English traders, go to war. The Creeks aid the Yamasees, but South Carolinians are reinforced by North Carolina and Virginia militia and the Cherokees. Peace is concluded between the Creeks and the English in November 1717, but the Yamasees remain at war until 1728.

September 9, 1730
The beleaguered Fox tribe, after escaping a monthlong siege of Fox Fort and weeks of near starvation, encounters a combined French and Native American force and loses 200–300 warriors and 300–600 women and children.

May 28, 1754–February 10, 1763
The French and Indian War pits England and France, with their various Native American allies, against each other.

May–November 1763
Ottawa chief Pontiac rouses natives from western New York to the Illinois River and unsuccessfully besieges Fort Detroit, while natives elsewhere capture Fort Sandusky, Fort Miami, and Fort Michilimackinac, capturing a total of eight forts within a two-week span.

August 5–6, 1763
To relieve Fort Pitt, Colonel Henry Bouquet leads 400 men from Fort Niagara and is set back in the Battle of Bushy Run, although not defeated by a large force of Delawares, Wyandots, Mingos, and Shawnees. Bouquet's advance forces the natives to lift the siege of Fort Pitt.

April–October 1774
Lord Dunmore's War erupts as numbers of frontiersmen attack native settlements in the Ohio River Valley. When the natives retaliate, Pennsylvanians and Virginians manipulate events as a means of subverting the Proclamation of 1763.

October 10, 1774
Chief Cornstalk of the Shawnees leads 1,000 Shawnee, Mingo, Delaware, Wyandot, and Ottawa warriors in an attack against Colonel Andrew Lewis and 1,100 unsuspecting militiamen in the Battle of Point Pleasant. Cornstalk fails to defeat the colonists and makes peace on October 19, 1774, surrendering all claims to lands south and east of the Ohio River.

April 19, 1775–September 3, 1783
The American Revolutionary War splits Native Americans' loyalties.

October 6–8, 1778
In direct response to Mohawk chief Joseph Brant's raid on German Flats, Lieutenant

Colonel William Butler raids and destroys the towns of Unadilla and Uquaga in the Mohawk Valley.

November 11, 1778
In response to Butler's destruction of Unadilla, Loyalists and their Iroquois allies massacre 47 people and capture 71 at Cherry Valley, New York.

October 18, 1790
Americans under Josiah Harmar come upon 2,500 Indians led by Miami chief Little Turtle in Ohio and are defeated.

November 4, 1791
Several factions of different tribes unite under Miami chief Little Turtle, and the new American nation suffers its greatest defeat against Native Americans in the Battle of the Wabash.

August 20, 1794
In retaliation for the defeat at the Wabash, American forces under General Anthony Wayne defeat another tribal coalition under Shawnee chief Blue Jacket in the Battle of Fallen Timbers, effectively ending Native American resistance in the Old Northwest Territory.

August 3, 1795
The Treaty of Greenville, which is essentially negated by settlers, is signed between General Anthony Wayne and several Northwest Indian tribes. The treaty calls for Indians to cede lands in the Ohio River Valley in return for cash payments.

April 30–December 20, 1803
French emperor Napoleon I and Thomas Jefferson conclude the Louisiana Purchase, in which the United States nearly doubles its existing territory for a price of $15 million.

November 7, 1811
Indiana governor William Henry Harrison defeats a confederation under Shawnee prophet Tenskwatawa and his absent half-brother, Tecumseh, in the Battle of Tippecanoe, helping to solidify the British–Native American alliance to combat American expansion.

June 1, 1812–February 17, 1815
The War of 1812 between the United States and Great Britain is fought.

1813–1814
The Red Stick War ignites a civil war between different factions of the Creek Nation. The White Sticks favor neutrality, while the Red Sticks want to strike back against the Americans, who they believe are more dangerous than the British.

January 18, 1813
After a British victory in the Battle of Frenchtown, between 30 and 60 captives are murdered by drunken Shawnees in what is dubbed the Raisin River Massacre.

July 27, 1813
In a surprise attack, Colonel James Caller routs a Red Stick force under Peter McQueen at the Battle of Burnt Corn Creek, marking the beginning of the Creek War between the Red Sticks on one side and the United States and their White Stick Creek allies in Alabama on the other side.

August 30, 1813
A Black slave warns the garrison at Fort Mims, Alabama, about approaching hostile Indians, but he is not believed. Some 800–1,000 Red Sticks, led by William Weatherford and Josiah Francis, surprise the garrison and kill hundreds of people there.

October 5, 1813
In the Battle of the Thames, the retreating British and Shawnee warriors make a stand against the Americans but are defeated, and Tecumseh is killed.

November 9, 1813
In the Battle of Talladega, Americans encircle the Creek Red Sticks, who suffer 299 deaths. Lacking supplies, the Americans are forced to move north to Fort Schlosser.

December 23, 1813
In the Battle of Econochaca, the Americans descend on Creek holy ground, proving false the claims of Creek prophets that it is surrounded by a magic barrier that will strike dead any white who crosses. This battle has a devastating effect on Creek morale.

March 27, 1814
Tennessee militia under Major General Andrew Jackson happens upon 1,200 Red Sticks by the Tallapoosa River. In the Battle of Horseshoe Bend, 557 Creeks are killed; another 350 are taken captive.

August 9, 1814
Jackson dictates terms to the defeated Creeks, forcing them to cede two-thirds of their lands and shift their villages outside of the settlers' path.

November 20, 1817–October 31, 1818
The First Seminole War is fought. After several indecisive battles, Andrew Jackson strikes south with an overwhelming force, eventually seizing a Spanish outpost and hanging two British subjects for allegedly inspiring native uprisings. Jackson's success convinces Spanish officials to sell Florida to the United States in 1819.

August 23, 1823
In the Arikara War, the Arikaras resist American encroachment up the Missouri River in a pitched battle but are defeated by Colonel Henry Leavenworth at the mouth of the Grand River.

September 1823
Treaty of Moultrie Creek between the United States and the Seminoles is signed. The treaty stipulates that in exchange for goods and supplies, the Seminoles will give up claims to land in Florida and move to a reservation in the center of the state.

May 28, 1830
The Indian Removal Act is passed at the request of President Andrew Jackson and calls for Indian nations to cede their lands east of the Mississippi River in exchange for lands west of the river in what would be called Indian Territory (present-day Oklahoma).

March 18, 1831
In *Cherokee Nation v. Georgia*, William Wirt attempts to defend Cherokee rights before the U.S. Supreme Court.

March 3, 1832
In *Worcester v. Georgia*, the Supreme Court rules that the Cherokee Nation is a distinct community possessing self-government, but Georgia ignores the ruling.

May–July 1832
When Sauk and Fox planters return to Rock Island, Illinois, to sow new crops, panicky American militiamen shoot down one of their men, prompting Sauk chief Black Hawk to authorize cross-border raids; they are defeated at Wisconsin Heights. Black Hawk flees west and is defeated in the Battle of Bad Axe.

May 9, 1832

The Treaty of Payne's Landing, an agreement between the United States and several Seminole chiefs, is signed and stipulates that the Seminoles are to relocate to the Creek Reservation in Arkansas Territory.

December 28, 1835–August 14, 1842

In the Second Seminole War, the Seminoles ravage farms, settlements, plantations, and army forts. The federal government sends in Brigadier General Winfield Scott.

March 26, 1836

Scott sends three columns into Seminole territory, but they are repeatedly harassed by Seminoles under Osceola, who strike isolated American outposts in the rear.

March 6, 1837

After several American victories, three Seminole chiefs request terms. A treaty is signed in which 1,000 Seminoles agree to be transported west of the Mississippi. The plans are publicly criticized, and the Seminoles resume hostilities.

October 27, 1837

Seminole war chief Osceola and 94 followers are treacherously seized near Fort Payton, despite having been asked to a parley.

December 25, 1837

Colonel Zachary Taylor launches a frontal assault on the Seminoles through a saw grass swamp. His force is riddled with counterfire, and the Seminoles escape.

1838

More than 17,000 Cherokees are rounded up at gunpoint, without provisions or belongings, to be relocated west to Indian Territory (present-day Oklahoma) along the infamous Trail of Tears, a distance of 1,200 miles; 424 Cherokees are officially recorded as having died during the journey, but actual estimates range from 4,000 to 8,000.

1838–1842

The Second Seminole War degenerates into a protracted brush war in which Americans attempt to hunt the Seminoles into extinction and deport hundreds of captives. Disgusted with the war, many U.S. regulars resign from service.

February 7, 1838

Major General Thomas Jesup meets with Seminole chief Tuskegee to persuade him to bring his followers to Fort Jupiter on the understanding that they will not have to abandon Florida. When Washington rejects these terms, Jesup sends the 2nd U.S. Dragoons to surround and imprison them, thus violating his promise.

1846–1864

Despite a treaty in 1846, 1,000 Navajos attack Fort Defiance. More raids follow, and when an ultimatum fails, Colonel Christopher Houston "Kit" Carson destroys food stores. The Navajos capitulate in January 1864 at Canyon de Chelly, beginning Carson's infamous Long Walk in which 9,022 Navajos are interned at Fort Sumner in New Mexico and thousands more die along the way.

1855–1858

Third Seminole War is the final clash between U.S. troops under Colonel William Harney and the Seminoles under Billy Bowlegs. Bowlegs surrenders on May 7, 1858, and although the hostilities are officially ended, the final remnant of Seminoles never surrenders.

August 17–September 23, 1862
The Dakota Sioux conduct surprise attacks against scores of settlements after not receiving their treaty-guaranteed food. Colonel Henry Sibley quells the uprising and soundly defeats the Sioux at the Battle of Wood Lake. Three hundred three natives are convicted and sentenced to hang, but President Abraham Lincoln commutes all but 38 of the sentences. The Sioux tribes are expelled from Minnesota.

April 1864–October 1867
Hoping to acquire statehood, Colorado officials provoke the Cheyenne-Arapaho War and create the 3rd Colorado Cavalry. The war ends with the Medicine Lodge Creek Treaty in 1867, wherein many Cheyennes and Arapahos agree to permanent relocation in Indian Territory.

July 28, 1864
In the Battle of Killdeer Mountain (also known as the Battle of Tahkahokuty Mountain), the U.S. 1st Brigade under Brigadier General Alfred Sully scatters a large number of Sioux warriors but is unable to keep them from continuing to raid American settlements.

November 29–December 1, 1864
The Cheyenne-Arapaho War's most notorious event, dubbed the Sand Creek Massacre, occurs. The 3rd Colorado Cavalry under Colonel John Chivington, a Methodist minister, attacks a peaceful Cheyenne camp; 148 Cheyennes die, only 60 of whom are men.

1866–1868
Oglala Sioux chief Red Cloud resists American efforts to build a series of forts along the Bozeman Trail, igniting Red Cloud's War.

December 21, 1866
Captain William Fetterman, attempting to relieve a wood train under attack and ignoring orders, leads his men into a Sioux ambush. All 81 are killed.

August 2, 1867
In the Wagon Box Fight, American soldiers under Captain James Powell hold off 1,500 Sioux led by Red Cloud in large part because of the new Springfield Model 1866 Trapdoor .50-caliber breech-loading rifle issued after the Fetterman Massacre.

Mid-August 1868
Cheyenne, Sioux, and Arapaho war bands under Cheyenne chief Roman Nose raid Kansas, killing more than 100 settlers. Major George Forsyth tracks the bands, and Roman Nose is mortally wounded, although the Indians prevail until Forsyth is rescued by the 10th Cavalry Regiment.

November 6, 1868
The Fort Laramie Treaty is signed, ending Red Cloud's War. A temporary victory for the Sioux, the treaty closes the Bozeman Trail, and U.S. forts along the trail are evacuated. In the Battle of the Washita, Lieutenant Colonel George Armstrong Custer's 7th Cavalry Regiment attacks Black Kettle's Cheyenne village. Black Kettle is killed, and the village is torched before the Indians regroup.

May 18, 1871
While on an inspection tour of Texas, Commanding General William T. Sherman with a small escort passes unmolested before a large Kiowa raiding party that instead strikes a large wagon train just hours later, some eight miles west of Fort Richardson, torturing and killing several teamsters. The experience prompts Sherman to intensify military activity on the southern Plains.

November 27, 1872–June 3, 1873

Clashes between California-Oregon border settlers and the Modocs bring a large regular military response. During a parley, Modoc leader Captain Jack produces a revolver from his jacket and kills Brigadier General Edward Canby, and more skirmishes ensue. The Modocs eventually lose their will to fight. Canby becomes the only general officer to be killed by Indians during the post–Civil War period.

December 1872

Major Joseph Brown runs down and massacres a band of Tonto Apaches at Salt River Ridge. Another victory shortly thereafter secures the surrender of the majority of the remaining Tontos.

May 17, 1873

Colonel Ranald Slidell Mackenzie leads a cavalry column into Mexico on an illegal incursion to curb Kickapoo, Lipan, and Lipan Apache raids. The Indians are completely surprised and are quickly defeated.

June 27, 1874–June 2, 1875

Native Americans of the southern Plains clash with the United States in the Red River War. The U.S. Army is called to end the uprising, and within five years, the southern Plains tribes are pacified.

June 27, 1874

Several hundred Comanche and Cheyenne warriors attack a group of 28 buffalo hunters at Adobe Walls in the Texas Panhandle. The hunters, skillfully employing their high-power rifles, hold out while inflicting substantial losses on the attackers.

September 28, 1874

Mackenzie wins a climactic engagement at Palo Duro Canyon against Comanche warriors, capturing 1,500 horses and greatly hampering Native American movement.

1876–1877

Discovery of gold in the Black Hills pits Americans against the northern Plains tribes in the Great Sioux War, despite the Fort Laramie Treaty of 1868 that guarantees ownership of the sacred land to Native Americans. The U.S. Army has major successes starting in late 1876.

March 1876

Brigadier General George Crook marches a column out of Fort Fetterman to stop Sioux and Northern Cheyenne raiding parties led by Hunkpapa Sioux chief Sitting Bull. Although the U.S. troops are initially successful, the Indian warriors counterattack and maul the 3rd Cavalry Regiment under Colonel J. J. Reynolds.

June 17, 1876

As part of a major three-pronged attack, Crook launches another expeditionary force that collides with 1,000 warriors under Chief Crazy Horse along Rosebud Creek. Crook withdraws to await reinforcements. In what is known as Custer's Last Stand, Custer inexplicably disobeys orders by attacking Sioux leader Sitting Bull's encampment along the Little Bighorn River. After Custer divides his force, his battalion is quickly overwhelmed by warriors under Hunkpapa chief Gall and Oglala Sioux chief Low Dog, and Custer's command is annihilated. The remainder of Custer's regiment under Major Marcus Reno holds out until rescued.

October 1876

Mackenzie's 4th Cavalry Regiment overruns the Northern Cheyenne village of Dull Knife by the Powder River.

June 1877–October 5, 1877
The Nez Perce War is fought between non-treaty Nez Perces under Chief Joseph and the U.S. Army under Brigadier General Oliver O. Howard and Colonel A. Nelson Miles, resulting in a running campaign that covers more than 1,600 miles before Joseph surrenders.

August 9–10, 1877
Nez Perce chief Looking Glass, believing that his band is temporarily safe from attack, insists that they stop to rest, against the judgment of Chief Joseph, and is surprised by a second army column under Colonel John Gibbon in the Battle of the Big Hole. The Nez Perces escape after 36 hours.

September 1877
About 300 Apaches under Victorio and Loco flee the San Carlos Reservation but surrender at Fort Wingate 11 days later and are taken to the Warm Springs Reservation.

September 30–October 5, 1877
Not far from the Canadian border, Nez Perce chief Looking Glass again insists that his band rest, only to be attacked by several companies under Miles. A dispirited Chief Joseph surrenders.

Mid-October 1878
When they learn that they will be repatriated back to the San Carlos Reservation, Victorio and 80 followers flee Warm Springs.

February 1879
Victorio surrenders at Mescalero.

July 1879
Victorio flees to Mexico.

September 1879
Some White River Utes in Colorado ambush a U.S. contingent, killing Major Thomas

Thornburgh and several troops before the uprising is put down by Mackenzie.

October 15, 1880
Victorio and most of his Apache warriors are killed in a battle with Mexican troops.

April 1882
Apache leaders Geronimo and Juh flee the San Carlos Reservation along with several hundred of Loco's Chiricahua followers. Chased by Colonel George Forsyth, they manage to reach Mexico but are ambushed by Mexican troops.

September 1882
Crook resumes command of the Department of Arizona and then crosses the Mexican border to pursue Geronimo.

March 1883
Geronimo's Apaches launch lightning raids throughout northern Mexico, southeastern Arizona, and New Mexico.

May 1, 1883
Crook pursues Geronimo into the northern Mexico highlands and along with loyal Apache scouts manages to locate the Apache base camp while the warriors are away raiding. The Apaches surrender, and eventually, Crook escorts several hundred back to the San Carlos Reservation. Geronimo again escapes San Carlos along with Chihuahua, Naiché, Nana, and Mangas. Despite the cavalry that Crook had stationed along the Mexican border, Geronimo succeeds in escaping into the Sierra Madres.

January 1886
Captain Emmet Crawford's scouts capture Geronimo's horses and provisions in Mexico, but shortly after opening negotiations

with Geronimo, Crawford is killed by Mexican scalp hunters.

March 25, 1886
Geronimo agrees to surrender to Crook and serve two years' imprisonment in the East. However, the War Department reneges on this promise and instead ships 77 Chiricahuas to Fort Marion in Florida. Crook resigns, and Geronimo again flees to Mexico. Crook is replaced by Brigadier General Miles.

September 4, 1886
Five thousand U.S. regulars and hundreds of Apache scouts hunt Apache leader Geronimo, who finally surrenders to Miles along with 33 followers. Geronimo is dispatched to Fort Pickens in Florida along with the other males, while their families are sent to Fort Marion, also in Florida.

December 29, 1890
Near the Pine Ridge Agency, Colonel James Forsyth's 7th Cavalry Regiment intercepts members of Miniconjou Sioux chief Big Foot's band. Fighting breaks out, and U.S. troops kill more than 150 Native Americans, including dozens of women and children. Twenty-five troops die, and 39 others are wounded. The Battle of Wounded Knee brings to a close major warfare between Native Americans and the U.S. Army.

Bibliography

Alvarez, Alex. *Native America and the Question of Genocide*. Studies in Genocide: Religion, History, and Human Rights. Lanham, MD: Rowman & Littlefield, 2014.

Ambrose, Stephen E. *Crazy Horse and Custer: The Parallel Lives of Two American Warriors*. New York: Anchor Books, 1996.

Anderson, Fred. *Crucible of War: The Seven Years' War and the Fate of the Empire in British North America, 1754–1766*. New York: Vintage Books, 2001.

Anderson, Gary Clayton. *Little Crow: Spokesman for the Sioux*. St. Paul: Minnesota Historical Society Press, 1986.

Atkinson, James R. *Splendid Land, Splendid People: The Chickasaw Indians to Removal*. Tuscaloosa: University of Alabama Press, 2004.

Axtell, James. *The Invasion Within: The Contest of Cultures in Colonial North America*. New York: Oxford University Press, 1985.

Bailey, John W. *Pacifying the Plains: General Alfred Terry and the Decline of the Sioux, 1866–1890*. Westport, CT: Greenwood, 1979.

Bailey, Lynn R. *The Long Walk: A History of the Navajo Wars, 1848–68*. Los Angeles: Westernlore, 1964.

Ball, Durwood. *Army Regulars on the Western Frontier, 1848–1861*. Norman: University of Oklahoma Press, 2001.

Barnes, Celia. *Native American Power in the United States, 1783–1795*. Teaneck, NJ: Fairleigh Dickinson University Press, 2003.

Barr, Daniel P., ed. *The Boundaries between Us: Natives and Newcomers along the Frontiers of the Old Northwest Territory, 1750–1850*. Kent, OH: Kent State University Press, 2006.

Beatty Medina, Charles, and Melissa Rinehart. *Contested Territories: Native Americans and Non-Natives in the Lower Great Lakes, 1700–1850*. East Lansing: Michigan State University Press, 2012.

Beck, Robin. *Chiefdoms, Collapse, and Coalescence in the Early American South*. Cambridge: Cambridge University Press, 2013.

Berthrong, Donald. *The Southern Cheyennes*. The Civilization of the American Indian Series. Norman: University of Oklahoma Press, 1963.

Black, Jason Edward. *American Indians and the Rhetoric of Removal and Allotment*. Jackson: University Press of Mississippi, 2015.

Blackhawk, Ned. *Violence over the Land: Indians and Empires in the Early American West*. Cambridge, MA: Harvard University Press, 2006.

Blyth, Lance R. *Chiricahua and Janos: Communities of Violence in the Southwestern Borderlands, 1680–1880*. Lincoln: University of Nebraska Press, 2012.

Bossy, Denise I., ed. *The Yamasee Indians from Florida to South Carolina*. Lincoln: University of Nebraska Press, 2018.

Brandão, José António. *Your Fyre Shall Burn No More: Iroquois Policy toward New France and Its Native Allies to 1701*. Lincoln: University of Nebraska Press, 1997.

Braund, Kathryn E. Holland, ed. *Tohopeka: Rethinking the Creek War and the War of 1812*. Tuscaloosa: University of Alabama Press, 2012.

Brown, Dee. *Bury My Heart at Wounded Knee*. New York: Holt, Rinehart and Winston, 1970.

Calloway, Colin G. *The Abenaki*. New York: Chelsea House, 1989.

Calloway, Colin G. *The American Revolution in Indian Country: Crisis and Diversity in Native American Communities*. Cambridge: Cambridge University Press, 1995.

Calloway, Colin G. *The Indian World of George Washington: The First President, the First Americans, and the Birth of the Nation*. New York: Oxford University Press, 2018.

Calloway, Colin G. *New Worlds for All: Indians, Europeans, and the Remaking of Early America*. Baltimore: Johns Hopkins University Press, 1997.

Calloway, Colin G. *The Shawnees and the War for America*. The Penguin Library of American Indian History. New York: Penguin Books, 2008.

Calloway, Colin G. *The Victory with No Name: The Native American Defeat of the First American Army*. Oxford: Oxford University Press, 2015.

Cameron, Catherine M., Paul Kelton, and Alan C. Swedlund, eds. *Beyond Germs: Native Depopulation in North America*. Amerind Studies in Anthropology. Tucson: University of Arizona Press, 2016.

Carley, Kenneth. *The Sioux Uprising of 1862*. 2nd ed. St. Paul: Minnesota Historical Society, 1976.

Carlos, Ann M., and Frank D. Lewis. *Commerce by a Frozen Sea: Native Americans and the European Fur Trade*. Philadelphia: University of Pennsylvania Press, 2010.

Carroll, John M., ed. *The Black Military Experience in the American West*. New York: Liveright, 1971.

Carter, Harvey Lewis. *The Life and Times of Little Turtle: First Sagamore of the Wabash*. Urbana: University of Illinois Press, 1987.

Cave, Alfred A. *Lethal Encounters: Englishmen and Indians in Colonial Virginia*. Santa Barbara, CA: Praeger, 2011.

Cave, Alfred A. *The Pequot War*. Amherst: University of Massachusetts Press, 1996.

Chartrand René, and Adam Hook. *Raiders from New France: North American Forest Warfare Tactics, 17th–18th Centuries*. Oxford: Osprey Publishing, 2019.

Clark, Jerry E. *The Shawnee*. Lexington: University Press of Kentucky, 2007.

Cole, D. C. *The Chiricahua Apache, 1846–1876: From War to Reservation*. Albuquerque: University of New Mexico Press, 1988.

Coleman, William S. E. *Voices of Wounded Knee*. Lincoln: University of Nebraska Press, 2000.

Connell, Evan S. *Son of the Morning Star: Custer and the Little Bighorn*. New York: North Point Press, 1984.

Cothran, Boyd. *Remembering the Modoc War: Redemptive Violence and the Making of American Innocence*. First Peoples: New Directions in Indigenous Studies. Chapel Hill, NC: University of North Carolina Press, 2014.

Covington, James W. *The Seminoles of Florida*. Gainesville: University Press of Florida, 1993.

Cozzens, Peter. *The Earth Is Weeping: The Epic Story of the Indian Wars for the American West*. New York: Alfred A. Knopf, 2016.

Cozzens, Peter, ed. *Eyewitnesses to the Indian Wars, 1865–1890*. 5 vols. Mechanicsburg, PA: Stackpole, 2001–2006.

Cress, Lawrence Delbert. *Citizens in Arms: The Army and the Militia in American Society to the War of 1812.* Chapel Hill: University of North Carolina Press, 1982.

Custer, George Armstrong. *My Life on the Plains: Or, Personal Experiences with Indians.* Introduction by Edgar I. Stewart. Norman: University of Oklahoma Press, 1962.

Debo, Angie. *Geronimo: The Man, His Time, His Place.* The Civilization of the American Indian Series. Norman: University of Oklahoma Press, 1976.

Decker, Peter. *The Utes Must Go: American Expansion and the Removal of a People.* Golden, CO: Fulcrum, 2004.

DeMontravel, Peter R. *A Hero to His Fighting Men: Nelson A. Miles, 1839–1925.* Kent, OH: Kent State University Press, 1998.

Dennis, Jeff W. *Patriots & Indians: Shaping Identity in Eighteenth-Century South Carolina.* Columbia: University of South Carolina Press, 2017.

Dennis, Matthew. *Cultivating a Landscape of Peace: Iroquois-European Encounters in Seventeenth-Century North America.* Ithaca, NY: Cornell University Press, 1993.

Densmore, Christopher. *Red Jacket: Iroquois Diplomat and Orator.* Syracuse, NY: Syracuse University Press, 1999.

Dixon, David. *Never Come to Peace Again: Pontiac's Uprising and the Fate of the British Empire in North America.* Campaigns and Commanders Series. Norman: University of Oklahoma Press, 2005.

Dobak, William A., and Thomas D. Phillips. *The Black Regulars, 1866–1898.* Norman: University of Oklahoma Press, 2001.

Dowd, Gregory Evans. *A Spirited Resistance: The North American Indian Struggle for Unity, 1745–1815.* Baltimore: Johns Hopkins University Press, 1992.

Dowd, Gregory Evans. *War under Heaven: Pontiac, the Indian Nations, and the British Empire.* Baltimore: Johns Hopkins University Press, 2002.

Downey, Fairfax. *Indian Wars of the U.S. Army, 1776–1865.* Garden City, NY: Doubleday, 1963.

Downey, Fairfax, and J. N. Jacobsen. *The Red-Bluecoats: The Indian Scouts.* Fort Collins, CO: Old Army, 1973.

Drake, James D. *King Philip's War: Civil War in New England, 1675–1676.* Amherst: University of Massachusetts Press, 1999.

Eccles, W. J. *The French in North America: 1500–1783.* Revised ed. Markham, ON: Fitzhenry and Whiteside, 2010.

Edmunds, R. David. *The Shawnee Prophet.* Lincoln: University of Nebraska Press, 1983.

Edmunds, R. David. *Tecumseh and the Quest for Indian Leadership.* Library of American Biography. Boston: Little, Brown, 1984.

Edmunds, R. David, ed. *American Indian Leaders: Studies in Diversity.* Lincoln: University of Nebraska Press, 1980.

Edmunds, R. David, and Joseph L. Peyser. *The Fox Wars: The Mesquakie Challenge to New France.* The Civilization of the American Indian Series. Norman: University of Oklahoma Press, 1993.

Englebert, Robert, and Guillaume Teasdale. *French and Indians in the Heart of North America, 1630–1815.* East Lansing: Michigan State University Press, 2013.

Ethridge, Robbie. *Creek Country: The Creek Indians and Their World.* Chapel Hill: University of North Carolina Press, 2003.

Faulk, Odie B. *The Geronimo Campaign.* New York: Oxford University Press, 1969.

Fenton, William N. *The Great Law and the Longhouse: A Political History of the Iroquois Confederacy.* The Civilization of the American Indian Series. Norman: University of Oklahoma Press, 1998.

Forbes, Jack D. *Apache, Navaho, and Spaniard.* 2nd ed. The Civilization of the American Indian Series. Norman: University of Oklahoma Press, 1994.

Fowler, Arlen L. *The Black Infantry in the West, 1869–1891.* Norman: University of Oklahoma Press, 1996.

Frey, Rodney. *The World of the Crow Indians: As Driftwood Lodges.* The Civilization of the American Indian Series. Norman: University of Oklahoma Press, 1987.

Gallay, Alan. *The Indian Slave Trade: The Rise of the English Empire in the American South, 1670–1717.* New Haven, CT: Yale University Press, 2002.

Galliker, Leslie. *Native American Wars on the Western Frontier, 1866–1890.* Major U.S. Historical Wars. Broomall, PA: Mason Crest, 2016.

Galloway, Patricia K., ed. *La Salle and His Legacy: Frenchmen and Indians in the Lower Mississippi Valley.* Jackson: University Press of Mississippi, 1982.

Garavaglia, Louis A., and Charles G. Worman. *Firearms of the American West, 1803–1865.* Niwot: University Press of Colorado, 1997.

Gibbon, Guy. *The Sioux: The Dakota and Lakota Nations.* Malden, MA: Blackwell, 2003.

Gibson, Charles. *Spain in America.* New American Nations Series. New York: Harper and Row, 1966.

Gleach, Frederic W. *Powhatan's World and Colonial Virginia.* Lincoln: University of Nebraska Press, 1997.

Gordon-McCutchan, R. C., ed. *Kit Carson: Indian Fighter or Indian Killer?* Niwot: University Press of Colorado, 1996.

Gray, John S. *Centennial Campaign: The Sioux War of 1876.* Norman: Oklahoma University Press, 1988.

Green, Michael D. *The Politics of Indian Removal: Creek Government and Society in Crisis.* Lincoln: University of Nebraska Press, 1982.

Greene, Jerome A. *American Carnage: Wounded Knee, 1890.* Norman, Oklahoma: University of Oklahoma Press, 2014.

Greene, Jerome A. *Morning Star Dawn: The Powder River Expedition and the Northern Cheyennes, 1876.* Campaigns and Commanders Series. Norman: University of Oklahoma Press, 2003.

Greene, Jerome A. *Nez Perce Summer, 1877: The U.S. Army and the Nee-Me-Poo Crisis.* Helena: Montana Historical Society Press, 2000.

Greene, Jerome A. *Washita: The U.S. Army and the Southern Cheyennes, 1867–1869.* Campaigns and Commanders Series. Norman: University of Oklahoma Press, 2004.

Gwynne, S. C. *Empire of the Summer Moon: Quanah Parker and the Rise and Fall of the Comanches, the Most Powerful Indian Tribe in American History.* New York: Scribner, 2010.

Haefeli, Evan, and Kevin Sweeney. *Captors and Captives: The 1704 French and Indian Raid on Deerfield.* Amherst: University of Massachusetts Press, 2003.

Hagan, William T. *Quanah Parker, Comanche Chief.* Norman: University of Oklahoma Press, 1993.

Hahn, Stephen C. *The Invention of the Creek Nation, 1670–1763.* Lincoln: University of Nebraska Press, 2004.

Hart, Siobhan M., and Paul A. Shackel. *Colonialism, Community, and Heritage in Native New England.* Cultural Heritage Studies. Gainesville: University Press of Florida, 2019.

Hartley, William, and Ellen Hartley. *Osceola: The Unconquered Indian.* New York: Hawthorne Books, 1973.

Hatch, Thom. *Black Kettle: The Cheyenne Chief Who Sought Peace but Found War.* Hoboken, NJ: Wiley, 2004.

Hauptman, Laurence M., James D. Wherry, and William T. Hagan, eds. *The Pequots in Southern New England: The Rise and Fall of an American Indian Nation.* The Civilization of the American Indian Series. Norman: University of Oklahoma Press, 1990.

Haveman, Christopher D. *Rivers of Sand: Creek Indian Emigration, Relocation, and Ethnic Cleansing in the American South.* Indians of the Southeast. Lincoln: University of Nebraska Press, 2016.

Heidler, David S., and Jeanne T. Heidler. *Old Hickory's War: Andrew Jackson and the*

Quest for Empire. Mechanicsburg, PA: Stackpole, 1996.

Hinderaker, Eric. *Elusive Empires: Constructing Colonialism in the Ohio Valley, 1673–1800.* New York: Cambridge University Press, 1997.

Hinderaker, Eric, and Peter C. Mancall. *At the Edge of Empire: The Backcountry in British North America.* Baltimore: Johns Hopkins University Press, 2003.

Hittman, Michael. *Wovoka and the Ghost Dance.* Expanded ed. Edited by Don Lynch. Lincoln: University of Nebraska Press, 1997.

Hoig, Stan. *The Peace Chiefs of the Cheyennes.* Norman: University of Oklahoma Press, 1980.

Hoig, Stan. *The Sand Creek Massacre.* Norman: University of Oklahoma Press, 1961.

Horsman, Reginald. *Expansion and American Indian Policy, 1783–1812.* East Lansing: Michigan State University Press, 1967.

Hoxie, Frederick E., Ronald Hoffman, and Peter J. Albert, eds. *Native Americans and the Early Republic.* Charlottesville: University Press of Virginia, 1999.

Hurt, R. Douglas. *The Indian Frontier, 1763–1846.* Albuquerque: University of New Mexico Press, 2002.

Hutton, Paul Andrew. *Phil Sheridan and His Army.* Lincoln: University of Nebraska Press, 1985.

Hutton, Paul Andrew, ed. *Soldiers West: Biographies from the Military Frontier.* Lincoln: University of Nebraska Press, 1987.

Ingram, Daniel Patrick. *Indians and British Outposts in Eighteenth-Century America.* Gainesville: University Press of Florida, 2012.

Inskeep, Steve. *Jacksonland: President Andrew Jackson, Cherokee Chief John Ross, and a Great American Land Grab.* New York: Penguin Press, 2015.

Ivers, Larry E. *This Torrent of Indians: War on the Southern Frontier, 1715–1728.* Columbia: University of South Carolina Press, 2016.

Jackson, Donald, ed. *Ma-ka-tai-me-she-kia-kiak, Black Hawk: An Autobiography.* Urbana: University of Illinois Press, 1955.

Jackson, Helen Hunt. *A Century of Dishonor: A Sketch of the United States Government's Dealings with Some of the Indian Tribes.* New York: Harper & Brothers, 1881.

Jacobs, Wilbur R. *Dispossessing the American Indian: Indians and Whites on the Colonial Frontier.* New York: Scribner, 1972.

Jennings, Francis. *Empire of Fortune: Crowns, Colonies, and Tribes in the Seven Years War in America.* New York: Norton, 1988.

Jennings, Matthew. *New Worlds of Violence: Cultures and Conquests in the Early American Southeast.* Knoxville: University of Tennessee Press, 2011.

Jortner, Adam Joseph. *The Gods of Prophetstown: The Battle of Tippecanoe and the Holy War for the American Frontier.* New York: Oxford University Press, 2012.

Josephy, Alvin M., Jr. *The Patriot Chiefs: A Chronicle of American Indian Resistance.* New York: Penguin, 1989.

Jung, Patrick J. *The Black Hawk War of 1832.* Campaigns and Commanders Series. Norman: University of Oklahoma Press, 2007.

Kaplan, Lawrence S. *Thomas Jefferson: Westward the Course of Empire.* Wilmington, DE: Scholarly Resources, 1999.

Keating, Susan Katz. *Native American Rivalries.* Native American Life. Philadelphia: Mason Crest, 2014.

Kelsay, Isabel Thompson. *Joseph Brant, 1743–1807: Man of Two Worlds.* Syracuse, NY: Syracuse University Press, 1984.

Kenner, Charles L. *Buffalo Soldiers and Officers of the Ninth Cavalry, 1867–1898: Black and White Together.* Norman: University of Oklahoma Press, 1999.

Knaut, Andrew L. *The Pueblo Revolt of 1680: Conquest and Resistance in Seventeenth-Century New Mexico.* Norman: University of Oklahoma Press, 1995.

Knetsch, Joe. *Florida's Seminole Wars, 1817–1858.* Charleston, SC: Arcadia Publishing, 2003.

Kopperman, Paul E. *Braddock at the Monongahela.* Pittsburgh: University of Pittsburgh Press, 1977.

Kraft, Louis. *Gatewood and Geronimo.* Albuquerque: University of New Mexico Press, 2000.

Laramie, Michael G. *The European Invasion of North America: Colonial Conflict along the Hudson-Champlain Corridor, 1609–1760.* Santa Barbara, CA: Praeger/ABC-CLIO, 2012.

Laramie, Michael G. *King William's War: The First Contest for North America, 1689–1697.* Yardley, PA: Westholme Publishing, 2017.

Larson, Robert W. *Red Cloud: Warrior-Statesman of the Lakota Sioux.* Norman: University of Oklahoma Press, 1997.

La Vere, David. *Contrary Neighbors: Southern Plains and Removed Indians in Indian Territory.* Norman: University of Oklahoma Press, 2000.

La Vere, David. *The Tuscarora War: Indians, Settlers, and the Fight for the Carolina Colonies.* Chapel Hill: The University of North Carolina Press, 2013.

Leach, Douglas Edward. *Flintlock and Tomahawk: New England in King Philip's War.* East Orleans, MA: Parnassus Imprints, 1992.

Leckie, William H., and Shirley A. Leckie. *The Buffalo Soldiers: A Narrative of the Black Cavalry in the West.* Norman: University of Oklahoma Press, 2003.

Lepore, Jill. *The Name of War: King Philip's War and the Origins of American Identity.* New York: Knopf, 1998.

Lindsay, Brendan C. *Murder State: California's Native American Genocide, 1846–1873.* Lincoln: University of Nebraska Press, 2012.

Lipman, Andrew. *The Saltwater Frontier: Indians and the Contest for the American Coast.* New Haven, CT: Yale University Press, 2015.

Mahon, John K. *History of the Second Seminole War, 1835–1842.* Rev. ed. Gainesville: University Press of Florida, 1991.

Mails, Thomas E. *Dog Soldiers, Bear Men, and Buffalo Women: A Study of the Societies and Cults of the Plains Indians.* Englewood Cliffs, NJ: Prentice Hall, 1973.

Malone, Patrick M. *The Skulking Way of War: Technology and Tactics among the New England Indians.* Lanham, MD: Madison Books, 2000.

Mancall, Peter C., and James H. Merrell, eds. *American Encounters: Natives and Newcomers from European Contact to Indian Removal, 1500–1850.* New York: Routledge, 2000.

Mandell, Daniel R. *King Philip's War: Colonial Expansion, Native Resistance, and the End of Indian Sovereignty.* Baltimore: Johns Hopkins University Press, 2010.

Mangum, Neil A. *Battle of the Rosebud: Prelude to the Little Bighorn.* El Segundo, CA: Upton, 1987.

Marshall, Joseph M., III. *The Journey of Crazy Horse: A Lakota History.* New York: Viking, 2004.

Marsico, Katie. *The Trail of Tears: The Tragedy of the American Indians.* New York: Marshall Cavendish Benchmark, 2010.

McConnell, Michael N. *A Country Between: The Upper Ohio and Its Peoples, 1724–1774.* Lincoln: University of Nebraska Press, 1992.

McGinnis, Anthony. *Counting Coup and Cutting Horses: Intertribal Warfare on the Northern Plains, 1738–1889.* Lincoln: University of Nebraska Press, 2010.

McNab, Chris. *The Native American Warrior, 1500–1890 CE.* Warriors of the World. New York: Thomas Dunne Books, 2010.

McNitt, Frank. *Navajo Wars: Military Campaigns, Slave Raids, and Reprisals.* Albuquerque: University of New Mexico Press, 1990.

Merritt, Jane T. *At the Crossroads: Indians and Empires on a Mid-Atlantic Frontier, 1700–1763.* Chapel Hill: University of North Carolina Press, 2003.

Merwick, Donna. *The Shame and the Sorrow: Dutch-Amerindian Encounters in New Netherland.* Philadelphia: University of Pennsylvania Press, 2006.

Miller, David Humphreys. *Ghost Dance.* Lincoln: University of Nebraska Press, 1985.

Missall, John, and Mary Lou Missall. *The Seminole Wars: America's Longest Indian Conflict.* Gainesville: University Press of Florida, 2004.

Monnett, John H. *Tell Them We Are Going Home: The Odyssey of the Northern Cheyennes.* Norman: University of Oklahoma Press, 2001.

Moore, William Haas. *Chiefs, Agents, and Soldiers: Conflict on the Navajo Frontier, 1868–1882.* Albuquerque: University of New Mexico Press, 1994.

Moulton, Candy. *Chief Joseph: Guardian of the People.* New York: Tom Doherty, 2005.

Murray, Keith A. *The Modocs and Their War.* The Civilization of the American Indian Series. 1959; reprint, Norman: University of Oklahoma Press, 2001.

Neeley, Bill. *The Last Comanche Chief: The Life and Times of Quanah Parker.* New York: Wiley, 1995.

Nelson, Paul David. *Anthony Wayne: Soldier of the Early Republic.* Bloomington: Indiana University Press, 1985.

Nerburn, Kent. *Chief Joseph and the Flight of the Nez Perce: The Untold Story of an American Tragedy.* New York: HarperCollins, 2005.

Nester, William R. *The Great Frontier War: Britain, France, and the Imperial Struggle for North America, 1607–1755.* Westport, CT: Praeger, 2000.

Nester, William R. *"Haughty Conquerors": Amherst and the Great Indian Uprising of 1763.* Westport, CT: Praeger, 2000.

Newcomb, William W. *The Indians of Texas: From Prehistoric to Modern Times.* Austin: University of Texas Press, 1995.

Nichols, Roger L. *Black Hawk: A Biography.* Wheeling, IL: Harland Davidson, 2000.

Oberg, Michael Leroy. *Dominion and Civility: English Imperialism, Native America, and the First American Frontiers, 1585–1685.* Ithaca, NY: Cornell University Press, 2018.

Oliphant, John. *Peace and War on the Anglo-Cherokee Frontier 1753–63.* Baton Rouge: Louisiana State University Press, 2001.

Olson, James C. *Red Cloud and the Sioux Problem.* Lincoln: University of Nebraska Press, 1965.

Owens, Robert M. *Mr. Jefferson's Hammer: William Henry Harrison and the Origins of American Indian Policy.* Norman: University of Oklahoma Press, 2011.

Parker, Arthur Caswell. *Red Jacket: Seneca Chief.* Lincoln: University of Nebraska Press, 1998.

Paul, R. Eli, ed. *Autobiography of Red Cloud: War Leader of the Oglalas.* Helena: Montana Historical Society Press, 1997.

Perdue, Theda. *The Cherokee.* Indians of North America. New York: Chelsea House, 1989.

Philbrick, Nathaniel. *The Last Stand: Custer, Sitting Bull, and the Battle of the Little Bighorn.* New York: Viking, 2010.

Piecuch, Jim. *Three Peoples, One King: Loyalists, Indians, and Slaves in the Revolutionary South, 1775–1782.* Columbia: University of South Carolina Press, 2008.

Pierce, Michael D. *The Most Promising Young Officer: A Life of Ranald Slidell Mackenzie.* Norman: University of Oklahoma Press, 1993.

Powers, Thomas. *The Killing of Crazy Horse.* New York: Alfred A. Knopf, 2010.

Prucha, Francis Paul. *American Indian Policy in the Formative Years: Indian Trade and Intercourse Acts, 1790–1834*. Cambridge, MA: Harvard University Press, 1962.

Prucha, Francis Paul. *American Indian Treaties: The History of a Political Anomaly*. Berkeley: University of California Press, 1994.

Prucha, Francis Paul. *The Sword of the Republic: The United States Army on the Frontier, 1783–1846*. New York: Macmillan, 1969.

Pulsipher, Jenny Hale. *Subjects unto the Same King: Indians, English, and the Contest for Authority in Colonial New England*. Philadelphia: University of Pennsylvania Press, 2005.

Remini, Robert Vincenti. *Andrew Jackson and His Indian Wars*. New York: Penguin, 2001.

Remini, Robert Vincenti. *The Life of Andrew Jackson*. New York: Harper and Row, 1988.

Remley, David A. *Kit Carson: The Life of an American Border Man*. Norman: University of Oklahoma Press, 2011.

Reséndez, Andrés. *The Other Slavery: The Uncovered Story of Indian Enslavement in America*. Boston: Houghton Mifflin Harcourt, 2016.

Richter, Daniel K. *Facing East from Indian Country: A Native History of Early America*. Cambridge, MA: Harvard University Press, 2001.

Richter, Daniel K. *The Ordeal of the Longhouse: The People of the Iroquois League in the Era of European Colonization*. Chapel Hill: University of North Carolina Press, 1992.

Richter, Daniel K. *Trade, Land, Power: The Struggle for Eastern North America*. Philadelphia: University of Pennsylvania Press, 2013.

Richter, Daniel K., and James H. Merrell, eds. *Beyond the Covenant Chain: The Iroquois and Their Neighbors in Indian North America, 1600–1800*. Syracuse, NY: Syracuse University Press, 1987.

Roberts, David. *Once They Moved Like the Wind: Cochise, Geronimo, and the Apache Wars*. New York: Touchstone, 1993.

Roberts, David. *The Pueblo Revolt: The Secret Rebellion That Drove the Spanish out of the Southwest*. New York: Simon and Schuster, 2004.

Robinson, Charles M., III. *Bad Hand: A Biography of General Ranald S. Mackenzie*. Austin, TX: State House Press, 1993.

Robinson, Charles M., III. *General Crook and the Western Frontier*. Norman: University of Oklahoma Press, 2001.

Robinson, Charles M., III. *A Good Year to Die: The Story of the Great Sioux War*. New York: Random House, 1995.

Robinson, Charles M., III. *Satanta: The Life and Death of a War Chief*. Austin, TX: State House Press, 1997.

Ronda, James P., ed. *Thomas Jefferson and the Changing West*. Albuquerque: University of New Mexico Press, 1997.

Rountree, Helen C. *Pocahontas, Powhatan, Opechancanough: Three Indian Lives Changed by Jamestown*. Charlottesville: University of Virginia Press, 2005.

Rountree, Helen C. *The Powhatan Indians of Virginia: Their Traditional Culture*. The Civilization of the American Indian Series. Norman: University of Oklahoma Press, 1989.

Ruby, Robert H. *The Oglala Sioux: Warriors in Transition*. New York: Vantage, 1955.

Sajna, Mike. *Crazy Horse: The Life behind the Legend*. New York: Wiley, 2000.

Salisbury, Neal. *Manitou and Providence: Indians, Europeans, and the Making of New England, 1500–1643*. New York: Oxford University Press, 1982.

Sandoz, Mari. *Crazy Horse: The Strange Man of the Oglalas*. 3rd ed. Lincoln: University of Nebraska Press, 2008.

Saunt, Claudio. *Unworthy Republic: The Dispossession of Native Americans and the*

Road to Indian Territory. New York: W.W. Norton & Company, 2020.

Schmidt, Ethan A. *Native Americans in the American Revolution: How the War Divided, Devastated, and Transformed the Early American Indian World*. Santa Barbara, CA: Praeger/ABC-CLIO, 2014.

Schmitt, Martin F., ed. *General George Crook: His Autobiography*. Norman: University of Oklahoma Press, 1986.

Schultz, Eric B., and Michael J. Tougias. *King Philip's War: The History and Legacy of America's Forgotten Conflict*. Rev. ed. Woodstock, VT: Countryman Press, 2017.

Shannon, Timothy J. *Indians and Colonists at the Crossroads of Empire: The Albany Congress of 1754*. Ithaca, NY: Cornell University Press, 2000.

Sheehan, Bernard W. *Seeds of Extinction: Jeffersonian Philanthropy and the American Indian*. Chapel Hill: University of North Carolina Press, 1973.

Silver, Peter. *Our Savage Neighbors: How Indian War Transformed Early America*. New York: Norton, 2008.

Simmons, Virginia McConnell. *The Ute Indians of Utah, Colorado, and New Mexico*. Niwot: University Press of Colorado, 2000.

Simmons, William S. *The Narragansett*. New York: Chelsea House, 1989.

Skaggs, David Curtis, and Larry L. Nelson, eds. *The Sixty Years' War for the Great Lakes, 1754–1814*. East Lansing: Michigan State University Press, 2001.

Sklenar, Larry. *To Hell with Honor: Custer and the Little Bighorn*. Norman: University of Oklahoma Press, 2000.

Smithers, Gregory D. *The Cherokee Diaspora: An Indigenous History of Migration, Resettlement, and Identity*. The Lamar Series in Western History. New Haven, CT: Yale University Press, 2015.

Smithers, Gregory D. *Native Southerners: Indigenous History from Origins to Removal*. Norman: University of Oklahoma Press, 2019.

Sonnichsen, C. L. *The Mescalero Apaches*. 2nd ed. The Civilization of the American Indian Series. Norman: University of Oklahoma Press, 1958.

Sonnichsen, C. L., ed. *Geronimo and the End of the Apache Wars*. Lincoln: University of Nebraska Press, 1990.

Staeger, Rob. *Native American Tools and Weapons*. Native American Life. Broomall, PA: Mason Crest, 2014.

Starkey, Armstrong. *European and Native American Warfare, 1675–1815*. Norman: University of Oklahoma Press, 1998.

Stockwell, Mary. *Interrupted Odyssey: Ulysses S. Grant and the American Indians*. Carbondale: Southern Illinois University Press, 2018.

Strobel, Christoph. *Native Americans of New England*. Santa Barbara, CA: Praeger/ABC-CLIO, 2020.

Sugden, John. *Blue Jacket: Warrior of the Shawnees*. Lincoln: University of Nebraska Press, 2000.

Sugden, John. *Tecumseh: A Life*. New York: Holt, 1997.

Sweeney, Edwin R. *Cochise: Chiricahua Apache Chief*. The Civilization of the American Indian Series. Norman: University of Oklahoma Press, 1991.

Sweeney, Edwin R. *From Cochise to Geronimo: The Chiricahua Apaches, 1874–1886*. The Civilization of the American Indian Series. Norman: University of Oklahoma Press, 2010.

Sweeney, Edwin R. *Mangas Coloradas: Chief of the Chiricahua Apaches*. The Civilization of the American Indian Series. Norman: University of Oklahoma Press, 1998.

Sword, Wiley. *President Washington's Indian War: The Struggle for the Old Northwest, 1790–1795*. Norman: University of Oklahoma Press, 1985.

Tate, Michael L. *The Frontier Army in the Settlement of the West*. Norman: University of Oklahoma Press, 1999.

Taylor, Colin F. *Native American Weapons.* Norman: University of Oklahoma Press, 2001.

Thompson, Gerald. *The Army and the Navajo: The Bosque Redondo Reservation Experiment, 1863–1868.* Tucson: University of Arizona Press, 1976.

Thrapp, Dan L. *The Conquest of Apacheria.* The Civilization of the American Indian Series. Norman: University of Oklahoma Press, 1967.

Thrapp, Dan L. *General Crook and the Sierra Madre Adventure.* Norman: University of Oklahoma Press, 1972.

Thrapp, Dan L. *Victorio and the Mimbres Apaches.* The Civilization of the American Indian Series. Norman: University of Oklahoma Press, 1974.

Tiller, Veronica E. Velarde. *The Jicarilla Apache Tribe: A History, 1846–1970.* Lincoln: University of Nebraska Press, 1983.

Trafzer, Clifford E. *The Kit Carson Campaign: The Last Great Navajo War.* Norman: University of Oklahoma Press, 1990.

Trask, Kerry A. *Black Hawk: The Battle for the Heart of America.* New York: Holt, 2006.

Turner, Frederick Jackson. *The Frontier in American History.* New York: Henry Holt, 1920.

Utley, Robert M. *Cavalier in Buckskin: George Armstrong Custer and the Western Military Frontier.* Rev. ed. Norman: University of Oklahoma Press, 2001.

Utley, Robert M. *The Commanders: Civil War Generals Who Shaped the American West.* Norman: University of Oklahoma Press, 2018.

Utley, Robert M. *Frontier Regulars: The United States and the American Indian, 1866–1891.* New York: Macmillan, 1973.

Utley, Robert M. *Frontiersmen in Blue: The United States and the Indian, 1848–1865.* Lincoln: University of Nebraska Press, 1967.

Utley, Robert M. *The Indian Frontier of the American West, 1846–1890.* Albuquerque: University of New Mexico Press, 1984.

Utley, Robert M. *The Lance and the Shield: The Life and Times of Sitting Bull.* New York: Ballantine, 1993.

Utley, Robert M. *The Last Days of the Sioux Nation.* 2nd ed. New Haven, CT: Yale University Press, 2004.

Vaughan, Alden T. *New England Frontier: Puritans and Indians, 1620–1675.* 3rd ed. Norman: University of Oklahoma Press, 1995.

Wallace, Anthony F. C. *Jefferson and the Indians: The Tragic Fate of the First Americans.* Cambridge, MA: Belknap Press of Harvard University Press, 1999.

Wallace, Anthony F. C. *Tuscarora: A History.* Tribal Worlds: Critical Studies in American Indian Nation Building Series. Albany: State University of New York Press, 2012.

Wallace, Ernest. *Ranald S. Mackenzie on the Texas Frontier.* College Station: Texas A&M University Press, 1993.

Wallace, Ernest, and E. Adamson Hoebel. *The Comanches: Lords of the South Plains.* The Civilization of the American Indian Series. 1952; reprint, Norman: University of Oklahoma Press, 1986.

Warren, Stephen. *The Worlds the Shawnees Made: Migration and Violence in Early America.* Chapel Hill: University of North Carolina Press, 2014.

Washburn, Wilcomb E. *The Indian in America.* New American Nation Series. New York: Harper and Row, 1975.

Weber, David J., ed. *New Spain's Far Northern Frontier: Essays on Spain in the American West, 1540–1821.* Albuquerque: University of New Mexico Press, 1979.

Weinstein-Farson, Laurie. *The Wampanoag.* New York: Chelsea House, 1988.

Wert, Jeffrey D. *Custer: The Controversial Life of George Armstrong Custer.* New York: Simon and Schuster, 1996.

White, Richard. *The Middle Ground: Indians, Empires, and Republics in the Great Lakes Region, 1650–1815*. New York: Cambridge University Press, 1991.

White, Richard. *The Roots of Dependency: Subsistence, Environment, and Social Change among the Choctaws, Pawnees, and Navajos*. Lincoln: University of Nebraska Press, 1983.

Wood, Peter H., Gregory A. Waselkov, and M. Thomas Hatley, eds. *Powhatan's Mantle: Indians in the Colonial Southeast*. Lincoln: University of Nebraska Press, 1989.

Woolford, Andrew John, Jeff Benvenuto, and Alexander Laban Hinton. *Colonial Genocide in Indigenous North America*. Durham, NC: Duke University Press, 2014.

Wooster, Robert. *The Military and United States Indian Policy, 1865–1903*. New Haven, CT: Yale University Press, 1988.

Wooster, Robert. *Nelson A. Miles and the Twilight of the Frontier Army*. Lincoln: University of Nebraska Press, 1993.

Worcester, Donald E. *The Apaches: Eagles of the Southwest*. The Civilization of the American Indian Series. Norman: University of Oklahoma Press, 1979.

Wright, J. Leitch, Jr. *Britain and the American Frontier, 1783–1815*. Athens: University of Georgia Press, 1975.

Wright, J. Leitch, Jr. *The Only Land They Knew: The Tragic Story of the American Indians in the Old South*. New York: Free Press, 1981.

About the Editor and Contributors

EDITOR

Dr. Justin D. Murphy is Dean of Arts and Sciences and Professor of History at Oakland City University in Indiana. He earned his M.A. in history with a specialization in Native American history and his PhD with a specialization in Modern European History from Texas Christian University in Fort Worth, Texas. Murphy is the author of *Military Aircraft, Origins to 1918: An Illustrated History of Their Impact*, coauthor of *Military Aircraft, 1919–1945: An Illustrated History of Their Impact*, and editor of *American Civil War: Interpreting Conflict through Primary Documents*. He has served on the Military History Advisory Board for ABC-CLIO and as an assistant editor of numerous encyclopedias on military history.

CONTRIBUTORS

Ralph Martin Baker
Independent Scholar

Daniel P. Barr
Robert Morris University

Dr. Jeffrey D. Bass
Quinnipiac University

Walter F. Bell
Aurora University

Marcia Schmidt Blaine
Plymouth State University

Dr. Thomas John Blumer
U.S. Navy

Dr. Stefan M. Brooks
Lindsey Wilson College

Dr. John Thomas Broom
Norwich University

William H. Brown
North Carolina Office of Archives and History

Dr. Jon L. Brudvig
Dickinson State University

Roger M. Carpenter
University of Louisiana

Dr. David Coffey
University of Tennessee at Martin

Chip Colwell-Chanthaphonh
Denver Museum of Nature and Science

David M. Corlett
The College of William and Mary

Dr. Rory T. Cornish
Winthrop University

Dr. Jennifer Nez Denetdale
University of New Mexico

Michael F. Dove
University of Western Ontario

Dr. Alan C. Downs
Georgia Southern University

Rick Dyson
Missouri Western State University

Billie Ford
Independent Scholar

Dr. Andrew K. Frank
Florida State University

Dr. John C. Fredriksen
Independent Scholar

Dr. Dixie Ray Haggard
Valdosta State University

Dr. John W. Hall
University of Wisconsin-Madison

Dr. Michael R. Hall
Armstrong Atlantic State University

Karl S. Hele
Concordia University

Dr. Bruce E. Johansen
University of Nebraska at Omaha

Andy Johns
Independent Scholar

Dr. Kathleen Kane
University of Montana

Robert B. Kane
Air Force Historical Research Center

Jerry Keenan
Independent Scholar

Dr. Martin Kich
Wright State University

Anna Kiefer
Independent Scholar

Matthew J. Krogman
Independent Scholar

Dr. Daniel W. Kuthy
Brescia University

Dr. Janne Lahti
University of Helsinki

Dr. Alan K. Lamm
Mount Olive College

Dr. Raymond W. Leonard
University of Central Missouri

Dr. Peter C. Luebke
Independent Scholar

Jason Lutz
Georgia Southern University

Robert W. Malick
Harrisburg Area Community College

Dr. Sarah E. Miller
University of South Carolina-Salkehatchie

Matthew S. Muehlbauer
Independent Scholar

Dr. Malcolm Muir Jr.
Virginia Military Institute

Dr. B. Keith Murphy
Fort Valley State University

Dr. Justin D. Murphy
Oakland City University

Dr. Paul David Nelson
Berea College

Dr. Dawn Ottevaere Nickeson
Michigan State University

Dr. Jennifer Bridges Oast
Bloomsburg University

Dr. Jaime Ramón Olivares
Houston Community College

Dr. Jim Piecuch
Kennesaw State University

Dr. Paul G. Pierpaoli Jr.
Associate Editor and Fellow, ABC-CLIO

Dr. Raeschelle Potter-Deimel
Independent Scholar

Barry M. Pritzker
Skidmore College

Steven J. Rauch
U.S. Army Signal Center

Charles Rosenberg
Independent Scholar

Dr. Anna Rulska
Old Dominion University

Dr. Patrick R. Ryan
Western Connecticut State University

Dr. Matt Schumann
Eastern Michigan University

Lorin Lowrie Scott
Howard Payne University

David Sloan
University of Kentucky

H. Henrietta Stockel
Independent Scholar

Dr. William Toth
Heidelberg College

Dr. Spencer C. Tucker
Senior Fellow, ABC-CLIO

Dallace W. Unger Jr.
Independent Scholar

Dr. Mark van de Logt
Texas A&M University at Qatar

Dr. Bruce Vandervort
Virginia Military Institute

Dr. Donald L. Walker Jr.
Arapahoe Community College

Dr. Andrew J. Waskey
Dalton State College

Tim J. Watts
Kansas State University

Dr. William Whyte
Lehigh University

Dr. Roberta Wiener
Pace University

Dr. Brett F. Woods
American Public University System

Dr. Kyle F. Zelner
University of Southern Mississippi

Index

Note: Page numbers in **bold** indicate the location of main entries.